BEUR

A GUIDE TO JEWISH

Rabbi Isaiah Wohlgemuth
1915–2008

ביאורי התפילה

Beurei HaTefillah

A Guide to Jewish Prayer

Rabbi Isaiah Wohlgemuth

Edited by
Asher Reichert and Rashie Reichert

Associate Editor
Eliyahu Krakowski

Coordinated by
Stephen Denker

EXPANDED AND UPDATED EDITION

KTAV PUBLISHING HOUSE

NOTE TO EDUCATORS

Rabbi Wohlgemuth's legendary success as a teacher was attributable as much to his educational methodology as to the substance of the material. A collection of Rabbi Wohlgemuth's teaching materials for his *Beurei HaTefillah* course is hosted online by sefaria.org at: https://www.sefaria.org.il/collections/wohlgemuth--guide-to-jewish-prayer.

Beurei HaTefillah
A GUIDE TO JEWISH PRAYER
EXPANDED AND UPDATED EDITION

OU Press
an imprint of the Orthodox Union
11 Broadway
New York, NY 10004
www.oupress.org

KTAV PUBLISHING HOUSE
527 Empire Blvd
Brooklyn, NY 11225
www.ktav.com
orders@ktav.com
Ph: (718) 972-5449 / Fax: (718) 972-6307

Set in Arno Pro by Raphaël Freeman MISTD, Renana Typesetting

ISBN 978-1-60280-456-2 (Hardcover)
ISBN 978-1-60280-462-3 (Paperback)

Printed and bound in the United States of America

This edition of
Rabbi Isaiah Wohlgemuth's
Guide to Jewish Prayer
is lovingly dedicated
to the memory of our dear parents

Abraham and Sylvia Wintman
אברהם צבי בן יצחק חיים
שרה בלומא בת קלמן מרדכי הכהן

Rabbi Wohlgemuth was an outstanding teacher who gave us, and all his students, a deep understanding and love of tefillah. Our parents were amazing role models who taught us the importance of hard work and connection to Hashem. Their close relationship with the Rav, Rabbi Joseph B. Soloveitchik, had a special part in our lives – he was more than just a teacher for us. The Rav was also a major force behind Rabbi Wohlgemuth's course in tefillah at Maimonides School and was a source of guidance in halachah and minhag for Rabbi Wohlgemuth's book. This book is a fitting way to honor our parents' legacy, ensuring that their values, Rabbi Wohlgemuth's teaching, and the Rav's wisdom reach a new audience and generations of students to come.

Kenny Wintman · **Sandy Welkes**

Contents

How this Book Came to Be

STEPHEN DENKER

The Maimonides School in Brookline, Massachusetts was founded in 1937 by the Rav, Rabbi Joseph B. Soloveitchik, *zt"l*. The Rav lived in Brookline, but commuted to New York City during the week, where he served as the head of Yeshiva University's Rabbi Isaac Elchanan Theological Seminary. When the Rav was at home in Brookline for weekends, neighbors would join him for davening as an informal Kehillah at Maimonides. One of the longtime members of what came to be known as "the Maimonides Kehillah" was Rabbi Isaiah Wohlgemuth, *zt"l*, a venerated member of the Maimonides School *Limudei Kodesh* faculty from 1945 to 1997, famous for his pioneering work in establishing the Maimonides *Beurei HaTefillah* curriculum. As events unfolded, the Maimonides Kehillah served as a catalyst for the development of Rabbi Wohlgemuth's *Guide to Jewish Prayer.* The book you have before you emerged as the result of decades of loving work by members of the Maimonides Kehillah and by Rabbi Wohlgemuth's students who had the privilege of personally knowing him.

The November 2013 edition of *Jewish Action* published a lengthy article by Steve Lipman, "Can Schools Do a Better Job of Teaching Tefillah?" The article wrote about Rabbi Wohlgemuth, and his *Beurei HaTefillah* course at Maimonides:

The Maimonides Beurei HaTefillah curriculum offers both the historical context and philosophical underpinnings of individual prayers. Additionally, it emphasizes the interpretation of the words and the structure of the siddur. The curriculum, say many people familiar with the Jewish educational field, is considered the gold standard of day schools in North America – one that offers depth and breadth, that engages adolescent students' interest, that inspires them to keep praying and understanding what they are saying after they have left the School.

Maimonides alumni often write that they have especially warm personal memories of Rabbi Wohlgemuth and of his class, and how what they learned has really stuck. "We can hear Rabbi Wohlgemuth's voice as we read his book and as we daven."

In an effort to preserve the value of the *Beurei HaTefillah* curriculum for the future and to make it more widely available as a resource, Rabbi Wohlgemuth determined to transform the curriculum into a book. As he approached retirement, Rabbi Wohlgemuth enlisted the aid of Rabbi Asher Reichert, a student of his from the Maimonides class of 1967. Over six years, they spent many afternoons in Brookline together as Rabbi Wohlgemuth dictated. Together, they revised and reorganized the material. After Rabbi Reichert went on *aliyah,* Rabbi Wohlgemuth came to Har Nof for three summers, where he and Rabbi Reichert continued writing and editing.

When Rabbi Wohlgemuth's health began to fail, Rabbi David Shapiro, then retired as the Principal of Maimonides, joined in the final editing in effort to accelerate the process. Rabbi Wohlgemuth read and approved all the text they produced. Later, Joel Robinson, a Maimonides Kehillah member, self-published this first edition of Rabbi Wohlgemuth's *Guide to Jewish Prayer* in 2001. Over 2,000 copies of the book were sold.

Rabbi Reichert, however, still had much additional material that was not included in the edition published by Joel Robinson. Rabbi Reichert and Rabbi Wohlgemuth discussed the details and overall scope of the project and how to include the additional material. Rabbi Wohlgemuth gave Rabbi Reichert very specific directions for those parts of the book that they didn't get to finish. Rabbi Reichert looked forward to when he could take the time to finish the project and do justice to fulfilling Rabbi Wohlgemuth's vision. It would be more than twenty years before this goal would be realized, during which time, in 2008, Rabbi Wohlgemuth passed away.

Maimonides writes (Mishneh Torah, Hilchot Talmud Torah 1:2): כְּשֵׁם שֶׁאָדָם חַיָּב לְלַמֵּד אֶת בְּנוֹ, כָּךְ הוּא חַיָּב לְלַמֵּד אֶת בֶּן בְּנוֹ, שֶׁנֶּאֱמַר "וְהוֹדַעְתָּם לְבָנֶיךָ, וְלִבְנֵי בָנֶיךָ" (דברים ד,ט), Just as it is a man's duty to teach his son, so it is his duty to teach his grandson, as it is written: "Make them known unto thy children and thy children's children" (Devarim 4:9). Several years ago, I wanted to purchase more copies of Rabbi Wohlgemuth's *Guide to Jewish Prayer* to study each Shabbat long distance with my four grandsons living in Staten Island, New York. I found, however, that it had been out of print for many years. So I posted an Internet request to the Jewish Boston Group list: "Does anyone have the files for the original edition?" Joel Robinson, publisher of the first two printings, now living in Israel responded. He had all the files, and he gave me permission to use them.

So, although I could create a reprint of Rabbi Wohlgemuth's book for my grandsons in New York City, I was concerned that, if the book were to go out of print again, and if Joel Robinson and I weren't around, Rabbi Wohlgemuth's important work would no longer be available. It seemed to me that if the Maimonides School were involved as publisher, that would ensure the continued availability of the book. I contacted Michael Rosenberg, Business and Development Officer at Maimonides, to discuss with him the possibility of making the book available again.

He told me that he had received many requests for copies of Rabbi Wohlgemuth's book.

Rabbi Wohlgemuth's son, Rabbi Shlomoh Wohlgemuth, granted permission for his father's book to be edited, annotated, and republished. Shlomoh Wohlgemuth approached Abe Katz, a 1971 Maimonides graduate and a student of Rabbi Wohlgemuth, to be involved in the project. Abe had established the Beurei HaTefillah Institute to assist educators in developing courses on Tefillah. Abe reviewed the entire manuscript and enhanced the edition with an index and with many additional footnotes to clarify Rabbi Wohlgemuth's commentary. Together, Abe Katz, Mike Rosenberg and I produced the second edition of Rabbi Wohlgemuth's *Guide to Jewish Prayer*, published by Maimonides School, which appeared in print in July 2014.

While the 2014 edition of Rabbi Wohlgemuth's book was a noteworthy achievement, I felt that the ultimate goal should be to publish an edition of the book edited by Rabbi Asher Reichert together with all of the additions and modifications that Rabbi Reichert had discussed with Rabbi Wohlgemuth that were not included in the 2014 edition. In the fall of 2017, my grandson Shmuel Denker entered Yeshivat Reishit in Beit Shemesh, Israel. He brought along a copy of the 2014 edition of *Guide to Jewish Prayer* for Rabbi Reichert and his wife Rashie Reichert, Reishit's Office Manager. (Rashie Reichert and my wife had taught together at Maimonides many years ago.) In reply to my suggestion that we embark on the project of editing, updating and expanding Rabbi Wohlgemuth's book, Rabbi Reichert agreed and stated, "I am committed to finishing this project as soon as I possibly can, as correct as I can make it, and consistent with what I believe Rabbi Wohlgemuth intended."

After several years of dedicated work by Rabbi Reichert and Mrs. Rashie Reichert, the result is this third edition of Rabbi Isaiah Wohlgemuth's *Guide to Jewish Prayer*, extensively expanded to include previously unpublished author's notes and supplementary material. Now that it has been published by OU Press, I fervently hope that this invaluable work will remain widely available to the Jewish community.

I would personally like to thank Rabbi Dov Huff, Judaic Principal at Maimonides School, Rabbi David Hellman of the Young Israel of Brookline and Rabbi Simon Posner of OU Press for their encouragement, support and thoughtful advice. I also extend thanks to the entire OU Press team and to Ktav Publishing House for their efforts in bringing this work to fruition. This project could not have been realized without the generous financial support provided by Kenny Wintman and his sister Sandy Welkes, both former students of Rabbi Wohlgemuth. As they have supported the publication of earlier editions of Rabbi Wohlgemuth's work, they have now lovingly endowed this new edition, a volume which is a major contribution to the Jewish community and a fitting tribute to the memory of Rabbi Isaiah Wohlgemuth, *zt"l.*

Stephen Denker

2021

Maimonides School and the Legacy of Rabbi Wohlgemuth

Jewish schools are renowned for their ambition, typically understood as their commitment to teach students two complete, yet independent, curricula over more than a decade of schooling – a full secular education along with a comprehensive Jewish education as well.

Rabbi Joseph B. Soloveitchik – the Rav *zt"l* – founder of Maimonides School and the *Gadol Hador* for American Orthodoxy in the 20th century, understood that the ambition of Jewish education does not merely extend to information or material learned in the classroom, it also includes a wide range of skills, beliefs, patterns of mind, and personal commitments as well. Students should practice halachic living, receive training in mitzvah observance, and develop a deep appreciation of the feelings and ideas of Judaism. Our mission is not only to study text, it is to help young men and women mature into Jewish adults, ready to live their own lives of Torah and mitzvot.

For that reason, Maimonides School has always been distinguished world-wide by its unique commitment to training its *talmidim* and *talmidot* in living life as observant Jews. It has always been an innovator in reducing the barrier between classroom and practice: it is one of the few Orthodox schools worldwide with school on Sukkot, a high school Talmud program focused on the practical laws of Shabbat and Chullin, and for many its crown jewel, the *Beurei Hatefillah* program associated for decades with Rabbi Isaiah Wohlgemuth.

The book before you is the legacy of the course that Rabbi Wohlgemuth built, simultaneously and ambitiously training students in the laws of prayer, the meaning of prayer, the philosophy of prayer and the how-to's of praying as an adult member of the Jewish people. Rabbi Wohlgemuth understood that *tefillah* is ideally learned not merely through osmosis, but through an explicit instruction covering the laws of prayer, the structure of prayer, and the ideas behind how prayer works. We hope this book serves as an opening to its readers for a window into our school, our educational vision, and our approach to learning *tefillah*.

Rabbi Dr. Yaakov Jaffe
Dean of Judaic Studies, Maimonides School

Editors' Foreword

In the early part of the twentieth century, Jews in America were escaping oppressive conditions in Europe where they had been the victims of anti-Semitism. When they came to America and found that, as Americans, they could escape that oppression, many actively tried to become more American, more assimilated.

When Rabbi Joseph B. Soloveitchik came to Boston, he responded to this phenomenon and founded Maimonides School to counteract the strong shifts toward assimilation and to provide an environment where Jews, who wanted to keep the Jewish traditions and beliefs, could grow. The people he selected to teach the new generations of American Jews were unique in their experiences and abilities. The idea of a Jewish day school in those days, however, was too new a concept to be easily accepted by either the community or Jewish parents. It took dedicated and brave people to go against the frame of mind of the community and support the Rav in this project. There were very few American Jews who were willing to send their children to this school. This was before it was acceptable for each ethnic group to keep its traditional heritage and values. Many of the parents and children would be ridiculed as being fanatics, specifically because this school went against the common trend to join the American melting pot philosophy.

Rabbi Moses J. Cohn was the principal of the Rav's day school. He escaped Europe with the Mirrer Yeshiva and went with the yeshiva to Shanghai. Rabbi Cohn was one of those who, in spite of his young age, was instrumental in arranging the move of the yeshiva across

Asia and away from Nazi capture. The Rav was aware of, among other qualities, Rabbi Cohn's knowledge and teaching abilities as well as his impressive organizational skills and appointed him to be the principal of Maimonides School.

Rabbi Cohn understood that Jewish high school students should learn to understand the davening that they say every day. That was just one of his very insightful realizations, and even today, the meaning of our prayers is not taught well in most Jewish day schools. Rabbi Cohn asked Rabbi Isaiah Wohlgemuth to create a curriculum for studying our prayers and to teach it to every grade in the upper school.

Rabbi Wohlgemuth turned out to be the perfect choice for this project. He was a rabbi in Bavaria before the war. He was a Holocaust survivor. He was a man of deep faith. Rabbi Wohlgemuth saw European Jewry destroyed, and wanted to help each surviving Jewish student grow in Jewish knowledge. Rabbi Wohlgemuth loved his students and had the intelligent mind and accompanying scholarship to transmit our heritage. Rabbi Wohlgemuth's wife, Berta, supported him in all of his efforts. She taught the students when they first came into the school, in kindergarten, and Rabbi Wohlgemuth taught Mrs. Wohlgemuth's students when they reached high school.

Rabbi Wohlgemuth created a singular program of study of prayer. His curriculum included a study of most of the topics that were discussed in the Gemara relating to the prayers. After learning the explanations of the prayers (בֵּאוּרֵי הַתְּפִלָּה) with Rabbi Wohlgemuth, students understood that the prayers contain significant conceptual issues with deep meaning and were able to draw on this knowledge in their attempts to come close to God.

Rabbi Wohlgemuth gave a solid basis for students to appreciate the siddur and the process of praying to God. His course of study enabled a student to be familiar with the prayer book; to feel comfortable as an insider with participating in one of the most central aspects of Jewish life. It helped each student understand how and when to turn to God in need. As well as teaching his prepared material, if any student had any question about tefillah or any other matter, Rabbi Wohlgemuth responded and addressed every issue.

Rabbi Wohlgemuth did not present *every* position from *every* primary, secondary or modern source on *every* topic in the prayers. That was not his goal. He selected the major positions, as well as many other very logical views, and transmitted his material in a cohesive structure so a student could have a deep understanding of the way to pray. His students became sophisticated enough to be able to examine any question on prayer in detail for further study. There are many complex subjects that are covered in the course of studying prayer. Rabbi Wohlgemuth asked Rabbi Soloveitchik's opinion about many of them. Many of Rabbi Soloveitchik's positions were included in Rabbi Wohlgemuth's classes.

Rabbi Wohlgemuth taught his class on בֵּאוּרֵי הַתְּפִלָּה to Maimonides School students for over thirty years. I was one of Rabbi Wohlgemuth's students. I loved him, as did many other students. When I returned to Boston after an absence of almost twenty years, I more fully understood Rabbi Wohlgemuth's greatness as an educator. I came back with rabbinical ordination, a master's degree in secondary Jewish education and with children of my own whom we sent to Maimonides School. Rabbi Wohlgemuth had just retired but was still, on a voluntary basis, teaching a Talmud class to high school students on Shabbat afternoons. We were living about a three-quarters of an hour walk from the school, but I walked with my two eligible children every Shabbat to Maimonides School so my children could learn from Rabbi Wohlgemuth. I happily attended as well.

When we study Chumash and want to understand a difficult verse, we start by studying Rashi's commentary on the text. It easily aids us in understanding the text. We sometimes think of it as simple. But if we do, we are forgetting that Rashi was one of the greatest scholars in our history. Throughout the Talmud, we will find the same Rashi explaining the basic underlying issues of each passage. Sometimes it takes a great scholar to present something complex in a way that is easy to understand. Taking that idea further, if you find a great scholar, with excellent skills of simplifying difficult material into an easy to understand explanation, it behooves you to try to study anything that scholar has to transmit. You will learn from it.

My children were able to learn from Rabbi Wohlgemuth, and I did too.

Rabbi Wohlgemuth had not decided what he would do after he retired. I suggested to him that his בֵּאוּרֵי הַתְּפִלָּה material was so important and so comprehensive that it would be a shame if students could no longer learn to understand the siddur in the way the previous thirty years of Maimonides School students had been able to do. I proposed that Rabbi Wohlgemuth write a book that included his material on the siddur. At first, he was hesitant. He was afraid it might be a very difficult undertaking. I offered to work with him on the project, and he agreed. I suggested that we meet every weekday for an hour and work on the book. Rabbi Wohlgemuth consented to the arrangment.

Rabbi Wohlgemuth had given a series of six public lectures on the topics of the siddur. Someone had transcribed the first lecture. I thought this might be a good starting point for us, so my wife transcribed the other five lectures, and I came with them to Rabbi Wohlgemuth's home to begin our work. As I sat before him in his living room, I realized that I didn't need to start with a transcription of a series that had not been as broad as our project. I was sitting before Rabbi Wohlgemuth himself, so I asked him to just start dictating, and I would start typing. We began. I went to Rabbi Wohlgemuth's home almost every day for at least an hour, and many times for longer, even much longer. Sometimes Rabbi Wohlgemuth gave me handwritten pages. I have a notebook full. Every time I came to his home, Rabbi or Mrs. Wohlgemuth would graciously welcome me, and the rabbi and I would start our work. He just spoke, and I typed. We discussed issues. I often asked him about sources. I worked on grammar. In those days, we didn't feel footnotes were generally necessary. Standards have changed, and today a book of this kind must include sources.[1]

1. Some of the source notes in this book were provided by Rabbi Wohlgemuth as we discussed the material. Some of the notes in this book reflect sources that Rabbi Wohlgemuth preferred. Some of the notes are sources that corroborate what Rabbi Wohlgemuth said, though they were not necessarily mentioned by him. The references to Rabbi Soloveitchik came from personal discussions

When I asked Rabbi Wohlgemuth about the basis for something, he always knew exactly where it was. He showed me the sources to answer each question I asked. I came to know which were his favorites. I came to understand his view in presenting the material. We became very close. Rabbi Wohlgemuth offered to list me as a co-author, but my goal went beyond a suggestion for how to spend his retirement. I was his student. I wanted to share Rabbi Wohlgemuth with future generations of Jewish students. I wanted to make Rabbi Wohlgemuth's students hear his voice as they read the book, and I wanted to make him appreciated by people who would never meet him. I didn't want to take any focus off my teacher. I agreed to be listed as the editor to Rabbi Wohlgemuth's legacy.

We worked together for about seven years before my family went to live in Israel. Rabbi Wohlgemuth came to Israel for two summers after that, and we continued our project. By now his health was starting to deteriorate. We understood the book was not yet finished, and I would have to take over the job. Rabbi Wohlgemuth outlined for me how I should proceed. We discussed what we should include and how I should structure the work and fill it in. My major concern was how to make the material seem as straightforward as Rabbi Wohlgemuth did. In my mind, I was writing for young high school students, senior high school students, and people who wanted to learn more about the siddur, both people who had a high-level background as well as those with little or no background. I rewrote the material several times: with translations, without translations, with different levels of explanation of terms, with different amounts of Hebrew text.

Meanwhile, people from the Maimonides community heard about our project. I was approached by a member of the Maimonides

---

that Rabbi Wohlgemuth had with the Rav, and Rabbi Wohlgemuth should be considered a source. There have been written records of the Rav's positions, and I have included corroborating statements of the Rav's opinions where I felt it would be helpful. The sources that I cited are largely articles that the Rav wrote himself, records of the Rav's positions or summaries of the Rav's *shiurim* at Yeshiva University.

community. He told me that Rabbi Wohlgemuth's health had deteriorated and there was a group who wanted to publish this book to show it to Rabbi Wohlgemuth while he could still appreciate it. My draft document was still not complete. I expressed my concerns that this was only an incomplete first draft. I hadn't been able to check it, and it was only a partial work. I was told that this was only for a limited edition, just so Rabbi Wohlgemuth could enjoy it being in print, and it would be good enough for that purpose. Under those circumstances, I agreed, but I wanted to review the changes before it was published to ensure that what was published would reflect properly on Rabbi Wohlgemuth and his scholarship. I handed over the document, but, after reviewing the initial changed pages, I was concerned that the project would not reflect the spirit in which Rabbi Wohlgemuth transmitted the material to me. The project went on without my involvement, but my fears were unfounded. A few years ago, Maimonides School was involved in republishing the book. I got a notice through the alumni network and ordered a copy. I briefly looked at it and was pleasantly surprised to see that errors that I had seen initially were not there. I indicated to the person who informed me about the book that I intended to finish the book as soon as I was able. Shortly after, I was contacted by Dr. Stephen Denker who was involved in producing that edition. He provided me with a file of the last edition. I compared that to my copy and found that it was very similar and essentially the same as my original copy. I no longer was afraid that Rabbi Wohlgemuth's teachings were misrepresented.

When I initially released my draft, I did not anticipate the course that events would take and that my draft, before I was completely finished with it, would be publicly available. I am very pleased that until I was able to finish our project, years of Jewish students have been able to learn from Rabbi Wohlgemuth's teachings. I see it in retrospect in the nature of a preview of Rabbi Wohlgemuth's and my work.

The way our book was previously published was unconventional, but it reflects the way the Maimonides community and those who learned about the prayers from Rabbi Wohlgemuth thirsted for what they had experienced. They were almost desperate to hear his Torah.

It reminds me of the Gemara in Sanhedrin 68a that describes the death of Rabbi Eliezer. Rabbi Akiva eulogized him and expressed what everyone was thinking: "I have many questions and no one to ask." The Gemara at the end of Sotah says when Rabbi Eliezer died, it was as if the Sefer Torah itself was buried. When Rabbi Akiva died, the deep understandings and fountains of wisdom were stopped up. When Rabbi Chanina ben Dosa died, there were no longer men of action. When Abba Yossi ben Ketonta died, the men of kindness were no more.

Rabbi Wohlgemuth was no longer able to teach. The Rav was gone. That generation of Torah giants had passed. I understand the motivation of those who published the book that I was working on before I was completely finished with it, and I am happy that it was available for Rabbi Wohlgemuth's students to review, relearn or even recreate those lessons that they heard from our teacher.

I know how important it is to finally publish this book, but I did not want it published until I had finished checking each statement and providing the backup sources. This was a necessary, but time-intensive endeavor, which delayed my finishing the book. There were many statements that Rabbi Wohlgemuth made that seemed strange or like a minority view but when researching the sources, I found that in virtually every case, he was correct. Rabbi Wohlgemuth made the complex simple, and quoted little known sources that were really the most logical option. Many positions of Rabbi Soloveitchik are found in the book. They are the results of personal conversations that Rabbi Wohlgemuth had with the Rav. The Rav taught many of the Gemaras upon which the subject matter is based, and Rabbi Herschel Reichman has published some volumes of the Rav's classes at Yeshiva University where many of these positions were also expressed. Some explanations of the Rav were only expressed in private conversations. Rabbi Wohlgemuth's knowledge that he transmitted in his classes was very simply explained, but very far reaching.

Rabbi Wohlgemuth's goal was not to provide an encyclopedic explanation of the sources on the siddur, but rather, a good explanation of topics that one must have to appreciate the prayer experience from the perspective of our tradition. This book should provide a student with sufficient understanding to make the prayers meaningful. If a student wants to find additional explanations of the prayers, many of the sources in this book can be used as a springboard to further understanding. These sources can hopefully assist in the goal of not having one's prayer become ossified, as we are enjoined by Rabbi Shimon in Pirkei Avot.[2] This book is an introduction to the sophisticated ideas contained in the siddur.

The former students of Rabbi Wohlgemuth who read this may remember him saying these things. They might even imagine hearing his voice as they read the words. But some will be disappointed. They will feel Rabbi Wohlgemuth left things out of the book. They will miss not being able to ask Rabbi Wohlgemuth as they did in class to elaborate about a point or ask a different question. They will feel this book is the glass half empty. They will be right. They will be expressing Rabbi Akiva's statement in the eulogy of Rabbi Eliezer, "I have questions and nobody to ask."

Rabbi Wohlgemuth did not intend to answer every question. That would have been impossible. There is no replacing the experience of being in class and hearing him in person. The Sefer Torah was buried. But he gave directions about how to finish, and that could lead the student to pursue, on his own, to find the answer. The glass is truly half empty.

The other kind of person who might read this book is someone who did not have the opportunity to hear Rabbi Wohlgemuth in person. He will read many things that, while all found in our sources, sometimes are obscure and hard to find. That reader will appreciate the material that gives a grounding in Jewish prayer in a way that is, hopefully, easy to follow and accessible. That reader will appreciate this book for being the glass half full.

I also ask, "Who can answer my questions?" I am grateful that Rabbi Wohlgemuth agreed to work with me, gave me his written material and charged me to finish the book, so we could have a companion

2. אבות פרק ב משנה יג: Rabbi Shimon said... Do not make your prayer fixed.

to the siddur for future Jewish students. I cherish the time we spent together and regret that we did not have more.

Kenny Wintman and his sister Sandy Welkes generously provided the financial support for this publication. The Wintman family has a long association with Maimonides and Rabbi Soloveitchik. When Rabbi Soloveitchik was struggling to start Maimonides School as an institution of advanced learning for Jewish students encompassing all grades through high school, there was a small group of committed parents who had the vision and commitment to support him and send their children to his school. Some of them understood that their children would be given the highest levels of education in both Jewish and core studies. The Wintmans were among this group of people who wanted these studies taught. They also understood the unique privilege it was to have a rabbi of Rabbi Soloveitchik's greatness live in Boston and leave his mark on Boston's Jewish community. It was well known that Mr. Abraham Wintman was Rabbi Soloveitchik's driver when the Rav was in Boston, and that he was one of those who helped the Rav in whatever way he could to build the Jewish community of Boston. Kenny and Sandy are former students of Rabbi Wohlgemuth who appreciated him then and want to carry on Rabbi Wohlgemuth's legacy. Kenny contributed a selection of this book on the subject of the difference between Sukkot and Shemini Atzeret, taken from his notes. He was a good student. I think Kenny and Sandy will appreciate this book and see it as more than a glass half full.

Dr. Stephen Denker has been instrumental in coordinating the publication of this book. Dr. Denker was not Rabbi Wohlgemuth's student but his children were. Dr. Denker told me how he had one of the versions of the book that was published from my first, unfinished draft. On Shabbat afternoons, he studied the book with his grandchildren. Dr. Denker is singularly and selflessly devoted to spreading Rabbi Wohlgemuth's Torah to as many Jewish students and possible. When we were considering publishers, Dr. Denker vigorously proposed that my finished work be published by the OU Press, and he committed to do what he could to make this book available to as wide a group of future Jewish students as possible. It became clear to me that Dr.

Denker and Kenny Wintman represented the best examples of people who would appreciate the finished book. I believe I could have no better espousers to enable Rabbi Wohlgemuth's Torah to help students understand the contents of the siddur.

I would like to thank a number of people who have been very helpful in enabling me to complete this work. Rabbi Yitzchak Lichtenstein answered a number of questions I had regarding Hallel, the Haggadah and the practices of his grandfather, the Rav. Rabbi Mayer Twersky, also a grandson of the Rav, likewise was very kind and answered a number of questions I had regarding his grandfather's opinions and positions of the Vilna Gaon. Professor Avraham Grossman was gracious in giving me his opinion about the possible origin of the berachah of שֶׁעָשַׂנִי כִּרְצוֹנוֹ. Rabbi Chayim Soloveichik was very helpful and served as a sounding board for me when I was struggling through a number of *sugyot*.

We also thank Rabbi Eliyahu Krakowski for his editing of our work. I believe Rabbi Wohlgemuth would have been very pleased with what Rabbi Krakowski has done. His scholarship, knowledge and insights are of the highest caliber, and we are honored by his involvement in this project.

Rabbi Asher Reichert
Rashie Reichert

This book could not have been written without the help of my wife, Rashie Reichert. I verified Rabbi Wohlgemuth's statements and finished some work that he and I discussed, but Rashie caught Rabbi Wohlgemuth's way of making the complex simple. She took my pedantry and brought it back to Rabbi Wohlgemuth's clear and straightforward style. She, in fact, made it readable.

Rabbi Asher Reichert

Preface

Some thirty years ago, the principal of Maimonides School in Boston, Rabbi Moses J. Cohn, asked me to develop and teach a course on prayer. We called it Be'urei Hatefillah, or Explanations of the Prayers. It was to be taught from eighth through twelfth grades. For the senior year, I worked out a special program that was a comprehensive review of the entire material. The students were also asked to present a term paper on a subject of their choice.

It is amazing how often former students, sometimes those who graduated more than a generation ago, come to me to discuss a fine point of the course. Some made it a ritual to go over the notes with their families. They often assure me that of all the religious subjects, Be'urei Hatefillah was the one that helped them most in life. It made the hours spent in shul more meaningful, and established their relationship with the Almighty on a more intimate basis.

Rabbi J.B. Soloveitchik (the Rav) enthusiastically endorsed the course and stated that no student could graduate from Maimonides School without passing it. The Rav encouraged me to discuss with him all problems that might come up in teaching this course. I took ample advantage of his invitation to consult him. I usually asked him questions in the morning when I had the privilege to drive him to and from shul. The Rav's interpretations and explanations thus became a major part of my understanding of prayer.

Why was the Rav so interested in Be'urei Hatefillah? Most likely it was because his soul thirsted for closeness to God. On one occasion, when he had resumed teaching his classes at Maimonides after serious abdominal surgery, he expressed his frustration with many of our brothers and sisters who go into surgery without a last-minute appeal to God to crown the effort of the surgeon with success.

"It is the gentile," the doctors told him, "who muster all their feelings to get God's assistance in their difficult ordeal."

"What a disgrace!" the Rav exclaimed. "We Jews, who taught the world to pray, have forgotten this art. For this reason," he explained, "I shall dedicate my Saturday evening classes to relearning the true meaning of prayer." It was indeed a year of great discoveries and spiritual heights.

The Rav often visited the classes in religious subjects. Understandably, the teachers did not feel so happy about it. However, the Rav did not come to class to criticize the instructors but rather to get a feel of the academic standing of that particular class. One day I had prepared a test for my senior students, and the Rav entered the class to listen to the lesson. I quickly explained the situation to him. "Just give me a copy of the test," the Rav said, and left the room. A few weeks later he called me and said, "By the way, I gave your test to my senior rabbinical students. None of them could give all the answers. It is a good course."

Naturally, I read and studied all books and sources on prayer that were available to me. The German Jewish movement, the Wissenschaft des Judentums, constantly dealt with this fascinating subject. The study of prayer started in Germany in the nineteenth century as a result of the development of the Reform and Conservative movements, which started during this period. As these movements appeared on the stage of Jewish history, they promoted the study of prayer. On the one hand, Reform and Conservative Jews wanted to show that our prayers were not always a part of our heritage, therefore, what wasn't always there could be eliminated. They didn't like long prayers, and they didn't like prayers in Hebrew. They liked to have sermons. They wanted to show that their reforms had a legitimate place.

On the other hand, the Orthodox tried to show that everything that we say is essential, that we have no right to make changes, and that we cannot skip anything. Great luminaries, great scholars, such as Rabbis Berliner, Landshut and Sachs, appeared in Germany who dealt with the subject. One of the last scholars in Germany was the late Dr. Ismar Elbogen. Although he was a Reform scholar, he was always fair and thorough in transmitting the Orthodox point of view. His contributions were based on the works of many scholars and are now available in an excellent Hebrew translation, הַתְּפִלָּה בְּיִשְׂרָאֵל בְּהִתְפַּתְּחוּתָהּ הַהִיסְטוֹרִית. Rav Soloveitchik said to me, "Read his books. Study his books. He is very traditional in his approach. He is very clever and he made very valuable contributions to the study of prayer." Yitzchak (Seligman) Baer was another early German-Jewish Orthodox scholar. His classic commentary on the prayers, עֲבוֹדַת יִשְׂרָאֵל, is an important work.

This book, *A Guide to Jewish Prayer,* is an outgrowth of, and a recapitulation of the Be'urei Hatefillah course and is meant to be a companion volume to the siddur. The systematic reading of this volume or an occasional review of it should keep the meaning of the prayers fresh in the mind of the reader.

This book is not meant to make new discoveries in the study of the prayers, but rather to keep the כַּוָּנָה (concentration) of the students at a high point. Since the purpose of this book is to inspire the reader, my method was to go over most of the materials on the various prayers and present a thorough summary of the problems therein that would be most interesting. As stated before, in most cases I have presented the philosophy of Rav Soloveitchik. However, the rabbinic sources that I found in the Talmudic literature will be cited in the notes.

Rabbi Isaiah Wohlgemuth
1986

Prologue

The Jewish people have faced persecution throughout the ages, and each generation has overcome many difficulties. There have, however, been several periods in history when Jewish communities have flourished. Those periods can be referred to as "Golden Ages of Judaism." There is general agreement that the Jews in Spain, under the Moorish rule, were able to develop their skills in many fields, such as government, poetry, philosophy, and language. Their achievements in this age are well known, and Jews are proud of those accomplishments.

I, surprisingly, have classified the years from 1933 to 1939 as another Golden Age in Jewish history. You might think it strange to refer to those years as a Golden Age. Are they not the beginning of the Hitler period, years of tragedy, the years that immediately preceded the Holocaust?

They were years in which the Jewish people were deprived of all basic rights and classified as second-class citizens. I lived through these years and think of them very often. Hitler came to power, and we knew there was no future for the Jewish people in Germany. We knew that the history of a thousand years in Europe had come to an end.

On the other hand, we thought the elimination of Jews from all activities would proceed in a fashion that would allow our escape. We thought our youth could be trained in skills that would help them to establish a new life in the free world. We thought the older generation would spend the last few years of their lives in comparative ease, living on their savings and hoping for a peaceful future. We thought that middle age people would be able to emigrate and start life anew.

The most significant aspect of this period, however, was our ability to study Judaism and observe the great spiritual heritage of our ancestors. The political oppression of those years might have frustrated most people in the world, but it did not frustrate the Jews in Germany, who, in spite of all the obstacles, difficulties, and hardships, dedicated all their free time to learn Torah, in the widest sense of the word.

I personally studied in those years at the great Telshe Yeshiva and Rabbinical Seminary in Berlin. My father, זצ״ל (of blessed memory), passed away in 1935, and the community invited me to become his successor. I was of the opinion that I had years of spiritual work ahead of me. In those years the Nazi dictatorship did not interfere with Jewish studies as long as we did not interfere with the Nazi plans for the future.

Suddenly, everyone in my congregation wanted to learn, תּוֹרָה שֶׁבִּכְתָב (the written word of Torah) and Torah שֶׁבְּעַל פֶּה (the oral law). They wanted to attend classes in the many fields of Jewish scholarship. They also wanted to improve their knowledge of English and modern Hebrew. They believed that these languages would make it easier for them to adjust in the countries to which they would immigrate.

I was busy every hour of the day, and what happened in my congregation happened all over Germany. The most assimilated Jews wanted to make up for their lack of knowledge of Jewish studies. There was a tremendous search for knowledge that was unequaled in all Jewish history. Martin Buber, Franz Rosenzweig, and Leo Baeck, to name a few, were leading scholars of this renaissance of Jewish learning.

In the Orthodox community, the Munks, the Wohlgemuths, the Cohens, the Breuers, the Biberfelds, the Freimans, the Carlebachs, and many others taught Talmud virtually all day long. We did not think of the dangers ahead of us, and we continued on the path that we set for ourselves.

The highlight of the week in every community was the weekly sermon of the rabbi. Today, people are rarely eager to hear rabbis' sermons. In those days, nobody wanted to miss one word of the rabbis' ideas, both in the Orthodox community and in the Liberal congregations. Here I was, just twenty-one years of age, and, I am embarrassed to say, people loved every idea I gave them. They discussed and absorbed each one. Some of the sermons I delivered in those days are still fresh in my mind.

For my part, I was not eager to deliver sermons, because I knew that every gentile in town could stop my "revolutionary ideas." In large communities like Berlin, where there were close to 200,000 Jews, delivering a sermon was very dangerous because the Gestapo sent their spies into synagogues to find out whether the rabbi said anything unfavorable about Hitler or the Nazis. The rabbi would never know who was listening to him, and each sermon he delivered was recorded by the Nazi spies. Those men, such as Rabbis Joachim Prinz or Max Nussbaum from prewar Berlin, actually risked their lives every time they spoke. We, in our naiveté, thought that this lifestyle, in which the love of learning was so powerful and great, would continue for a few years and that we rabbis and other teachers had a great task ahead of us. There were very few eras in history where a total commitment to learning was the guiding light.

One Shabbat, I overheard people discussing the depression they suffered because of the uncertainty of the future. This inspired me to deliver sermons that were geared to restoring their courage, self-confidence, and hope for the future. One sermon I delivered has stayed with me ever since.

I began by quoting פָּרָשַׁת וַיֵּצֵא, where Rashi asks about the verse, וַיֵּצֵא יַעֲקֹב מִבְּאֵר שָׁבַע וַיֵּלֶךְ חָרָנָה ("And Jacob went out of Beersheva and went to Haran").[1] Why does it say, "And Jacob went out of Beersheva"? It would have been sufficient just to say, "And Jacob went to Haran." Thus, we see that the departure of a righteous person from a city leaves a deep impression. As long as the righteous person lives in the city, the city enjoys his or her glory and fame. The moment that the righteous person leaves the city, the city loses its importance and greatness.

Starting with this interpretation of Rashi, I stated that our emigration from Germany would make a great impression; it would turn Germany, a country of scientific achievements, into a second-rate

1. בראשית כח:י

community. Sermons of this nature boosted peoples' self-confidence and gave them the strength to live through those difficult years. Our emigration from Germany was Germany's loss.

On another occasion, I raised the question, why is the second book of the Torah, Exodus, called Shemot in Hebrew, which literally means "Names"? Is it not strange that the Hebrew name given to each book of the Holy Scriptures is the first word of that book, without any connection to the context of the chapter or book as a whole? Sometimes we can find a connection in the choice of names. Bereshit (Genesis), which literally means "In the beginning," is the first word of the Torah and explains to us what the parashah is all about. However, what does "Names" have to do with the second book of the Torah?

The Hebrew word not only means "names" but also the "fame and glory" of a people. Therefore, I explained that Shemot is the book that shows how a despised people became, with the help of God, the chosen people of Israel.

When the Jews were in Egypt, many were abused, insulted, beaten, and murdered. By the time the narrative moved from the Exodus from Egypt to the giving of the law on Mount Sinai, everyone spoke with great awe of the Jewish people. Suddenly they had turned into the most important society in the ancient world. We can therefore translate Shemot as "the Book of the Name of Israel": how oppressed slaves became the nation that God chose to lead humanity from darkness into light, from oppression to liberty.

I addressed the congregation, saying, "Today we are the despised people of Israel. Tomorrow we will yet be the chosen people of God." I told them, "The short period of servitude will be turned into the era of a super nation of Israel that would set an example for the rest of the human race." I predicted that history would repeat itself. It took courage to say these words in those days, but it made life tolerable for the Jews of Germany in those terrible years.

Sometimes I substituted those sermons of encouragement with words of reprimand. For instance: when the Jews were safe in Egypt, they listened to Moshe and the laws that he taught them. They had the courage to defy the power of Pharaoh, as they showed Moshe great respect and appreciated their ancestors' philosophy. After crossing the Red Sea, they sang the famous Song of the Sea, which expressed the closeness of Israel to God: "And Israel saw the powerful hand that God unfolded in Egypt, the people feared God, and they believed in God and in Moshe."[2] Soon after, the Jewish people complained to Moshe about the bitter water.[3]

Before crossing the Red Sea, the Jews listened to Moshe as God commanded them. The attitude of the Jewish people changed tremendously, however, once they crossed the Red Sea. They refused to listen to Moshe and carry out his commands.

The Torah says: וַיַּסַּע מֹשֶׁה אֶת־יִשְׂרָאֵל (He made Israel travel).[4] Moshe was in a rush, but the Jewish people were in no rush to arrive at Mount Sinai. They were busy picking up the booty of the Egyptian army. Moshe had to use all his persuasion to have them follow him to Mount Sinai.

I told my congregants: it seems that the Jews have not changed much in 3,000 years. When we fear our enemies, we turn to God and pray. But the moment that we cross the Red Sea, we set out on the road of assimilation and forget God.

I said, "You, my friends, must show that you are different. Today you are oppressed, so you fill the synagogues and study halls. But once you cross the line into freedom, I fear that you will go back to your old ways. Let us show the world that we love God and the Torah not only in days of distress but also in years of freedom."

I told a nice anecdote about the famous Rothschild family in Frankfurt. The Rothschild family overcame the poverty of the ghetto, built a beautiful palace, and had a good life. But they never strayed from the words of the Torah, and they always showed their gratitude to God for their good fortune by carrying out the laws of the Torah. In their home they had a synagogue and a מִקְוֶה (ritual bath) and everything necessary to lead a good Jewish life.

---

2. שמות יד:לא
3. שמות טו:כד
4. שמות טו:כב

Anshel Rothschild often invited rabbis, and especially the chief leaders among the rabbis, to visit him and spend a few days with him. On one occasion he boasted somewhat about his piety. He showed his guests and the Rosh Yeshiva through his house while relating to them how he maintained the Yiddishkeit of his ancestors. He expected a word of praise from the Rosh Yeshiva.

Instead of praise the Rosh Yeshiva said, "There was one commandment in the Torah that you did not keep." Reb Anshel, surprised, looked at him and said, "Which word of the Torah did I not observe?" The Rosh Yeshiva answered with a smile, וַיִּשְׁמַן יְשֻׁרוּן וַיִּבְעָט ("And Jeshurun waxed fat and kicked").[5] Here the Torah tells us, the Rosh Yeshiva continued, that when Jews are successful they go back on the road of assimilation. You, Reb Anshel, waxed fat. But you have never yet broken a law of the Torah willingly.

Then I concluded: Today we are looked down upon and threatened with extinction. Let us be like Anshel Rothschild; when God's kindness will have redeemed us, let us carry on with the life of Torah and its commandments, learning and scholarship. May God grant us the wisdom to continue in these ways even when we will again be a free nation. וּבָא לְצִיּוֹן גּוֹאֵל וּלְשָׁבֵי פֶשַׁע בְּיַעֲקֹב נְאֻם ה׳ (And a Redeemer will come to Zion and to the people among Israel who turn away from sin).[6] This is a prophecy of God. We have anxiously been waiting for the coming of the Redeemer. May we all live through these years of oppression and hardship and lead a life based on the words of the Torah.

Unfortunately, the scholarship of the years 1933 to 1939 did not grant us the freedom that we desired. The tragedy of the Holocaust followed those years of second-class citizenship. But those years will always show the tremendous potential of the Jewish community.

Rabbi Isaiah Wohlgemuth
1986

---

5. דברים לב:טו
6. ישעיהו נט:כ

The Elements of Prayer

WHAT'S IN A NAME?

When reciting the prayer known as the שְׁמוֹנֶה עֶשְׂרֵה (or Amidah), many Jews practice a strange custom. Before reciting the concluding sentence, יִהְיוּ לְרָצוֹן אִמְרֵי פִי וְהֶגְיוֹן לִבִּי לְפָנֶיךָ ה׳ צוּרִי וְגֹאֲלִי ("May my words and thoughts be acceptable to You, God, my source of strength and my Savior"), they quote a verse from the Bible that either contains their Hebrew name or starts and ends with the same letters as their Hebrew name. This practice goes back to the mystic known as the Shelah.[1] He claimed that recitation of this sentence would help us to remember our name after we die and are called before the Divine tribunal to give an account of our activities in this world. Many versions of the siddur still print a list of verses containing the most popular Jewsh names. The minhag does not really make sense, however. Why should a person have to identify oneself before the Almighty? After all, the Almighty is omniscient.

I would interpret this custom the following way: When Jews name a child, it is not simply a way of identifying the child; it is a way to find a goal for the child in life and to determine his or her spiritual make-up.

Among Ashkenazi Jews, parents usually name a child after a beloved person who has departed this life. If the family members

1. See *Siddur Otzar Hatefillot* (Hebraica Press: New York, 1966), p. 372.

admired the departed for piety, good deeds, love of God and Torah, they would give their child the name of the departed, indicating that there is somebody new who will continue the excellent way of life of the person they mourn. Naming a child after a departed person has a twofold purpose: first, the child has been identified, and second, the child has been told what is expected of him or her in life. A child who has been named after a biblical figure has been told to make the aspirations of this biblical figure his or her own (in addition to adopting the virtues of the departed relative of that name).

To the Rabbis, a person's name was indicative of his or her character. The Talmud tells us a delightful story.[2] Rabbi Meir and his colleagues, Rabbi Yehudah and Rabbi Yossi, came to a certain town shortly before Shabbat. They went to the local inn to reserve a room and to deposit their valuables with the innkeeper. Before they handed over their valuables, Rabbi Meir asked the innkeeper for his name. When the innkeeper relied, "Kiddor," Rabbi Meir turned to his friends and said, "I don't trust this man." His name reminded Rabbi Meir of the verse (Devarim 32:20): כִּי דוֹר תַּהְפֻּכֹת הֵמָּה ("Because they are a generation [– in Hebrew, *Ki dor*] that does everything the wrong way").

"If this is all you have against him," the friends said to Rabbi Meir, "we shall deposit our money with him. It is foolish to suspect a person of wrongdoing because of his name." "Have it your way," Rabbi Meir said, and he looked for a place to hide his valuables.

His friends, without giving it another thought, left their money with the innkeeper. The townspeople had an inspiring Shabbat with Rabbi Meir. On Sunday morning, the rabbis got ready to continue their trip. Rabbi Meir went to his hiding place and recovered his money, while his friends asked Kiddor for their funds.

"What funds?" the innkeeper asked, and denied all knowledge of the transaction. Since there were no witnesses, it was their word against his. "Why did we not listen to Rabbi Meir?" his colleagues bemoaned.

In our context, the same way that a person's name might reflect on

---

2. יומא דף פג עמ׳ ב

his or her personality, when we refer to God, the specific name we use when we do so, reflects the attribute of God that He displays when revealing Himself to us.

WHAT'S IN GOD'S NAME?

God is known to us by many names. Some are actual names of God, such as the Tetragrammaton (שֵׁם הַמְּפֹרָשׁ, which we abbreviate as ה׳ and read as "Hashem," or "the Name"). Others indicate God's activities, such as הָרַחֲמָן ("the All-Merciful") or הַמָּקוֹם ("the Omnipresent").

It is alright to write and erase these last two names, since they are not real names but only characteristics of God.[3] The real names of God should not be written and certainly never erased. The Rabbis mention seven names of God to which this applies.[4] One should not pronounce these names of God except in the framework of reciting a verse, berachah, or prayer. To do so at any other time is a violation of the mitzvah to fear God, which includes not uttering God's name in vain.[5]

The שֵׁם הַמְּפֹרָשׁ cannot even be properly pronounced today, for we no longer know how to do so. It was only pronounced in the Temple in Jerusalem. Since then the pronunciation has been forgotten. The שֵׁם הַמְּפֹרָשׁ consists of the following letters: Yud-Keh-Vav-Keh. Even in writing this, we change Heh to Keh. Whenever we recite a verse, berachah, or prayer, we use the substitute name "Ado-nay"; otherwise, as noted, we say "Hashem."

We take a similar action with any of the other six names of God, such as Elokim (again replacing the H with a K); these names can be, and often are, pronounced, but it is still a sin to erase them. We are therefore very careful not to write the name correctly, if it will

3. רמב"ם הלכות יסודי התורה פרק ו הל׳ ה

4. רמב"ם הלכות יסודי התורה פרק ו הל׳ ב and שולחן ערוך יורה דעה סימן רעו סעיף ט. The seven names are the שֵׁם הַמְּפֹרָשׁ as it is written and as it is pronounced (הוי"ה and אדנות), as well as אהי־ה, א־ל, אלו־ה, אל־הים; ש־די, צב־אות.

5. רמב"ם הלכות שבועות פרק יב הל׳ יא

eventually be thrown away. If we do write a name of God by mistake, it must be buried, not thrown away. We do this with a siddur and other holy books that contain God's names when they are so old and torn that they cannot be used anymore. In the Middle East, many synagogues used an attic for this purpose. It was called a genizah. The most famous genizah was the one discovered in Cairo, Egypt. To this day, many scholars are engaged in deciphering manuscripts that have been found there.

In order to have the proper כַּוָּנָה, or concentration, in our prayers and berachot, we must always think of the real meaning of the name of God that we are using. For instance, when we pronounce אֱלֹקִים, we must think of its meaning, that God is all-powerful. When we pronounce the שֵׁם הַמְּפֹרָשׁ as Ado-nai, we must recognize God as the Master and Owner of everything.[6]

The Shulchan Aruch contains an interesting controversy: Should we think of the meaning of the שֵׁם הַמְּפֹרָשׁ as it is written or as it is pronounced? The Shulchan Aruch recommends doing both. The Gaon of Vilna suggests that we should think of the name that we actually pronounce except when we recite the first verse of שְׁמַע, when one should have in mind both meanings.[7]

We see the importance of God's names in Shacharit, beginning with the prayer בָּרוּךְ שֶׁאָמַר ("Blessed is the One who spoke"). בָּרוּךְ שֶׁאָמַר, the berachah that opens פְּסוּקֵי דְזִמְרָה, should logically start like any other berachah, with בָּרוּךְ אַתָּה ה׳ ("Blessed are You, Hashem"). However, a whole paragraph of the prayer comes before this berachah. Why is this so?

Rabbi David Zvi Hoffmann, the teacher of my late father, solved this problem in his essay on sacrifices.[8] At the beginning of Shacharit, we clarify to whom we pray. We turn in prayer to Hashem; therefore, in the beginning of בָּרוּךְ שֶׁאָמַר, there is an introduction before we

---

6. שולחן ערוך אורח חיים סימן ה

7. ביאור הגר"א אורח חיים סימן ה

8. R. David Zvi Hoffmann, *Sefer Vayikra*, vol. 1, pp. 59–68. See also R. David Zvi Hoffmann, *Al Hatefillah*, pp. 65–67.

begin the actual berachah. There we interpret God's proper name in seven different ways. For instance, the phrase שֶׁאָמַר וְהָיָה הָעוֹלָם ("who spoke and the world came into being") is a reference to God as the Creator of the Universe. By saying בָּרוּךְ חַי לָעַד ("Blessed be the One who lives forever"), we refer to God as the Eternal: הָיָה, הֹוֶה, יִהְיֶה (He was, is, and will be).[9]

Similarly, when we refer to ourselves in our prayers as the Jewish people, we also use different names. For instance, in the section לְעוֹלָם יְהֵא, we call our people יִשְׂרָאֵל and יְשֻׁרוּן. Israel, because our father Yaakov fought with an angel and triumphed;[10] יְשֻׁרוּן, derived from יָשָׁר (right), because we are dedicated to doing what is right in the eyes of God.[11]

In Shacharit, in the berachah preceding the שְׁמוֹנֶה עֶשְׂרֵה, we refer to the Jewish people as Israel, while in Maariv, in the parallel berachah, we identify ourselves as Jacob. Why is there this change of name? In the evening, when Jacob was attacked by the angel, he was still Jacob, fighting for his very existence; by the morning, after defeating his enemy, his name had been changed to Israel.[12]

A BERACHAH UTTERED IN VAIN

Since אַנְשֵׁי כְּנֶסֶת הַגְּדוֹלָה formulated the prayers, we are no longer allowed to create new berachot. Only אַנְשֵׁי כְּנֶסֶת הַגְּדוֹלָה, which included prophets and the greatest scholars, had that right.[13] They established the rabbinic obligation to recite blessings and they coined their format.[14] After their establishing the berachot, no one had the authority to add berachot. If there is no obligation to say the berachah and

9. See *The World of Prayer* by Rabbi Dr. Elie Munk (Feldheim: New York, 1961), pp. 60–65, based on the explanation of R. David Zvi Hoffmann.

10. בראשית לב:כט

11. אבן עזרא דברים לב:טו ד"ה וישמן ישורון

12. *The World of Prayer*, p. 204.

13. מגילה דף יז עמ׳ ב

14. רמב"ם הלכות ברכות פרק א הלכה ב-ג

you do say it, it would be a violation of the prohibition of reciting a berachah in vain (בְּרָכָה לְבַטָּלָה).

However, the Geonim – the rabbis who followed the Talmudic period – living much closer to the source, had a more intimate knowledge of Talmudic practice than we do. The Geonim knew of many berachot whose source we have lost. It is possible that they knew that a specific berachah was, in fact, composed by אַנְשֵׁי כְּנֶסֶת הַגְּדוֹלָה. Some give weight to the fact that a berachah became an established practice, no matter what its source. Once it became a tradition or minhag, this view maintains that it gained an official status. This view allows saying such a berachah, even though it may not have been instituted by אַנְשֵׁי כְּנֶסֶת הַגְּדוֹלָה.[15]

What happens if we say a berachah and then we realize that there was no need for it – for instance, suppose I want to eat a piece of fruit, but as I say the berachah I realize that I have no fruit to eat? The Rabbis advised us, in such a case, to immediately say, בָּרוּךְ שֵׁם כְּבוֹד מַלְכוּתוֹ לְעוֹלָם וָעֶד ("Blessed be the renown of His kingship forever").[16] In other words, we praise God's name.

Why does this relieve us of our sin? I would suggest the following reason. When I say, "Blessed are You, Hashem our God, King of the universe, who created the fruits of the trees," I thank God for giving me the opportunity to enjoy one of His creations. By adding בָּרוּךְ שֵׁם כְּבוֹד מַלְכוּתוֹ לְעוֹלָם וָעֶד, I am not thanking God for doing me a special favor but rather praising God for creating fruits for the benefit of humanity.

---

15. Rav Ovadiah Yosef (שו"ת יביע אומר חלק ב - אורח חיים סימן כה ד"ה והנה) writes that the two views are those of the kabbalists on the one hand and the halachists on the other, and the question of how to decide remains unresolved (והנה במקום שרבני המקובלים סוברים היפך דברי הפוסקים, לא יצא הדבר מידי מחלוקת אם יש לפסוק כהמקובלים או כהפוסקים).
The two sides of the issue are represented by very serious authorities. To list a few in no particular order: In favor: ר"ת, רא"ש, רמ"א, אר"י, עטרת זקנים, ט"ז, משנה ברורה, בן איש חי. Opposed: רמב"ם, סמ"ק, רוקח, ב"י, מהרש"ל, גר"א, גר"ח מוואלוז'ין, עטרת צבי. The מגן אברהם says to recite the berachah without שֵׁם וּמַלְכוּת.

16. שלחן ערוך אורח חיים סימן רו סעיף ו

FOCUSING ONE'S ATTENTION: כַּוָּנָה

There are different types of כַּוָּנָה, intention or awareness. One type of awareness means that I am aware of doing the action in order to fulfill the mitzvah (commandment). For example, if I blow the shofar on Rosh Hashanah with the intention of performing a mitzvah rather than blowing it as a musical instrument, if I recite the Shema specifically to fulfill the mitzvah rather than reciting it as reading sentences from the Torah, or if I pick up the lulav and esrog in order to perform the mitzvah rather than just to carry it from one place to another, then I am having the kind of awareness that is called the כַּוָּנָה לָצֵאת (intention to fulfill the commandment).

The second type of awareness consists of understanding and focusing on the meaning of every word of our prayers. This kind of concentration is very difficult, since the human mind finds it almost impossible to focus for any length of time on any one idea.[17] The Rabbis warn us not to "throw" a berachah out of our mouths. By this they declare that we must understand and think about its meaning.

With regard to Shema, there may be another form of כַּוָּנָה as well. This is the intention to accept God's mastery of the world (קַבָּלַת עֹל מַלְכוּת שָׁמַיִם). The mitzvah of Shema is not merely reciting certain words. Having this כַּוָּנָה to "accept the yoke of heaven" is actually part of the mitzvah of Shema.[18] The Rabbis declared that only if one lacks this awareness in the first verse, one must repeat the Shema.[19] We have a similar law regarding the Amidah, or שְׁמוֹנֶה עֶשְׂרֵה. When reciting the Amidah, we must clear our minds of other thoughts and have כַּוָּנָה that we are standing in God's presence,[20] at least for the first berachah of the שְׁמוֹנֶה עֶשְׂרֵה. If we don't even have כַּוָּנָה for that, strictly speaking, we should go back and repeat the שְׁמוֹנֶה עֶשְׂרֵה again with concentration

---

17. שלחן ערוך אורח חיים סימן צח סעיף ב
18. בית יוסף אורח חיים סימן סג בשם הרשב״א; מגן אברהם סימן ס ס״ק ד; חידושי ר׳ עקיבא איגר, ברכות דף יג עמ׳ א ד״ה ראיתי
19. שלחן ערוך אורח חיים סימן ס סעיף ה
20. רמב״ם, הל׳ תפילה פרק ד הל׳ טז

and awareness.[21] However, the Rama says, and we follow his opinion, that we might not even be able to have כַּוָּנָה the second time we recite the שְׁמוֹנֶה עֶשְׂרֵה either, so we don't repeat it.[22]

Jewish folklore contains many stories about the importance of כַּוָּנָה. One story tells of a child who could not master the skill of reading the machzor (the High Holiday prayer book). During the High Holiday services, his father pressed a machzor into his hands, hoping that he could at least follow the chazzan (prayer leader) during part of the prayers. Suddenly, during the most solemn part of the services, the boy whistled loudly. His father, deadly embarrassed, shrieked at his son.

The rabbi who had witnessed the scene calmed the father, saying, "If the Almighty has accepted our prayers today, it is because of your son's whistling. None of us reached complete כַּוָּנָה during today's service. Your son did. He is aware that he cannot daven (pray) properly, but he knows how to whistle better than anyone else. He put all of his love of Hashem into his whistling, meaning, 'Everything I know and all I have belongs to God.' Our prayers may not have reached God, but your son's whistling pierced the very heavens."[23]

The Shulchan Aruch[24] says that a congregation can pray in any language. The Shulchan Aruch cites two opinions about whether an individual can pray in any language or whether an individual must pray in Hebrew. Later authorities write that prayer in Hebrew is strongly

---

21. This is actually subject to a dispute. According to R. Chaim Soloveitchik (חידושי ר׳ חיים הלוי, הל׳ תפילה פרק ד הל׳ א), the כַּוָּנָה required especially for the first berachah of the Amidah is to understand the words you are saying. But the awareness that one is standing in God's presence is necessary for the entire Amidah; otherwise, it is as if no prayer was recited at all. However, others (see גליונות החזון איש שם) argue that this would place an almost impossible requirement of concentration on those praying. Rather, if one is aware of being in God's presence for the first berachah of the Amidah alone, it is not ideal but it is sufficient to fulfill the obligation of prayer.

22. Here, the Rama quotes the Tur: רמ״א אורח חיים סימן קא, סעיף א.

23. Many attribute this story to the Baal Shem Tov.

24. שולחן ערוך אורח חיים סימן קא סעיף ד

preferred.[25] In summary, we certainly should not make an official policy to pray in another language, but if necessary, we could do so until we are able to learn to pray in Hebrew.

THE MEANING OF THE WORD תְּפִילָּה

Usually the word תְּפִילָּה is translated as prayer. In the Talmud, תְּפִילָּה is the technical term for the Amidah, or Shemoneh Esreh. What does תְּפִילָּה really mean? Rabbi Samson Raphael Hirsch points out that the root of תְּפִילָּה is פלל, which he says is related to the root בלל, which means mixing or combining.[26] In prayer, we infuse ourselves with true ideas about God and His relationship with us. These ideas are integrated into our personalities through our תְּפִילָּה.

This explains how we can have fixed times to pray. If תְּפִילָּה were primarily about our internal feelings, then it would not make sense to be obligated to pray when we did not feel the impulse to do so. But since תְּפִילָּה is about integrating into our personalities true ideas about God, we can be obligated to pray even when we don't feel the need to pour out our souls. תְּפִילָּה is intended to shape us spiritually, even when we are not in the mood.

THE WRITTEN SIDDUR

The Rambam[27] understands that prayer is a mitzvah from the Torah. The Ramban disagrees.[28] The Ramban says that if there is any Torah obligation to pray, that is only when a person is in trouble, either as an individual or when a calamity befalls the community or nation. Otherwise, it is a Rabbinic mitzvah.

The Rambam writes that everyone expressed the ideas of the prayers in their own words, as best they could, until the Anshei

25. משנה ברורה סימן קא ס"ק יג
26. פירוש רש"ר הירש בראשית מח:יא
27. ספר המצוות לרמב"ם מצות עשה ה
28. השגות הרמב"ן לספר המצוות לרמב"ם מצות עשה ה

Knesset Hagedolah established the text of the prayers.[29] But the siddur was still not written down, as indicated by the fact that Shimon Hapakuli had to reinstitute the order of the blessings of the Amidah, because it had been forgotten.[30] Writing the text of the prayers happened many centuries later;[31] there are no written siddurim until the times of the Geonim.[32]

The first prayerbook that we have was written in response to a question addressed to Rav Natronai Gaon, who lived in the 9th century. Jews had begun moving away from Babylonia, then the center of Jewish scholarship, across the Mediterranean Sea to Spain. The Jews of Lucena wrote a letter to Rav Natronai Gaon and said, "Please explain to us about the one hundred berachot." There is a rabbinic edict to recite at least one hundred berachot a day.[33] If we pray properly, we certainly recite a hundred berachot a day. The one day on which we would not say a hundred berachot is Yom Kippur, since we can't eat and because the Amidah has only seven berachot instead of the usual nineteen.[34]

Rav Natronai Gaon gave them a long answer. This answer was, more or less, the first written record of the prayer service. Later, Rav Amram Gaon, who also lived in the ninth century, and Rav Sa'adia Gaon, who lived in the tenth century, wrote the first actual prayer books. The Geonim wrote these prayer books as guides; they primarily

---

29. רמב"ם הלכות תפילה פרק א הלכה ד

30. ברכות דף כח עמוד ב

31. *Toldot Hatefillah Be'Yisrael*, p. 12 (תולדות התפלה בישראל, יצחק משה אלבוגן, הוצאת דביר, ירושלים - ברלין, תרפד).

32. The Gemara was completed around 500 C.E., ending the Talmudic period and heralding in the Gaonic period, which lasted from 500 to 1000 or 1040 C.E. This period is called the Gaonic period because the heads of the two great yeshivas in Sura and in Pumpedita were given the title Gaon.

33. מנחות דף מג עמ' ב

34. This is why people sometimes take an etrog, put cloves in it and smell it a few times during the day on Yom Kippur. It may not make the fast easier, but it enables one to recite the berachah over smelling spices, providing another few berachot to recite.

focused on the laws of the prayer service. We have gained invaluable benefits by having the prayer books that were in use during this early period. Both are extant, although we can't be certain that they have been transmitted exactly as Rav Amram and Rav Sa'adia Gaon wrote them. Nevertheless, both Rav Amram Gaon's book and Rav Sa'adia Gaon's book strongly influenced both the Sephardic and Ashkenazic version of the prayers.

The actual davening of Shacharit consists primarily of two components: to recite the Shema with its accompanying berachot and to say the prayer of nineteen berachot called the שְׁמוֹנֶה עֶשְׂרֵה, or Amidah.

During the First Temple period, the Shema was said the same way we say it, because it is all verses from the Torah; it was not composed by the Rabbis. The שְׁמוֹנֶה עֶשְׂרֵה, on the other hand, was a totally individualized prayer.

Our ancestors knew that when praying before God, the prayer had to have three components: praise, petition, and thanks.[35] But even though the Torah commands us to pray, each person could formulate the prayer according to his or her own style, feelings, temperament, and devotion.[36] A formalized, set prayer was not yet established. The Jewish people were in the Babylonian exile for nearly seventy years, and during this time they forgot much of Judaism. They stopped using Hebrew in favor of Aramaic. They lost the fluency they had in quoting verses from the Bible. They found it very difficult to express themselves in a traditional Jewish manner.

With this background we can now understand why the leaders of the Jewish people instituted the formal שְׁמוֹנֶה עֶשְׂרֵה. The leaders were the אַנְשֵׁי כְּנֶסֶת הַגְּדוֹלָה, Men of the Great Assembly, and the way they composed the שְׁמוֹנֶה עֶשְׂרֵה is the way that we recite it to this day. In the course of time, the אַנְשֵׁי כְּנֶסֶת הַגְּדוֹלָה also put the Shema within the framework of its accompanying berachot.

We know that this version of the Shema was developed during

35. רמב"ם הלכות תפילה פרק א הלכה ב

36. רמב"ם הלכות תפילה פרק א הלכה ב-ד

the early times of the Second Temple, for the Mishnah mentions it.[37] Although the Mishnah was codified in 200 C.E., the various mishnayot had been recited orally for many centuries.

The Shema and the שְׁמוֹנֶה עֶשְׂרֵה did not originally form one unit but were two separate parts. A person would say the Shema at one time and the שְׁמוֹנֶה עֶשְׂרֵה at another time. By establishing the rule that as soon as you conclude the Shema and its accompanying berachot, you must immediately begin the recitation of the שְׁמוֹנֶה עֶשְׂרֵה, the Gemara required that the two observances be combined into one performance.[38] Although they represent separate commandments, these two elements, the Shema and the שְׁמוֹנֶה עֶשְׂרֵה, both fulfill the the commandment of accepting God's sovereignty.

In the Shema, we clearly proclaim to all the world that we have accepted the yoke of Divine kingship (קַבָּלַת עֹל מַלְכוּת שָׁמַיִם). In the שְׁמוֹנֶה עֶשְׂרֵה, we declare our dependence on God. By making so many requests in the שְׁמוֹנֶה עֶשְׂרֵה, we are demonstrating that without God we couldn't exist. God is the One who provides us with food, grants us health, and accepts many of our prayers.

In ancient times, different versions of the prayer service emerged. This occurred easily since the prayers were not written down. The Jews of Babylonia had one version, and the Jews in Israel had another. Today as well, there are differences between the Ashkenazic and Sephardic versions of prayer, and differences within each group as well.

TO WHICH DIRECTION DO WE PRAY?

When we pray we always face toward Israel. If you are in Israel, you should face toward Jerusalem. If you are in Jerusalem, you should face the Temple. Within the Temple, you should face toward the Holy of Holies.[39] The Shulchan Aruch adds that while facing Israel, you should

37. See, for example, משנה ברכות דף יא עמ׳ א: Also see: תמיד דף לב עמוד ב.

38. ברכות דף ד עמ׳ א and see Rashi ד״ה זה הסומך.

39. ברכות דף ל עמ׳ א

also have in mind Jerusalem, the Temple, and the Holy of Holies.[40] A person without any points of reference should intend his heart toward the Presence of the Holy One and pray.[41]

The Gemara quotes a number of פְּסוּקִים as sources for why we face Israel, Jerusalem, the Temple and the Holy of Holies while praying. One of these is:

וְשָׁבוּ אֵלֶיךָ בְּכָל לְבָבָם וּבְכָל נַפְשָׁם בְּאֶרֶץ אֹיְבֵיהֶם אֲשֶׁר שָׁבוּ אֹתָם וְהִתְפַּלְלוּ אֵלֶיךָ **דֶּרֶךְ אַרְצָם** אֲשֶׁר נָתַתָּה לַאֲבוֹתָם **הָעִיר** אֲשֶׁר בָּחַרְתָּ **וְהַבַּיִת** אֲשֶׁר בָּנִיתִי לִשְׁמֶךָ.

"And they will return to You with all their hearts and souls in the land of the enemies who took them captive, and they will pray to You in the direction of the **land** that You gave to their fathers, the **city** You have chosen, and the **house** I built for Your Name."[42]

TIMES OF DAVENING

We daven three times daily: Shacharit, Minchah and Ma'ariv. On Shabbat, Yom Tov, and Rosh Chodesh, we add Musaf. Each of these tefillot has specific times during which they must be said. In addition, the Shema, which is part of Shacharit and Ma'ariv, has its own time requirements.

Time in halachah follows its own rules; an hour is not necessarily 60 minutes. Each halachic hour is 1⁄12 of the time from הָנֵץ הַחַמָּה (sunrise) to שְׁקִיעַת הַחַמָּה (sunset). In the summer, when the daytime is longer than the night, these hours are longer than 60 minutes, and in the winter, they are shorter than 60 minutes. These hours are called שָׁעוֹת זְמַנִּיּוֹת (variable hours).

The mitzvah of קְרִיאַת שְׁמַע entails reciting the Shema twice a day: once in the morning and once at night.[43] The times are, as the verse says, when you go to sleep and when you wake up (בְּשָׁכְבְּךָ וּבְקוּמֶךָ). In

40. שולחן ערוך אורח חיים סימן צד סעיף א
41. ברכות דף ל עמ׳ א
42. מלכים א פרק ח פסוק מח
43. רמב״ם הלכות קריאת שמע פרק א הל׳ א

the morning, ideally it should be said with the rising sun, but it can be said even earlier than sunrise and up to three halachic hours after sunrise.[44]

As mentioned, it is best to recite the Shema when the sun first starts to rise. This was the practice of the וָתִיקִין.[45] Reciting Shema at this time enables a person to recite קְרִיאַת שְׁמַע וּבִרְכוֹתֶיהָ immediately before the sunrise, and then start saying the שְׁמוֹנֶה עֶשְׂרֵה just at the sunrise, in fulfillment of the verse (Tehillim 72:5) יִירָאוּךָ עִם שָׁמֶשׁ, "They will fear You with the [rising] sun."[46]

The Gemara tells us that the prayer services were modeled after the sacrifice services in the Temple. Rabbi Yehudah says that the תָּמִיד שֶׁל שַׁחַר (morning sacrifice) was brought through the fourth hour, so we are allowed to pray Shacharit through the fourth hour.[47]

In order to understand when we can daven Minchah, we must introduce some other terms.

- מִנְחָה גְּדוֹלָה – The first possible time that we can daven Minchah. It begins half an hour after חֲצוֹת (the midpoint of daylight).[48]
- מִנְחָה קְטַנָּה – The תָּמִיד שֶׁל בֵּין הָעַרְבַּיִם (afternoon sacrifice) could be brought from מִנְחָה גְּדוֹלָה and onward, but in actuality it was slaughtered at 8½ hours and sacrificed at 9½. מִנְחָה קְטַנָּה occurs at 9½ hours.
- שְׁקִיעַת הַחַמָּה – Sunset, the time until which we can daven Minchah.
- פְּלַג הַמִּנְחָה – Halfway between מִנְחָה קְטַנָּה (9½ hours) and sunset (12 hours). In other words, 1¼ hours before sunset.[49]

We can start saying Minchah from מִנְחָה גְּדוֹלָה. There are differences of opinion about the latest time we can say it. Rabbi Yehudah

---

44. שולחן ערוך אורח חיים סימן נח סעיף א

45. Rashi explains that they are modest people who cherish the commandments.

46. ברכות דף ט עמוד ב

47. ברכות דף כו עמוד ב; רמב"ם הלכות תפילה פרק א הלכה ה

48. שולחן ערוך אורח חיים סימן רלג סעיף א

49. ערוך השולחן אורח חיים סימן רלג סעיף א

maintains that it can be said until פְּלַג הַמִּנְחָה, while the Sages maintain that it can be said until שְׁקִיעַת הַחַמָּה.[50] The Gemara states that one can follow either opinion.[51]

There was a time when it was dangerous to go to shul when it was dark and the synagogues were located outside the towns. People used to daven Ma'ariv when it was still light, and go home in a group. When people say Ma'ariv early, they can only say Minchah until פְּלַג הַמִּנְחָה. When they say Ma'ariv after dark, they can say Minchah until שְׁקִיעַת הַחַמָּה.

The nighttime Shema ideally should be said at nightfall (צֵאת הַכּוֹכָבִים, when the stars come out). There are a number of opinions about when צֵאת הַכּוֹכָבִים is. The Gemara[52] states that צֵאת הַכּוֹכָבִים is when three medium-sized stars become visible in the sky. The question is how to calculate this time, and there are different opinions about this.

Afterwards, Shema can still be recited the whole night, but as a safeguard against falling asleep without having said the Shema, the Rabbis decreed that it should be said before halachic midnight (חֲצוֹת, the midpoint of the night).[53]

If it is not possible to say Ma'ariv, including קְרִיאַת שְׁמַע וּבִרְכוֹתֶיהָ by חֲצוֹת, it is acceptable to say Ma'ariv, including קְרִיאַת שְׁמַע וּבִרְכוֹתֶיהָ, until עֲלוֹת הַשַּׁחַר, the time of night that borders on day and starts taking on the characteristics of day.[54] If there were extenuating circumstances, you could say Ma'ariv until that time.

We saw that sometimes a congregation might daven Ma'ariv early. This happens very often in the summertime. If you attend a minyan like that, you are accepting that Ma'ariv can be said from פְּלַג הַמִּנְחָה on. This is an acceptable solution and an acceptable way of saying Ma'ariv. But you have not fulfilled your obligation of reciting Shema at night.

---

50. ברכות דף כו עמ' א
51. ברכות דף כז עמ' א
52. שבת דף לה עמוד ב
53. שולחן ערוך אורח חיים סימן רלה סעיף ג
54. שולחן ערוך אורח חיים סימן רלה סעיף ג

If you daven Ma'ariv before צֵאת הַכּוֹכָבִים, you must repeat the three paragraphs of Shema once it gets dark.

The time for Ma'ariv was established to be all night long, because the sacrifices could be burned all night long.

The additional sacrifice for holidays, the Musaf, could be sacrificed immediately following the תָּמִיד שֶׁל שַׁחַר, and the Musaf service should be recited immediately following Shacharit as well. It should not be delayed past the seventh hour, but if one did delay it can still be said all day long, as the offering is valid the entire day.[55]

בֵּין הַשְּׁמָשׁוֹת (dusk), a period of time before nightfall, has the status of סָפֵק (doubt) as to whether it is day or night.[56] If you missed saying Minchah before שְׁקִיעָה, you can say Minchah until close to צֵאת הַכּוֹכָבִים, though that would not be ideal.[57]

There is a similar phenomenon in the morning. The ideal time for Shacharit begins at sunrise. However, if you have no other choice, you can say Shacharit after עֲלוֹת הַשַּׁחַר, before הָנֵץ הַחַמָּה.[58] If you accidentally missed saying Ma'ariv until the end of the night, as long as it is before הָנֵץ הַחַמָּה, you can still say Ma'ariv then, but the paragraph of הַשְׁכִּיבֵנוּ ("Let us lie down") would not be said because it is not relevant, as that is not a time when most people are still going to sleep.[59]

---

55. שולחן ערוך אורח חיים סימן רפו סעיף א
56. שבת דף לד עמוד ב
57. שולחן ערוך אורח חיים סימן רלג סעיף א ומשנה ברורה שם ס"ק יד
58. שולחן ערוך אורח חיים סימן פט סעיף א, סימן נח סעיף ג
59. שולחן ערוך אורח חיים סימן רלה סעיף ד ומשנה ברורה שם ס"ק לג

Preliminary Berachot

The siddur developed slowly, over centuries. In general, during the First Temple period, most Jews did not yet daven using a formal text; they made up their own prayers. Before the Babylonian exile,[1] Jews were capable of expressing themselves freely in Hebrew. During the Babylonian exile, they lost that skill. After the Jews returned from Babylonia and settled again in Eretz Yisrael, the אַנְשֵׁי כְּנֶסֶת הַגְּדוֹלָה[2] fixed most of the texts of the prayers.

The Rambam[3] writes that during the First Temple period, the שְׁמוֹנֶה עֶשְׂרֵה was a fluid prayer with a certain framework to be followed. One began by praising God, then you brought your requests before God, finally you expressed your gratitiude to God. But within that structure, you phrased your prayers in your own way. If you had a hard time expressing your ideas and thoughts, you said a very short prayer. If you could express them more eloquently, you said a longer prayer.

The Jews lived in Babylonia for seventy years, or almost four generations. In four generations there was a great deal of assimilation. When the Jews returned to Israel, they had mostly forgotten Hebrew.

---

1. In 597 B.C.E., Nebuchadnezzar, the king of Babylonia, began exiling the Jews of Judea. In 586 B.C.E., his armies destroyed the Temple. In 537 B.C.E., Cyrus, the Persian conqueror of Babylonia, decreed that the Jews could return to Israel and rebuild the Temple. This sixty-year period (commonly referred to as seventy years) is known as the Babylonian exile.
2. Ezra, Nechemiah, and the other great scholars of that age.
3. רמב״ם הלכות תפילה פרק א הל׳ ד

Most of them spoke Aramaic by that time, and they had great difficulty expressing themselves in Hebrew. They had not had a proper Hebrew education. אַנְשֵׁי כְנֶסֶת הַגְּדוֹלָה said that since the Jews were having such a hard time saying the prayers, they would give them set texts.

These set texts that they established are more or less the versions that we have today. This seems to be true for the שְׁמוֹנֶה עֶשְׂרֵה as well the texts of berachot and other prayers as well. Since many of the berachot that we will study in this book were formulated by the Rabbis of the Talmud, they were obviously not said before Talmudic times. Little by little, the Rabbis introduced those berachot, and they became part of our daily prayers. Because most people had memorized the prayers, the part of the oral law that was written down later than anything else was the set prayers. The standardization of the prayers happened during the eighth and ninth centuries. The prayer books of Rav Amram Gaon and Rav Sa'adia Gaon were the first two siddurim,[4] and were written around the ninth century.

The first subject that we shall study is called in every siddur בִּרְכוֹת הַשַּׁחַר (the morning berachot). Actually, this is a misnomer. If anything, they should be called בִּרְכוֹת הַיּוֹם (berachot of the day) because we do not say berachot that apply only to the morning; we say berachot for things that apply to the entire day. If I forgot to say these berachot in the morning, and I only remembered them at 4:00 p.m., I am still entitled to say them, with certain exceptions.[5] We say them at the first opportunity, which is usually early in the morning.

There are also certain sections in the siddur that were put before these prayers, such as מַה טֹּבוּ and אֲדוֹן עוֹלָם, but since these are not an essential part of the siddur, I am ignoring them in this book.

It is common practice today, if you are going to shul, to say several berachot at home and several in shul. We say עַל נְטִילַת יָדָיִם ("upon washing the hands"), אֲשֶׁר יָצַר ("Who made humanity with wisdom"), אֱלֹקַי נְשָׁמָה ("My God, the soul that you gave me is pure"), and בִּרְכוֹת

---

4. Siddur comes from the Hebrew root סדר, meaning "to organize." The siddur organized the prayer service for the Jewish people.

5. משנה ברורה סימן נב ס"ק י

בָּרוּךְ אַתָּה ה׳...אֲשֶׁר נָתַן לַשֶּׂכְוִי בִינָה הַתּוֹרָה at home. In shul, we start with בָּרוּךְ אַתָּה ה׳...אֲשֶׁר נָתַן לַשֶּׂכְוִי בִינָה ("Who gave the rooster understanding"). You can say this berachah and those that follow it at home as well.[6]

THE NATURE OF BERACHOT

Many of our berachot begin with the following formula: בָּרוּךְ אַתָּה ה׳ אֱלֹקֵינוּ מֶלֶךְ הָעוֹלָם אֲשֶׁר קִדְּשָׁנוּ בְּמִצְוֹתָיו וְצִוָּנוּ. The format is problematic, however. First of all, we are not being grammatically correct when we switch from the second person to the third person. We say, בָּרוּךְ אַתָּה, "Blessed are *You*...who sanctified us with *His* commandments."

We make this grammatical switch because we are imitating King David who did so. When we pray to God, we are doing something very irrational. Who am I to speak to God? Does God want to listen to me? Why should God be interested in my conversations? How do we have the chutzpah, the nerve, to address God? If I wanted to address a king or if I wanted to go to Washington to speak with the president, I wouldn't have a chance to see him. If I were an important person, perhaps I would, but it would be weeks or even months until I could do so. Yet when we want to speak to God, we just get up and say, "Listen, God, to what I have to tell you." It's a bit presumptuous. Is my language adequate to address God? Do I use the proper terms? Fortunately, we have great people in our history to use as models.

King David is known as נְעִים זְמִירוֹת יִשְׂרָאֵל, "the sweet singer of Israel,"[7] because he wrote the Psalms. He had a special relationship with God and reached levels of religious inspiration that we cannot. We rely on his example. In Psalm 145, King David switches from the second person to the third and then back again: כְּבוֹד מַלְכוּתְךָ יֹאמֵרוּ וּגְבוּרָתְךָ יְדַבֵּרוּ ("They speak of the glory of *Your* kingdom, and talk about *Your* mighty deeds"). The next verse is לְהוֹדִיעַ לִבְנֵי הָאָדָם גְּבוּרֹתָיו וּכְבוֹד הֲדַר מַלְכוּתוֹ ("to make known to mankind *His* mighty deeds and

---

6. See further.
7. שמואל ב פרק כג פסוק א

the glory of *His* kingship"). It is followed by מַלְכוּתְךָ מַלְכוּת כָּל־עֹלָמִים ("*Your* kingship is a kingship for all eternity").

The rationale for the switch is based on the notion that our approach to God is a dual one. On the one hand, God is the great Being, the Omnipotent and the Omniscient, whom no human being can fathom. There is no point in speculating about the essence of God; we'll never be able to understand it. When we speak of God, how can we say, בָּרוּךְ אַתָּה ("Blessed are You")? The One to whom I am speaking is above the cosmos, beyond my experience.

At the same time, we instinctively know that if we are in trouble, we can turn to God. If I am sick, I turn to God and ask to be healed; if there are problems in Israel, we turn to God and ask for help. We know that אֵין לָנוּ מוֹשִׁיעַ אֶלָּא אָבִינוּ שֶׁבַּשָּׁמַיִם, we have no savior other than our Father in heaven. We approach God as our parent as well as our king. We pour out our hearts like children to parents, but we stand in respect and awe as subjects before a king at the same time. On the one hand, we feel very close to God; on the other hand, God is completely beyond our reach.[8] The grammatical switch in persons represents this dual approach.[9]

Is it our place to declare that God is blessed? Again we learn from the example of King David, who actually coined this phrase in Psalm 119: בָּרוּךְ אַתָּה ה׳ לַמְּדֵנִי חֻקֶּיךָ ("Blessed are You, Hashem, teach me Your laws"). We borrowed this phrase from King David; we would not have the nerve to say "Blessed are You" otherwise.

Can We Bless God?

What does בָּרוּךְ אַתָּה ה׳ אֱלֹקֵינוּ מֶלֶךְ הָעוֹלָם ("Blessed are You, Hashem our God, King of the universe") really mean? Can I give God a berachah? Does God need my blessing? On the contrary, we need God's

---

8. The עיון תפלה, found in the *Otzar Hatefillot* (p. 110), cites the Machzor Vitry (מחזור ויטרי, סימן פח) who gives this explanation.

9. This dual approach to God is distinctly Jewish. Other religions have never understood it. The most essential difference between Judaism and Christianity is that Christians pray to a mediator between humanity and God.

berachah! Who should be blessing whom? A person of higher status blesses a person of lower status; a parent blesses a child.[10] We appeal to God to do something for those we love, to give them something that may be lacking; that is what it means to bless a person. If I bless a child, I am asking God to please give this child understanding, wisdom, health, long life, and so on. But is there something that God doesn't have? That would be blasphemy. God has everything. He is the Creator of the universe! What then are we doing when we "bless" God?

Rav Soloveitchik said in the name of Rav Chaim,[11] his grandfather, "There is something God does not have that He needs. That is the respect of the world. If God had the respect of the world, the world would be better. There would be no wars, there would be no anti-Semitism, there would be no hatred; it would be a different world. When we bless God, we are saying, 'Please God, we wish that You receive what You are still missing: that people worship You, recognize You, accept You, reject evil, and choose good.' Naturally, God could force the human race to do this, but God doesn't want to do that. God wants the human race to reach that understanding on its own. God hopes that everybody, in due time, will understand on his or her own the greatness of God, worship God, and make this world a better place."

Another explanation from Rav Soloveitchik is that the word בָּרוּךְ (blessed) means abundance. When we give a person a berachah, we pray that God will grant that person an abundance of something good, such as long life or good health. When we say to God, בָּרוּךְ אַתָּה (Blessed are You), we are saying that we recognize the source of good, that God is the source of abundance, and that we receive goodness from God's abundance.[12]

---

10. There is a minhag for parents to bless their children on Friday night or, if one doesn't have that custom, before Yom Kippur.

11. Rav Chaim Soloveitchik (1853–1918) innovated a revolutionary, analytical approach to Talmud study.

12. See ספר החינוך מצוה תל.

מִצְוֹות דְּרַבָּנָן

Back to the berachah on washing our hands: When we say אֲשֶׁר קִדְּשָׁנוּ בְּמִצְוֹתָיו וְצִוָּנוּ ("Who has commanded us to wash our hands") is this the truth? It does not appear to be so, for if you look through the whole Torah, from beginning to end, there is no commandment to wash our hands. It is not a Divine commandment.

There are 613 commandments in the Torah.[13] In addition to these, there are several commandments that the Rabbis introduced (מִצְוֹות דְּרַבָּנָן). There is a common list of seven מִצְוֹות דְּרַבָּנָן that includes: נְטִילַת יָדַיִם, to wash our hands before we eat; נֵר שַׁבָּת, to kindle a light on Friday night; נֵר חֲנֻכָּה, to kindle a light on Chanukah; מְגִלָּה, to hear the Megillah (Book of Esther) on Purim; הַלֵּל, to recite Hallel on the holidays;[14] בִּרְכַּת הַנֶּהֱנִין, to recite berachot (for example over food); and עֵרוּבִין, to make an eruv.[15]

If I perform a commandment from the Torah, I can reasonably say וְצִוָּנוּ ("Who commanded us...") since the Torah is God's words. But since the Rabbis commanded us to wash our hands, how can we say that God commanded us? The answer is very simple: The Almighty authorized the Rabbis to make laws for the Jewish people. If the Rabbis made these laws by the authority of God, it is as if God established them. Therefore, we can say, "Who commanded us..."[16]

Aren't there more than just seven rabbinic commandments, however? For instance, what about מֻקְצֶה (the law that items that may not be used on Shabbos are forbidden to be touched on Shabbos)? The seven rabbinic commandments that I have listed were entirely new and have no basis in the Torah. מֻקְצֶה is of rabbinic origin, but it is

---

13. מכות דף כג עמ׳ ב-כד עמ׳ א

14. Hallel consists of songs of thanksgiving to God (Psalms 113–118). It is discussed in its own chapter below.

15. An עֵרוּב is a halachic mechanism that allows a person to carry from one property to another on Shabbat; that allows a person to cook on a holiday for Shabbat when Shabbat falls out right after the holiday or allows a person to extend the distance on which one can walk on Shabbat.

16. See שבת דף כג עמ׳ א.

based on a law of the Torah (i.e., the laws of Shabbat). This is called a "fence" around the Torah.

The Rambam sees a parallel between בִּרְכוֹת הַנֶּהֱנִין and בִּרְכוֹת הַמִּצְווֹת in that in both cases you must recite a berachah before performing the activity on which the berachah is recited. Rav Soloveitchik derived from the wording of the Rambam that it is forbidden to perform a mitzvah until one has first said the berachah. The berachah is what gives us permission to approach God through the performance of a mitzvah.[17]

נְטִילַת יָדָיִם

Now, let's take one berachah at a time. The Jew should begin his morning with the berachah for washing the hands, עַל נְטִילַת יָדָיִם. It is our practice that as soon as we awaken, we pour water over our hands as a ritual washing.[18] Some people are very strict and have water right next to their beds. Many poskim (halachic arbiters) rule, however, that since your whole home is the place where you wake up, you may wash your hands at the sink and say the berachah of עַל נְטִילַת יָדָיִם.

God commanded us through the Rabbis to wash our hands. Yet the berachah says נְטִילַת יָדָיִם, which literally means *lifting* of the hands. Why don't we say what we really mean? From this we learn that part of the commandment of the pouring water is to hold our hands up. The reason is that if I am טָמֵא, there is only one way to become טָהוֹר.[19] I dip my whole body in a mikveh, or ritual pool. If only my hands are טָמֵא

17. Rav Soloveitchik derived this from the Rambam, הלכות ברכות פרק א הלכה ג–ב. See רשימות שיעורים (ר״י"ד סולובייצ׳יק) מסכת ברכות דף יא עמוד ב.

18. שולחן ערוך אורח חיים סימן ד, סעיף יח: אֵלּוּ דְּבָרִים צְרִיכִין נְטִילָה בַּמַּיִם: הַקָּם מֵהַמִּטָּה; וְהַיּוֹצֵא מִבֵּית הַכִּסֵּא וּמִבֵּית הַמֶּרְחָץ; וְהַנּוֹטֵל צִפָּרְנָיו; וְהַחוֹלֵץ מִנְעָלָיו; וְהַנּוֹגֵעַ בְּרַגְלָיו; וְהַחוֹפֵף רֹאשׁוֹ. וי״א אַף הַהוֹלֵךְ בֵּין הַמֵּתִים; וּמִי שֶׁנָּגַע בְּמֵת; וּמִי שֶׁמַּפְלִיא כֵּלָיו; וְהַמְשַׁמֵּשׁ מִטָּתוֹ; וְהַנּוֹגֵעַ בַּכִּנָּה; וְהַנּוֹגֵעַ בְּגוּפוֹ בְּיָדוֹ.

19. טָמֵא and טָהוֹר really have no English translations. They are foreign concepts in our culture. טָמֵא is a spiritual term that relates to mortality; it is conveyed through the reproductive functions, death, and certain types of diseases. Immersion in the water of a mikveh or a natural body of water, or in some

rather than my entire body, it is sufficient if I pour a certain quantity of water from a vessel over my hands. That has the same effect for my hands as the mikveh does for my body. But if I wash my fingers and then let my hands hang down so that water that has run onto the back of my hand comes back on my fingers, it makes my hands טָמֵא again.[20] Therefore, I must hold my hands up and let the water run the opposite way so my hands remain טָהוֹר until I dry them.

A berachah must be said for a commandment *before* you perform the commandment.[21] With נְטִילַת יָדָיִם, however, we are not so exact about it. We wash our hands first and say the berachah afterward. This is an exception to the rule.[22] One of the reasons that we have to wash our hands is that they are not pure enough for us to pronounce God's name. Thus, I cannot say the berachah before washing. I am therefore caught in a dilemma. What should I do? The solution is to divide the commandment into two: washing and drying. When I wash my hands and say the berachah, the commandment is not yet completed; I complete the commandment by drying my hands. People who are in a big rush and dry their hands while saying the berachah are wrong. You should wash your hands, say the berachah, and dry them afterward.

Our siddur is written in Hebrew, and our prayers are in Hebrew. One exception is Kaddish, the prayer said by mourners. יְקוּם פּוּרְקָן ("May salvation come")[23] is also not in Hebrew, but it is not a prayer in the strict sense of the word. Since occasionally Aramaic can creep into our usage, some commentators view the Hebrew word נְטִילָה (lifting) as an Aramaic word. The Aramaic word for the measure of the cup required for washing is אַנְטַל. These people believe that you do not say עַל רְחִיצַת יָדָיִם (concerning the washing of the hands), but

---

cases with the additional sprinkling of ashes from a red heifer, would make a טָמֵא person טָהוֹר.

20. סוטה דף ד עמוד ב; שולחן ערוך אורח חיים סי׳ קסב סעיף א

21. פסחים דף ז עמוד ב; שולחן ערוך אורח חיים סי׳ כה סעיף ח

22. שלחן ערוך ורמ״א אורח חיים סי׳ קנח סעיף יא

23. This prayer introduces the Shabbat Musaf service.

עַל נְטִילַת יָדַיִם because you have to use a cup for it; you have to have the proper quantity of water to make your hand טָהוֹר. They would translate the word נְטִילָה not as lifting the hands but as using a cup for washing the hands.[24]

We have to wash our hands every morning. During the night our hands may have become טָמֵא when we touched parts of our body, so we have to purify our hands before davening. Washing the hands before davening is a requirement. Rambam is of the opinion that washing with a cup applies not only to Shacharit but also to Minchah and Ma'ariv.[25] That is why, in every shul, some people can be seen washing their hands with a cup before Minchah and Ma'ariv.

Suppose you forgot to say the berachah for נְטִילַת יָדַיִם, and after the davening you remember that you didn't say it. Can you now say the berachah? The answer is no. It only makes sense before the davening. After the davening, it would be a berachah uttered in vain.

Rashi provides us with a different possible idea about the purpose of washing our hands before davening. The Gemara[26] asks: from where do we know that we should wash our hands before davening? It quotes the verse, אֶרְחַץ בְּנִקָּיוֹן כַּפָּי וַאֲסֹבְבָה אֶת־מִזְבַּחֲךָ ה׳[27] ("I shall wash my hands in purity, and I will go around Your altar, God"). "I will go around Your altar" is a figure of speech meaning, "I will pray." First, I wash my hands, and then I pray.

Then the Gemara asks the question: why does the Psalm say אֶרְחַץ בְּנִקָּיוֹן כַּפָּי ("I shall wash my hands in purity")? Why doesn't it say אֶרְחַץ בְּמַיִם כַּפָּי ("I shall wash my hands with water")? It would be much simpler. The Gemara says that there are circumstances, such as when Jews lived in the desert and there was a shortage of water, when you can rub your hands in sand to clean them. There are certain occasions, such as if you know that you can find water within a short distance, that you should walk the distance to wash your hands; otherwise you

24. מרדכי, ברכות פרק אלו דברים רמז קצב, based on a Gemara in ב"ב דף נח א.
25. רמב"ם הלכות תפילה פרק ד הלכה א-ב, הלכות ברכות פרק ו הלכה ב
26. ברכות דף טו עמוד א
27. תהלים פרק כו פסוק ו

can use sand or something else. In order to permit this, the verse says אֶרְחַץ בְּנִקָּיוֹן כַּפָּי, meaning not necessarily in water but in anything that will make my hands טָהוֹר.

Rashi on this verse makes a strange comparison.[28] Rashi states that the verse means that I have not committed theft in performing mitzvot. If I steal a lulav to perform the mitzvah, that mitzvah would not be accepted by God. It's what we call a מִצְוָה הַבָּאָה בַּעֲבֵירָה (a mitzvah that is fulfilled by committing a sin in the process).[29] God does not want that kind of fulfillment of the commandments.

Based on Rashi, we can explain that the washing of the hands in the morning is not only a physical cleansing but symbolically, it is a spiritual cleansing as well, to free ourselves from guilt and sin. Before davening we should do teshuvah (repent). Who am I to go before God if I am a sinful human being? We are all sinful, but we should try to reduce this as much as possible. When a person prays in the morning to God and says a berachah, he or she should think, אֶרְחַץ בְּנִקָּיוֹן כַּפָּי, what did I do yesterday? As a teacher, did I insult a child in front of his or her friends? Did I give somebody a poor grade when it was not really justified? We all have our confessions; we all do some little sin every day. Before davening, we should ask ourselves what we did wrong that we could do better today and not let it happen again.

אֶרְחַץ בְּנִקָּיוֹן כַּפָּי means that before I can approach God to daven, I have to rid myself of impurity; I have to improve myself, I have to become a better human being, closer to God. Then I can "go around Your altar" – I can pray.

אֱלֹקַי נְשָׁמָה AND אֲשֶׁר יָצַר

There are two berachot that make up a unit of "formation of the body and restoration of the soul." They are the berachot of אֲשֶׁר יָצַר ("Who made humanity with wisdom"), and the berachah of אֱלֹקַי נְשָׁמָה ("My God, the soul that You gave me").

---

28. רש"י תהלים פרק כו פסוק ו: שאין גזל במצות שאני מקיים לולב הגזול פסול
29. סוכה דף ל עמוד א

In many siddurim there is the following sequence of morning berachot: first, the berachah of עַל נְטִילַת יָדָיִם, followed by אֲשֶׁר יָצַר, then בִּרְכוֹת הַתּוֹרָה, and then אֱלֹקַי נְשָׁמָה. I use the following sequence after עַל נְטִילַת יָדָיִם: First אֲשֶׁר יָצַר then the berachah of אֱלֹקַי נְשָׁמָה, and then בִּרְכוֹת הַתּוֹרָה.[30]

Unlike the berachah over washing the hands which, if I omitted it in the morning, I cannot make up, I may say אֲשֶׁר יָצַר at any time during the day. We say this berachah whenever we use the bathroom. Our ability to take care of our physical needs is a special kindness from God, so when we leave the bathroom, we say אֲשֶׁר יָצַר each time.

The rest of the berachah reads as follows: וּבָרָא בוֹ נְקָבִים נְקָבִים חֲלוּלִים חֲלוּלִים ("...Who created in the human body many openings and many cavities").[31] גָּלוּי וְיָדוּעַ לִפְנֵי כִסֵּא כְבוֹדֶךָ שֶׁאִם יִפָּתֵחַ אֶחָד מֵהֶם אוֹ יִסָּתֵם אֶחָד מֵהֶם אִי אֶפְשַׁר לְהִתְקַיֵּם וְלַעֲמוֹד לְפָנֶיךָ אֲפִילוּ שָׁעָה אֶחָת ("It is known before the throne of Your glory that if one [of those places in the body that should be closed] is open or if one [of the places that should be open] is closed, it is impossible to live and to stand before God even for one hour") – we know that if a person gets a heart attack, if there is a blockage in the blood flow, or if anything that should be closed opens up, it may lead to death. בָּרוּךְ אַתָּה ה׳ רוֹפֵא כָל בָּשָׂר וּמַפְלִיא לַעֲשׂוֹת ("Blessed are You, healer of all flesh who works miracles").

A berachah usually follows a certain format. There is a short format and a long format of berachot. A short berachah has one subject. It only has the beginning phrase and an appropriate ending. An example

---

30. This was the Vilna Gaon's practice and the practice of Rav Soloveitchik as well.

31. You might find in different siddurim the word spelled as חֲלָלִים or חֲלוּלִים. The Gemara in Berachot 60b quotes the text of the berachah as חֲלָלִים, but the Rif's version of the Gemara said חֲלוּלִים. The Avudraham thinks it should be חֲלִים חֲלִים, derived from a verse in Isaiah (2:19), וּבִמְחִלּוֹת עָפָר, which means a cavity. The Tur (אורח חיים סימן ו) prefers חֲלוּלִים because the gematria (numerical value of the letters) equals 248, corresponding to the number of organs in the body. Either way, both words have very similar meanings: hollows, veins, cavities, empty spaces.

of a short berachah is בָּרוּךְ אַתָּה ה׳ אֱלֹקֵינוּ מֶלֶךְ הָעוֹלָם מַלְבִּישׁ עֲרֻמִּים in which there is only one idea, in this case, that God clothes the naked.

A long berachah includes many subjects. It starts with בָּרוּךְ אַתָּה ה׳ אֱלֹקֵינוּ מֶלֶךְ הָעוֹלָם, talks of the many subjects, has a closing summary of the main theme of the berachah, and ends with בָּרוּךְ אַתָּה ה׳ and a phrase that is related to the opening theme.

An example of a long berachah is the first paragraph of the Birkat Hamazon – בָּרוּךְ אַתָּה ה׳ אֱלֹקֵינוּ מֶלֶךְ הָעוֹלָם הַזָּן אֶת הָעוֹלָם כֻּלּוֹ ("Blessed are You, Hashem our God, King of the universe, who feeds the whole world"). The summary phrase is כִּי הוּא אֵ־ל זָן וּמְפַרְנֵס לַכֹּל וּמֵטִיב לַכֹּל וּמֵכִין מָזוֹן לְכָל בְּרִיּוֹתָיו אֲשֶׁר בָּרָא ("He is the Lord who feeds and provides for all, and does goodness for all and prepares food for all His creations that He created"). It ends with בָּרוּךְ אַתָּה יְיָ, הַזָּן אֶת הַכֹּל ("Blessed are You, Hashem our God, Who feeds all").

In the case of the berachah of אֲשֶׁר יָצַר, it seems that this berachah has a double ending: רוֹפֵא כָל בָּשָׂר וּמַפְלִיא לַעֲשׂוֹת. The Gemara instructs us to end a berachah, even if it is a complex berachah, with a single theme. The Gemara discusses how this specific berachah should end. Rav suggested[32] that the berachah should focus on God who is a healer of sick people, רוֹפֵא חוֹלִים. Shmuel responded that this would imply that everyone in the world is sick. Rather, Shmuel maintains, we should end it רוֹפֵא כָל בָּשָׂר ("Healer of all flesh"). Rav Sheshet says we should end this berachah focusing on a different matter: מַפְלִיא לַעֲשׂוֹת ("who acts wondrously"). Both Rashi and Tosafot explain that the berachah is talking about how the body removes waste and functions to enable a person to live. They both cite a Midrash that explains in normal circumstances, if there is a pitcher with a hole in it, it cannot keep air inside, yet people have many openings and are still able to keep in their life force (רוּחַ).

Rav Pappa says we should combine them. God is wondrous for the complex way He has enabled people to live. The body removes waste and takes in nourishment and oxygen. This keeps people healthy

32. ברכות דף ס׳ עמ׳ ב

and able to thrive. He suggests the berachah should end: רוֹפֵא כָל בָּשָׂר וּמַפְלִיא לַעֲשׂוֹת.

The berachah of אֱלֹקַי נְשָׁמָה is also a long berachah that deals with many ideas. In translation it reads: אֱלֹקַי נְשָׁמָה שֶׁנָּתַתָּ בִּי טְהוֹרָה הִיא ("My God, the soul that You gave me is pure"). אַתָּה בְרָאתָהּ. אַתָּה יְצַרְתָּהּ. אַתָּה נְפַחְתָּהּ בִּי. וְאַתָּה מְשַׁמְּרָהּ בְּקִרְבִּי ("You created it. You formed it. You breathed it into me and You watch over it in my body"). וְאַתָּה עָתִיד לִטְּלָהּ מִמֶּנִּי וּלְהַחֲזִירָהּ בִּי לֶעָתִיד לָבוֹא ("In the future, You will take it away from me, but in the time of the resurrection of the dead,[33] You will restore it to me"). כָּל זְמַן שֶׁהַנְּשָׁמָה בְּקִרְבִּי מוֹדֶה אֲנִי לְפָנֶיךָ ה׳ אֱלֹקַי וֵאלֹקֵי אֲבוֹתַי. רִבּוֹן כָּל הַמַּעֲשִׂים אֲדוֹן כָּל הַנְּשָׁמוֹת ("As long as the soul is within me, I thank You, my God and God of my ancestors, Master of all creation, Lord of all souls"). It ends with בָּרוּךְ אַתָּה ה׳ הַמַּחֲזִיר נְשָׁמוֹת לִפְגָרִים מֵתִים ("Blessed are You, Hashem, who restores the souls to the dead").

This berachah also refers to restoring our souls to us every morning, because at night we are almost like dead; our body does not function fully. The Greeks used to call sleep *adelphos thanatos*, the brother of death, so we thank God for the daily – as well as the ultimate, in the time of the resurrection of the dead – restoration of our souls.

אֱלֹקַי נְשָׁמָה is a long berachah with many ideas, so why doesn't it begin with בָּרוּךְ אַתָּה ה׳ אֱלֹקֵינוּ מֶלֶךְ הָעוֹלָם? The best answer is given by the Rosh.[34] He says we have a rule that is known as בְּרָכָה הַסְּמוּכָה לַחֲבֶרְתָּהּ (berachot next to each other). In such a case, you do not have to repeat the standard opening formula at the beginning of each berachah. You say it once, at the beginning of the first berachah, and it covers the other berachot as well.[35]

An example of this is found in the Grace after Meals. The first berachah starts with בָּרוּךְ אַתָּה ה׳ אֱלֹקֵינוּ מֶלֶךְ הָעוֹלָם. The next berachah,

---

33. Maimonides lists the belief that God will eventually reawaken the righteous dead to live another physical existence in this world as one of the thirteen cardinal principles of faith in Judaism. These thirteen principles of faith are found in most siddurim.

34. שו״ת הרא״ש כלל ד סימן א

35. ברכות דף מו עמוד א

נוֹדֶה לְּךָ ("We will thank You"), relies on the first berachah and does not have to start with the standard opening formula.

Therefore, the Rosh says, אֱלֹקַי נְשָׁמָה is not an independent berachah; it follows the berachah of אֲשֶׁר יָצַר.[36] Those two berachot are intimately connected. They belong together because the human being is body and soul. So, we thank God for both. It is nonsensical, the Rosh says, to interrupt this with other berachot in between. He tells us to first say אֲשֶׁר יָצַר and, immediately after that, אֱלֹקַי נְשָׁמָה שֶׁנָּתַתָּ בִּי טְהוֹרָה הִיא. You do not need the formula בָּרוּךְ because it relies on the preceding berachah; the two are connected.

If you forgot to say the berachah of אֱלֹקַי נְשָׁמָה, it should no longer be said after reciting שְׁמוֹנֶה עֶשְׂרֵה, because it is covered by the second berachah of the שְׁמוֹנֶה עֶשְׂרֵה, in which we say מְחַיֵּה מֵתִים אַתָּה ("You raise the dead").[37]

אֱלֹקַי נְשָׁמָה has a slight problem. It appears that we are not telling the truth. We say that "the soul that You gave me is pure." Can we really say that our soul is pure, that we have not sinned, that we do not speak לָשׁוֹן הָרַע (gossip) or do other bad deeds? It is a bold statement to make.

Because of that, Yitzchak (Seligman) Baer (1825–1897) removes the word הִיא ("it" in the feminine) that appears in some versions.[38] He felt the version with the word הִיא implies, "The soul that You gave me is pure now." But if הִיא is omitted, then the words mean, "The pure soul which You placed in me"; in other words, it was pure when You placed it in me, but it might not be so pure anymore.

The various versions of the text, whether including the word הִיא or not, say, "The soul that You gave to me is pure." Rabbi Dr. Elie

---

36. See the Beur HaGra which cites the disagreement between Tosafot and the Rosh (ביאור הגר"א אורח חיים סימן ו סעיף ג: ברכת כו'. כ"כ תוס' מ"ו א' ד"ה כל כו' דלא כהרא"ש ריש כלל ד' שכתב מפני שסמוכ' לאשר יצר).

37. פרי חדש אורח חיים סי' מו

38. Seder Avodat Yisrael (סדר עבודת ישראל, הוצאת שוקן, שנת תרצ"ז, עמ' 39). He cites Chida (R. Chaim Yosef David Azulai) as saying that this word should not be included as a part of the text. Baer brings many versions that omit it, and says that although our versions of the Rif include this word, it must be due to a scribal error that the word is included in his version.

Munk explained that the Rabbis used the siddur, and this berachah in particular, as a vehicle for discussion about a major difference between Christianity and Judaism.[39] Since Jews lived in a Christian world and were constantly under attack, they could not explain their philosophy publicly, so it was quietly put into the siddur.

The Christians teach the doctrine of "original sin," that every human being is born sinful. Judaism disagrees. When we say נְשָׁמָה שֶׁנָּתַתָּ בִּי טְהוֹרָה הִיא, it is quite possible that the Rabbis wished to emphasize the difference between Christianity and Judaism. Nothing impure comes from God's hands. God did not create people with sinful souls. Perhaps we have sinned since our creation, but we can then purify our souls again by repentance and the absolution from sin.

We each have a soul but we are all different. We have different minds, different interests, but we each have a soul that is Divine. This is why the siddur here uses two expressions, בְּרָאתָהּ and יְצַרְתָּהּ, which basically mean the same thing – You created it, You formed it. These terms actually have two different meanings. בְּרָאתָהּ is usually used to indicate that something was made from nothing. God brought our soul from nonexistence into existence. יְצַרְתָּהּ means that God made me different from anybody else.[40] I have different ideas and a unique personality. Thus, God created my soul in its body and then gave the soul its individual endowments. We are all created differently, and that's why we need both words.

וּלְהַחֲזִירָהּ בִּי לֶעָתִיד לָבוֹא ("You will restore it to me"): in this phrase of the prayer, we emphasize our belief in the resurrection of the dead. The nations of antiquity did not believe in this concept; they thought it was ridiculous and made fun of it. In the Talmud,[41] there are discussions between the Rabbis and the Greek and Roman philosophers who did not believe in the resurrection of the dead. Therefore, the Rabbis always emphasized this concept. When we say the second berachah of the Amidah, we repeat the phrase מְחַיֵּה הַמֵּתִים ("who resurrects the

---

39. *The World of Prayer*, p. 21.

40. עיין רמב״ן בראשית פרק א פסוק א

41. סנהדרין דף צ עמ׳ ב

dead") many times. Once is not enough; we repeat it over and over to demonstrate how basic this belief is in Judaism.

In אֱלֹקַי נְשָׁמָה, there is an interesting expression: וְאַתָּה עָתִיד לִטְּלָהּ מִמֶּנִּי ("In the future, You will take it away from me"). We are realistic; we know that we will not live forever. We are not despondent about this, however, because we know that there will come a time when we will be reawakened to a new life. This berachah is a clear affirmation of the beliefs that our soul is pure, that there is no original sin, and that the resurrection of the dead will indeed occur.

After these two berachot, one recites בִּרְכוֹת הַתּוֹרָה. Although I follow this sequence, and it was the custom of the Vilna Gaon,[42] everybody should follow the minhag of one's family.

בִּרְכוֹת הַתּוֹרָה

Next, we are required to recite בִּרְכוֹת הַתּוֹרָה. We must say them before we learn Torah in the morning, so they are said as close to the time we get up as possible.

The Torah is a great gift, so just as we thank God for the benefit we get from eating an apple or a steak, for instance, we certainly must thank God for having the benefit, privilege, and spiritual satisfaction of studying Torah. I am not supposed to study Torah before thanking God for it, just as I am not supposed to eat an apple before saying a berachah for it.[43] Before we say a berachah, everything belongs to God, so if we don't say the berachah, we have no right to use the object. It is like stealing.

King David says in Tehillim,[44] לַה׳ הָאָרֶץ וּמְלוֹאָהּ; תֵּבֵל, וְיוֹשְׁבֵי בָהּ ("The earth belongs to God; the world and all who live in it"). Tehillim also says,[45] הַשָּׁמַיִם שָׁמַיִם לַה׳ וְהָאָרֶץ נָתַן לִבְנֵי־אָדָם ("The heavens belong to God,

---

42. משנה ברורה סימן ו ס"ק יב, citing the Gra, ביאור הגר"א בסימן מ"ו.

43. This means that the בִּרְכוֹת הַתּוֹרָה fall into the category of בִּרְכוֹת הַנֶּהֱנִין (berachot recited upon receiving a benefit from something), as opposed to berachot of thanks or praise (בִּרְכוֹת שֶׁבַח וְהוֹדָאָה).

44. תהלים כד:א

45. תהלים קטו:טז

and the earth He gave to humanity"). That seems like a contradiction; to whom does the earth belong? The Rabbis say that it is very simple: before we say a berachah, everything belongs to God and we can't benefit from it. The moment that we say a berachah, we acquire it, or start paying for it, as it were, so we have a right to benefit from it.[46] The same is true of the בִּרְכוֹת הַתּוֹרָה.

Suppose I forgot to say these berachot in the morning, do I recite them later? During the berachot that precede the Shema, we say the phrase, אָבִינוּ הָאָב הָרַחֲמָן הַמְרַחֵם רַחֵם עָלֵינוּ וְתֵן בְּלִבֵּנוּ לְהָבִין וּלְהַשְׂכִּיל לִשְׁמֹעַ לִלְמֹד וּלְלַמֵּד לִשְׁמֹר וְלַעֲשׂוֹת וּלְקַיֵּם אֶת כָּל דִּבְרֵי תַלְמוּד תּוֹרָתֶךָ בְּאַהֲבָה ("Our Father, merciful Father, who shows mercy, have mercy on us and help us to understand, to apply, to hear, to learn, to teach, to protect, to observe, and to fulfill all the words of your Torah with love"). The Gemara tells us that if we missed saying the בִּרְכוֹת הַתּוֹרָה in the morning, then they are indeed included in this berachah before the Shema. Therefore, we need not go back to say those berachot, because that would be considered saying berachot unnecessarily. However, there is one condition. In order for the berachah preceding Shema to take the place of בִּרְכוֹת הַתּוֹרָה, one must study Torah immediately following davening.[47]

Regarding when we should recite the בִּרְכוֹת הַתּוֹרָה, there are different customs. The Tur cites a custom to say the berachot just before reciting the verses about the sacrifices.[48] But, he continues, his practice was to recite the בִּרְכוֹת הַתּוֹרָה right after the berachot of אֲשֶׁר יָצַר and אֱלֹקַי נְשָׁמָה. The Shulchan Aruch writes: "One must be very careful regarding בִּרְכוֹת הַתּוֹרָה."[49] The Levush explains[50] that reciting the בִּרְכוֹת הַתּוֹרָה before one learns demonstrates the importance of the Torah.

How many berachot are contained in the בִּרְכוֹת הַתּוֹרָה? The Rambam and the Tosafot differ on how to count them. The Tosafot are of the

46. ברכות דף לה עמוד א
47. ברכות דף יא עמוד ב; שולחן ערוך סי׳ מז סעיף ז ומשנה ברורה שם ס״ק טו
48. טור אורח חיים סימן מו
49. אורח חיים סימן מז סעיף א
50. לבוש אורח חיים סימן מז סעיף א

opinion that there are only two berachot.[51] The first berachah, according to the Ashkenazi version, begins, בָּרוּךְ אַתָּה ה׳, אֱלֹקֵינוּ מֶלֶךְ הָעוֹלָם אֲשֶׁר קִדְּשָׁנוּ בְּמִצְוֹתָיו וְצִוָּנוּ לַעֲסוֹק בְּדִבְרֵי תוֹרָה ("Blessed are You, Hashem... who has commanded us to be involved with words of Torah"). It continues with וְהַעֲרֶב נָא ("And please make sweet"). In most siddurim, this phrase begins a new paragraph, but according to Tosafot, it is not a new berachah. The word *and* means that it is all one berachah. It concludes with בָּרוּךְ אַתָּה ה׳ הַמְלַמֵּד תּוֹרָה לְעַמּוֹ יִשְׂרָאֵל ("Blessed are You, Hashem, who teaches Torah to His people, Israel").

The second berachah, according to the Tosafot, is בָּרוּךְ אַתָּה ה׳ אֱלֹקֵינוּ מֶלֶךְ הָעוֹלָם, אֲשֶׁר בָּחַר בָּנוּ מִכָּל הָעַמִּים וְנָתַן לָנוּ אֶת תּוֹרָתוֹ: בָּרוּךְ אַתָּה ה׳, נוֹתֵן הַתּוֹרָה ("Blessed are You, Hashem... who chose us from all the people and gave us His Torah. Blessed are You, Hashem, Giver of the Torah").

Actually, we should have only one berachah, not two. Whenever we fulfill a commandment, we say a berachah, but only one berachah for each commandment. That makes the position of the Tosafot, who seem to say we have two berachot for the commandment of Torah study, problematic. The answer is very simple. There are two aspects of Torah, the written part and the oral part, so each one needs a berachah.[52]

The first berachah, לַעֲסוֹק בְּדִבְרֵי תוֹרָה, refers to the Oral Torah, because the word לַעֲסוֹק means "to be involved with, to discuss," and the Oral Torah implies one person talking with another. The second berachah says: אֲשֶׁר בָּחַר בָּנוּ מִכָּל הָעַמִּים וְנָתַן לָנוּ אֶת תּוֹרָתוֹ. This speaks about מַתַּן תּוֹרָה (the giving of the Torah); thus, it refers to the written Torah.

The Rif had an alternative text of the berachah to be said. His blessing reads: אֲשֶׁר קִדְּשָׁנוּ בְּמִצְוֹתָיו וְצִוָּנוּ עַל דִּבְרֵי תוֹרָה ("for the words of the Torah"). This version was adopted by the Sephardic world, and the first version, לַעֲסֹק בְּדִבְרֵי תוֹרָה, was adopted by the Ashkenazic world.[53]

The Rambam counts three berachot in the בִּרְכוֹת הַתּוֹרָה.[54] The

51. תוספות ברכות דף מו עמוד א ד״ה כל הברכות
52. רבינו יונה על הרי״ף מסכת ברכות דף ה עמוד ב
53. טור אורח חיים סימן מז
54. רמב״ם הלכות תפילה פרק ז הלכה י

first one is וְצִוָּנוּ עַל דִּבְרֵי תוֹרָה. Like the Rif, Rambam's text does not read לַעֲסוֹק בְּדִבְרֵי תוֹרָה but rather עַל דִּבְרֵי תוֹרָה. The second berachah, according to the Rambam, is וְהַעֲרֶב נָא ה׳ אֱלֹקֵינוּ אֶת דִּבְרֵי תוֹרָתְךָ. The third berachah is בָּרוּךְ אַתָּה ה׳...אֲשֶׁר בָּחַר בָּנוּ מִכָּל הָעַמִּים. If the Tosafot counted two berachot, why did the Rambam count three? According to the Rambam, the three berachot may correspond to the three different kinds of Torah study: one for the Written Torah, one for the Mishnah, and one for Talmud.

But there is still something that bothers us according to the Tosafot. Why do we first thank God for the Oral Torah and only then for the Written Torah? It should be the other way around. Logically, the Written Torah was given first, and then God gave Moshe the interpretations little by little, and Moshe taught them to the Jewish people. We seem to be changing the sequence.

Here again we have an example of the Rabbis fighting against people who were deviating from mainstream Judaism. During the time of the Second Temple, there were many Jews who denied the validity and existence of the Oral Torah. That was the basis of the great controversy between the צְדוּקִים (Sadducees) and the פְּרוּשִׁים (Pharisees).[55] Because of such movements, the Rabbis decided that the first berachah should emphasize the oral law.[56] There can be no Judaism without the oral law. The Christians appropriated the written law and claimed that they understood its true meaning. The Muslims did, too. History has shown us what happens to the Torah without the oral law. The oral law is what makes us Jews. As a result, we first thank God for the oral law.

We say in this berachah the phrase וְנִהְיֶה אֲנַחְנוּ...וְצֶאֱצָאֵי עַמְּךָ בֵּית יִשְׂרָאֵל כֻּלָּנוּ יוֹדְעֵי שְׁמֶךָ וְלוֹמְדֵי תוֹרָתְךָ לִשְׁמָהּ ("May we...and the whole

55. The Pharisees studied both the Written Torah and the Oral Torah, while the Sadducees studied and observed only the Written Torah. Controversies between the two factions, therefore, emerged on issues like the counting of the Omer, צִיצִית (ritual fringes), and the permissibility of benefiting from light and heat on Shabbat. Over time, other sects developed, such as the Karaites, who also believed only in the Written Torah.

56. Tikkun Tefillah in Otzar Hatefillot, ד״ה לעסוק.

house of Israel be knowledgeable of Your name and learners of Your Torah for its own sake"). What does it mean to "be knowledgeable of Your name"? We already know God's names. It's a strange expression. When it says we should learn the Torah, we know what that means; we have to sit down and work hard. When it says וְהַעֲרֶב נָא, "And please make it sweet," in the mouths of our children, we know this means that we have to lighten the workload a little.[57] But what does it mean that we should know God's name? There are two possible interpretations. The word יוֹדְעֵי (knowers of) may be used as a substitute for "lovers of," such as וְהָאָדָם יָדַע אֶת חַוָּה אִשְׁתּוֹ ("Adam knew Chavah, his wife"). The phrase seems to mean that we should not only know God's name but also love God, as in וְאָהַבְתָּ אֵת ה׳ אֱלֹקֶיךָ ("You should love Hashem your God").[58] This is a very great level to reach. It is very simple to know God's name, but to love God and give everything we have to God is a bit more complicated.[59]

Another interpretation of knowing God's name is that we should know the meaning of God's name. We have already noted that God has several names, and each name represents a particular attribute of God. אֱלֹקִים means that God is a judge, utilizing the attribute of justice. The שֵׁם הַמְּפֹרָשׁ refers to God's attribute of mercy. אֲדֹנָ־י is God as the Owner of everything. ה׳ צְבָקוֹת is God as the Creator of the heavenly and earthly hosts. Whenever we say a prayer, we can reach full כַּוָּנָה only if we understand the meaning of the particular name of God.[60]

Whenever we say a berachah for a mitzvah, we must fulfill the mitzvah immediately after the recitation of the berachah. There should be as little time as possible between the berachah and the performance of the mitzvah. According to Tosafot, an exception to this rule is the בִּרְכוֹת הַתּוֹרָה. When we say these berachot, we don't have

---

57. We used to give children an apple baked with honey when they started learning Torah.

58. דברים פרק ו פסוק ה

59. See רד"ק תהלים פרק צא פסוק יד: וידיעת שם המפורש שהוא בן ארבע אותיות היא אהבת הא־ל יתברך.

60. For a list of examples, see Avot D'Rabbi Natan, Chapter 38 (נוסחא ב פרק לח).

to immediately follow the berachah with the mitzvah; we can fulfill the mitzvah at a later time.[61] If, for example, you say the בִּרְכוֹת הַתּוֹרָה in the morning, you can have breakfast, go to work, come home, eat dinner, and attend a Torah class at 8:00 P.M., and the berachot from the morning are still valid.

The reason for this is that our activities during the day are not actually a distraction. This has to do with the nature of the berachot of Torah study. If a busy physician goes to shul in the morning, rushes home, sees patients, and then finally, in the evening, sits down and learns Torah, ten hours might have elapsed between the berachah and the Torah study. But there was really no interruption, because healing the sick is a commandment in the Torah. Similarly, the berachah is valid for a businessperson who rushes from davening in the morning to work all day and only sits down to study Torah in the evening. The purpose of making money is to support one's family and to give to the poor. The laws of business relations are described in the Shulchan Aruch. Therefore, whatever your profession is, it is somehow connected to Torah. There is never an interruption. Saying this berachah once in the morning covers me all day and all night, until the next morning when I get up and say it again, because all our activities should ideally be directed toward one goal: following the teachings (i.e., being "involved with the words") of the Torah.

Nevertheless, the siddur includes a short "study session" after the בִּרְכוֹת הַתּוֹרָה. After the concluding phrase, בָּרוּךְ אַתָּה ה׳ נוֹתֵן הַתּוֹרָה, we include verses from the Torah. The first verses are the Priestly Blessing, יְבָרֶכְךָ ה׳ וְיִשְׁמְרֶךָ ("May Hashem bless you and protect you").[62] The second selection is a Mishnah, אֵלּוּ דְבָרִים שֶׁאֵין לָהֶם שִׁעוּר ("The following things have no minimum amount"), with the addition of a supplementary passage in the Talmud.[63] The scholars of the Middle Ages introduced these study sessions into the siddur.[64]

61. תוספות ברכות דף יא עמוד ב, ד"ה שכבר נפטר באהבה רבה
62. במדבר פרק ו:כד-כו
63. פאה א, א; שבת דף קכז עמוד א
64. תקון תפלה ד"ה לעסוק בדברי תורה

Whatever you give of these things listed in the Mishnah, you have fulfilled your duty. If you are a farmer, you have to leave the corner of the field for the poor. No matter how little you leave, you have fulfilled the Biblical requirement of the commandment. In the season of Shavuot, our ancestors brought the בִּכּוּרִים (first fruits of their harvest) to Jerusalem. This commandment also has no minimum amount. Whatever you give is enough. The Rabbis said that even though, from the Torah's perspective, you can give as little as you want, you should never be too stingy. They said to give one-sixtieth.[65] This is the rabbinic requirement.

Regarding acts of kindness, here the phrase "no minimum amount" doesn't really refer to a minimum but to a maximum. When I do an act of kindness, there is no limit to it. I should do as many kindnesses as I can. Similarly, with Torah study, there is no maximum. The more you learn the better. צְדָקָה (charity), however, does have a maximum. It is one-fifth of one's income.[66] The Rabbis set a limit because they did not want a person's family to suffer because of this generosity. Rich people can certainly give more if they are so inclined.

This Mishnah was chosen to be included in the siddur because it mentions Torah study and acts of kindness. It may also have been chosen because these are laws that have no arguments about them.[67] Anybody who learns Mishnah knows that there are always arguments. One rabbi says one thing, and another one says something else. There are very few laws which have no arguments; these are the laws that should be learned in the morning prior to davening, because they inspire us and give us more כַּוָּנָה. If we get caught up in an argument, we will not concentrate as well on our davening.

Next comes the passage,[68] אֵלוּ דְבָרִים שֶׁאָדָם אוֹכֵל פֵּירוֹתֵיהֶן בָּעוֹלָם הַזֶּה ("These are the things from which a person benefits in this world"), meaning that God rewards us in this world, but just slightly. The

---

65. רמב"ם, הלכות מתנות עניים פרק א הל' טו; הלכות ביכורים פרק ב הל' יז
66. שולחן ערוך יורה דעה סי' רמ"ט סעי' א
67. סדר עבודת ישראל עמוד 38 ד"ה יברכך
68. פאה א א. See also קידושין דף לט עמ' ב.

principal reward is in the next world. A person should not say, however, "I am such a wonderful person; I give so much charity and learn so much Torah; why am I not doing so well? Why am I sick or poor?" The real reward for doing mitzvot is given in the next world. If we look at rich people, we might feel that we too should receive more benefit in this world. Why does God not give us more reward in this world sometimes? If there were a reward in this world for each commandment, everyone would be righteous in order to benefit from the immediate reward. Since there is usually no immediate reward in this world for doing the mitzvot, people must observe them for unselfish reasons and not abstain from doing them even if they suffer. People should do the mitzvot because they love the Torah, not to get a reward.[69]

Nevertheless, sometimes we do get a slight reward in this world for certain commandments, and this passage explains which ones. Respect for one's parents is one of the deeds that the Torah specifically says a person will be rewarded for in this world.[70] For instance, if your parents are old and feeble, and they have to be taken care of, you should gladly do that. The reward could be that your own children will learn from it, and later in life they will take care of you. This is a simple explanation of this passage.

Why did our scholars choose these specific "study sessions"? There are thousands of verses to choose from in the Torah and the Talmud. Our Rabbis[71] explain that there are sixty letters in the Priestly Blessing. Thus, the Priestly Blessing is related to the number sixty. The oral law consists of sixty parts: the Mishnah has sixty volumes.[72] Referring to the sixty volumes is a hint to us, saying that it is alright to study the

---

69. אבות פרק א משנה ג

70. דברים פרק ה פסוק טז. Also see דברים פרק יא פס׳ יח-כא.

71. במדבר רבה פרשת קרח פרשה יח

72. סדר עבודת ישראל עמוד 38 ד״ה יברכך. There are really sixty-three volumes, but originally there were only sixty. Some volumes were so long that they were split. The volumes called Bava Kama, Bava Metzia, and Bava Batra were originally one, but the material was so extensive that it was divided it into three volumes. The volumes of Sanhedrin and Makkot also used to be one. This, too, had so much material that it was divided into two volumes.

way we do, but we are never doing enough. There are sixty volumes. We can spend years, a whole lifetime, studying and never finish all sixty volumes. Whatever we are studying, we should never feel too proud of ourselves because there is always more to do. We can never reach the goal of learning everything.

The Gemara[73] says that people should spend their lives devoting one third to the study of מִקְרָא (Bible), one third in the study of Mishnah, and one third in the study of Talmud. But, the Gemara asks, how can a person know when he will die? How can he decide how much time to spend on any one discipline? The Gemara answers its question: לֹא צְרִיכָא - לְיוֹמֵי. Don't divide your study by years, but divide it by days. Rashi explains this means to divide the days of the week in thirds, so that you spend two days a week in each discipline. Tosafot[74] believe that every day we should study each of these disciplines. Tosafot explain that this is the reason that Rav Amram's siddur includes study of each of these disciplines before פְּסוּקֵי דְזִמְרָה. In that way, we can have at least some of each kind of Torah study in case we are too busy later to continue.

Rabbenu Tam cites a Gemara in Sanhedrin[75] that says the study of the Babylonian Talmud includes all three categories. According to Rabbenu Tam, the study of the Babylonian Talmud is sufficient to fulfill the requirement of studying the three different components of the Torah.

The Other בִּרְכּוֹת הַתּוֹרָה

When we go to shul and are given the honor of being called to the Torah, this is considered public Torah study.[76] At that time, we say two berachot. Before the reading we say אֲשֶׁר בָּחַר בָּנוּ מִכָּל הָעַמִּים ("Who

73. קידושין דף ל עמוד א

74. תוספות קידושין דף ל עמ׳ א לא צריכא ליומי

75. סנהדרין דף כד עמ׳ א

76. See רשימות שיעורים (רי״ד סולובייצ׳יק) מסכת ברכות דף ב עמוד א בענין שומע כעונה בקריאת שמע ותפלה א בא״ד.

chose us from all the nations"), and after the reading we say אֲשֶׁר נָתַן לָנוּ תּוֹרַת אֱמֶת ("Who gave us the Torah of truth").

Before we study, we thank God for giving us the great gift of the Torah. After we study, we thank God for giving us the ability to study it. Shouldn't the same be true throughout the day? When we get up in the morning, we say the בִּרְכוֹת הַתּוֹרָה before we study. Maybe we should say another berachah before we go to bed, thanking God that we accomplished something and learned some Torah?

We don't do this for an obvious reason. When I am called to the Torah in shul, I know exactly how many verses I am getting for my aliyah (the section read for the person called to the Torah). Each weekly portion is divided into seven parts and the aliyah is a fixed number of verses.

Because my section is finite, I am entitled to say a berachah afterward. But when it comes to the בִּרְכוֹת הַתּוֹרָה in the morning, even if I am very industrious and study the whole day, can I really say that I studied "enough"? If I were to say a berachah on the Torah afterward, it would be as if I were saying, "I did all that I could do." But that isn't the case. Therefore, there is no berachah at the end of the day that signifies the completion of Torah study because there is no end to learning.

When comparing the בִּרְכוֹת הַתּוֹרָה in the morning to the בִּרְכוֹת הַתּוֹרָה that we say before an aliyah, we can ask another question. Before an aliyah, we start with בָּרְכוּ אֶת ה׳ הַמְבֹרָךְ ("Blessed is Hashem who is blessed"). Everybody then answers, בָּרוּךְ ה׳ הַמְבֹרָךְ לְעוֹלָם וָעֶד ("Blessed is Hashem who is blessed forever"). In the morning when we say the בִּרְכוֹת הַתּוֹרָה, we don't do that. Is it because we need a minyan (a quorum for prayer) for בָּרְכוּ (the exhortation to bless God), and we are saying these בִּרְכוֹת הַתּוֹרָה in the privacy of our homes where we do not have a minyan? If that were the reason, we could say the berachot in shul with a minyan, and then we could say בָּרְכוּ.

That we do not do this points to a very important difference between studying Torah and reading from the Torah. When I am called up to the Torah and the *ba'al koreh* (reader) rushes through the week's portion, it is not easily understood, but it is nevertheless a public demonstration of Torah study. When I study Torah on an individual basis, I have a different standard. I enrich myself intellectually. It isn't an intellectual activity unless I understand it. When we read from the Torah, this is not "studying" as much as it is a demonstration of our dedication to the Torah as an aspect of our dedication to God. It might be קַבָּלַת עֹל מַלְכוּת שָׁמַיִם (accepting God as our Sovereign), since we sanctify ourselves to carry out the Torah and renew our commitment to it. It is a more emotional approach. Therefore, when I am called up to the Torah, I am telling the congregation that they are supposed to listen to a certain portion, to which we are all committing ourselves. We will do everything in our power to carry it out, no matter what happens, even if our lives are threatened. That is קַבָּלַת עֹל מַלְכוּת שָׁמַיִם.

This is the same commitment that Rabbi Akiva had when the Romans came to him and said, "If you study Torah, you will be executed." He demonstrated the ultimate in accepting God as our King in refusing to give up the right and need to study Torah. We say, "So too will we accept God to any extreme." The reading of the Torah in shul is thus preceded by בָּרְכוּ, which means a commitment and a dedication to the Torah and to God.

When the person called up to the Torah says בָּרְכוּ אֶת ה׳ הַמְבֹרָךְ, you would expect people to stand up for the response, as they do when בָּרְכוּ is recited before the berachot of Shema. Strictly speaking, according to Ashkenazic custom, people should stand up because this is considered accepting the sovereignty of God over our lives, and for that we customarily stand. But people rarely do. Some people sit and make a slight motion as if they are rising. We should, however, stand up fully, out of respect for God.[77]

Are Women Obligated to Study Torah?

In describing the morning berachot, R. Yosef Karo points out something very important: women are obliged to say the בִּרְכוֹת הַתּוֹרָה every morning.[78] If the Shulchan Aruch says that women are obliged to say the בִּרְכוֹת הַתּוֹרָה, then clearly women are obliged to study Torah;

---

77. ט״ז אורח חיים סימן קמו ס״ק א, משנה ברורה שם ס״ק יח

78. שולחן ערוך אורח חיים סימן מז, סעיף יד

otherwise they would be saying a berachah in vain. The fact that women did not study Torah for so many centuries had serious consequences. We still pay the price for that neglect, as many Jewish women lack important Torah knowledge and have even drifted away from their religion.

Some men, nevertheless, still say that women should study only the written law and not the oral law.[79] All kinds of explanations are given to rationalize this view. But it is obvious that women have to learn oral as well as written Torah. Women too have to understand the laws that apply to them (and the vast majority of laws apply to all Jews).[80]

Years ago, I discussed this with Rav Soloveitchik, who told me a story that is fairly well known.[81] In Poland before World War I, women rarely studied Torah because the opportunity was not given to them. They did not even know how to daven. They had special prayer books in Yiddish called *Techinos* instead of the regular Hebrew siddur. The education of women was sorely neglected.

The Chafetz Chayim[82] once said at a rabbinic conference, "My dear colleagues and friends: the time has come to break with the tradition not to teach women. Women have to learn Torah. If we don't teach women to learn Torah, the future generations won't know anything and Judaism will suffer."

The other rabbis said, "How can you go against the law? Does it not say in the Gemara, כָּל הַמְלַמֵּד אֶת בִּתּוֹ תּוֹרָה כְּאִלּוּ לִמְּדָהּ תִּפְלוּת ('He

---

79. This view is based on the Rambam, הלכות תלמוד תורה פרק א הלכה יג. See also יורה דעה סימן רמו סעיף ו.

80. רמ"א, יורה דעה סימן רמו סעיף ו; ספר חסידים (מרגליות) סימן שיג

81. Rav Aharon Lichtenstein independently corroborated this narrative. See *Seeking His Presence: Conversations with Rabbi Aharon Lichtenstein*, by R. Haim Sabato (Tel Aviv, 2016), in the chapter titled "Why Should Her Portion be Diminished? On Torah study for women and feminism," especially p. 213 and note 37.

82. The "Chafetz Chayim," Rabbi Yisrael Meir HaKohen (1838–1933), was a saintly scholar and ethicist, who, among other works, was the author of the Mishnah Berurah. He is often referred to by the title of his work "Chafetz Chayim" on the laws of forbidden speech.

who teaches his daughter Torah is like the one who teaches her foolishness')?"[83] The Chafetz Chayim said, "What would the law be if a gentile woman came to you and said, 'I want to convert'?" The rabbis answered, "You have to teach her the Torah. She must accept the observance of the commandments."

The Chafetz Chayim asked, "Do you all agree to that?" The rabbis replied, "Of course. How else can she know what Shabbat is? She has to know what is forbidden, and she has to know what is permissible. She has to know how to keep a kosher kitchen. There are many things to learn."

The Chafetz Chayim responded, "You mean to say that for a non-Jewish woman to become Jewish, it is alright for her to learn Torah, but a woman who is born Jewish may not learn?"[84]

In part because of the Chafetz Chayim's strong stand, the Bais Yaakov schools for women were founded in Poland before World War I where they continued to exist until the Nazis destroyed them during the Holocaust.

83. סוטה דף כ עמוד א

84. See also the Chafetz Chayim's discussion in לקוטי הלכות, סוטה פרק ג, עמ' 22–21.

Morning Berachot

Now we are ready to discuss the portions of Shacharit called בִּרְכוֹת הַשַּׁחַר, the berachot of the morning. These berachot consist of two different types: berachot over activities that we do upon getting up in the morning and berachot of being or status.

WHERE DO WE SAY THESE BERACHOT?

In Talmudic times, these berachot were not said together in the synagogue. They were said at home as the occasion arose, and it might have taken an hour or more to say them. If you awoke early in the morning and heard the rooster crow, you would say the berachah of אֲשֶׁר נָתַן לַשֶּׂכְוִי בִינָה לְהַבְחִין בֵּין יוֹם וּבֵין לָיְלָה ("Who gives the rooster understanding"). When you finally opened your eyes for the day, you would say the berachah of פּוֹקֵחַ עִוְרִים ("Who opens the eyes of the blind"); when you got dressed, you would say the berachah of מַלְבִּישׁ עֲרֻמִּים ("Who clothes the naked"); and so on, with each berachah.[1] These berachot were said as each activity was performed. A Jew knows that nothing should be taken for granted, that every good thing is a special kindness from God. We sometimes forget that we have to thank God for all those little things that are part of our daily ritual.

In the Shulchan Aruch, R. Yosef Karo records the Talmud's rules about when to say each berachah. It states that the proper place to say these berachot is in the home as the occasion arises. However, he

---

1. ברכות דף ס עמ׳ ב

adds that today because people may not know the different berachot, it has become customary to say all the berachot together as part of the synagogue service instead.[2] According to R. Yosef Karo, the berachot represent the various activities performed at home at different times. Therefore, if you did not experience those things for which the berachot are recited, such as if you did not get dressed that day, you would not recite the corresponding berachah. In other words, these are בִּרְכוֹת הֲנָאָה (berachot recited upon receiving some benefit), and if you did not receive the benefit you do not recite the berachah.[3]

The Rama understood the nature of these berachot differently. The Rama says that even if I did not perform the activity which corresponds to the berachah, I should nevertheless say the berachah.[4] He sees them as berachot of praise and thanks for what God does for the whole human race; whether I personally put on my clothes is immaterial.

One example of the difference between these two approaches arises on Yom Kippur. On this day we are not supposed to wear leather shoes. According to R. Yosef Karo, who says that I must thank God for the special kindness of the moment, on Yom Kippur I should skip the berachah for putting on shoes. According to the Rama, I am praising God for creating shoes for human beings in general, so I should say the berachah even on Yom Kippur. Ashkenazic Jews therefore say all the berachot every day.

The berachah for putting on shoes is שֶׁעָשָׂה לִּי כָּל צָרְכִּי ("Who provided for me all my needs"). Only when I am wearing shoes can I go where I have to go and do what I have to do. Without shoes, I am stuck in the house. The next berachah we say is הַמֵּכִין מִצְעֲדֵי גָבֶר ("Who prepares the steps of a man"), or who gives us the power to walk. We thank God that we are not paralyzed or lame.

In the Talmud, the order of these two berachot is reversed. The reason for this is that the Talmud was written in Babylonia, where

---

2. שולחן ערוך אורח חיים סימן מו סעיף ב
3. שולחן ערוך אורח חיים סימן מו, סעיף ח
4. שולחן ערוך אורח חיים סימן מו, סעיף ח

people did not put on shoes when they got up in the morning. They only wore shoes when they left the house and went into the street. At home they did not wear their shoes. Therefore, in those days the first berachah to be said was the berachah for walking. Since our habit is to put on our shoes right away when we get dressed, because most of us wear our shoes in the house, we reverse the order of the berachot.[5]

BERACHOT OVER ACTIVITIES

The berachot over activities each begin with בָּרוּךְ אַתָּה ה׳ אֱלֹקֵינוּ מֶלֶךְ הָעוֹלָם. The first berachah ends with אֲשֶׁר נָתַן לַשֶּׂכְוִי בִינָה לְהַבְחִין בֵּין יוֹם וּבֵין לָיְלָה ("Who gave the rooster the understanding to distinguish between day and night"), and the last ends with הַמַּעֲבִיר שֵׁנָה מֵעֵינַי וּתְנוּמָה מֵעַפְעַפָּי ("Who removes sleep from my eyes and slumber from my eyelids").

The first berachah, that God gave the rooster the understanding to distinguish between day and night, refers to the fact that the rooster is the first creature to welcome the morning. The rooster instinctively knows that morning has come.

Even though this is the way most siddurim translate this berachah, there is a better translation. The word שֶׂכְוִי (usually translated as rooster) is found in the book of Job[6] and there it means "human heart." This would render the translation of our berachah: "Who gave the human heart the understanding to distinguish between day and night."[7] I prefer this translation because most of us don't hear a rooster these days; and if we don't, the question is what benefit have we derived for which we recite this berachah? Are we even permitted to say it? But if it means that God gave the human heart understanding, then I am saying the berachah for a personal benefit. In other words, the first thing we thank God for is the ability to discern between day and night. All human scholarship, learning, and understanding starts

5. שולחן ערוך הרב אורח חיים סימן מו סעיף ה
6. איוב לח:לו
7. רא״ש ברכות פרק ט סימן כג

with the ability to discern one thing from another. We are therefore thanking God for giving us a thinking mind.

Most of the berachot that we say every morning are universal berachot. In other words, I thank God for what He did not for me as a Jew but for me as a human being. We don't say פּוֹקֵחַ עֵינֵי יִשְׂרָאֵל ("Who opens the eyes of the Jews"). We recite a universal berachah that says פּוֹקֵחַ עִוְרִים ("Who opens the eyes of the blind"). Every human being has eyes. Any person, Jew or gentile, should sense the benefits that we receive from God.

There are two berachot, in this section of berachot of activities, however, that are not universal and do refer to Jews alone: אוֹזֵר יִשְׂרָאֵל בִּגְבוּרָה ("Who girds Israel with strength") and עוֹטֵר יִשְׂרָאֵל בְּתִפְאָרָה ("Who crowns Israel with glory"). We say אוֹזֵר יִשְׂרָאֵל בִּגְבוּרָה when we put on a belt, and we say עוֹטֵר יִשְׂרָאֵל בְּתִפְאָרָה when we cover our heads. Why is that particular to Jews? These two berachot are actually referring to two commandments that Jews fulfill every morning.

Our philosophy in prayer is that we must separate the lower, animal part of our body from the higher, spiritual part of our body.[8] Chasidic men demonstrate this by wearing a gartel (sash) around the midriff. Non-Chasidic Jews believe in this principle, too, but think that an ordinary belt serves the same purpose. For other people, a belt is just a garment; for us it is an expression of spirituality. We want to rise above the animal level to higher realms, where we come close to the angels and to God.

The same is true with עוֹטֵר יִשְׂרָאֵל בְּתִפְאָרָה. A Jewish man should not walk around with an uncovered head, so he wears a yarmulke. A yarmulke for us is an expression of our acceptance of the yoke of Heaven, or God's sovereignty, wherever we are.

When Rav Soloveitchik davened as שְׁלִיחַ צִבּוּר (chazzan), he recited the blessing הַנּוֹתֵן לַיָּעֵף כֹּחַ ("Who gives strength to the weak") without שֵׁם וּמַלְכוּת (that is, without mentioning God's name, ה׳ אֱלֹקֵינוּ מֶלֶךְ הָעוֹלָם, in the berachah). He said instead, בָּרוּךְ הַנּוֹתֵן לַיָּעֵף כֹּחַ, because

8. ספר אבודרהם ברכות השחר, in the section starting כששומע קול תרנגול.

this berachah is not mentioned in the Talmud.[9] It seems that this berachah was added in the Middle Ages, probably as an aftermath of the first Crusade.[10] Until the Crusades, the life of the Jews in Europe was not too bad. It wasn't ideal, but a Jew could make a living. Jews were respected and had certain rights. With the Crusades, all of this ended. Jews had no more rights and were massacred in large numbers. After the First Crusade, when a Jew woke up in the morning, still alive, he or she said הַנּוֹתֵן לַיָּעֵף כֹּחַ. The Jews added this berachah on their own. They wondered how could they exist in such a world, and they needed God to give them strength. They believed that if they could function at all, it was a miracle. Rav Soloveitchik did not believe that we should say berachot that are not mentioned in the Talmud, so he didn't recite it as a full berachah.

The last berachah, which begins הַמַּעֲבִיר שֵׁנָה מֵעֵינַי וּתְנוּמָה מֵעַפְעַפָּי ("Who removes sleep from my eyes and slumber from my eyelids") is very long in comparison to the other berachot. It concludes with בָּרוּךְ אַתָּה ה׳, גּוֹמֵל חֲסָדִים טוֹבִים לְעַמּוֹ יִשְׂרָאֵל ("Blessed are You, Hashem, who bestows acts of kindness on His people, Israel").

This berachah seems to go against a basic rule. When a berachah is a "long berachah" (בְּרָכָה אֲרוּכָה), its ending must directly follow from, or be related to the opening theme. We may digress and mention different themes in the middle of the berachah, but the end and the beginning must be the same topic. This unifies the berachah under one major theme.

---

9. Communicated to Rabbi Wohlgemuth by Rabbi Soloveitchik in a private conversation. It is also mentioned in R. Hershel Schachter, נפש הרב, עמ׳ קז.

10. The commentary Iyun Tefillah, in the Otzar Hatefillot on this berachah, explains the unusual circumstances of coining a berachah in such a late period after the conclusion of the Talmud: He noted the period of terrible suffering in the aftermath of the Crusades, and the response of the rabbis to the suffering of the people. Even though we say that new berachot cannot be coined after the conclusion of the Talmud, there is an overriding principle that God listens to the cries of the downtrodden. That is the reason, according to the Iyun Tefillah, for coining the berachah of הַנּוֹתֵן לַיָּעֵף כֹּחַ during the Middle Ages at this point in the davening.

Here we don't seem to abide by this rule. At the beginning we say, "Blessed are You, Hashem our God, King of the universe, who removes sleep from my eyes and slumber from my eyelids." At the end we say, "Blessed are You, Hashem, who bestows acts of kindness on His people Israel." That is something entirely different. At the beginning we talk about waking up, and at the end we speak of acts of kindness. The Tosafot raised the issue,[11] and they answered that although it may seem to be two different themes, in reality it is only one theme. When we go to bed at night, we are not guaranteed that we will wake up healthy the next morning. God performs a great kindness by allowing me to open my eyes at all. I am still alive. A new day is here, and I can accomplish great things.

In this long berachah, there is one idea that is a little puzzling. It says, וְכֹף אֶת יִצְרֵנוּ לְהִשְׁתַּעְבֶּד לָךְ ("and force our inclinations to subjugate ourselves to You"). In other words, we are asking God to force us to perform the commandments. This seems to be against everything we know. We know that we have free will, yet here we seem to be yielding it and saying, "Please, God, force me to be good." Why do we ask God to force us to do something that we should do on our own? Actually, the most we can ask from God is to remove any obstacles that might prevent us from reaching our intended goal.[12]

This is not the only time that we deal with this issue. We have a similar problem in the שְׁמוֹנֶה עֶשְׂרֵה. In the fifth berachah of the שְׁמוֹנֶה עֶשְׂרֵה, the berachah of repentance, we say: הֲשִׁיבֵנוּ אָבִינוּ לְתוֹרָתֶךָ. We ask God to "bring us back to Your Torah, bring us closer to Your service, and bring us back in complete repentance before You." Again, we seem to be asking God to compel our good behavior. The same explanation applies to this case as well. Sometimes we need some help in serving God, so we ask God to remove any obstacles in our path. Nevertheless, it still poses a serious problem in our prayers.

The Talmud says that a person should always pray for other people

11. תוספות ברכות דף מו עמ׳ א ד״ה כל הברכות כולן
12. *The World of Prayer*, p. 35.

in the congregation when they pray for their own needs.[13] I never say, for example, "Forgive me, God, for I have sinned," because I am not that important in the scheme of things for God to make an exception for me.[14] If I am sick, I say, "Heal us." No Jew has special privileges before God. When we say the prayer for the sick in the morning in shul for a specific individual, we never ask for that person alone. We always ask that God cure this person בְּתוֹךְ שְׁאָר חוֹלֵי יִשְׂרָאֵל (together with all the sick people of Israel). I am obligated to pray for every Jew. If I want God's mercy, I should ask for others first, and then, perhaps because they are deserving, God will grant my personal request, too.

The berachah of הַמַּעֲבִיר שֵׁנָה מֵעֵינַי וּתְנוּמָה מֵעַפְעַפָּי breaks the rule of praying for the whole community. It says *my* eyes and *my* eyelids. Here, I am thanking God for letting me, in the singular, wake up. Shouldn't it be in the plural? However, as we continue this berachah, we do make a transition from the singular to the plural, for example, we say שֶׁתַּרְגִּילֵנוּ בְּתוֹרָתֶךָ (accustom *us* to study Your Torah), וְהַרְחִיקֵנוּ מֵאָדָם רָע (keep *us* away from evil people), וְכֹף אֶת יִצְרֵנוּ (and force *our* wills), וְתִגְמְלֵנוּ חֲסָדִים טוֹבִים (do acts of kindness for *us*). It ends with בָּרוּךְ אַתָּה ה' הַגּוֹמֵל חֲסָדִים טוֹבִים לְעַמּוֹ יִשְׂרָאֵל. We start on the wrong foot, so to speak, in the singular, and we catch ourselves, as it were, and skip to the plural. Why do we do this?

The words הַמַּעֲבִיר שֵׁנָה מֵעֵינַי וּתְנוּמָה מֵעַפְעַפָּי are adopted directly from Psalm 132.[15] This reflects the tension about our wanting to pray for

---

13. ברכות דף כט ע"ב - דף ל ע"א. See רש"י ברכות דף ל ע"א ד"ה לישתף נפשיה. The Mishnah Berurah (סימן קי ס"ק כ) qualifies that this rule applies when we are reciting an established prayer, but when a person is praying in his own words for his own private needs, he needn't pray in the plural.

14. One example of this kind of praying in the plural tense is when we even change the Scriptural source of the berachah for health, רְפָאֵנוּ ("Heal us") in the Amidah. The verse from Jeremiah (ירמיהו יז:יד) on which the berachah is based states: רְפָאֵנִי ה' וְאֵרָפֵא הוֹשִׁיעֵנִי וְאִוָּשֵׁעָה ("Heal me, Hashem, and I will be healed; save me and I will be saved"), but in the Amidah it is changed to: רְפָאֵנוּ ה' וְנֵרָפֵא. הוֹשִׁיעֵנוּ וְנִוָּשֵׁעָה ("Heal *us*, Hashem, and *we* will be healed; save *us* and *we* will be saved").

15. אִם־אֶתֵּן שְׁנַת לְעֵינָי לְעַפְעַפַּי תְּנוּמָה :תהלים פרק קלב פס' ד

the whole Jewish people, not just for in individual, but at the same time, being very hesitant to change a Biblical text. Perhaps we feel that we have no right to change a text that is derived directly from a biblical verse. When we say a prayer, we say it in the plural, but when we borrow from the Book of Psalms, we don't change the wording.

There are many places in the davening where we do change biblical verses from the singular to the plural. The Rishonim[16] say that when we utilize biblical verses for a prayer or plea to God, we are allowed to do this, especially if it is a single verse rather than a whole Biblical chapter. However, it is still difficult to change a Biblical text.[17]

BERACHOT OF BEING OR STATUS

There are three berachot we have skipped which I consider בִּרְכוֹת יְצִירָה (berachot of being or status), and they are very controversial:

- שֶׁלֹּא עָשַׂנִי אִשָּׁה ("Who has not made me a woman") for men, and שֶׁעָשַׂנִי כִּרְצוֹנוֹ ("Who has made me according to His will") for women;
- שֶׁלֹּא עָשַׂנִי עָבֶד ("Who has not made me a slave"); and
- שֶׁלֹּא עָשַׂנִי גּוֹי ("Who has not made me a gentile").

Rav Soloveitchik taught that these three berachot are statements of gratitude about the levels of obligation to perform as many commandments as possible.[18] A non-Jew is obligated to perform only

16. The Rishonim are the rabbis of the post-Gaonic period until the late Middle Ages, roughly from the eleventh century to the middle of the fifteenth century of the Common Era.

17. See טור אורח חיים סימן קטז. In Selichot, we do change the words from the verse יִהְיוּ לְרָצוֹן אִמְרֵי־פִי וְהֶגְיוֹן לִבִּי לְפָנֶיךָ ה׳ צוּרִי וְגֹאֲלִי to the plural and say: יִהְיוּ לְרָצוֹן אִמְרֵי פִינוּ וְהֶגְיוֹן לִבֵּנוּ לְפָנֶיךָ ה׳ צוּרֵנוּ וְגוֹאֲלֵנוּ. However, I listened to Rav Soloveitchik say this verse, and he always said this verse in the singular as it appears in Psalms. He believed that, although some Rishonim permitted the change, we really should avoid as much as possible trying to "improve" the work of King David.

18. Based on לבוש אורח חיים סימן מו סעיף ה.

the seven Noachide laws. An *eved kena'ani* (quasi-Jewish slave) and a Jewish woman are obligated to perform all commandments except מִצְוַת עֲשֵׂה שֶׁהַזְּמַן גְּרָמָא, Torah obligations requiring the observance of a particular action that must be fulfilled within a specific time.[19]

The text שֶׁלֹּא עָשַׂנִי גּוֹי may be incorrect. Some argue that the word for gentile in the berachah, גּוֹי, should really be נָכְרִי.[20] This is because in Biblical Hebrew, גּוֹי means *people,* while נָכְרִי means *gentile.* The intention of this berachah is to thank God that we are not gentiles, which is a statement of gratitude for the fact that we are obligated to perform more of God's commandments.[21]

Many of the Conservative rabbis believe that it is terrible to thank God for not making us a gentile. They feel that we are saying that we are better than non-Jews. They think it is necessary to "correct" this berachah and say שֶׁעָשַׂנִי יִשְׂרָאֵל ("Who has made me a Jew"). Seemingly, they have a point. If you look in the Talmud,[22] the text says שֶׁעָשַׂנִי יִשְׂרָאֵל. These Conservative rabbis have simply changed the prayer to follow the Talmud. Why won't Orthodox rabbis change it? The Talmud was often under censorship by Christians even as late in history as nineteenth-century Czarist Russia. Most versions of the Talmud were printed only after a censor approved it. The censors were usually Jews who had left their faith. The original text of the Gemara was שֶׁלֹּא עָשַׂנִי גּוֹי, but censors forced the change to שֶׁעָשַׂנִי יִשְׂרָאֵל.[23]

Suppose, however, that I live in a non-Jewish neighborhood, and I personally feel bad if I insult my neighbors. Perhaps I should say שֶׁעָשַׂנִי יִשְׂרָאֵל? Would that be so bad? Actually, it would. Because the phrase

---

19. ספר אבודרהם ברכות השחר

20. Based on the Ibn Ezra's explanation of נָכְרִי as found in Exodus 21:8, Yitzchak Baer in the siddur Avodat Yisrael points out that a גּוֹי refers to a nation and a נָכְרִי refers to someone who is not Jewish. Baer insists that we must be precise in our usage of words, and the focus of this berachah is to praise and give thanks to God for choosing us and giving us the mitzvot that enrich us in this world and in the next.

21. Seder Avodat Yisrael, p. 40.

22. מנחות דף מג ע"ב

23. See Dikdukei Sofrim, Menachot 43b.

means that I am bragging to God that I am a *good* Jew. יִשְׂרָאֵל means "fighter for God." I am giving myself praise that I may not deserve. I can only say I am not a gentile. To be a *real* Jew – יִשְׂרָאֵל – takes work, struggle, and years of study. It is not so simple.

The berachah of שֶׁלֹּא עָשַׂנִי עָבֶד deals with a complex topic. We are saying that God did not make me a slave. But what does it really mean? Is the purpose of this berachah to insult someone? No. We only want to say that there are different obligations. There is a system of seven commandments known as the Noachide laws, which are obligatory for all gentiles.[24] If a non-Jewish person became a slave to a Jew and underwent *tevilah* as a slave,[25] he also became obligated to fulfill Jewish law, but was exempt from performing the מִצְוֹות עֲשֵׂה שֶׁהַזְּמַן גְּרָמָא, Torah obligations requiring the observance of a particular action that must be fulfilled within a specific time.[26] A slave, by definition, cannot say to his master, "Look, I can't work for you right now. I have to say the Shema. If I don't say it, I will miss the time."

Jewish women are also exempt from the מִצְוֹות עֲשֵׂה שֶׁהַזְּמַן גְּרָמָא.[27] One explanation for this is that mothers of infants or small children are busy with child rearing, which is a mitzvah in itself.[28] Yet all women (including those with grown children or no children at all) are exempt. Others have explained why men in particular require these additional mitzvot, while women do not.[29]

All Jewish men must observe the מִצְוֹות עֲשֵׂה שֶׁהַזְּמַן גְּרָמָא. When

24. Based on Sanhedrin 56b, the Rambam (Hilchot Melachim, Chapter 9) tells us that God transmitted to Adam, the first person, the prohibitions of idolatry, cursing God, bloodshed, incest, robbery and the requirement to set up enforcement of these laws. Noah was given an additional prohibition against eating meat of an animal taken from it while it was still alive.

25. שולחן ערוך יורה דעה הלכות עבדים סימן רסז, סעיף ג, יז

26. חגיגה דף ד עמוד א

27. For a list of mitzvot that are restricted to a specific time that women are nevertheless obligated to perform, see the section "Are Women Obliged to Say Hallel?" below.

28. אגרות משה אורח חיים חלק ד סימן מט

29. See, for example, R. Samson Raphael Hirsch's commentary, ויקרא פרק כג

Jewish men and women say שֶׁלֹּא עָשַׂנִי גּוֹי or שֶׁלֹּא עָשַׂנִי נָכְרִי, they are thanking God that they have more than the seven Noachide laws to fulfill. When Jewish men say שֶׁלֹּא עָשַׂנִי אִשָּׁה, they are thanking God for the extra commandments that they are obligated to do.[30] They are not supposed to feel superior to women by saying this; rather, they are supposed to feel gratitude for the privilege they have, because they have the burden of extra mitzvot.

Many women feel uncomfortable about the berachah of שֶׁלֹּא עָשַׂנִי אִשָּׁה. In the Middle Ages, women gave expression to this discomfort by adding an alternative berachah, שֶׁעָשַׂנִי כִּרְצוֹנוֹ. Many years ago, Rav Soloveitchik explained this in a remarkable way. These three berachot – שֶׁלֹּא עָשַׂנִי נָכְרִי; שֶׁלֹּא עָשַׂנִי עָבֶד and שֶׁלֹּא עָשַׂנִי אִשָּׁה – are all mentioned in the Gemara.[31] Rabbi Meir was the one who taught us to say these berachot. Rabbi Meir's wife was Beruria. She was a most remarkable woman who was a scholar in her own right. When she felt her husband was wrong in Talmudic learning, she told him so, and he accepted her word. Obviously, the berachah of שֶׁלֹּא עָשַׂנִי אִשָּׁה did not come from a place of disparagement toward women.

Beruria's father was Rabbi Chanina ben Tradyon. He was one of the עֲשָׂרָה הֲרוּגֵי מַלְכוּת (ten martyrs killed by the Romans) that we read about in our liturgy on Yom Kippur and Tisha B'Av. Under Roman rule, the Romans were successful in preventing their conquered nations from rebelling. There was just one stubborn little nation that rebelled against them time and time again, and the Romans got sick and tired of it. So, they asked, what makes the Jews so courageous? Why are they such good fighters? Why don't they accept our rule like everybody else? They found out that it was the Torah and the mitzvot. Hadrian, the Roman general who was in charge of quelling the Jewish rebellion (and who later became the Emperor of Rome, 117–138 C.E.) decreed, "No more Torah and no more mitzvot. Anyone

---

פסוק מג; R. Emanuel Rackman, "Arrogance or Humility in Prayer," *Tradition* 1:1, p. 17.

30. תוספתא ברכות פרק ו

31. מנחות דף מג עמוד ב

who observes them will be executed." The Romans were especially strict against the rabbis who taught the people and gave them new courage. Rabbi Akiva was murdered in those days, as was Rabbi Chanina ben Tradyon. When Rabbi Chanina ben Tradyon was caught teaching Torah, the Romans tied him down on a pile of wood. They lit the wood and arranged the fire so he would slowly burn to death. They made sure the whole town was watching so that they should see what happens if you teach Torah. These Roman legionaires stood around the person to be executed so no one would be able to rescue him. The Romans also knew that smoke would kill a person much quicker than the fire, so they bared Rabbi Chanina's chest and placed a lot of wet wool on his chest to prevent the smoke from killing him prematurely. Rabbi Chanina was supposed to suffer for an hour or two, however one Roman soldier said to him, "What will you do for me if I put an end to your suffering?" Rabbi Chanina promised him a share in the world to come. The Roman soldier removed the wet wool from Rabbi Chanina's chest, and Rabbi Chanina died quickly from smoke inhalation. The Roman soldier then jumped into the fire after him, because he knew what would happen to him, and he was ready for the next world.

When the Romans killed Jews, they almost always killed just the men. They had a special respect for womanhood. When you look through history, you see that the Romans seldom killed women. When did all this change? Women became martyrs as well as men in the Christian countries during the first Crusade. In 1096, the Jews in the great communities of Worms, Speyer and Mainz (or, as they were called, קְהִלּוֹת שו״ם[32]) were massacred. The Christians did not make any distinction between men and women. The "Religion of Love" did not have the same respect and love that the pagan Romans did for womanhood.

When Rabbi Meir saw what happened to his father-in-law, he introduced this berachah, שֶׁלֹּא עָשַׂנִי אִשָּׁה, because men could fulfill one mitzvah that women could not: dying עַל קִדּוּשׁ הַשֵּׁם (to sanctify

32. מ=מאגנצא; ו=ורמיזא; ש=שפירא

God's name). Women did not have such an opportunity. When the Christian Crusaders in the Middle Ages started massacring all Jews, including women, the women introduced a new berachah: שֶׁעָשַׂנִי כִּרְצוֹנוֹ, meaning You made me also in such a way that I can do Your will now, that also I can die עַל קִדּוּשׁ הַשֵּׁם. This explanation of Rav Soloveitchik shows us a different picture of this berachah.

RABBI YEHUDAH HANASI'S PRAYER

After these berachot, we come to a short prayer: יְהִי רָצוֹן מִלְּפָנֶיךָ...בֵּין שֶׁהוּא בֶן בְּרִית וּבֵין שֶׁאֵינוֹ בֶן בְּרִית: "May it be Your will, Hashem my God and the God of my ancestors, that You rescue me this and every day from shameless people and from shamelessness of my own, from an evil person and from an evil companion, from an evil neighbor, from a bad accident, from the satan [prosecuting angel], from a difficult legal case, and from a difficult opponent in court, whether or not a fellow Jew."

This brief prayer defies the rule that all of our prayers should be in the plural, and it is also somewhat repetitious. This prayer can only be understood if we know who composed it and why. It was the private prayer of Rabbi Yehudah HaNasi,[33] who lived around the year 200 C.E. and was the redactor of the Mishnah. He lived during the Roman persecution. A Jew could not sit down and quietly, peacefully, study or teach Torah. The political situation did not permit it.

Rabbi Yehudah HaNasi, however, was not only a great scholar but also a great politician. He was somehow able to create a modus vivendi with the Romans, who respected him and let him teach. The Talmud tells us there was one Roman, Antoninus, who was a close friend of Rabbi Yehudah HaNasi.[34] We are not certain who Antoninus was; he may have been the emperor of Rome who spent some time in the Near East, or he may have only been a governor. But during this

---

33. ברכות טז עמ׳ ב

34. ברכות דף נז עמ׳ ב and עבודה זרה דף יא עמ׳ א

period of favorable relations, Rabbi Yehudah HaNasi took advantage of the opportunity and compiled the Mishnah.

It was common among the Rabbis in those days to add special meditations at the end of the שְׁמוֹנֶה עֶשְׂרֵה. Every day Rabbi Yehudah HaNasi said the above-mentioned prayer at the end of his שְׁמוֹנֶה עֶשְׂרֵה. We can understand this prayer from a historical perspective and in light of his accomplishments for the Jewish people.

He said, "Rescue me this and every day from shameless people." This referred to the Romans. Rabbi Yehudah HaNasi had to worry every day that the peace that he was able to establish between Judea and Rome might be disturbed. With the phrase, "Rescue me from shamelessness of my own," Rabbi Yehudah HaNasi meant that he hoped not to offend the Romans. "Rescue me from an evil companion, from an evil neighbor" meant that if he had a fight with the Romans, all his goals could not be carried out. "A difficult legal case" referred to his status as the supreme judge of the Jewish people. Sometimes a difficult case came before him and he did not know what to decide. "A difficult opponent in court" meant that sometimes a person came to court who would argue and make life miserable for him so that he could not do what he needed to do.

Even though this was the private prayer of Rabbi Yehudah HaNasi, it was later adopted into the morning service. This is an example of a personal prayer so eloquent that Chazal felt everyone should partake of its beauty. Throughout our siddur, we find many examples of prayers which were borrowed from our rich history of addressing God. After the prayer of Rabbi Yehudah HaNasi, the siddur continues with the עֲקֵדָה, or binding of Isaac. This reflects the influence of the Zohar, the central work of Jewish mysticism.[35]

THE SECRET SHEMA

We then continue with לְעוֹלָם יְהֵא אָדָם יְרֵא שָׁמַיִם ("A person should always be God-fearing"). This section ends with the Shema, שְׁמַע יִשְׂרָאֵל

35. Siddur Otzar Hatefillot, p. 130.

ה׳ אֱלֹקֵינוּ ה׳ אֶחָד ("Hear, Israel, Hashem is our God, Hashem is one"), and בָּרוּךְ שֵׁם כְּבוֹד מַלְכוּתוֹ לְעוֹלָם וָעֶד.

How did this unit get into our prayer book? Though its original form is found in the Midrash תַּנָּא דְּבֵי אֵלִיָּהוּ, which dates back to the end of Talmudic times, it is not as integral a part of the service as other sections. If I come a bit late to shul and skip this section, it is not such a terrible thing. If I were to skip the berachot of the Torah, on the other hand, that would be more serious. Or if I were to skip the morning berachot, that too would be more serious. But if I were to skip this, it wouldn't be so terrible. Nevertheless, it should be said if possible.

There are three explanations for why לְעוֹלָם יְהֵא אָדָם יְרֵא שָׁמַיִם is included at this point in the service: a historical explanation, a halachic explanation, and a liturgical explanation.

The historical explanation is that in Talmudic times, when our prayers were formed (the second to sixth centuries C.E.), the majority of the Jewish people lived in Babylonia. Only a minority of the Jewish people lived in Eretz Yisrael because they were persecuted there by the Romans. The Jews were being driven off the land, and it was very difficult to remain there.

One of the most fanatical kings of Byzantium (the eastern Roman Empire) was Justinian. He hated Jews, made life miserable for them and directly ruled over the Jews who lived in Israel. He was both pious and intolerant. He was very upset, for example, when the Jews prayed and said, קָדוֹשׁ קָדוֹשׁ קָדוֹשׁ ה׳ צְבָקוֹת מְלֹא כָל־הָאָרֶץ כְּבוֹדוֹ ("Holy, holy, holy, Hashem, God of legions..."). When Jews pray, they refer to only one God. Justinian considered it unacceptable that anyone should recite this verse and not be referring to the Christian doctrine of the trinity. Thus, he was very harsh to the Jews.

In Babylonia, where people were still pagans, life was much easier for the Jews. The Babylonian Talmud is much larger than the Jerusalem Talmud because the Jews had the peace of mind to study and teach in Babylonia. They could sit down and discuss issues at length, while in Israel they were always in fear that the Romans were after them.

The situation of the Jews was not ideal in Babylonia, however. The most popular religion there was Zoroastrianism. This was a belief in dualism, or two gods: the god of good and the god of evil, or the god of light (Ahura Mazda) and the god of darkness (Angra Mainyu).

The Jews had arrived at an arrangement with the Babylonian rulers. However, in the fifth century, there was a king named Yezdegerd II.[36] He said, "The Jews are terrible. They believe in only one God and deny the basis of our faith. There are two gods, and the Jews have the nerve to get up every morning and say שְׁמַע יִשְׂרָאֵל, ה׳ אֱלֹקֵינוּ, ה׳ אֶחָד. They say there is only one God." He issued a decree that no Jew could recite the Shema anymore because it was against the official religion. Thus, even in Babylonia there was religious persecution.

What could the Jews do? Soldiers were posted as guards in shuls, and they had been trained to understand the line שְׁמַע יִשְׂרָאֵל, ה׳ אֱלֹקֵינוּ, ה׳ אֶחָד. If a Jew said the Shema, the consequences could be grave. How could Jews not say it, not accept upon themselves the responsibilities and duties of being subject to the sovereignty of God? Yet to say the Shema and be killed was not a pleasant thought, either.

The Jews learned to outsmart their enemies. They said the Shema quietly before leaving their houses to go to shul. Then in shul, they just skipped it.[37] The prayer "A Jew should always be God-fearing" was to be said secretly, at home where the enemy soldiers wouldn't see them. This is the meaning of לְעוֹלָם יְהֵא אָדָם יְרֵא שָׁמַיִם בַּסֵּתֶר וּמוֹדֶה עַל הָאֱמֶת וְדוֹבֵר אֱמֶת בִּלְבָבוֹ – you should fear God even in secret and speak the truth in your heart.

Yezdegerd II died suddenly at a very young age. The early Jewish chronicles say that he was swallowed by a snake. The Jews said that it was a miracle. The Almighty killed him because he didn't let us say the Shema. It was then decided that this special section would be said at this point every day in shul to remind us of the miracle. Once the king died, Jews were no longer forbidden from reciting the Shema. This prayer is actually a historical section that reminds us of the miracle

36. *The World of Prayer*, pp. 38–39.

37. At this time the rabbis also instituted reciting the Shema in the Kedushah of Musaf on Shabbat when everyone was in shul, but after the guards had left.

God performed on the Jews’ behalf.[38] According to this view, this section culminates in the Shema.

Yitzhak Baer, in his prayer book, עֲבוֹדַת יִשְׂרָאֵל, says that the line לְעוֹלָם יְהֵא אָדָם יְרֵא שָׁמַיִם בַּסֵּתֶר וּמוֹדֶה עַל הָאֱמֶת וְדוֹבֵר אֱמֶת בִּלְבָבוֹ should not be said. He claims that saying it is a mistake that crept in; this sentence is merely an instruction. It should be followed, not said. When you say the berachot after meals on a holiday and you come to the prayer of יַעֲלֶה וְיָבוֹא, the siddur says, “Add the following on festivals.” But you don’t recite the phrase “Add the following on festivals.” These words are instructions that tell us what to do, but we don’t say them.[39]

Some editors of the siddur have found it necessary to add the word יְרֵא שָׁמַיִם בַּסֵּתֶר "וּבַגָּלוּי" (God-fearing secretly and publicly) because they thought, “What does this mean, ‘fear God secretly’? Does this mean that you should not fear God in public?” What they didn’t understand is that this sentence has a historical reason. The point was to say the Shema in secret only, to fulfill the commandment without being killed for doing so.[40] Thus, the prayerbooks that add the word וּבַגָּלוּי are wrong. In fact, the original text of this section did not say either “in private” or “in public.”[41]

The second reason for reciting the Shema before Shacharit, the halachic reason, is to make sure that it is said in its proper time.[42] This emphasizes the importance of doing mitzvot in the way that God commands us to do them and not necessarily in the ways that are most convenient for us. If I want to sleep late and get up at noon and say the Shema, I haven’t fulfilled the commandment, because the Shema can only be said in the first three hours of the day. We recite this paragraph of Shema at this point to make sure that it is said in its

---

38. *Tikun Tefillah* in *Otzar Hatefillot*, p. 132.
39. *Avodat Yisrael*, p. 44.
40. סדר אליהו רבה וסדר אליהו זוטא, מהדורת מאיר איש שלום הערה 28
41. The original text comes from the Midrash Tanna D’vei Eliyahu (סדר אליהו רבה, פרק יט סעי׳ כא אות יז): מכאן אמרו, לעולם יהא אדם ירא שמים יראה גמורה, יראה על האמת, ומודה על האמת, ודובר אמת בלבבו.
42. שולחן ערוך אורח חיים סי׳ נח סעי׳ א

proper time. Since the "official" Shema (recited in the framework of the berachot of Shema) is said later in the morning, we might miss fulfilling the commandment if we only said it then.[43]

While we are discussing the halachic reason, we must also talk about whether or not to say בָּרוּךְ שֵׁם כְּבוֹד מַלְכוּתוֹ לְעוֹלָם וָעֶד at this point, when we come to the paragraph in the siddur:

> לְפִיכָךְ אֲנַחְנוּ חַיָּבִים לְהוֹדוֹת...אַשְׁרֵינוּ מַה טּוֹב חֶלְקֵנוּ וּמַה נָּעִים גּוֹרָלֵנוּ וּמַה יָּפָה יְרֻשָּׁתֵנוּ. אַשְׁרֵינוּ שֶׁאֲנַחְנוּ מַשְׁכִּימִים וּמַעֲרִיבִים עֶרֶב וָבֹקֶר וְאוֹמְרִים פַּעֲמַיִם בְּכָל יוֹם שְׁמַע יִשְׂרָאֵל ה׳ אֱלֹקֵינוּ ה׳ אֶחָד. בָּרוּךְ שֵׁם כְּבוֹד מַלְכוּתוֹ לְעוֹלָם וָעֶד
>
> ("Therefore, we must thank You... How happy we are; how good is our lot, how sweet our portion... How happy are we to arise early... and say Shema...")

In all siddurim, following the verse of Shema is the verse of בָּרוּךְ שֵׁם כְּבוֹד מַלְכוּתוֹ לְעוֹלָם וָעֶד. Whether we should in fact say בָּרוּךְ שֵׁם כְּבוֹד מַלְכוּתוֹ לְעוֹלָם וָעֶד depends on the reason that we say Shema here. If I say Shema for the historical reason, then I don't need to say בָּרוּךְ שֵׁם כְּבוֹד מַלְכוּתוֹ לְעוֹלָם וָעֶד at all. If I am saying Shema for the halachic reason of saying it on time, then I must say בָּרוּךְ שֵׁם כְּבוֹד מַלְכוּתוֹ לְעוֹלָם וָעֶד. Even though you have performed the mitzvah of Shema at this point, when you reach the point in the regular service where you recite the Shema with its berachot according to the rabbinic requirements, you should still say the Shema again.[44]

What if I forget to say בָּרוּךְ שֵׁם כְּבוֹד מַלְכוּתוֹ לְעוֹלָם וָעֶד? Have I fulfilled the commandment? You might think that I certainly have because that line is not part of the section in the Torah; it was added later. On the other hand, perhaps there is a rabbinic reason why I must say it, and I haven't fulfilled the commandment if I don't say it. There are different opinions. The Levush says that if you don't say it, you don't fulfill the obligation of saying the Shema.[45] Nevertheless, the requirement to say it is very puzzling.

---

43. רמ"א, אורח חיים סימן מו סעיף ט
44. עטרת צבי אורח חיים סימן מו ס"ק כד
45. לבוש אורח חיים סימן מו סעיף ח

Where does בָּרוּךְ שֵׁם כְּבוֹד מַלְכוּתוֹ לְעוֹלָם וָעֶד come from? Most of the prayerbook can be traced back to verses in the Torah or Psalms. This is not a biblical verse. For this reason, we recite it silently when we say the Shema. Obviously, it does not have the same value as the rest of the Shema.

There are actually three sources for בָּרוּךְ שֵׁם כְּבוֹד מַלְכוּתוֹ לְעוֹלָם וָעֶד. The first source can be traced back to the Temple. In the Temple, people never said Amen. Instead, when they heard the name of God, they recited this phrase.[46]

On Yom Kippur, we recount that the high priest used to recite the ineffable name of God, "and all the priests and the people would prostrate themselves and bow down to the ground, and say, בָּרוּךְ שֵׁם כְּבוֹד מַלְכוּתוֹ לְעוֹלָם וָעֶד."[47] In the Temple, the actual name of God was said and therefore Amen was not the proper response. The proper response was בָּרוּךְ שֵׁם כְּבוֹד מַלְכוּתוֹ לְעוֹלָם וָעֶד, meaning, "This name of God, which we just heard, shall be blessed forever." Now we don't have a Temple, and we cannot say the real name of God. According to the Levush, since the Shema is so important, we add בָּרוּךְ שֵׁם כְּבוֹד מַלְכוּתוֹ לְעוֹלָם וָעֶד, which gives our recitation of God's name the holiness of the actual name of God.[48]

The second source is the Midrash, which tells us that when God was giving the Torah, Moshe heard the angels sing this praise: בָּרוּךְ שֵׁם כְּבוֹד מַלְכוּתוֹ לְעוֹלָם וָעֶד. According to the Midrash, it was one of the songs by which the angels praised God. Moshe loved it and thought, "I am going to keep it for the people of Israel." When he came down from Mount Sinai, he said, "I have a beautiful song to sing for you; it is a song of the angels. Naturally, the angels might be angry if we steal their song, so we must say it softly." To this day we say it softly, with the one exception of Yom Kippur. On that day we raise ourselves to angelic heights by not eating or drinking and by spending the day in prayer. Then we have the chutzpah to say it aloud.[49]

---

46. תענית דף ט"ז עמוד ב
47. יומא דף סו עמוד א
48. לבוש אורח חיים סימן מו סעיף ח
49. דברים רבה (וילנא) פרשת ואתחנן, לו

The third source of the statement is the Talmud.[50] When Jacob was on his deathbed, he called his sons to give them a berachah. According to the Talmud, Jacob wanted to do more than just bless his children. He wanted to reveal to them the future of the Jewish people, such as when the Messiah would come. He was about to tell his children, when he lost his ability to prophesy and forgot what he was about to say. He looked at his children and said, "If I forgot what I knew a moment ago, there must be a reason. Perhaps you are not as pious or as God-fearing as I think you are; perhaps one of you is unfit and has caused God's presence to depart from me."

His children looked at him and said: שְׁמַע יִשְׂרָאֵל ("Hear, [Father] Israel"). ה׳ אֱלֹקֵינוּ ("Hashem is our God"), ה׳ אֶחָד ("Hashem is the only God"). In other words, "We have faith in Him. We carry out whatever you taught us. We are not responsible for your forgetting." So, Jacob said, בָּרוּךְ שֵׁם כְּבוֹד מַלְכוּתוֹ לְעוֹלָם וָעֶד, "Thank God that all my children are all good, and I don't have to worry in this respect."[51]

If we want to fulfill our obligation to say the Shema here, then at this point we should say the paragraph of וְאָהַבְתָּ אֵת ה׳ אֱלֹקֶיךָ בְּכָל־לְבָבְךָ as well. Some prayer books rely on the opinion of Rabbi Yehudah HaNasi, who believed that if you say only the first line of the Shema, you have fulfilled the Torah requirement.[52] According to him, the rest was added on by rabbinic decree.

In an emergency, when you are late, one may perform the commandment according to the Torah's minimal requirements. If possible, I would recommend that you say the whole Shema in this particular place. After all, why should we not fulfill the commandment according to the rabbinic requirement also? Rashi says that the first paragraph is necessary to fulfill the commandment.[53] Some prayer books reflect

---

50. פסחים נו עמוד א

51. פסחים דף נו עמ׳ א. See also the similar description in דברים רבה פרשת ואתחנן.

52. ברכות יג עמוד ב

53. The first Tosafot in ברכות ב עמוד א states that Rashi believes that the primary Shema is recited at night before one goes to bed [קְרִיאַת שְׁמַע עַל הַמִּטָּה]. In Rashi's siddur (סימן תכט) he says that at night, before one goes to bed, you

this view as well. There are Rishonim who are of the opinion that the first two paragraphs are necessary because both mention the commandment of the Shema,[54] while the Rambam seems to say that it is necessary to say all three paragraphs in order to fulfill the commandment.[55]

There is one more reason why this section, לְעוֹלָם יְהֵא אָדָם יְרֵא שָׁמַיִם, is said, which I call a liturgical reason. This has to do with the prayer known as Kaddish, which is said by mourners. One version of the Kaddish has a distinctive phrase: עַל יִשְׂרָאֵל וְעַל רַבָּנָן וְעַל תַּלְמִידֵיהוֹן וְעַל כָּל תַּלְמִידֵי תַלְמִידֵיהוֹן... יְהֵא לְהוֹן וּלְכוֹן שְׁלָמָא רַבָּא חִנָּא וְחִסְדָּא וְרַחֲמִין וְחַיִּין אֲרִיכִין וּמְזוֹנֵי רְוִיחֵי וּפֻרְקָנָא מִן קֳדָם אֲבוּהוֹן דְּבִשְׁמַיָּא וְאַרְעָא ("May Israel and the rabbis and their students and all the students of their students – have much peace and pleasantness, grace, and mercy, and long life, and sustenance in plenty, and deliverance – from their Father who is in the heavens and earth"). This version of the Kaddish is recited at the end of the section of the Morning Berachot, and it has a prerequisite in order to be able to recite it. The section לְעוֹלָם יְהֵא אָדָם יְרֵא שָׁמַיִם contains the prerequisite, a paragraph of Aggadah, that enables us to recite that Kaddish. We will explain the different Kaddishes at the end of this section.

The next paragraph reads: אַתָּה הוּא מִשֶּׁנִּבְרָא הָעוֹלָם אַתָּה הוּא עַד שֶׁלֹּא נִבְרָא הָעוֹלָם ("You were there before the world was created, and You are here since the world was created"). It concludes, בָּרוּךְ אַתָּה ה׳, הַמְקַדֵּשׁ אֶת שִׁמְךָ בָּרַבִּים ("Blessed are You, Hashem, who widely sanctifies Your name").

Should we recite this berachah or should we skip it? This is the subject of a debate between Ashkenazic siddurim, which include the

---

read Shema and the first paragraph up to וְהָיָה אִם שָׁמֹעַ. See also Magen Giborim (שלטי גבורים סימן רלט) who explains Rashi's position on Shema.

54. See טור אורח חיים סימן רלט who cites the view that one should recite both paragraphs of Shema when going to sleep. See also Rabbenu Yonah (תלמידי רבינו יונה ברכות דף א. בדפי הרי״ף בסוף ד״ה ואיפסיקא).

55. This is how Rav Soloveitchik explains the Rambam's position. See *Shiurim Lezecher Abba Mari z"l* (Mosad Harav Kook: Jerusalem, 2002), pp. 15–16.

berachah, and Sephardic siddurim, which do not.[56] The Rambam did not say it with the name of God.[57] If there should be a berachah here, we have to understand why. This berachah is for Kiddush Hashem, sanctifying God's name, by dying if necessary.

In the historical reason described above, we learned that people said the Shema at the risk of their lives. Even if they said it in the privacy of their own homes, a window might be open, a soldier might come by, and they might have been overheard. One's life was always at risk. Thus, in those days, when people said the Shema, they were fulfilling the commandment of sanctifying God's name. They were ready to die for God. Perhaps, in those days, it would have been appropriate to say בָּרוּךְ אַתָּה ה׳, הַמְקַדֵּשׁ אֶת שִׁמְךָ בָּרַבִּים using God's name.

But we don't risk our lives today, so it would be better not to make this into an official berachah by using the standard closing, but rather to say בָּרוּךְ הַמְקַדֵּשׁ אֶת שִׁמְךָ בָּרַבִּים, leaving out "Hashem."

However, we must recall the principle שְׁאַל אָבִיךָ וְיַגֵּדְךָ זְקֵנֶיךָ וְיֹאמְרוּ לָךְ ("Ask your father and he will tell you; your elders, and they will instruct you").[58] The best thing is to maintain the existing tradition of one's family and not change the way that one currently recites this paragraph.

קָרְבָּנוֹת

As we mentioned earlier, a person should always divide one's study into three parts: Bible, Mishnah, and Talmud.[59]

Although this is a halachah, not every Jew is able to fulfill it. Ideally, every Jew would have time to attend a class two or three times a day in order to learn everything. But people must earn a living, and before the day is over, they are too tired to learn all three of these topics. The Rabbis knew this, so they included a section in the prayer book that

56. See ערוך השולחן אורח חיים סימן מו סעיף טז.

57. רמב"ם סדר תפילות כל השנה

58. דברים לב:ז

59. קידושין דף ל עמוד א

contains passages from Bible, Mishnah, and a little Talmud. Even if we don't get around to studying every day, we have fulfilled the precept through our prayers.[60]

The first section, from the Bible, discusses the sacrifices. The second section, from the Mishnah, also concerns the sacrifices. The third section consists of the thirteen rules of Rabbi Yishmael for interpreting the Torah.

Why was the subject of sacrifices chosen? Why not the laws of charity? The Rabbis tell us that we have two ways of worshiping or approaching God. One is the sacrificial service, and the other is prayer, what the Rambam calls "worship of the heart."[61] Although we have lost the sacrifices because we no longer have the Temple, we still have prayer. This is why, when we finish the שְׁמוֹנֶה עֶשְׂרֵה, we say: יְהִי רָצוֹן מִלְּפָנֶיךָ...שֶׁיִּבָּנֶה בֵּית הַמִּקְדָּשׁ בִּמְהֵרָה בְיָמֵינוּ...וְשָׁם נַעֲבָדְךָ בְּיִרְאָה כִּימֵי עוֹלָם וּכְשָׁנִים קַדְמוֹנִיּוֹת ("May it be Your will... that the Temple be rebuilt soon... and there we will worship You with awe, as in the days of old and years long ago"). Our worship is deficient since we only have the worship of the heart, and we hope soon we will also once again have the Temple and the sacrifices.

The Rabbis say that although we cannot offer a sacrifice because there is no Temple, if we study the laws of sacrifices, it is considered as though we have offered the sacrifice.[62] Therefore, even though we could read other laws for our "learning session," in the prayer service we learn about the sacrifices so that God will credit us for having offered a sacrifice.

Many people think that our prayers today take the place of the sacrifices. This is a common misconception. The Rabbis said that תְּפִלּוֹת כְּנֶגֶד תְּמִידִין תִּקְנוּם (prayer corresponds to the sacrificial services),[63] not that prayer replaces the sacrifices. Both the sacrificial service and the prayer service are important.

---

60. שולחן ערוך אורח חיים סימן נ סעיף א
61. רמב"ם הלכות תפילה פרק א הלכה א
62. תענית דף כז עמוד ב
63. ברכות דף כו עמוד ב

In the middle of the section dealing with the sacrifices, most prayer books include the description of the incense that was offered every day with the sacrifices. This explains how the incense was made for the Temple service.

Sephardic Jews and most Israelis say this section every day, at this point and at the end of the service. On weekdays, Ashkenazic Jews say it here, but not at the end of the service. Ashkenazic Jews only say it at the end of the service on Shabbat and Yom Tov.[64]

This portion, which details which ingredients we use for the incense offering and how to mix them, is strictly Halachah. When we say it at the end of the service, we follow it with the Aggadah, אָמַר רַבִּי אֶלְעָזָר אָמַר רַבִּי חֲנִינָא תַּלְמִידֵי חֲכָמִים מַרְבִּים שָׁלוֹם בָּעוֹלָם ("Rabbi Eliezer said in the name of Rabbi Chanina, Torah scholars increase peace in the world").[65] This is the same Aggadah that we say on Friday night after בַּמֶּה מַדְלִיקִין. Why do we use this same Aggadah?

All of the spices have a pleasant odor but one. Why do we use an ingredient that doesn't smell good? Is this respectful to God? The Rabbis[66] told us that there is a good reason for it. We can learn something from it. Many Jews have a "good fragrance," meaning that they observe the commandments and do good deeds. There are Jews whose "fragrance" (essence) is not so good. They are sinful. But they are still Jews. Every Jew is a Jew and must be accepted. Just like the spices, of which there was one that was malodorous, so too we have some members who are "malodorous." We have no right to exclude them. Every Jew is part of the community of Israel. This is why the Rabbis introduced this particular Aggadah, to explain to us the importance of peace among the Jewish people.

64. רמ"א אורח חיים סימן קלב סעיף ב

65. תנא דבי אליהו אליהו זוטא פרשה יז

66. כריתות דף ו עמוד ב

קַדִּישׁ

Over the course of a day, there are seven obligatory recitations of Kaddish.[67] As the Aruch Hashulchan explains[68]: Originally there were only seven times Kaddish was recited each day – three during the Shacharit: one after יִשְׁתַּבַּח, the second after תַּחֲנוּן, and the third after וּבָא לְצִיּוֹן גּוֹאֵל; and two more during Minchah: one after אַשְׁרֵי, and the second one after תַּחֲנוּן; and two in Ma'ariv: one before the שְׁמוֹנֶה עֶשְׂרֵה and the second one after the שְׁמוֹנֶה עֶשְׂרֵה. Then three more were added: one at the end of each service following עָלֵינוּ, for the mourners who couldn't lead the services. This was called the Mourner's Kaddish. And on days when the Torah was read [in the service], another Kaddish is said after reading the Torah. And another Kaddish was added after the Psalm of the Day for when there were a lot of mourners.

There are different kinds of Kaddish:

1. חֲצִי קַדִּישׁ (Half-Kaddish) creates a separation between two parts of davening: for example, between פְּסוּקֵי דְזִמְרָה and קְרִיאַת שְׁמַע וּבִרְכוֹתֶיהָ or between the Torah reading and the resumption of the service.[69]
2. קַדִּישׁ תִּתְקַבַּל is a concluding קַדִּישׁ, identified by the phrase תִּתְקַבַּל צְלוֹתְהוֹן וּבָעוּתְהוֹן דְּכָל בֵּית יִשְׂרָאֵל קֳדָם אֲבוּהוֹן דִּי בִשְׁמַיָּא ("May the prayers and requests of all the House of Israel be accepted before our Father in Heaven"). This is recited following the Amidah, at the conclusion of the service.
3. קַדִּישׁ יָתוֹם – In the aftermath of the Crusades, this Kaddish was recited as the prayer of orphans.[70] It expresses their faith and belief

67. According to one interpretation in the Midrash Tehillim (on Psalm 6), the verse שֶׁבַע בַּיּוֹם הִלַּלְתִּיךָ, "Seven during the day will I praise You" (Psalm 119:164), refers to the seven times that the leader of the service recites Kaddish each day.

68. ערוך השולחן אורח חיים סימן נה סעיף ד

69. Many shuls give this privilege of saying Kaddish after we read the Torah to a mourner if there is one in shul.

70. The *Or Zarua* (2:50) states: "Our custom in the land of Canaan [=Bohemia], and also the custom of the Rhineland, is that after the congregation says

that there will be an end to Jewish suffering and that the Almighty will fulfill all of the promises found in the Holy Scriptures.

4. Another kind of added Kaddish is recited after someone is buried.[71] This Kaddish is also recited today at a *siyum* (completion of a Talmudic tractate).
5. In the קַדִּישׁ דְּרַבָּנָן, we ask for God's blessings upon all those who study Torah. It is probably the original Kaddish, and it was recited following the rabbi's sermon.[72] Without the dedication of the rabbis, we would not have the oral law. Therefore, after studying the oral law, we say קַדִּישׁ דְּרַבָּנָן; we give thanks to those who enabled us to learn and understand the Torah properly and hand it down to our children.

There is a dispute about קַדִּישׁ דְּרַבָּנָן: May we say it after studying Halachah, or is it necessary to learn a bit of Aggadah (non-legal sections of the Talmud) also? According to the Rambam in his siddur, any section of oral law is sufficient.[73] However, Rashi writes that one only recites קַדִּישׁ דְּרַבָּנָן after studying Aggadah. In order to say קַדִּישׁ דְּרַבָּנָן, we therefore conclude the communal study of Mishnayot with an Aggadic statement: רַבִּי חֲנַנְיָא בֶּן עֲקַשְׁיָא אוֹמֵר רָצָה הקב"ה לְזַכּוֹת אֶת יִשְׂרָאֵל לְפִיכָךְ הִרְבָּה לָהֶם תּוֹרָה וּמִצְוֹת, "Rabbi Chananyah b. Akashya said: God wished to bring merit to Israel; therefore, He enlarged the Torah and increased its commandments."[74]

In the morning, we say קַדִּישׁ דְּרַבָּנָן as soon as we are through with the section of the sacrifices, following the section of "Rabbi Yishmael says." This section is all law. We need to recite a little Aggadah to satisfy Rashi's opinion. That's why we say לְעוֹלָם יְהֵא אָדָם יְרֵא שָׁמַיִם ("A person

---

אֵין כֵּאלֹקֵינוּ, the mourner rises and says Kaddish, but in France, I saw that they aren't careful about whether someone who is a mourner or not [recites it]..."

71. שולחן ערוך יורה דעה סימן שעו סעיף ד

72. See סוטה דף מט עמוד א.

73. Rambam, Seder Hatefillah, Kaddish Derabbanan.

74. See Rashi at the end of the fifth chapter of Avot, explaining the recitation of רבי חנניה בן עקשיא אומר.

should always be God-fearing"). This is Aggadah and enables us to say קַדִּישׁ דְּרַבָּנָן.

What is the aggadic content of this particular section? In this paragraph, we say that we are not worth much, we are mortal, we don't live long, and we don't accomplish much. There is no difference between man and beast, for both are born; both eat; both propagate and both die.

When we belittle ourselves on purpose and say that we are unworthy, we use the word מַה (what) seven times: (1) מָה אֲנַחְנוּ ("What are we"); (2) מֶה חַיֵּינוּ ("what are our lives"); (3) מֶה חַסְדֵּנוּ ("what is our kindness"); (4) מַה צִּדְקֵנוּ ("what is our righteousness"); (5) מַה יְשׁוּעָתֵנוּ ("what is our salvation"). Some prayer books put this (מַה יְשׁוּעָתֵנוּ) in parentheses. It should not be parenthetical. It belongs here. (6) מַה כֹּחֵנוּ ("what is our strength"); and (7) מַה גְּבוּרָתֵנוּ ("what is our power"). Then we continue with a normal sentence structure: מַה נֹּאמַר לְפָנֶיךָ ה' אֱלֹקֵינוּ ("What can we say before you, Hashem our God?") Nothing. We are no better than the beast in the field.

Why do we belittle ourselves specifically seven times? In Kohelet it says, הֲבֵל הֲבָלִים אָמַר קֹהֶלֶת הֲבֵל הֲבָלִים הַכֹּל הָבֶל. ("Vanity of vanities, said Kohelet, vanity of vanities, everything is vanity").[75] These are the seven vanities of human existence. Counting each singular word (הבל) as one and each plural of this word (הבלים) as two, this adds up to seven vanities.[76] Everybody translates הֶבֶל as vanity, but that doesn't give us the full flavor and meaning of the Hebrew word: הֶבֶל means much more than being vain. "Worthlessness" is perhaps better. It is a very difficult word.

Kohelet, the author of this biblical book, is, in fact, King Solomon according to Jewish tradition. Why did King Solomon tell us that there are seven vanities? One opinion is that they correspond to the seven days of the week. Whatever we accomplish in the seven days of the week isn't worth much. Another opinion is that the seven

---

75. קהלת פרק א פסוק ב

76. *Eitz Yosef* in *Otzar Hatefillot*, p. 134.

vanities stand for the seven decades of the average human lifespan.[77] Whatever we do in the first, second, or even last decade of our lives is really worthless. What have we actually accomplished? This is a very pessimistic outlook on life.

However, the accomplishments of Abraham, Isaac, and Jacob are indeed worthwhile, and we seek to emulate their achievements. So we continue: לְפִיכָךְ אֲנַחְנוּ חַיָּבִים ("Therefore, we must"): (1) לְהוֹדוֹת לְךָ ("thank You"); (2) וּלְשַׁבֵּחֲךָ ("praise You"); (3) וּלְפָאֶרְךָ ("glorify You"); (4) וּלְבָרֶכְךָ ("bless You"); (5) וּלְקַדֵּשׁ אֶת שְׁמֶךָ ("sanctify Your name"); (6) וְלָתֵת שֶׁבַח ("and give praise"); (7) וְהוֹדָיָה לִשְׁמֶךָ ("and gratitude to Your name"). There are seven tasks.

The seven vanities of the average human life can be overcome by the seven tasks of a Jew. This means that we should lead a life that gives glory to the name of God. We should be the most honest people in business so that everybody will say, "It is good to be a Jew. They are a great people, the children of Abraham, Isaac, and Jacob." It means that we should not waste our time doing foolish things. Instead, we should sit together and study Torah, or try to help people. To praise God does not mean just by words but also by actions. If we dedicate our lives to the actions of learning Torah, fulfilling God's will, carrying out His commandments, and doing deeds of benevolence and kindness, then our lives will not be in vain and we will have overcome the seven vanities. Our lives will have been a preparation for the next world.

This explanation makes the passage לְעוֹלָם יְהֵא אָדָם an aggadic one. Thus, according to the opinion of Rashi, we can say קַדִּישׁ דְּרַבָּנָן.[78]

---

77. קהלת רבה (וילנא) פרשה א

78. This is the position of Tosafot as well. See ברכות דף ג עמוד א תוס׳ ד״ה ועונין and רשימות שיעורים שם.

פְּסוּקֵי דְזִמְרָה

The Mishnah and the beraita that accompanies it tell us that we should be in a proper frame of mind before we pray.[1] They relate how the חֲסִידִים רִאשׁוֹנִים (early pious ones) used to prepare themselves for davening by coming to shul early, waiting an hour before they started davening to get themselves into the proper frame of mind, and waiting another hour after they finished before they took up the ordinary daily activities.

The Tur[2] says: Before one approaches prayer, one should stop for a little while, just like those early righteous people. A person should set one's mind to be serious, and not frivolous or involved in irrelevant matters, nor full of anger. One should feel the joy of performing a mitzvah, and subjugate oneself to God so one can properly address Him. Afterwards, one should wait before resuming one's normal activities to demonstrate that the prayer is not a burden that one wants to run away from, as if to escape from it. This is why the אַנְשֵׁי כְּנֶסֶת הַגְּדוֹלָה established פְּסוּקֵי דְזִמְרָה (Verses of Song) before the core of the morning prayer, the Shema and the שְׁמוֹנֶה עֶשְׂרֵה, to parallel the preparations of the חֲסִידִים רִאשׁוֹנִים before davening. That is also why we say עָלֵינוּ לְשַׁבֵּחַ after davening, to ease away from the davening.[3]

פְּסוּקֵי דְזִמְרָה is introduced by בָּרוּךְ שֶׁאָמַר and concludes with יִשְׁתַּבַּח. The heart of פְּסוּקֵי דְזִמְרָה is תְּהִלָּה לְדָוִד, Psalm 145, to which we add two

1. ברכות דף ל עמוד ב
2. טור אורח חיים הלכות תפלה סימן צג
3. ט"ז אורח חיים קלב ס"ק ב

verses beforehand which begin with the word אַשְׁרֵי (Psalm 84:5 and 144:15). Following this we recite Psalms 146–150. This group of psalms are considered as "the everyday Hallel," הַלֵּל שֶׁל כָּל יוֹם.[4]

There are a number of reasons why פְּסוּקֵי דְזִמְרָה is so important as a prelude to the main section of Shacharit. First, it helps us focus our concentration on prayer, thereby preparing us to say the Shema and the שְׁמוֹנֶה עֶשְׂרֵה with the proper כַּוָּנָה (frame of mind).[5] The concept of פְּסוּקֵי דְזִמְרָה goes back to the earliest history of the Second Temple period. As the Mishnah states,[6] חֲסִידִים הָרִאשׁוֹנִים הָיוּ שׁוֹהִין שָׁעָה אַחַת וּמִתְפַּלְּלִין, כְּדֵי שֶׁיְּכַוְּנוּ לִבָּם לַאֲבִיהֶם שֶׁבַּשָּׁמַיִם ("The early pious ones used to wait an hour before their prayers in order to pray with concentration"). What did they do during that hour? Presumably, they were reciting Psalms and other verses to get the proper feeling for the prayers. פְּסוּקֵי דְזִמְרָה literally means "verses that sing God's praises." It has been suggested that the word זִמְרָה is connected to the verb זמר, meaning to prune.[7] Thus, those pious ones spent this hour "pruning" all thoughts and ideas from their minds in order to think only of one thing: the holiness and greatness of God.

A second reason for reciting פְּסוּקֵי דְזִמְרָה is that humanity can't really praise God. What do we actually know about God's greatness? In order to praise somebody, you must understand him or her. No human being understands the Almighty, and yet praise of the Almighty is an essential part of the שְׁמוֹנֶה עֶשְׂרֵה.[8] Rav Soloveitchik explained that פְּסוּקֵי דְזִמְרָה functions as our "license" to praise God. Since King David did it so beautifully in his Book of Psalms, we are not concerned about the *logic* of praising God; we know that King David *did* praise God. He set a precedent for us to follow. Since King David praised God, so may we praise God.

---

4. שבת קי"ח עמ׳ ב

5. This is in line with the dictate of the Gemara (ברכות דף לב עמ׳ א) that a person should organize his praises of God before reciting his prayers.

6. ברכות דף ל עמוד ב

7. *The World of Prayer*, p. 65.

8. The first three berachot of the Amidah are praise.

Rav Soloveitchik provided a third reason for the institution of פְּסוּקֵי דְזִמְרָה. Before we pray, we have to learn Torah.[9] Which prinicples do we learn in פְּסוּקֵי דְזִמְרָה? We learn that "God feeds every living thing willingly," that God is kind to human beings, and that "God straightens up the hunched-over and opens the eyes of the blind." By studying God's ways, we gain insight into the principle that "Just as God is merciful and full of grace, so too should you be merciful and full of grace."[10]

Before we can call upon God's mercy in the prayers, we must first learn to imitate the Almighty. Once we have absorbed this lesson, we have a right to stand before God in prayer and ask for His heavenly guidance. On this idea is based a custom which, at first glance, doesn't seem very proper. During the חֲזָרַת הַשַּׁ"ץ of the שְׁמוֹנֶה עֶשְׂרֵה (the repetition by the chazzan), there is often somebody who goes around with a pushke and collects charity. This is not conducive to good concentration in shul. It is really not at all respectful to do this in the middle of the repetition of the שְׁמוֹנֶה עֶשְׂרֵה when one should be listening and answering "Amen." But we want to show that we have learned our lesson. We give charity, so, therefore, we have a right to ask for God's charity. It would, of course, be wiser to collect the charity at a time other than the middle of the שְׁמוֹנֶה עֶשְׂרֵה, such as at the beginning of davening. In fact, the Ari *z"l* suggested that you should give to tzedakah while reciting the paragragph beginning וַיְבָרֶךְ דָּוִיד in פְּסוּקֵי דְזִמְרָה.[11] The Rabbis tell us[12] that by giving even a small amount to charity, I enable myself to stand before God.[13]

---

9. See Rabbi Joseph B. Soloveitchik, *Blessings and Thanksgiving: Reflections on the Siddur and Synagogue*, pp. 35–47.

10. Shabbat 133b; Rambam, Hilchot De'ot, 1:6.

11. See מגן אברהם אורח חיים סימן נא ס"ק ז.

12. בבא בתרא דף י עמוד א, רמב"ם הל' מתנות עניים פרק י הלכה טו, שולחן ערוך אורח חיים סי' צב סעיף י

13. Rav Amram Gaon writes that although it is forbidden to interrupt between Yishtabach and the berachot of Shema, it is permitted to give charity at that time to the needy: סדר רב עמרם גאון קריאת שמע וברכותיה: ודקא אמרינן אסור

Standing for Prayers

Do we sit or stand for פְּסוּקֵי דְזִמְרָה? The most logical position would be to sit, because there is really only one prayer where it is obligatory to stand: the שְׁמוֹנֶה עֶשְׂרֵה, which is also called the עֲמִידָה (standing).

For everything else, then, shouldn't we be able to sit? In the Rambam's shul, they didn't stand until they got to the שְׁמוֹנֶה עֶשְׂרֵה. Even then, the only one who stood up was the chazzan, the leader, for the שְׁמוֹנֶה עֶשְׂרֵה. There was not even a chazzan for פְּסוּקֵי דְזִמְרָה. Everyone recited the prayers at an individual speed; some were faster and said a little more, some were slower and said a little less. Before יִשְׁתַּבַּח, the chazzan stood up and began to lead. Everyone else remained seated until they reached the שְׁמוֹנֶה עֶשְׂרֵה.[14] Today we conduct the service differently: We stand more often. The Rama writes that the custom is to stand for בָּרוּךְ שֶׁאָמַר, וַיְבָרֶךְ דָּוִיד, and יִשְׁתַּבַּח.[15] Ashkenazic Jews follow this practice.

These three sections are all berachot, or similar to berachot. King David, in fact, is the originator of the format of our berachot – we know that it is proper to say such a thing as בָּרוּךְ אַתָּה ה׳ because King David gave us this precedent.[16] The Rama considers it proper to stand up for all berachot[17]; therefore, he considers it proper to stand up for the section of the prayers where King David teaches us how to utter a berachah as well. This shows some halachic development. Originally everyone used to sit, but now for certain sections, the Ashkenazim stand. Customarily, we stand through the section of the אָז יָשִׁיר as well.[18]

לאשתעויי בין ישתבח לפריסת שמע, הני מילי דלא צרכי צבור נינהו. אבל לצרכי צבור או לצורך מי שבא להתפרנס מן הצבור ובעו למיפסק ליה צדקה איסורא ליכא.

14. רמב״ם הלכות תפילה פרק ט הלכה א

15. רמ״א אורח חיים סימן נא סעיף ז

16. In וַיְבָרֶךְ דָּוִיד, we say: וַיְבָרֶךְ דָּוִיד אֶת ה׳ לְעֵינֵי כָּל הַקָּהָל. וַיֹּאמֶר דָּוִיד בָּרוּךְ אַתָּה ה׳ אֱלֹקֵי יִשְׂרָאֵל אָבִינוּ ("And David blessed Hashem before the entire congregation. David said, 'Blessed are You, Hashem, God of Israel, our Father'").

17. The Ateret Zekenim (עטרת זקנים סימן נג ס״ק א) says we should stand for any ברכת המצות, though not a ברכת הנהנין.

18. See ערוך השולחן אורח חיים סימן נא סעיף ח.

COMPONENTS OF פְּסוּקֵי דְזִמְרָה

בָּרוּךְ שֶׁאָמַר

There is a question about who actually instituted the practice of saying בָּרוּךְ שֶׁאָמַר that was established to introduce פְּסוּקֵי דְזִמְרָה.

The Pri Chadash[19] says it was introduced during the period of the Geonim, but that would be problematic from a few standpoints: First, we are hesitant to accept berachot coined after the close of the Talmud. אַנְשֵׁי כְּנֶסֶת הַגְּדוֹלָה, who established most of our prayers, had the authority to establish berachot. Even though there are many who do not recite berachot coined after the close of the Talmud, there is no one who objects to saying בָּרוּךְ שֶׁאָמַר on these grounds.

Furthermore, פְּסוּקֵי דְזִמְרָה was known in the period of the Gemara. As we have seen, the Gemara[20] says that Rabbi Yossi aspired to recite hallel every day, and what he meant was that he aspired to recite פְּסוּקֵי דְזִמְרָה every day. As a result, it became accepted to recite פְּסוּקֵי דְזִמְרָה every day before we began the berachot of the Shema. After פְּסוּקֵי דְזִמְרָה was universally accepted into the prayers, a berachah was added before and after. The berachah at the end is יִשְׁתַּבַּח, and we have no record of any berachah before פְּסוּקֵי דְזִמְרָה other than בָּרוּךְ שֶׁאָמַר.[21] The Rif ascribes בָּרוּךְ שֶׁאָמַר to "the Rabbis," presumably referring to the sages of the Talmud, and the kabbalists ascribe it to אַנְשֵׁי כְּנֶסֶת הַגְּדוֹלָה.[22]

The Or Zarua tells us[23] how אַנְשֵׁי כְּנֶסֶת הַגְּדוֹלָה came to write it. He says a note fell down from Heaven with 87 words on it. The 87 words of בָּרוּךְ שֶׁאָמַר are alluded to in the verse (Shir Hashirim 5:11) רֹאשׁוֹ כֶּתֶם פָּז, "His head is finest gold." The numerical value of פָּז is 87, and רֹאשׁוֹ refers to the beginning of פְּסוּקֵי דְזִמְרָה. In other words, the פָּז, "finest gold," is the tefillah that אַנְשֵׁי כְּנֶסֶת הַגְּדוֹלָה composed, containing 87

---

19. פרי חדש אורח חיים סימן נא

20. שבת דף קיח עמוד ב

21. שבת קיח עמ׳ ב, רי״ף, רא״ש טור אורח חיים נא

22. See *Tikkun Tefillah* in *Otzar Hatefillot*, p. 172. See also Mishnah Berurah (סימן נא ס״ק א).

23. מטה משה עמוד העבודה בית הכנסת, ברכות ופסוקי דזמרה סימן מד

words to be recited at the beginning of פְּסוּקֵי דְזִמְרָה. It encompasses the theme of the פְּסוּקֵי דְזִמְרָה: the creation of the world, and attributes of the Holy One, blessed be He.

The Gemara[24] explains that a blessing must begin with the word בָּרוּךְ except a בְּרָכָה הַסְּמוּכָה לַחֲבֶרְתָּהּ (a blessing in a series with another). Tosafot explain[25] that יִשְׁתַּבַּח does not begin with בָּרוּךְ because it is a בְּרָכָה הַסְּמוּכָה לַחֲבֶרְתָּהּ with בָּרוּךְ שֶׁאָמַר. All of פְּסוּקֵי דְזִמְרָה that is recited in between the two berachot is not an interruption. Tosafot compare it to the berachot before and after קְרִיאַת שְׁמַע. The blessing after קְרִיאַת שְׁמַע similarly does not start with בָּרוּךְ, because it is considered a בְּרָכָה הַסְּמוּכָה לַחֲבֶרְתָּהּ with the first blessing before קְרִיאַת שְׁמַע.

יְהִי כְבוֹד and הוֹדוּ and Other Individual Verses

The Ashkenazim say הוֹדוּ לַה׳ קִרְאוּ בִשְׁמוֹ ("Give thanks to Hashem, call in His name") after בָּרוּךְ שֶׁאָמַר, because, after all, these are verses of praise. הוֹדוּ consists of verses of praise from Chronicles and from Psalms. King David composed these verses. They were recited daily as the Psalm of the Day after he brought the Ark of the Covenant to Jerusalem before the Temple was built.[26] According to the Sephardic *nusach* (version), הוֹדוּ is said before בָּרוּךְ שֶׁאָמַר. The reason הוֹדוּ belongs before בָּרוּךְ שֶׁאָמַר is the proximity of הוֹדוּ to the section dealing with the sacrifices. It serves as a transition to פְּסוּקֵי דְזִמְרָה. This is one of the places where we can easily see the difference between the Ashkenazic and the Sephardic versions.

There is also a collection of individual verses from the Book of Psalms beginning בָּרוּךְ יְיָ לְעוֹלָם אָמֵן וְאָמֵן, in addition to the sections of וַיְבָרֶךְ דָּוִיד from Chronicles[27] and אַתָּה־הוּא יְיָ לְבַדֶּךָ from Nechemia.[28] Finally, פְּסוּקֵי דְזִמְרָה includes the description of the destruction of

24. פסחים דף קד ב
25. תוס׳ פסחים דף קד ב ד״ה חוץ
26. See Divrei Hayamim 1, Chapter 16.
27. דברי הימים א׳ פרק כט
28. נחמיה פרק ט

Pharaoh in the selection called the Song at the Sea, אָז יָשִׁיר.[29] On Shabbat and holidays, we add additional Psalms to the basic framework.

מִזְמוֹר לְתוֹדָה

There is one other place in פְּסוּקֵי דְזִמְרָה where many stand: מִזְמוֹר לְתוֹדָה.[30] What is the relevance of מִזְמוֹר לְתוֹדָה (Psalm 100) to פְּסוּקֵי דְזִמְרָה, which was meant to praise God? The Psalm of Thanksgiving obviously thanks God. But the reason for saying the Psalm of Thanksgiving is more specific. When we finish the previous prayer, הוֹדוּ, we say in the last verse, וַאֲנִי בְּחַסְדְּךָ בָטַחְתִּי. יָגֵל לִבִּי בִּישׁוּעָתֶךָ. אָשִׁירָה לה׳ כִּי גָמַל עָלָי ("I place my faith in Your kindness; my heart rejoices in Your salvation; I sing unto God because He did acts of kindness for me"). The moment I mention that He did acts of kindness for me, I have to think, "Did He do acts of kindness for me today? Did I thank Him for them? Perhaps on the way to shul I was driving carelessly and God saved me. Perhaps I had to fight a thousand germs and I overcame a sickness that I didn't even know about." Every moment miracles happen, and we are unaware of them.[31]

The Psalm of Thanksgiving is said for all personal miracles, the innumerable times that God saves us without our awareness.[32] A person doesn't know how many miracles occur for him or her in a day. When we are in real trouble, we are aware of it, but God also saves us every day from many troubles of which we are not aware. A thanksgiving sacrifice was offered by our ancestors in the Temple for a personal miracle.[33] At that time the Kohanim (priests) stood for

---

29. שמות טו

30. The *Otzar Hatefttillot* quotes the *Derech Hachaim* (30:9) that one should recite מִזְמוֹר לְתוֹדָה while standing. See also *Sha'arei Teshuvah* (Orach Chaim 51:4).

31. *Seder Avodat Yisrael*, p. 61.

32. In the שְׁמוֹנֶה עֶשְׂרֵה we say the berachah of וְכֹל הַחַיִּים יוֹדוּךָ סֶּלָה ("All the living thank You") for miracles of which we are aware.

33. Today we say a berachah instead of bringing a thanksgiving sacrifice, i.e., בִּרְכַּת הַגּוֹמֵל. There are four instances for which a person should recite the בִּרְכַּת הַגּוֹמֵל: one who made a sea voyage and returned safely, one who traveled over

the entire service. Any part of our prayer service that is connected to the Temple service should therefore be said while standing. The Psalm of Thanksgiving was recited during the Temple times when a person brought a sacrifice for having been delivered from danger. This psalm was the heartfelt, verbal response that accompanied the קָרְבָּן, and there are those who believe that we should stand for it, just as the Kohanim stood for the sacrificial service. Today, we have no sacrifices, but when we think of the last verse of the previous prayer, and we are grateful for kindnesses that we might not have even been aware of, this psalm is the best response.[34]

There are a few times during the year when we do not say the Psalm of Thanksgiving: Shabbat, Yom Tov (including all of Passover), the day before Passover and the day before Yom Kippur. Logically, it would seem that if I have to thank God every day for His miracles, I certainly should thank God on these days as well. So why don't we say it on these days? The answer is that there are certain days of the year when you could not offer a Thanksgiving sacrifice. On Shabbat and Yom Tov, it is forbidden to slaughter a non-obligatory animal sacrifice.[35]

However, why is מִזְמוֹר לְתוֹדָה omitted on the day *before* Passover, and on the intermediate days of Passover? When the thanksgiving sacrifice was brought, it was accompanied with forty loaves of bread, ten of which were *chametz* (leavened). On the day before Passover, we are only allowed to eat *chametz* until a certain hour. Therefore, bringing it on the day before Passover would limit the amount of time that one could eat the bread and possibly cause it not to be eaten.

Similarly, since the thanksgiving sacrifice had to be eaten during

---

a desert and reached his destination safely, one who was ill and recovered, and one who was imprisoned and was released (Orach Chaim 219:1).

34. This is consistent with the verse that we recite in the Hallel: לֹא אָמוּת כִּי־אֶחְיֶה וַאֲסַפֵּר מַעֲשֵׂי קָהּ – when God saves my life I am compelled to tell of His kindnesses.

35. סידור רש"י סימן תיז.

the day and the following evening, the day before Yom Kippur was another time when the thanksgiving sacrifice couldn't be offered.[36]

אַשְׁרֵי

Actually, אַשְׁרֵי is a misnomer. Psalm 145 should be called תְּהִלָּה לְדָוִד ("A psalm of David"), because those are its first words. Even though Psalm 145 starts with the words תְּהִלָּה לְדָוִד, we commonly refer to this Psalm as אַשְׁרֵי, because of the verses that precede it. Two verses were added to Psalm 145 to begin the prayer. The first comes from Psalm 84:5, אַשְׁרֵי יוֹשְׁבֵי בֵיתֶךָ. עוֹד יְהַלְלוּךָ סֶּלָה ("Happy are those who dwell in Your house; may they continually praise You"). From this verse, the early Chasidim concluded that we should prepare ourselves slowly for davening. First, they dwell in God's home (in shul), and only then are they ready to pray.[37] The second addition comes from Psalm 144:15, אַשְׁרֵי הָעָם שֶׁכָּכָה לּוֹ. אַשְׁרֵי הָעָם שֶׁה' אֱלֹקָיו ("Happy are the people for whom this is so. Happy are the people for whom Hashem is their God").

The Talmud says that, "Anybody who recites אַשְׁרֵי three times a day is certain to have a share in the world to come."[38] Therefore, we recite the אַשְׁרֵי three times a day in the course of the prayer services: in פְּסוּקֵי דְזִמְרָה, after the שְׁמוֹנֶה עֶשְׂרֵה of Shacharit, and before Minchah.

The Rabbis say that whenever King David liked one of his Psalms especially well, he started and ended it with the same words. Thus, all those Psalms that start and end with the word הַלְלוּקָהּ ("Praise God") were especially important to David.[39] Psalm 145 starts with תְּהִלָּה לְדָוִד ("A psalm of praise by David") and ends with תְּהִלַּת ה' יְדַבֶּר פִּי ("My mouth will speak Hashem's praise"). That both verses start with תְּהִלָּה, praise, indicates that this too was especially dear to David. What did David intend to express by this? The words *Psalm of praise* (תְּהִלָּה) and *Hallel* both mean to praise God. Thus, David uses this psalm to discuss the nature of praising God. This is another instance where

---

36. רמ"א אורח חיים סימן נא סעיף ט

37. ברכות לב עמ' ב

38. ברכות דף ד עמוד ב

39. See ברכות דף י עמוד א, תוספות ד"ה כל פרשה.

King David instructs us and gives us a precedent with which to praise God. But we do not praise Him with our own words; we borrow the words from King David, who, we have noted, was called "the sweet singer of Israel, נְעִים זְמִרוֹת יִשְׂרָאֵל."[40]

David starts this Psalm by saying, אֲרוֹמִמְךָ אֱלוֹקַי הַמֶּלֶךְ ("I will praise you, My God, the King"); בְּכָל יוֹם אֲבָרְכֶךָּ ("every day I will bless You"). God's greatness can't be probed because it is beyond human understanding. So how is it possible for us to praise God by mentioning His greatness? We simply follow in the footsteps of our great ancestors. Since דּוֹר לְדוֹר יְשַׁבַּח מַעֲשֶׂיךָ. וּגְבוּרֹתֶיךָ יַגִּידוּ ("one generation praises Your works and tells of Your greatness to the next generation"), then וְדִבְרֵי נִפְלְאֹתֶיךָ אָשִׂיחָה ("I too will speak of Your wondrous deeds").

David says that it is impossible to do justice to God's greatness. Since the former generations such as Abraham did it, we too can do it. We rely on historical precedent. This explains the switch from the third person plural to the first person singular, as we discussed in an earlier chapter. "They" refers to the former generations. "I will speak" and "I will tell" is David's way of explaining his praises of God. The best way to praise God would be to keep quiet; as David himself says, לְךָ דֻמִיָּה תְהִלָּה ("To You, silence is praise").[41] But David then says that it is impossible to keep quiet. Seeing the great universe and feeling God's closeness to us, we have to speak up. The essence of God can never be described, but we do know His acts of kindness to us and can enumerate them. This Psalm mentions many of the daily acts of kindness that God performs, such as being חַנּוּן וְרַחוּם (gracious and merciful) and אֶרֶךְ אַפַּיִם (slow to anger).

Psalm 145 ends with the words, תְּהִלַּת ה׳ יְדַבֶּר פִּי. וִיבָרֵךְ כָּל בָּשָׂר שֵׁם קָדְשׁוֹ לְעוֹלָם וָעֶד ("My mouth will speak Hashem's praise, and all flesh will bless His holy name forever"). It is in itself a nice ending for a psalm, but we add an additional verse from Hallel to end אַשְׁרֵי: וַאֲנַחְנוּ

40. שמואל ב כג:א. Rashi explains that "sweet singer of Israel" refers to the fact that in the Temple, only his songs were used.

41. תהלים פרק סה פס׳ ב

נְבָרֵךְ קָהּ מֵעַתָּה וְעַד עוֹלָם. הַלְלוּקָהּ ("And we shall bless Hashem from now on and forever; praise Hashem").

Why do we need this additional verse? David always uses the full שֵׁם הַמְפֹרָשׁ in speaking about God's acts of kindness, but in this verse of Hallel he uses only the first half of it, the "Yud" and the "Heh." The full name indicates the whole world's acceptance of God. The time will come when the whole human race will pay homage to God. This will be the Messianic Era. Unfortunately, that time has not yet come, so right now God's name is incomplete. Today is not a time of supernatural miracles, but of faith. If this were a time of overt miracles, it would be easy to accept God, and everyone would do so. Since there are no miracles today, most of the world has not accepted God. David notes, however, that Jews do God's will today, despite not having witnessed any supernatural miracles.

Another reason why we need this verse is to incorporate אַשְׁרֵי into the הַלֵּל שֶׁל כָּל יוֹם. Each of the other Psalms begin and end with the word הַלְלוּקָהּ. By adding this verse, אַשְׁרֵי becomes part of the everyday Hallel.

In אַשְׁרֵי, King David appears to ignore the rules of grammar to teach us ways to praise God. In the verse beginning with the word יוֹדוּךָ, he uses an unusual spelling of the word יְבָרְכוּכָה (וַחֲסִידֶיךָ יְבָרְכוּכָה, and Your righteous ones will bless You) to give us a message. יְבָרְכוּכָה (will bless You) should be spelled with a ךָ, which is second person singular. Instead we spell it with a כה. King David wrote this word in a way that could be divided into two words: יְבָרְכוּ כָה (they will bless you in the following way) to tell us that in אַשְׁרֵי he will tell us how to praise God.

Before we spoke of our praising God and explained a switch from the third person plural to the first person singular. Sometimes we have a different switch in case when we refer to God in the second person and then in the third person. For example, the following two verses speak about God in the second person: אֲרוֹמִמְךָ אֱלוֹקַי הַמֶּלֶךְ וַאֲבָרְכָה שִׁמְךָ ("I will extol You, my God and king, and bless Your name") and בְּכָל יוֹם אֲבָרְכֶךָּ וַאֲהַלְלָה שִׁמְךָ לְעוֹלָם וָעֶד ("Every day I will bless You and praise Your name forever and ever"). But the next verse switches to the third person: גָּדוֹל ה׳ וּמְהֻלָּל מְאֹד וְלִגְדֻלָּתוֹ אֵין חֵקֶר ("Great is Hashem and much acclaimed; and it is not possible to comprehend His greatness").

This use of the different persons of speech teaches us that one can bless God directly. He is close to us, our Friend, our Protector, and our Guide. But He is also distant from us. "It is not possible to comprehend His greatness" and we cannot become too familiar with Him. We should always be aware of this dual relationship between God and His people.

To the Rabbis, Psalm 145 was very special for two reasons. First, it contains the verse, פּוֹתֵחַ אֶת יָדֶךָ וּמַשְׂבִּיעַ לְכָל חַי רָצוֹן ("You open Your hand and feed all living things willingly"). Without this we couldn't live. Second, it contains an acrostic of the letters of the Alef Bet. This indicates that we are not able to do justice to God's greatness with our power of expression. Therefore, we offer Him the letters of the Alef Bet, as if to say, "You, God, will have to formulate Your own praises from these letters, as we are not adequately able to do so." Each of these ideas is mentioned in other Psalms, but אַשְׁרֵי is the only Psalm that combines both themes in one.

A conspicuous omission in אַשְׁרֵי, however, is a line beginning with the letter "נ". The Gemara[42] explains that David did not want to include "נ" in Ashrei because it is the first letter of a verse that predicted the downfall of the Jewish people: נָפְלָה לֹא-תוֹסִיף קוּם בְּתוּלַת יִשְׂרָאֵל ("The virgin Israel fell and will no longer be able to get up").[43] Therefore, King David skipped "נ" and proceeded directly to the next letter, "ס", to say, סוֹמֵךְ ה׳ לְכָל הַנֹּפְלִים ("Hashem supports all who fall"). This is in line with the explanation of the verse by the Sages who broke up the phrase differently: "She will not continue to fall: Arise, the virgin Israel."

הַלֵּל שֶׁל כָּל יוֹם

The Talmud declares, "A person who recites Hallel every day blasphemes the Almighty."[44] The statement of the Talmud means that the

---

42. ברכות דף ד עמוד ב

43. עמוס ה:ב

44. שבת דף קיח עמוד ב

הַלֵּל הַמִּצְרִי (the "Egyptian Hallel") should only be said on the festivals for which it is required. If we said the festival Hallel every day, and mentioned the miracles of the splitting of the sea, the bringing forth of water from the rocks, and so on, it would seem that we believe in God only because of all the great miracles that He performs. But isn't nature itself one great miracle? A person who really loves and believes in God doesn't need the miracles of the Exodus from Egypt to feel in awe of God. We can just look around every morning at the great and beautiful universe in which we live, and that should be enough to strengthen our faith. For the miracles of every day we should, and do, praise and thank God in פְּסוּקֵי דְזִמְרָה.

פְּסוּקֵי דְזִמְרָה as another form of Hallel thanks God for the miracles of Creation and for daily miracles. An examination of the last five chapters of the Book of Psalms shows that they speak about the daily miracles that are done for each individual. For example, Psalm 146 says, "He opens our eyes, He lets us stand straight," and so on. Psalm 148 mentions miracles that God does in nature: fire and hail, snow and wind. Wherever we look, we can see miracles, great and wonderful things happening all the time.

We repeat the verse כֹּל הַנְּשָׁמָה תְּהַלֵּל קָהּ הַלְלוּקָהּ at the end of the selections of Psalms that are the heart of פְּסוּקֵי דְזִמְרָה, just like we repeat the last verse of אָז יָשִׁיר.[45] This is to indicate that we are not trying to

---

45. There are two opinions about where the chapter of אָז יָשִׁיר ends. One position believes that this section ends with Shemot chapter 15 verse 18: יְיָ יִמְלֹךְ לְעֹלָם וָעֶד. Another opinion is that the chapter of אָז יָשִׁיר ends with verse 19: כִּי בָא סוּס פַּרְעֹה בְּרִכְבּוֹ וּבְפָרָשָׁיו בַּיָּם וַיָּשֶׁב יְיָ עֲלֵהֶם אֶת־מֵי הַיָּם וּבְנֵי יִשְׂרָאֵל הָלְכוּ בַיַּבָּשָׁה בְּתוֹךְ הַיָּם. Some siddurim end it one way and some the other. The Rav, during the year he taught about the siddur in his Motzaei Shabbat shiurim, explained that אָז יָשִׁיר in the Torah is written with spaces in each line, alternating so the whole section looks like it is made of bricks. He then asked someone to take out first one Torah from the אֲרוֹן הַקֹּדֶשׁ and showed us how אָז יָשִׁיר was written and then had someone take out another Torah and showed us the same section. In the first Torah, it was clear that אָז יָשִׁיר ended at verse 18: יְיָ יִמְלֹךְ לְעֹלָם וָעֶד. But in the other Torah, the bricks were structured differently and the end of אָז יָשִׁיר might have included כִּי בָא סוּס פַּרְעֹה. Our siddurim that repeat verse

finish quickly with the davening and hurry out of shul. For this reason we repeat many of the final verses in the davening.[46]

יִשְׁתַּבַּח

יִשְׁתַּבַּח, the berachah at the end of פְּסוּקֵי דְזִמְרָה, is a bit unusual in that the word יִשְׁתַּבַּח is in the reflexive form (הִתְפַּעֵל), meaning "Your name should be praised." Why do we not say נְשַׁבֵּחַ, meaning "We will praise Your name"? By using the reflexive form, we make it clear that humanity cannot praise God. Only God knows His own greatness. This is why we say, in the conclusion, הַבּוֹחֵר בְּשִׁירֵי זִמְרָה ("Who chooses songs of praise"). Although we can't comprehend it, God chooses to listen to our praises, incomplete and deficient as they are.

In this prayer, we use fifteen terms for the praises that we offer to God. There are fifteen such praises because in the Temple there were fifteen steps that led from the women's court to the courtyard of the Israelites.[47] On Sukkot, during the water-drawing ceremony, the Levites used to stand on these steps with their musical instruments. They created the joyous mood that we experienced on one of the happiest days of the year. Ever since then, the number fifteen has been associated with happiness and rejoicing.[48]

It is also possible that we want to express something else with these fifteen terms. The Priestly Blessing contains fifteen words.[49] Perhaps we want to indicate that we praise God with fifteen expressions and hope that God in return will activate all the berachot contained in the Priestly Blessing. In addition, the incomplete form of God's name adds up, in the value of its letters, to fifteen.

18, יְיָ יִמְלֹךְ לְעֹלָם וָעֶד, at the end of אָז יָשִׁיר, follow the opinion that אָז יָשִׁיר ends with יְיָ יִמְלֹךְ לְעֹלָם וָעֶד.

46. See רמ״א אורח חיים סימן נא סעיף ז; *Siddur Otzar Hatefillot*, p. 228, citing Avudraham.

47. אבודרהם

48. See *The World of Prayer*, pp. 86–87.

49. Seder Avodat Yisrael, p. 75.

The Shema and Its Berachot

After יִשְׁתַּבַּח, the chazzan recites the half-Kaddish. This Kaddish designates the end of the previous section of the prayers, פְּסוּקֵי דְזִמְרָה, and the beginning of the next section, the Shema with its berachot.

The berachot of Shema begin with the call to bless God, בָּרְכוּ. A person is not supposed to talk between יִשְׁתַּבַּח and the berachot of Shema. This is a serious enough sin to excuse a man from going to war.[1] Since some people might consider that a benefit, let me hasten to explain that one is excused from battle because he cannot assume that God will protect him.[2]

The Shulchan Aruch discusses the rules of interrupting the davening.[3] We should be very careful not to talk once we start saying בָּרוּךְ שֶׁאָמַר until we finish the שְׁמוֹנֶה עֶשְׂרֵה. The Mishnah Berurah adds[4] that we should not talk until after we finish Tachanun.

Interrupting in the Middle of Davening

There are some instances under which we might have to interrupt. The halachot regarding interrupting your davening differ depending

---

1. טור אורח חיים סימן נ״א, citing the Yerushalmi.
2. סוטה דף מד עמוד א. The Or Hachaim explains that to be saved by a miracle, one might need to be worthy of having God change the whole natural order of things. Even a minor offense can therefore cause a person not to be worthy of receiving a miracle. See also מנחות לו עמ׳ א and Rashi there ד״ה עבירה היא.
3. שולחן ערוך אורח חיים סימן נא סעי׳ ד-ו
4. משנה ברורה סימן נא ס״ק ט

on where you are in the davening. In the middle of פְּסוּקֵי דְזִמְרָה, we might have to say the blessing of אֲשֶׁר יָצַר, or might have to answer מוֹדִים דְּרַבָּנָן or might have to say the blessing for hearing thunder. The Aruch Hashulchan[5] tells us it would be alright to interrupt as long as we finish the verse we are saying first. If you are in the middle of פְּסוּקֵי דְזִמְרָה, and you are called up to the Torah, you can certainly go up to the Torah and receive that עֲלִיָּה.

A problem arises if someone interrupts you in the middle of your davening, or you feel you have to respond to an important matter.

There are a couple of terms we must define, and these categories are not always clear. Many times you must decide on your own how you define the person who is interrupting you. The following definitions are based on the Aruch Hashulchan[6]:

מִפְּנֵי הַכָּבוֹד – The category of person who interrupts is someone to whom you must respond because of his honor. Rashi explains that this is a person deserving our respect. Rambam describes מִפְּנֵי הַכָּבוֹד as someone whom we are obligated to honor, like a parent or teacher.

מִפְּנֵי הַיִּרְאָה – The category of person who interrupts is someone to whom you must respond because you are afraid. Rashi says it is someone of whom you are afraid of mortal danger. Rashba says that what we mean here is someone like a parent or teacher whom we are commanded to fear. The Terumas Hadeshen[7] adds to this someone who is awe-inspiring, like a person who is exceptionally brilliant.

The Aruch Hashulchan explains that in the middle of פְּסוּקֵי דְזִמְרָה, between chapters, we can say hello to someone if he is a person you should address מִפְּנֵי הַכָּבוֹד, and we are allowed to respond to anyone who says hello to us (וּמֵשִׁיב שָׁלוֹם לְכָל אָדָם).

If, however, we are in the middle of a chapter, we should not interrupt our own prayers to ask after someone's welfare, unless it is for someone whom you would address מִפְּנֵי הַיִּרְאָה. If someone who is described as מִפְּנֵי הַכָּבוֹד interrupts us, we can respond (מֵשִׁיב מִפְּנֵי הַכָּבוֹד).

The halachah seems to be the same regarding interrupting during

---

5. ערוך השולחן אורח חיים סי׳ נא סעי׳ ו

6. אורח חיים סימן סו סעיף ב

7. תרומת הדשן סי׳ קל״ה

קְרִיאַת שְׁמַע וּבִרְכוֹתֶיהָ as for interrupting during פְּסוּקֵי דְזִמְרָה. As we said, we cannot interrupt between בָּרְכוּ and קְרִיאַת שְׁמַע וּבִרְכוֹתֶיהָ. That is a very serious matter. Yet, there is really only one other major difference, relating to the actual Shema, between interrupting in Shema and פְּסוּקֵי דְזִמְרָה. That exception is if we are in the middle of either שְׁמַע יִשְׂרָאֵל or בָּרוּךְ שֵׁם כְּבוֹד מַלְכוּתוֹ לְעוֹלָם וָעֶד. There, we should not interrupt at all unless we are afraid for our lives. Once we have started a section, we should only ask after someone who is categorized as someone to whom we would respond מִפְּנֵי הַיִּרְאָה.

The similarity of the response to interruptions in these two sections strikes us as strange, because קְרִיאַת שְׁמַע וּבִרְכוֹתֶיהָ is much more important than פְּסוּקֵי דְזִמְרָה, and yet, our behavior does not reflect the increased importance of the prayer. The Taz suggests[8] that the Shulchan Aruch's language is not coincidental. The Torah itself requires us to hold our parents in awe.[9] That does not mean to be afraid of them necessarily, but certainly not to take them for granted, to treat them with great respect. A person should also honor and fear his Rebbe, his teacher, even more than he does his parents. His parents bring him into this world, while his teacher brings him into the next world.[10] It says in the Mishnah,[11] מוֹרָא רַבָּךְ כְּמוֹרָא שָׁמָיִם ("The fear you have for your teacher should be similar to the fear you have for Heaven"). The comparison that the Torah set up between honoring parents, teachers and God Himself leads us to view our interactions, even in the middle of קְרִיאַת שְׁמַע וּבִרְכוֹתֶיהָ in a different light.

Nowadays people don't stand on ceremony the way they once did, so we shouldn't answer another person's greeting, even a parent or teacher, and even if we are in between paragraphs.[12] We should not make any sort of interruption. There is an exception if a person comes to ask his rabbi a halachic question. Most people will wait until their

---

8. ט"ז אורח חיים סימן סו ס"ק א
9. ויקרא פרק יט פסוק ג
10. שולחן ערוך יורה דעה סימן רמב סעיף א
11. אבות פרק ד משנה יב
12. מגן אברהם סימן ס"ו ס"ק א; משנה ברורה סימן נ"א ס"ק י"ב; ערוך השולחן סימן ס"ו סעיף ד

rabbi finishes davening unless it is an emergency or if the person who asks doesn't realize he should wait. In such cases, the rabbi should answer between paragraphs.[13]

We cannot just brush aside the importance of our prayers. The Levush, in a cautionary rebuke,[14] says even if it is for something as important as doing a different mitzvah, we may not interrupt. However, there are exceptions to this statement of the Levush that might cause us to interrupt our קְרִיאַת שְׁמַע וּבִרְכוֹתֶיהָ. The Shema should be said while wearing tallit and tefillin,[15] but if we didn't have them with us, we would still say Shema because it is an independent mitzvah. The Gemara says[16] that if you say Shema, and you don't wear tefillin, it is like giving false testimony, because in Shema we speak about the obligation to wear tefillin. But if you have no choice, you have no choice.

It might happen that you didn't have tefillin with you, and it was time to say Shema and you started saying Shema. Then somebody walked over to you and gave them to you to put on. If you are between the chapters, the Shulchan Aruch says[17] that you are allowed to interrupt to put on a tallit and tefillin with their blessings and continue to say Shema. The Rama believes you can put on the tallit right away, but recite the berachah after שְׁמוֹנֶה עֶשְׂרֵה. As far as tefillin, you should finish the chapter, put on the tefillin with their berachot and continue the Shema.[18]

Another case where one might have to interrupt is a case of delaying the congregation: If a Kohen came late to shul and was still saying Shema while the rest of the minyan was up to reading the Torah, it would be better to call another Kohen. If he was the only Kohen in shul, and the gabbai called him up for an aliyah, what should he do?

---

13. ערוך השולחן אורח חיים סימן סו סעיף ד
14. לבוש אורח חיים סימן נא סעי׳ ה
15. שולחן ערוך אורח חיים סי׳ כה סעי׳ ד
16. ברכות דף יד עמ׳ ב
17. שולחן ערוך אורח חיים סימן סו סעי׳ ב
18. מגן גיבורים אלף המגן סימן סו ס״ק ד

The Shulchan Aruch[19] quotes two opinions about whether he should interrupt and rules that he should not. Many others, including the Levush, rule that since it is a matter of showing honor to the Torah, he should go up to the Torah if he is called.[20]

During the Aseret Yemei Teshuvah (from Rosh Hashanah to Yom Kippur), many congregations recite Psalm 130, שִׁיר הַמַּעֲלוֹת מִמַּעֲמַקִּים קְרָאתִיךָ ה׳ ("Song of ascents. From the depths I call to You") right after יִשְׁתַּבַּח. Rav Soloveitchik suggested that in order to avoid any interruption between יִשְׁתַּבַּח and the berachot of Shema this Psalm should be recited before יִשְׁתַּבַּח, thereby making it part of פְּסוּקֵי דְזִמְרָה.

בָּרְכוּ

The Kaddish and בָּרְכוּ that come between the end of פְּסוּקֵי דְזִמְרָה and the berachot of the Shema are not considered interruptions and have a specific purpose there that relates to the first berachah of Shema.

The berachot of Shema begin with the call to bless God, בָּרְכוּ. This call to bless God is a דָּבָר שֶׁבִּקְדוּשָּׁה (a holy passage which requires a minyan), and neither the בָּרְכוּ nor the Kaddish that precedes it can be said if there is no minyan. If there is no minyan, each person continues with the berachot of the Shema individually.

We have already explained that most Ashkenazic Jews today stand during a דָּבָר שֶׁבִּקְדוּשָּׁה because of its special holiness.[21]

What is the purpose of בָּרְכוּ here? בָּרְכוּ is a call to a congregation to publicly accept עוֹל מַלְכוּת שָׁמַיִם (God's rule over us). It is an introduction to the Shema whose core is the acceptance of God's rule.[22]

In בָּרְכוּ, we say, בָּרְכוּ אֶת ה׳ הַמְבֹרָךְ ("Bless God, who is blessed"). What is the need for the word הַמְבֹרָךְ? Shouldn't "Bless God" be

19. שולחן ערוך אורח חיים סימן סו סעיף ד

20. לבוש אורח חיים סימן ס״ו סעיף ד; משנה ברורה שם ס״ק כו; ערוך השולחן שם סעיף ט

21. רמ״א אורח חיים סימן נו סעיף א

22. This connection of Torah and קַבָּלַת עוֹל מַלְכוּת שָׁמַיִם is also the reason for having בָּרְכוּ at the beginning of the first berachah of Shema. See: רשימות שיעורים ברכות דף יא עמוד ב.

sufficient? The word הַמְבֹרָךְ eliminates a misunderstanding. If the chazzan said only, "Bless God," we might think that the chazzan is instructing others to bless God but is not doing so himself. The word הַמְבֹרָךְ makes it clear that he, too, is blessing God and is being consistent with Hillel's dictum, אַל תִּפְרוֹשׁ מִן הַצִּבּוּר ("Don't separate yourself from the community").[23] The Gemara[24] says that when a person invites others to bless God, he should include himself and also bless God at the same time.

THE BLESSINGS OF THE SHEMA

In Shacharit there are three berachot that accompany the Shema: The first is יוֹצֵר אוֹר ("Who formed light"), which ends with יוֹצֵר הַמְּאוֹרוֹת ("Creator of the luminaries"); the second is אַהֲבָה רַבָּה ("A great love"); and the third is בִּרְכַּת גְּאוּלָּה (the blessing of redemption). Each of these berachot is an elaboration of one of the three paragraphs of the Shema.[25] The berachah of יוֹצֵר הַמְּאוֹרוֹת is clearly an extension of the Shema. God is the only Creator of the heavens and the earth. In the conclusion of this berachah we accept God as our Sovereign. The berachah of אַהֲבָה רַבָּה is an elaboration of the second paragraph of the Shema, the paragraph of וְהָיָה אִם שָׁמֹעַ ("And it will be if you listen"). In its conclusion we accept the commandments as described in the second paragraph of the Shema. In both the second berachah of Shema and the second paragraph of Shema, we emphasize the importance of the study of Torah to enable us to carry out the commandments properly.[26] The third berachah of the Shema has the same theme as the third paragraph of the Shema, the Exodus from Egypt.[27]

---

23. אבות פרק ב משנה ד

24. ברכות דף מט עמוד ב - נ עמ׳ א

25. רשימות שיעורים מסכת ברכות דף ב עמוד א בענין שומע כעונה בקריאת שמע ותפלה

26. לְהָבִין וּלְהַשְׂכִּיל. לִשְׁמֹעַ. לִלְמֹד וּלְלַמֵּד. לִשְׁמֹר וְלַעֲשׂוֹת וּלְקַיֵּם אֶת כָּל דִּבְרֵי תַלְמוּד תּוֹרָתֶךָ in אַהֲבָה רַבָּה, and וְלִמַּדְתֶּם אֹתָם אֶת בְּנֵיכֶם לְדַבֵּר בָּם in the second paragraph of the שְׁמַע.

27. רשימות שיעורים ברכות, עמ׳ יח. The berachot of Shema and the Shema itself have the same theme.

Some commentators[28] think that the berachot of the Shema demonstrate the influence of King David's Psalm 19.[29] This psalm contains two themes. The first half of the psalm describes how the natural world speaks the praises of God: הַשָּׁמַיִם מְסַפְּרִים כְּבוֹד־קֵל וּמַעֲשֵׂה יָדָיו מַגִּיד הָרָקִיעַ ("The heavens declare the glory of God, the sky proclaims His handiwork"). The second half of the psalm describes how the Torah reflects God's perfection: תּוֹרַת ה׳ תְּמִימָה מְשִׁיבַת נָפֶשׁ עֵדוּת ה׳ נֶאֱמָנָה מַחְכִּימַת פֶּתִי ("The Torah of Hashem is perfect, renewing life; the decrees of Hashem are trustworthy, making the simple wise"). This accounts for the two berachot before Shema. The first berachah, which is about God's creation of the natural world, corresponds to the first theme of Psalm 19, and the second berachah, which is about God's gift of the Torah, corresponds to the second.

יוֹצֵר אוֹר

בָּרוּךְ אַתָּה ה׳, אֱלֹקֵינוּ מֶלֶךְ הָעוֹלָם, יוֹצֵר אוֹר וּבוֹרֵא חֹשֶׁךְ עֹשֶׂה שָׁלוֹם וּבוֹרֵא אֶת הַכֹּל....אוֹר חָדָשׁ עַל צִיּוֹן תָּאִיר וְנִזְכֶּה כֻלָּנוּ מְהֵרָה לְאוֹרוֹ. בָּרוּךְ אַתָּה ה׳, יוֹצֵר הַמְּאוֹרוֹת.

("Blessed are You, Hashem, who formed light and created darkness... Blessed are You, Hashem, Creator of the luminaries")

The berachot of יוֹצֵר הַמְּאוֹרוֹת, אַהֲבָה רַבָּה and אֱמֶת וְיַצִּיב are a series of long berachot, so they must adhere to the specific criteria of long berachot. They are also בְּרָכוֹת הַסְּמוּכוֹת לַחֲבֶרְתָּהּ (a long berachah in proximity to another long berachah). That's why only the first one begins with the phrase בָּרוּךְ אַתָּה ה׳.

אֱמֶת וְיַצִּיב is the berachah that immediately follows the Shema. Is it really a בְּרָכָה הַסְּמוּכָה לַחֲבֶרְתָּהּ? Yes. The Shema is not an interruption, just like פְּסוּקֵי דְזִמְרָה is not an interruption between the berachah of בָּרוּךְ שֶׁאָמַר and יִשְׁתַּבַּח.

The opening words of the berachah of יוֹצֵר אוֹר are borrowed from Isaiah,[30] but the words of the prophet are slightly different. Isaiah

---

28. See *Tikkun Tefillah* in *Otzar Hatefillot*, עמ׳ קכה.

29. תהלים פרק יט

30. ישעיהו מה פסוק ז

says, יוֹצֵר אוֹר וּבוֹרֵא חֹשֶׁךְ עֹשֶׂה שָׁלוֹם וּבוֹרֵא רָע ("Who forms light and creates darkness, makes peace and creates evil"). Our prayer book has changed וּבוֹרֵא רָע ("and creates evil") to וּבוֹרֵא אֶת הַכֹּל ("and creates everything") to indicate that everything that God creates is good, even though, with our limited understanding, it may seem to be evil.

The prophet Isaiah and the Rabbis were engaged in an ongoing battle against Zoroastrianism, the religion of dualism whose major tenet is that there is a god of light and good, and a god of darkness and evil. This religion had a simple answer to the most difficult question: Why do righteous people suffer while wicked people prosper? They said that when the god of light has the upper hand, there is peace and prosperity. When the god of darkness has the upper hand, there is suffering and misery in the world. A belief in two gods is idolatry, which is why Isaiah took such pains to explain to the Jewish people that there is only one God, who "makes peace and creates evil," who is responsible for good and for what seems to be evil. In establishing the text of the prayer book, the Rabbis utilized Isaiah's phrase, which enabled them to renew their struggle against that particular form of idol worship every day. Only one God is the Originator of darkness and light, not two as the Zoroastrians said.

The Gemara says[31] that we include darkness in the daytime blessing and light in the nighttime blessing in order to interject a mention of day into the night and an element of night into the day, as we say יוֹצֵר אוֹר וּבוֹרֵא חֹשֶׁךְ in the morning and גּוֹלֵל אוֹר מִפְּנֵי חֹשֶׁךְ וְחֹשֶׁךְ מִפְּנֵי אוֹר ("who rolls away light in the face of darkness and darkness in the face of light") at night. The Shulchan Aruch explains[32] that the blessing was specifically designed like this in order to counter those who say that the one who created light could not create darkness and the one who created darkness could not have created light.

The berachah of יוֹצֵר אוֹר is a berachah of praise. Quite unexpectedly, in the middle of this berachah of praise, we switch to asking God to fill our needs: אֱלֹקֵי עוֹלָם בְּרַחֲמֶיךָ הָרַבִּים רַחֵם עָלֵינוּ ("God of the Universe, in

---

31. ברכות דף יא עמ׳ ב
32. אורח חיים סימן נ״ט סעיף א

Your great mercy, have compassion on us"). Then we continue again with praise. Why is there this interruption? The customary answer is that the stars and planets (הַמְּאוֹרוֹת) were created on the fourth day. The word הַמְּאוֹרוֹת (heavenly bodies that give off light) in Genesis is spelled missing the vavs (ו), as מְאֹרֹת. This could therefore be read as מְאֵרוֹת (curses). According to the Rabbis, this alludes to the fact that sickness was created along with the stars and planets. In our daily prayers, we want to praise God for the מְאוֹרוֹת (stars and planets), and we also implore God to save us from the מְאֵרוֹת (curses).[33]

Perhaps we can also see in this request the Rabbis' polemic against Christianity, which, like paganism, taught that the Almighty had withdrawn from the world into His heavenly abode after Creation. The distance between humanity and God was so great that it could not be bridged. Christianity therefore invented a godlike figure to overcome this chasm. In this berachah in which we praise God for Creation, we include a plea to show that we believe that God has not forsaken us, that the chasm can be overcome. Every human being has access to God, and in a miraculous way that we cannot understand, God lowers Himself to our level and we can feel close to Him.

Included in the berachah of יוֹצֵר אוֹר is an acrostic of the Alef Bet. On weekdays each word starts with a different letter of the Alef Bet, in order. On Shabbat, the prayer is expanded so that each letter of the Alef Bet starts a full line. What did the Rabbis want to teach us by including an acrostic? The Alef Bet is always the symbol of the Torah. This berachah raises the old and difficult question, "Why did God bring the world into being?" The answer seems to be so that we will live up to the Alef Bet, or carry out the demands of the Torah.

יוֹצֵר אוֹר continues with the description of the Kedushah that the angels sing in heaven. Normally, recitation of the Kedushah requires being summoned to do so, as well as a minyan and recitation while standing.[34] An individual who says this Kedushah does none of these.

33. *Anaf Yosef*, in *Otzar Hatefillot*.

34. According to the Sephardic tradition, for a דָּבָר שֶׁבִּקְדֻשָּׁה if you are standing,

Consequently, the Rambam ruled that an individual who is praying without a minyan should skip the Kedushah here.[35]

Ashkenazim, however, rely on the Rama's opinion, which permits an individual to recite this Kedushah. He says that here, we are not really reciting Kedushah ourselves but merely describing the Kedushah that the angels sing. The Shulchan Aruch recommends reciting it with its cantillation, so that it is considered reading from the Torah and not reciting Kedushah.[36]

This Kedushah is actually preliminary to the Kedushah in the שְׁמוֹנֶה עֶשְׂרֵה, which we introduce with the words, כְּשֵׁם שֶׁמַּקְדִּישִׁים אוֹתוֹ בִּשְׁמֵי מָרוֹם ("just as they sanctify Him in the heights of the heavens"). We know what the angels do by describing, here, in יוֹצֵר הַמְּאוֹרוֹת, their way of singing praises to God. It is also possible that our rabbis introduced the Kedushah in יוֹצֵר הַמְּאוֹרוֹת to teach us a basic truth, namely the existence of עוֹלָם הַבָּא (the World to Come). There exists a world of angels and souls of which we know very little. Nevertheless, we firmly believe that God created two worlds: עוֹלָם הַזֶּה (this world) and עוֹלָם הַבָּא (the next world).[37]

This Kedushah has two verses: קָדוֹשׁ קָדוֹשׁ קָדוֹשׁ ה׳ צְבָקוֹת מְלֹא כָל הָאָרֶץ כְּבוֹדוֹ ("Holy, holy, holy is the Lord, Creator of the heavenly and earthly hosts, the whole earth is filled with His glory") and בָּרוּךְ כְּבוֹד ה׳ מִמְּקוֹמוֹ ("Blessed be the glory of Hashem from His place"). We do not add the usual third verse of the standard Kedushah, that of יִמְלֹךְ ה׳ לְעוֹלָם אֱלֹקַיִךְ צִיּוֹן לְדֹר וָדֹר. הַלְלוּקָהּ ("May Hashem rule forever...") since we are just describing what the angels recite, and the angels do not recite the third verse of our Kedushah. This third verse is the song of King David in Psalm 146.[38]

---

you remain standing, and if you are sitting, you remain sitting. According to the Rama (whom the Ashkenazic Jews follow), you always stand for דָּבָר שֶׁבִּקְדֻשָּׁה.

35. רמב״ם הלכות תפילה פרק ז הלכה יז

36. שולחן ערוך ורמ״א אורח חיים סימן נט סעיף ג

37. See רמב״ם פירוש משניות, סנהדרין, הקדמה לפרק החלק.

38. Abraham Katz says, "I once heard the Rav explain that the third verse of Kedushah is not missing at all from this Kedushah. The first two verses, 'Holy, Holy, Holy...' and 'Blessed be the glory...' both refer to God as the

The angelic song קָדוֹשׁ קָדוֹשׁ קָדוֹשׁ ה׳ צְבָקוֹת מְלֹא כָל הָאָרֶץ כְּבוֹדוֹ was revealed to us by the prophet Isaiah.[39] The second angelic song, בָּרוּךְ כְּבוֹד ה׳ מִמְּקוֹמוֹ, is part of the famous vision of the Chariot, מַעֲשֵׂה הַמֶּרְכָּבָה from the Book of Ezekiel.[40]

The Kedushah of the angels also teaches us the rules of prayers that contain special holiness, דָּבָר שֶׁבִּקְדוּשָּׁה. When we talk about the angels, we emphasize כֻּלָּם עוֹמְדִים ("they all stand"): you have to stand for a דָּבָר שֶׁבִּקְדוּשָּׁה. The phrase וְנוֹתְנִים רְשׁוּת זֶה לָזֶה ("and they give permission one to another"), tells us that a דָּבָר שֶׁבִּקְדוּשָּׁה requires that one person call out to the others to recite the statement about God, the congregation responds, and then the leader repeats the statement. כֻּלָּם אֲהוּבִים ("they are all beloved"): the angels are united in their purpose of praising God, and there are no arguments between them. כֻּלָּם בְּרוּרִים ("they are all clear"): they know exactly what their task is. Finally, וְכֻלָּם מְקַבְּלִים עֲלֵיהֶם עֹל מַלְכוּת שָׁמַיִם זֶה מִזֶּה ("and each one accepts upon himself the sovereignty of God, one from the other").

When we want to say that the angels praise God, we use six synonyms[41] where one word would have been sufficient. To Isaiah, the angels appeared as six-winged beings. By repeating six times that they praise God, we show that they praise God with all their being, with all that they have, with all six wings.[42]

The attributes of God that were chosen by the Men of the Great Assembly to be included in this Kedushah were first chosen by Moshe: In this blessing, we proclaim that the angels praise "the name of the great, mighty and awesome king, God" (אֶת שֵׁם הָקֵל הַמֶּלֶךְ הַגָּדוֹל הַגִּבּוֹר

---

creator and sustainer of the universe, and therefore they are found in the berachah which describes God as the Creator. The third verse, 'May Hashem rule forever…' concerns the Redemption, and it can be found in our prayers, appropriately, in the third and final berachah of the Shema, the berachah of Geulah, or Redemption."

39. ישעיהו ו:ג

40. יחזקאל ג:יב

41. וּמְבָרְכִים וּמְשַׁבְּחִים וּמְפָאֲרִים וּמַעֲרִיצִים וּמַקְדִּישִׁים וּמַמְלִיכִים ("And they bless, praise, glorify, revere, sanctify, enthrone").

42. *Otzar Hatefillot*, עמ׳ קל אחרית לשלום ד"ה ומברכים.

וְהַנּוֹרָא). Likewise, Moshe spoke of God as הָקֵל הַגָּדוֹל הַגִּבּוֹר וְהַנּוֹרָא ("the great, mighty and awesome God").[43] In the time of Jeremiah, however, when the Jews suffered the destruction of the First Temple, Jeremiah omitted the attribute of נּוֹרָא (awesome)[44] because the Babylonians had destroyed the Temple, so obviously, the Babylonians did not fear God. Daniel omitted the attribute הַגִּבּוֹר (mighty) because he believed that God could not be called mighty when the nations of the world had enslaved His people.[45] The Gemara[46] tells us that the Men of the Great Assembly were given their title because they "restored" God's attributes. They explained that these terms are indeed appropriate, and thus we use them both here and in the שְׁמוֹנֶה עֶשְׂרֵה. God is called הַגִּבּוֹר (mighty), because He conquers His anger and does not destroy the wicked. We call Him הַנּוֹרָא (awesome), because the continued existence of the Jewish people attests to God's fear being imposed on the nations.

In describing the song of the angels, we are not quite sure how to understand a few words: בְּנַחַת רוּחַ ("with a calm spirit"), בְּשָׂפָה בְרוּרָה ("with a clear language"), וּבִנְעִימָה ("melodically"), and קְדֻשָּׁה ("holiness"). Most prayer books explain the words to mean, "In a clear and melodic language, the angels recite the Kedushah" In other words, קְדוּשָׁה is a noun in the objective case, meaning the prayer called Kedushah. Others vowelize the word as קְדוֹשָׁה, which would mean: "In a clear voice and with a holy melody. . . . " In this version, the word is an adjective.[47]

---

43. דברים י:יז: כִּי ה׳ אֱלֹקֵיכֶם הוּא אֱלֹקֵי הָאֱלֹקִים וַאֲדֹנֵי הָאֲדֹנִים הָקֵל הַגָּדֹל הַגִּבֹּר וְהַנּוֹרָא אֲשֶׁר לֹא־יִשָּׂא פָנִים וְלֹא יִקַּח שֹׁחַד

44. ירמיהו לב:יח: עֹשֶׂה חֶסֶד לַאֲלָפִים וּמְשַׁלֵּם עֲוֹן אָבוֹת אֶל־חֵיק בְּנֵיהֶם אַחֲרֵיהֶם הָקֵל הַגָּדוֹל הַגִּבּוֹר ה׳ צְבָקוֹת שְׁמוֹ

45. דניאל ט:ד: וָאֶתְפַּלְלָה לַה׳ אֱלֹקַי וָאֶתְוַדֶּה וָאֹמְרָה אָנָּא אֲד־נָי הָקֵל הַגָּדוֹל וְהַנּוֹרָא שֹׁמֵר הַבְּרִית וְהַחֶסֶד לְאֹהֲבָיו וּלְשֹׁמְרֵי מִצְוֹתָיו

46. יומא דף סט עמוד ב

47. *Seder Avodat Yisrael* quotes the Avudraham (אבודרהם ברכות קריאת שמע), who says that this means "a sweet and holy sound," making it an adjective. In the Siddùr Benè Romi (סדור בני רומי, סדור כמנהג איטליאני של ק״ק רומא יע״א) of the Roman *nusach* in Italy, it says: בְּנַחַת רוּחַ, בְּשָׂפָה בְּרוּרָה, בִּנְעִימָה, וּבִקְדֻשָּׁה כֻּלָּם

In translating the words ה' צְבָקוֹת most prayer books translate the word צְבָקוֹת as modifying the name of God, so that the two words ה' צְבָקוֹת are translated as "the Lord of Hosts." This is imprecise. The word צְבָקוֹת is itself one of the seven names of God that cannot be erased.[48] The proper translation then, is, "Hashem, Who is also known as Tzvakos." God is indeed called צְבָקוֹת because He created the hosts," or, "Hashem, Creator of the multitudes of the heavens and the earth." We must understand צְבָקוֹת to be one of the names of God.

After this Kedushah, we return to praising God. Here we use three different phrases for praising God: נְעִימוֹת יִתֵּנוּ (they offer pleasant melodies), זְמִירוֹת יֹאמֵרוּ (they say songs of praise), וְתִשְׁבָּחוֹת יַשְׁמִיעוּ (and they proclaim praises"). These parallel the threefold Kedushah (קָדוֹשׁ קָדוֹשׁ קָדוֹשׁ).

We then enumerate eight activities that God performs: (1) He performs mighty acts, פּוֹעֵל גְּבוּרוֹת; (2) He creates new things, עוֹשֶׂה חֲדָשׁוֹת; (3) He wages wars, בַּעַל מִלְחָמוֹת; (4) He plants seeds of righteousness, זוֹרֵעַ צְדָקוֹת; (5) He brings salvation to sprout, מַצְמִיחַ יְשׁוּעוֹת; (6) He creates cures, בּוֹרֵא רְפוּאוֹת; (7) He performs awe-inspiring and praiseworthy acts, נוֹרָא תְהִלּוֹת; and (8) He performs works of wonders, אֲדוֹן הַנִּפְלָאוֹת.

Why do we list eight actions that God performs? Any one would have been sufficient to continue our theme. Here again, the Rabbis were continuing their polemic against paganism. The ancient pagans thought that Earth and the seven visible "planets" (meaning, the sun, the moon, Mercury, Venus, Mars, Jupiter, and Saturn) orbited around it. For the ancients, these seven planets represented the powers of nature. They considered themselves dependent on the heavenly bodies and tried to appease them. One planet, for instance, was thought to be in charge of human health, another responsible for wars, and so on.

כְּאֶחָד עוֹנִים בְּאֵימָה וְאוֹמְרִים בְּיִרְאָה - "...With a calm spirit, in a clear voice, with a sweet melody and with holiness, they all answer as one..." In this version, וּבִקְדֻשָּׁה is a noun, but it does not refer to the prayer called Kedushah. *Avodat Yisrael* says that this was the text of Rav Natronai Gaon as well.

48. רמב"ם הלכות יסודי התורה פרק ו הל' ב.

The Rabbis teach us that the planets are not deities. They have no power over us but only carry out God's wishes. God alone is responsible for all the activities enumerated. God alone is responsible for our fate. Thus, these eight descriptions of God correspond to the powers attributed by the pagans to Earth and the seven visible planets.[49]

Before the close of this berachah, we emphasize, הַמְחַדֵּשׁ בְּטוּבוֹ בְּכָל יוֹם תָּמִיד מַעֲשֵׂה בְרֵאשִׁית ("Who daily renews with His goodness the act of creation"). God created the world ex nihilo and continues to make sure that the world exists from day to day. Without God's creative power, the world would collapse into nonexistence.[50]

If we remember the rule that the closing of a long berachah must have the same theme as the opening of the berachah, then we have to ask, is this section consistent with that rule? We started this berachah by saying יוֹצֵר אוֹר ("who forms light") and we end with אוֹר עַל צִיּוֹן תָּאִיר חָדָשׁ ("Shine a new light on Zion"), which is a request for the Messianic Era. How is this related to the opening of the berachah, which refers to the creation of light? The answer is that the light at the beginning of the berachah probably refers to the primordial light that God created and put away for the righteous in the next world. Humanity does not yet deserve this light. Perhaps in our closing, אוֹר חָדָשׁ ("a new light"), our prayer for new light is a request to God to restore the primordial light, since in the Messianic Era, we will be more worthy.[51]

The berachah of אַהֲבָה רַבָּה is rich in synonyms. In it we ask God to give us Torah wisdom in many different ways: לְהָבִין means to understand the complete ideas and difficult aspects of Torah study; וּלְהַשְׂכִּיל

49. See *The World of Prayer*, pp. 105–106.

50. *Etz Yosef* in *Otzar Hatefillot*, p. 263.

51. See טור אורח חיים סימן נט. The Midrash (שמות רבה פרשת תרומה פרשה לה) explains that there were a number of items that God created at the time of the Creation of the World, that He decided were good, but that the world wasn't yet ready for. One of these was the primordial light (אור הגנוז), which will be restored in the time of the Messiah. This idea is alluded to in a number of places in the Gemara (e.g. חגיגה יב א), and is a major theme in the Zohar (זהר ח"ב דף קנ"ו ע"א) and other important rabbinic sources (e.g., של"ה תולדות אדם בית חכמה).

means to understand in order to be able to carry out in practice what we learn in theory;[52] לִשְׁמֹעַ means that we have to be ready to listen to the Rabbis; לִלְמֹד means that we have to review our learning until it becomes part of our Torah knowledge; וּלְלַמֵּד means that we must share our knowledge with others; לִשְׁמֹר means that we have to guard our Torah knowledge lest we forget it; וְלַעֲשׂוֹת means to carry out the commandments; וּלְקַיֵּם tells us to fulfill the commandments in such a way that we change a purely mechanical action into a meaningful performance.

After we have thanked God for having enabled us to study the Torah, we quite unexpectedly change the subject and ask God to gather in our exiled people from the four corners of the earth. How are these subjects related? In the diaspora, we cannot carry out the Torah in its entirety. Many commandments depend on living in the Land of Israel. In this berachah, where we speak about studying and carrying out the Torah, we express our hope that our observance of the Torah will soon be complete, including the commandments that can only be observed in the Holy Land.

It has become a very popular practice to bring our deceased relatives for burial in the Land of Israel. Included in אַהֲבָה רַבָּה is our wish to have the merit to live in Israel while we are still alive: וְתוֹלִיכֵנוּ קוֹמְמִיּוּת לְאַרְצֵנוּ ("and bring us upright to our land") and to contribute to the rebuilding of the Land of Israel. Our forefather Jacob, on his death bed, asked his children to bury him in the land of Canaan and not in the land of Egypt. At the time of the resurrection of the dead, Jews will first have to go to the Land of Israel before they will enjoy a new life. This process is called צַעַר גִּלְגּוּל נְשָׁמוֹת ("the pain of the rolling of souls [to Israel]"). It will be a painful process to "roll" to Israel. Those who are already buried there will be spared this suffering.[53] This is another reason for our request to bring us to our land while we are alive and to find our eternal rest in holy soil. We conclude this berachah by proclaiming God's unity, which creates a smooth transition to the Shema.

---

52. *Etz Yosef* in *Otzar Hatefillot*, p. 267.

53. כתובות דף קי"א עמוד א

סְמִיכַת גְּאוּלָה לִתְפִלָּה

Rav Soloveitchik explained that one focus of Shema is accepting God's sovereignty together with song and praise, in the manner in which the angels sing His praise. The other focus of Shema is recognizing the unity of God. The placement of Shema next to the שְׁמוֹנֶה עֶשְׂרֵה brings an added element not just to Shema, but to the שְׁמוֹנֶה עֶשְׂרֵה as well. Rav Soloveitchik said[54] that Shema is recited immediately before the שְׁמוֹנֶה עֶשְׂרֵה (called סְמִיכַת גְּאוּלָה לִתְפִלָּה) because there is a connection between the two. Shema provides us with the permission to approach the Ruler of the heavens and the earth with our individual prayers.

We have noted that the chazzan used to say the whole berachah out loud, and now he just says the last few words out loud. As far as the berachah of יוֹצֵר אוֹר, we should try to finish our recitation of this berachah before the chazzan and say Amen after his conclusion. Everyone agrees with this. However, regarding the other berachot of the Shema,[55] there is a difference of opinion in the Shulchan Aruch between R. Yosef Karo and the Rama. R. Yosef Karo writes, "One should not answer Amen after the berachah of הַבּוֹחֵר בְּעַמּוֹ יִשְׂרָאֵל בְּאַהֲבָה because it would be an interruption."[56] He feels that it is a preliminary berachah for the performance of the commandment to recite the Shema, and we may not answer Amen afterwards. This follows the rule that there may be no interruption between a berachah for a commandment and the performance of the commandment. The Rama, on the other hand, maintains that Amen is recited after הַבּוֹחֵר בְּעַמּוֹ יִשְׂרָאֵל בְּאַהֲבָה.[57] The Rama seems to be of the opinion that the berachot of Shema are an elaboration of the paragraphs of the Shema itself, and not the preliminary berachah for the performance of a commandment.[58] Many Ashkenazic Jews follow this practice.

---

54. See רשימות שיעורים (רי״ד סולובייצ׳יק) מסכת ברכות דף ד עמוד ב: בענין סמיכת גאולה לתפלה, ביסוד הדין דתפלה בעי מתיר, עמ׳ נט-ס
55. אֱמֶת וְיַצִּיב and אַהֲבָה רַבָּה.
56. שולחן ערוך אורח חיים הלכות קריאת שמע סימן נט סעיף ד
57. רמ״א אורח חיים סימן סא סעיף ג
58. The Rav pointed this fact out many times. The basis of Keriat Shema

Similarly, R. Yosef Karo writes in the Shulchan Aruch,[59] "One should not say Amen after the berachah of גָּאַל יִשְׂרָאֵל ('Redeemer of Israel') [before the שְׁמוֹנֶה עֶשְׂרֵה] because it would be an interruption [between גָּאַל יִשְׂרָאֵל and the שְׁמוֹנֶה עֶשְׂרֵה]." The Rama then adds, "There is an opinion that one should answer Amen, and our custom is to answer Amen after the chazzan. But if one is praying alone, then one should not answer Amen."

The Rama's opinion is hard to understand. There is a principle that we must not interrupt between גָּאַל יִשְׂרָאֵל and the שְׁמוֹנֶה עֶשְׂרֵה. Doesn't the Rama accept this principle? How can he permit the saying of Amen after the berachah of גָּאַל יִשְׂרָאֵל?

The answer is that the Rama is following the position of Rashi.[60]

Rashi approves of saying "Amen" after your own berachah if it is at the end of a series of berachot, and he would therefore say "Amen" after גָּאַל יִשְׂרָאֵל. Rashi would have us say "Amen" after the last berachah in the שְׁמוֹנֶה עֶשְׂרֵה. He would also have us say "Amen" at the end of the last berachah of the Shema in the evening, for the same reason. According to him, when we reach the end of the berachah of גָּאַל יִשְׂרָאֵל in Shacharit, we should proclaim Amen. Tosafot doesn't disagree with Rashi, but he says that nevertheless what the people have adopted is

---

is accepting God's rule over us (קַבָּלַת עֹל מַלְכוּת שָׁמַיִם). The three berachot of Shema parallel the three paragraphs of Shema. The first berachah, in the morning, יוֹצֵר אוֹר וּבוֹרֵא חֹשֶׁךְ ("Who forms light and creates darkness") and at night, הַמַּעֲרִיב עֲרָבִים ("Who brings the evenings"), have as their main focus that God created everything. This is the theme of the first paragraph of the Shema: that God is One. The second berachah, both in the morning and night, have as their theme the study of Torah. This is the theme of the second paragraph of Shema: וְלִמַּדְתֶּם אֹתָם אֶת בְּנֵיכֶם לְדַבֵּר בָּם, "teach them to your children..." The third berachah, גָּאַל יִשְׂרָאֵל ("Redeemer of Israel"), is parallel to the third paragraph of Shema, which reminds us of how God took us out of Egypt. See Rabbi Zvi Yosef Reichman, רשימות שיעורים (רי"ד סולובייצ'יק) מסכת ברכות דף ב עמוד א בענין שומע כעונה בקריאת שמע ותפלה.

59. אורח חיים הלכות קריאת שמע סימן סו, סעיף ז

60. תוספות הא בבונה ירושלים and מסכת ברכות דף מה עמוד ב: רש"י הא בבונה ירושלים הא בשאר ברכות.

to only say "Amen" after the series of berachot at the end of birkat hamazon. That means that Tosafot believes practically we would not recite "Amen" after גָּאַל יִשְׂרָאֵל when davening without a minyan. The Rama follows Tosafot's position and therefore he holds that one does not say "Amen" after his own berachah of גָּאַל יִשְׂרָאֵל, but one would say "Amen" if he heard the chazzan finish the berachah.[61]

The best practice for us would be to conclude גָּאַל יִשְׂרָאֵל concurrently with the chazzan, since one generally does not answer "Amen" to one's own berachah. This would avoid the problem.[62] This was also the practice of Rav Soloveitchik.[63] The chazzan who tries to avoid the problem by saying גָּאַל יִשְׂרָאֵל softly is incorrect. As a chazzan, it is his task to say every word out loud, especially the conclusions of berachot.

בִּרְכוֹת קְרִיאַת שְׁמַע שֶׁל מַעֲרִיב

The commandment of reciting the Shema is twofold: We must recite it both in the morning and in the evening. Just as we say the berachot of the Shema for Shacharit, we also say the berachot of the Shema in Ma'ariv. The berachot of the morning Shema and the evening Shema have a lot in common. In both Shacharit and Ma'ariv, the berachot elaborate on the themes of the Shema. But there is also an essential difference. In Shacharit we list God's innumerable acts of kindness for the Jewish people, while in Ma'ariv we proclaim our unshakable faith in Him.[64] This difference is based on the verse לְהַגִּיד בַּבֹּקֶר חַסְדֶּךָ וֶאֱמוּנָתְךָ בַּלֵּילוֹת ("To proclaim Your kindness in the morning, Your faithfulness each night").[65]

---

61. אורח חיים הלכות קריאת שמע סימן סו, סעיף ז

62. מגן אברהם סימן ס"ו ס"ק יא; משנה ברורה שם ס"ק לה; ערוך השולחן שם סעיף יד-טו

63. סדור הגר"א [סדור אשי ישראל], ירושלים, עמוד 115, אות ב. However, if you are fulfilling your obligation to say the berachot of Shema through the recitation of the chazzan, then you should say Amen.

64. See רש"י ברכות דף יב עמוד א ד"ה שנאמר להגיד בבקר חסדך and תוספות שם ד"ה להגיד בבקר חסדך.

65. תהלים פרק צב פסוק ג

Rashi formulates this difference by stating that in Shacharit, the berachah following the Shema enumerates God's past kindnesses to us, but the berachah following Shema at night speaks about the future redemption as well.[66]

In Ma'ariv, we also add an extra berachah, הַשְׁכִּיבֵנוּ ("Let us, Hashem, our God, lie down in peace"). The Gemara[67] wonders why we add the berachah of הַשְׁכִּיבֵנוּ. It seems to be an interruption between the berachah of גָּאַל יִשְׂרָאֵל and the שְׁמוֹנֶה עֶשְׂרֵה. The Gemara concludes that it is not an interruption, and it calls הַשְׁכִּיבֵנוּ an extension of the theme of redemption. In the berachah of גָּאַל יִשְׂרָאֵל, we thank God for the redemption of the entire Jewish people, while in the berachah of הַשְׁכִּיבֵנוּ, we ask God for a personal redemption, such as וְהָסֵר מֵעָלֵינוּ אוֹיֵב דֶּבֶר וְחֶרֶב וְרָעָב ("And remove from upon us enemies, pestilence, the sword, and famine").[68]

RECITATION OF THE SHEMA

According to most authorities, the recitation of the Shema is an obligation ordained by the Torah.[69] The commandment derives from the verse וְדִבַּרְתָּ בָּם...וּבְשָׁכְבְּךָ וּבְקוּמֶךָ ("Recite them...when you lie down and when you get up"),[70] which requires reciting the text of Shema every evening and every morning.

There is a disagreement about how much of the Shema must be recited to fulfill the commandment. According to Rabbi Yehudah HaNasi, the requirement is fulfilled with the recitation of the first line alone.[71] Others believe that the first line of Shema together with the

66. רש״י ברכות דף יב עמוד א: שנאמר להגיד בבקר חסדך

67. ברכות דף ד עמוד ב

68. See רשימות שיעורים [רי״ד סולובייצ׳יק] מסכת ברכות דף ד עמוד ב: בענין סמיכת גאולה לתפלה.

69. Based on the Gemara: ברכות דף כא, עמוד א, the Rambam lists it among the 613 mitzvot: ספר המצוות לרמב״ם מצות עשה י. For another opinion, see תוספות סוטה דף לב עמוד ב, ד״ה ורבי.

70. דברים ו:ז

71. ברכות דף יג עמוד ב

whole first paragraph[72] are necessary to fulfill the Torah commandment,[73] and there are those who are of the opinion that the first two paragraphs[74] of the Shema constitute the commandment, since both paragraphs contain the biblical source of the commandment, וּבְשָׁכְבְּךָ וּבְקוּמֶךָ.[75] According to the Rambam, it seems that all three paragraphs[76] fulfill the Torah's requirement for this commandment.[77]

The three paragraphs that make up the Shema are not arranged according to their order in the Torah. The third section, פָּרָשַׁת צִיצִית (Numbers 15:37–41), precedes the other two in the Torah (וְאָהַבְתָּ, Deuteronomy 6:4–9; and וְהָיָה אִם שָׁמוֹעַ, Deuteronomy 11:13–21). In reading the Megillah, we would not fulfill our obligation if we changed the order of the chapters, because it must be read in its proper order.[78] In reciting the Shema, however, the paragraphs were arranged according to their conceptual order rather than in a sequence that tells a story, as in the Megillah.[79] Nevertheless, if a person were to change the order of the verses within each paragraph, the Shema would not be valid.[80]

The intention of the first verse of the Shema is to convey the idea of יִחוּד ה' (that Hashem is one).[81] Rashi explains that ה' אֱלֹקֵינוּ ה' אֶחָד

---

72. דברים, פרק ו', פס' ד'-ט'

73. See תלמידי רבינו יונה ברכות דף ט עמוד א; שאגת אריה סימן ב. The first Tosafot in Berachot (ברכות ב עמוד א ד"ה מאימתי) states that Rashi believes that the primary קְרִיאַת שְׁמַע is recited at night before one goes to bed (קְרִיאַת שְׁמַע עַל הַמִּטָּה), and in Rashi's siddur (סימן תכט) he says that at night before one goes to bed you only read Shema and the first paragraph up to וְהָיָה אִם שָׁמֹעַ.

74. דברים, פרק י"א, פס' י"ג-כ"א and דברים, פרק ו', פס' ד'-ט'

75. See R. Shmuel b. Meshulam Gerondi, ספר אהל מועד דף כא עמוד א; פרי חדש אורח חיים סימן סז.

76. במדבר, פרק ט"ו, פס' ל"ז-מ"א and דברים, פרק י"א, פס' י"ג-כ"א; דברים, פרק ו', פס' ד'-ט'

77. רמב"ם הלכות קריאת שמע פרק א, הלכה ב, הלכה ג. See *Shiurim Lezecher Abba Mari z"l* (Mosad Harav Kook: Jerusalem, 2002), pp. 15–16, and קרית ספר הל' קריאת שמע.

78. שולחן ערוך אורח חיים סימן תרצ סעיף ו

79. ברכות דף יג עמוד א, רמב"ם הלכות קריאת שמע ב:יא

80. שולחן ערוך אורח חיים סימן סד סעיף א

81. Since so many parts of the Shema have different nuances that would be

means, "Hashem, who is now only our God and rejected by the rest of the world, will soon be recognized and worshipped by the whole human race."[82] According to Rashi, then, the first verse is a prayer for the future.[83]

In the Torah, two letters of the first line of the Shema are larger than the other letters: the ע (ayin) of שְׁמַע and the ד (dalet) of אֶחָד. The Avudraham points out that the ע and ד can be read as עֵד (witness) meaning, "You[Israel] are My witnesses."[84] In the first verse of the Shema, we testify that God is what the philosophers termed the Prime Mover, which means the Creator of the cosmos. Others explain that the ד of אֶחָד is larger than the other letters so that we should not misread it as a ר (resh) and say אַחֵר (another), which would be heresy. A third view suggests that those two letters have been written larger to direct our attention to the fact that the statement framed by them expresses the foundation of Judaism.[85]

The Avudraham points out that the word שְׁמַע contains allusions to major Jewish concepts. It is an acrostic for שְׂאוּ מָרוֹם עֵינֵיכֶם ("Lift up your eyes to the heavens"), which we should do שַׁחֲרִית מִנְחָה עַרְבִית (morning, afternoon and night). The message is that שד־י מֶלֶךְ עוֹלָם (the Almighty is the Supreme King). If you do this, you will accept עוֹל מַלְכוּת שָׁמַיִם (acceptance of God's sovereignty), a backward acrostic of שְׁמַע.

---

ignored by a translation, we preferably should not read the Shema in a foreign language. The Hebrew text naturally includes all possible interpretations. However, the Shulchan Aruch does make provisions for when there is no alternative (שולחן ערוך אורח חיים הלכות קריאת שמע סימן סב, סעיף ב). You should be careful when you read the Shema in another language that you understand its meaning. See Mishnah Berurah (משנה ברורה סימן סב סעיף ב ד"ה בכל לשון).

82. רש"י דברים פרק ו פסוק ד

83. Rashi's explanation fits well in Musaf of Rosh Hashanah. There, the last verse of the middle berachah of the Musaf Amidah, Malchiyot, acknowledging God as Ruler of the world, is the Shema. The last verse in each of the three middle sections is a request, so the explanation of Rashi fits in perfectly with this theme.

84. ספר אבודרהם דיני קריאת שמע

85. בעל הטורים, דברים ו:ד

The Gemara[86] tells us that when we recite the Shema, we should extend the pronunciation of אֶחָד and our lives will be extended. Rabbi Acha bar Yaakov says that we should especially extend the last letter of the word, ד (dalet). Rav Ashi adds that we must not thereby shorten the pronunciation of the letter before, ח (chet).

After the first line of the Shema, we continue with the first paragraph, וְאָהַבְתָּ. Strangely, we interrupt the continuity of the biblical passage by saying בָּרוּךְ שֵׁם כְּבוֹד מַלְכוּתוֹ לְעוֹלָם וָעֶד. It is our custom to say this silently, except on Yom Kippur when we recite it aloud.

If one forgets to say בָּרוּךְ שֵׁם כְּבוֹד מַלְכוּתוֹ לְעוֹלָם וָעֶד, does that invalidate the recitation of the Shema? There are different opinions regarding this issue. The Levush says that if you do not say it, or even if you say it without the proper intention, you have not fulfilled the requirement to say the Shema properly.[87] He believes that בָּרוּךְ שֵׁם כְּבוֹד מַלְכוּתוֹ לְעוֹלָם וָעֶד has been included as part of the requirement of the mitzvah of Shema because it is also an expression of קַבָּלַת עֹל שָׁמַיִם מַלְכוּת. Others disagree.[88]

The Shema should contain 248 words, which correspond to the number of organs in the human body as well as the number of positive mitzvot in the Torah.[89] Actually, it is three words short. The Rama rules that one who recites the Shema alone (without a minyan) should add three words, קֵל מֶלֶךְ נֶאֱמָן ("God, faithful King"), at the very beginning of the Shema. Thus, even without a chazzan, an individual says 248 words. When you daven with a congregation, however, you should definitely not say these three words because the chazzan repeats the three words ה׳ אֱלֹקֵיכֶם אֱמֶת.[90]

Rav Soloveitchik, even when praying privately without a minyan,

---

86. ברכות יג עמ׳ ב

87. לבוש אורח חיים סימן סג סעיף ה

88. ב"ח אורח חיים סימן סא. See also ביאור הלכה סימן סא סעיף יג.

89. שולחן ערוך אורח חיים סימן סא, סעיף ג. This originates in מדרש תנחומא [בובר] פרשת קדושים סימן ו, ו: קדושים תהיו.

90. רמ"א על שולחן ערוך אורח חיים סימן סא, סעיף ג: ויש שכתבו

never said קֵל מֶלֶךְ נֶאֱמָן because he considered it an interruption between the berachot and the recitation of the Shema.[91]

The first full paragraph of the Shema begins: וְאָהַבְתָּ אֵת ה׳ אֱלֹקֶיךָ. We should love God, at least for all the good that He does for us. He nourishes us and watches over us. What is the definition of love? When we say that parents love their children, or a husband loves his wife, we mean that they are ready to make sacrifices for one another. Similarly, in the recitation of the Shema we are asked to make sacrifices for God. Sometimes they are small sacrifices, such as not eating certain food because we are not sure if it is kosher. Sometimes they are bigger sacrifices, such as giving up a well-paying job in order to observe Shabbat. Sometimes it even means giving our life for God. According to Rabbi Akiva,[92] it means dying עַל קִידּוּשׁ הַשֵּׁם (a martyr's death). While the Romans tortured him to death, he recited the Shema and accepted the sovereignty of God. Rabbi Akiva's students asked him, "Do you have to be reciting the Shema even under these difficult circumstances?" Rabbi Akiva explained to them, "All my life I agonized that I could not serve God בְּכָל נַפְשְׁךָ ('with all your soul'). Now that I have the opportunity to do so, should I not carry it out?"

The Talmud also interprets וְאָהַבְתָּ אֵת ה׳ אֱלֹקֶיךָ in the following way: שֶׁיְּהֵא שֵׁם שָׁמַיִם מִתְאָהֵב עַל יָדֶךָ (make God's name beloved through your actions). If a person lives up to the high standards of Judaism, people will say, "See how pleasant are his ways, how proper are his deeds." The verse states about such people: "You are My servant, Israel, in whom I will be glorified" (Isaiah 49:3).[93]

The verse וְאָהַבְתָּ אֵת ה׳ אֱלֹקֶיךָ demands of us that we love God בְּכָל לְבָבְךָ ("with all your heart"), which the Rabbis interpret to mean "with both the evil inclination and the good inclination";[94] בְּכָל נַפְשְׁךָ ("with all your soul") which Rabbi Akiva interpreted as "even if you have to give your life for it"; and וּבְכָל מְאֹדֶךָ ("with all your property"). Rabbi

---

91. See חידושי הרמב״ן ברכות דף יא עמוד ב.
92. ברכות דף סא עמוד ב
93. יומא דף פו עמוד א
94. ברכות דף נד עמוד א

Eliezer explains why the Torah demands your life, if necessary, and your property: Sometimes a person's body is his dearest possession. In that case he must give his life to God. Sometimes a person's property is his dearest possession. Then he must sacrifice all his property to God.[95]

The verse וְאָהַבְתָּ אֵת ה׳ אֱלֹקֶיךָ is in the second-person singular. At the beginning of the second paragraph of the Shema, we are also asked to love God בְּכָל לְבַבְכֶם וּבְכָל נַפְשְׁכֶם ("with all your hearts and with all your souls").[96] Why is this verse in the second-person plural, and why doesn't this verse also add וּבְכָל מְאֹדְכֶם? It has been suggested that there are some people who value their property more than their lives, but that is not the normal way of thinking. The reason that the second paragraph of the Shema is in the plural is because in the second paragraph of the Shema, God does not address an individual but the entire community. That is why וּבְכָל מְאֹדְכֶם (with all your property) was left out of the series listed in the first paragraph. An entire community would never be so foolish as to value its possessions more than everyone's lives.[97] When anti-Semitism has arisen, there have been cases where people could have saved their lives by leaving all their possessions behind, but they valued them too much to do so. In the end, they lost both their lives and their property.

In the first paragraph of the Shema, we say וְשִׁנַּנְתָּם לְבָנֶיךָ which means "you shall teach them to your children so they know them well"; in the second paragraph, we say וְלִמַּדְתֶּם אֹתָם אֶת בְּנֵיכֶם, "you shall teach them to your children." What is the difference between these verses? Rav Soloveitchik pointed out that the first verse refers to the relationship between a rebbe and his students. Rashi interprets וְשִׁנַּנְתָּם as "if someone asks you a question, you should be able to answer immediately," and לְבָנֶיךָ as "your students."[98] In short, this verse speaks about the kind of deep Torah scholarship that only a rebbe can impart

95. ברכות דף נד עמוד א.
96. דברים יא:יג
97. See שפתי חכמים, דברים י"א.
98. רש"י דברים פרק ו פסוק ז

to his students. In the second paragraph, Rashi writes[99] that "a child old enough to speak should be taught to recite תּוֹרָה צִוָּה־לָנוּ מֹשֶׁה מוֹרָשָׁה קְהִלַּת יַעֲקֹב ('Moshe commanded us the Torah, an inheritance to the community of Jacob'[100])." Thus, וְלִמַּדְתֶּם אֹתָם אֶת בְּנֵיכֶם refers to such a parent-child relationship.[101]

The Gemara also derives another principle from the word וְלִמַּדְתֶּם: The Amora Rav Ovadyah explains the word to mean שֶׁיְּהֵא לִמּוּדְךָ תָּם, that your teaching must be complete, i.e., that the words should not be slurred together.[102] One should take care to enunciate the words properly. For example, when saying עַל לְבָבֶךָ, we would ordinarily only sound one "lamed" at the juncture of the two words, *al le*. However, when reading Shema, one must pause between the two words so that each word is recited completely.[103] Similarly, the Rabbis explain וּכְתַבְתָּם: This word can also be divided into two words, וּכְתַב תָּם (write completely) as meaning that each letter must be written exactly according to its specifications.[104]

The phrase וְלִמַּדְתֶּם אֹתָם אֶת בְּנֵיכֶם was interpreted by the Rabbis as "sons," meaning, "not your daughters."[105] This verse is the source for women's exemption from the mitzvah of studying Torah. However, as we have noted, the Chafetz Chayim pointed out that if we must teach Torah to a gentile woman for her to convert to Judaism, we certainly have the right and the obligation to teach the basics of Judaism to Jewish women and girls. There are many opinions among the leading rabbis about how much Torah to teach girls. Rav Soloveitchik always wanted to give girls the maximum Torah education possible.

The Gemara[106] tells us that אַנְשֵׁי כְּנֶסֶת הַגְּדוֹלָה included the paragraph

---

99. רש"י דברים פרק יא פסוק יט

100. דברים לג:ד

101. קידושין כט עמוד ב

102. ברכות דף טו עמוד ב

103. See שולחן ערוך אורח חיים סימן סא סעיף כ.

104. רש"י מסכת ברכות דף טו עמוד ב: וכתבתם - שתהא כתיבה תמה ושלימה. See also מסכת שבת דף קג עמוד ב: מיתיבי: וכתבתם - שתהא כתיבה תמה.

105. קידושין כט עמוד ב

106. ברכות דף יב עמוד ב

of וַיֹּאמֶר in the Shema. In addition to mentioning the Exodus from Egypt, it contains the mitzvah of tzitzit and the obligation of accepting the commandments. It also warns us not to be swayed by thoughts of heresy, immorality or idolatry. There is an obligation to remember the Exodus from Egypt each day.[107] The Rambam[108] connects the mitzvah of Shema with the obligation of remembering the Exodus from Egypt. Rav Soloveitchik explained[109] that according to the Rambam, remembering the Exodus from Egypt is not its own mitzvah but part of the mitzvah of Shema. The Gemara[110] explains that the words אֲנִי ה׳ אֱלֹקֵיכֶם refer to God's sovereignty. In the third paragraph of Shema we say אֲנִי ה׳ אֱלֹקֵיכֶם in mentioning the Exodus. The mitzvah of Shema includes the obligation to accept God's sovereignty by mentioning the Exodus from Egypt. In other words, part of קַבָּלַת עוֹל מַלְכוּת שָׁמַיִם is recognizing God's redemptive role in our lives.

The Gemara[111] tells us that we must not interrupt between the words ה׳ אֱלֹקֵיכֶם at the end of the paragraph of וַיֹּאמֶר and the word "אֱמֶת" of the following blessing, which is not from the Torah. The Gemara ties this phrase to the verse which says ה׳ אֱלֹקִים אֱמֶת.[112] If you have to interrupt (for example, to answer the Kedushah), it must be after you say the word אֱמֶת.[113] The Erech Lechem[114] explains that we must not interrupt between the paragraph of וַיֹּאמֶר and the word אֱמֶת because אֱמֶת means truth, and God's signature characteristic, is truth.

When the chazzan repeats ה׳ אֱלֹקֵיכֶם and adds אֱמֶת, it brings the number of words in the three paragraphs of Shema to equal 248, the number of parts of the body. An individual who prays without a minyan cannot rely on the chazzan's recitation to reach the number

---

107. Berachot 12b.
108. רמב"ם הלכות קריאת שמע פרק א הלכה ג
109. See *Shiurim Lezecher Abba Mari z"l*, pp. 13–16.
110. ראש השנה דף לב עמ׳ א
111. ברכות דף יד עמ׳ א
112. ירמיהו י:י
113. שולחן ערוך אורח חיים סימן סו סעיף ה
114. ערך לחם אורח חיים סימן סא

248. The Shulchan Aruch gives a somewhat complicated solution: The 15 words following אֱמֶת each begin with the letter ו, the sixth letter of the alef beit. In gematria, "ו" stands for 6. Fifteen vavs equals 90. The gematria of Hashem's name is 26 (5 = ה + 6 = ו + 5 = ה + 10 = י 26 =) and the addition of the four letters themselves brings us to 30. By reciting these fifteen vavs which equal 90, it is as if we are reciting Hashem's name three more times and thus filling in the three missing words from the count of 248.[115] The Rama cites another opinion according to which one praying alone adds the words אֵ־ל מֶלֶךְ נֶאֱמָן before Shema, in place of the Amen that one would have answered to the Chazzan's blessing. However, as we discussed earlier regarding Amen, others maintain that one shouldn't interrupt between the berachot before Shema and the Shema itself.[116]

115. שולחן ערוך אורח חיים סימן סא סעיף ג

116. מגן אברהם סימן סא ס"ק ד; ערוך השולחן סימן סא סעיף יב

The Amidah: Introduction

The שְׁמוֹנֶה עֶשְׂרֵה is the central prayer in every service. Its most common form, recited on weekdays, consists of nineteen berachot, the original eighteen which give it its name, plus one berachah added on at a slightly later date. Because it must be recited while standing, it is also called the עֲמִידָה (the Hebrew word for standing). These names are synonymous.[1]

The Amidah is the core of a prayer service. While the Shema is specifically recited only at two specific times of the day, the Amidah is included in every Jewish prayer service: morning, afternoon and evening services of weekdays, Shabbat and Yom Tov, as well as Musaf and Ne'ilah.

Originally, there was no set text. One praised God, made requests of God, and then thanked God in his or her own words. When the Jewish people came back to Israel at the beginning of the Second Commonwealth, they had lost their ability to express themselves freely in Hebrew. This was because of widespread ignorance due to assimilation in the exile. The אַנְשֵׁי כְּנֶסֶת הַגְּדוֹלָה, the 120 scholars that included, among others, Ezra, Nechemiah, Haggai, Zechariah, Malachi, and Mordechai,[2] were responsible for standardizing the שְׁמוֹנֶה עֶשְׂרֵה.[3] Their format is the one that we follow today.[4]

1. רמב"ם הלכות תפילה ונשיאת כפים פרק ה' הל' א
2. ר' עובדיה מברטנורא אבות פרק א משנה א
3. מגילה דף יז עמוד ב
4. רמב"ם הלכות תפילה ונשיאת כפים פרק א הלכה ד. Also see יד המלך הלכות תפילה ונשיאת כפים פרק א הלכה ד.

The Amidah begins with the phrase ה׳ שְׂפָתַי תִּפְתָּח וּפִי יַגִּיד תְּהִלָּתֶךָ ("Hashem, open my lips, and my mouth will tell Your praise"). People who think that the first words of the Amidah are בָּרוּךְ אַתָּה ה׳ אֱלֹקֵינוּ וֵאלֹקֵי אֲבוֹתֵינוּ ("Blessed are You, Hashem, our God and God of our ancestors") are mistaken. Many people recite כִּי שֵׁם ה׳ אֶקְרָא הָבוּ גֹדֶל לֵאלֹקֵינוּ ("When I call on the name of Hashem, ascribe greatness to our God") before ה׳ שְׂפָתַי תִּפְתָּח during Musaf and Minchah. I do not say it, and most sources also do not suggest it.[5] The last words of the שְׁמוֹנֶה עֶשְׂרֵה are: יִהְיוּ לְרָצוֹן אִמְרֵי פִי וְהֶגְיוֹן לִבִּי לְפָנֶיךָ. ה׳ צוּרִי וְגוֹאֲלִי ("May the words spoken by my mouth and the intention of my heart come before You, Hashem, my Rock and Redeemer"[6]). This verse as well as ה׳ שְׂפָתַי תִּפְתָּח were added by the Rabbis of the Talmud.[7]

The chazzan must start repeating the שְׁמוֹנֶה עֶשְׂרֵה with ה׳ שְׂפָתַי תִּפְתָּח וּפִי יַגִּיד תְּהִלָּתֶךָ, as it is part of the שְׁמוֹנֶה עֶשְׂרֵה.[8] This means that the chazzan must recite the ה׳ שְׂפָתַי תִּפְתָּח out loud, because we have no need for a chazzan to daven silently. Similarly, at the end, יִהְיוּ לְרָצוֹן אִמְרֵי פִי וְהֶגְיוֹן לִבִּי לְפָנֶיךָ ה׳ צוּרִי וְגוֹאֲלִי is part of the שְׁמוֹנֶה עֶשְׂרֵה, and it should be said aloud by the chazzan.[9]

---

5. See טור אורח חיים סימן קיא who quotes this custom. The שולחן ערוך אורח חיים הלכות תפלה סימן קיא, סעיף א says one should not add sentences after the berachah of גָּאַל יִשְׂרָאֵל and before the Amidah except for the sentence ה׳ שְׂפָתַי תִּפְתָּח וּפִי יַגִּיד תְּהִלָּתֶךָ (תהלים נא, יז). The עטרת צבי אורח חיים סימן קיא ס״ק ב notes specifically that one should not add (דברים ל:ג) כִּי שֵׁם ה׳ אֶקְרָא הָבוּ גֹדֶל לֵאלֹקֵינוּ in Shacharit or Ma'ariv, because one must not interrupt between גָּאַל יִשְׂרָאֵל and the Amidah. He also quotes the Maharshal (שו״ת מהרש״ל סימן סד) who writes that he did not say it even before Musaf and Minchah, when there is no problem of interruption.

6. תהלים פרק יט:טו

7. ברכות דף ד עמ׳ ב. See also רמב״ם הלכות תפילה פרק ב הלכה ט.

8. שולחן ערוך אורח חיים סימן קיא סעיף ב

9. The Rama (אורח חיים סימן קכג סעיף ו) maintains that the chazzan does not need to recite the verse יִהְיוּ לְרָצוֹן אִמְרֵי פִי וְהֶגְיוֹן לִבִּי לְפָנֶיךָ, because he can rely on the fact that he will ask for his prayer to be accepted when he says Kaddish at the end of the service (משנה ברורה סימן קכג ס״ק כא). But the Mishnah Berurah (שם) quotes the view of the Shelah and Vilna Gaon who maintain that the chazzan should recite this verse.

Why did the Rabbis choose these two specific verses to serve as the beginning and the end of the שְׁמוֹנֶה עֶשְׂרֵה? The opening verse, ה׳ שְׂפָתַי תִּפְתָּח וּפִי יַגִּיד תְּהִלָּתֶךָ, has the same theme as many other verses. The ending verse, יִהְיוּ לְרָצוֹן אִמְרֵי פִי וְהֶגְיוֹן לִבִּי לְפָנֶיךָ ה׳ צוּרִי וְגוֹאֲלִי, could just as nicely have served as the opening verse. Placing these verses in their context in the Book of Psalms, however, will help us to understand why they were chosen here.

ה׳ שְׂפָתַי תִּפְתָּח וּפִי יַגִּיד תְּהִלָּתֶךָ is found in Psalm 51.[10] There King David asks God for forgiveness for his great sin with Batsheva when he caused her husband, Uriah, to be killed. The verse following ה׳ שְׂפָתַי תִּפְתָּח is כִּי לֹא־תַחְפֹּץ זֶבַח וְאֶתֵּנָה עוֹלָה לֹא תִרְצֶה ("You do not want me to bring sacrifices; You do not desire burnt offerings"). Rabbenu Yonah[11] explains that David was unable to bring a sacrifice for his sin because it was committed intentionally.[12] Only sincere repentance could free David from this sin, as the following verse states: זִבְחֵי אֱלֹקִים רוּחַ נִשְׁבָּרָה לֵב נִשְׁבָּר וְנִדְכֶּה אֱלֹקִים לֹא תִבְזֶה ("Repentance is what God desires as much as sacrifices; a broken and remorseful heart is the essence of repentance").[13] Nowadays, that we cannot offer sacrifices for our sins, we are all in a situation similar to that of King David. Our sincere prayers must take the place of sacrifices. The introductory verse that the Rabbis chose implies that if our sins are impediments to our prayers being accepted by God, then ה׳ שְׂפָתַי תִּפְתָּח, let us trust that in Your Divine grace, You will free us from our sins.

יִהְיוּ לְרָצוֹן אִמְרֵי פִי וְהֶגְיוֹן לִבִּי לְפָנֶיךָ ה׳ צוּרִי וְגוֹאֲלִי is the last verse of Psalm 19, one of the Psalms that we say on Shabbat morning. Our use of this verse as the end of the שְׁמוֹנֶה עֶשְׂרֵה indicates that we imitate King David's method of prayer as much as possible. Our praise of God is faulty. If any human being came close to the paradigm of the proper understanding of God's greatness, it was King David, and we imitate him in our prayer service whenever we can. This is his nineteenth

---

10. תהלים נא:יז
11. רבינו יונה על הרי״ף ברכות דף ג עמוד א
12. See רמב״ם הלכות שגגות פרק א הלכה א.
13. Based on Ibn Ezra, תהלים נא:יט.

Psalm, so after our nineteenth berachah, we conclude with the same words that he did. Our hesitancy to innovate comes from a fear that we have no right even to pray at all. How can we, after all, speak to God? Nobody is as great as King David in praising God. It is only by following the precedent of our ancestors that we feel we can be so bold.

The berachot of שְׁמוֹנֶה עֶשְׂרֵה are divided into three parts. The first part praises God, the middle part consists of petitions to God to fill our needs, and the last part gives thanks.

The first berachah of the שְׁמוֹנֶה עֶשְׂרֵה, known as אָבוֹת (Patriarchs), is also referred to by its closing, מָגֵן אַבְרָהָם ("Shield of Abraham"). The second berachah, known as גְּבוּרוֹת (Powers of God), is sometimes referred to by its closing, מְחַיֵּה הַמֵּתִים ("who revives the dead"). The third berachah of the שְׁמוֹנֶה עֶשְׂרֵה, known as קְדוּשַּׁת הַשֵּׁם (Holiness of God) is sometimes referred to by its closing, הָקֵל הַקָּדוֹשׁ ("the holy God"). These three berachot of praise are present in every Amidah.[14]

Similarly, the last three berachot are also constant in every שְׁמוֹנֶה עֶשְׂרֵה. It is the middle section that changes, based on the occasion. On weekdays we have thirteen berachot where we ask God for help in specific matters. On Shabbat and Yom Tov, we have only one berachah in the middle, which is called קְדוּשַּׁת הַיּוֹם (Holiness of the Day). This berachah discusses the sanctity of that particular day.[15] The only exception to this rule is Musaf on Rosh Hashanah, when there are three berachot in the middle section.

If I were to mistakenly say the weekday שְׁמוֹנֶה עֶשְׂרֵה on Shabbat or Yom Tov, the Shulchan Aruch rules that I would have fulfilled my obligation, because the obligation is simply to say the שְׁמוֹנֶה עֶשְׂרֵה. I must, however, make some mention of Shabbat or the appropriate Yom Tov.[16]

Why did the אַנְשֵׁי כְּנֶסֶת הַגְּדוֹלָה introduce a different שְׁמוֹנֶה עֶשְׂרֵה for Shabbat and the holidays? If we pray sincerely, the middle berachot

---

14. רש״י עבודה זרה דף ז עמוד ב
15. רמב״ם הלכות תפילה ונשיאת כפים פרק ב הלכה ה
16. שולחן ערוך אורח חיים סימן רסח סעיף ד

can sometimes upset us. When we say רְפָאֵנוּ ה׳ ("Heal us, Hashem"), we might think of someone dear to us who is sick. When we say בָּרֵךְ עָלֵינוּ ה׳ אֱלֹקֵינוּ אֶת הַשָּׁנָה הַזֹּאת ("Bless us this year") regarding our livelihood, if we are having a hard time making a living, then that berachah might distress us. These "weekday worries" would disturb the harmony of Shabbat.[17] Our Rabbis, therefore, wrote a more neutral berachah for Shabbat. After Shabbat, we can again return to our weekday worries.

Bowing in the שְׁמוֹנֶה עֶשְׂרֵה

When praying the שְׁמוֹנֶה עֶשְׂרֵה, there are four times that we bow. We bow at the beginning and the end of the first blessing and at the beginning and the end of the blessing of thanks, מוֹדִים.[18] There is a symbolism for bowing down in the beginning and the end of the שְׁמוֹנֶה עֶשְׂרֵה. The custom used to be that when a person approached a king to ask a favor, he would bow one or more times when he first came into the king's presence, and after he made his petition, when leaving the king, he would likewise bow one or more times as well. To bow when we come into God's presence follows ancient and well-established practices. It shows that we are subjugating ourselves to our King.[19]

Ordinary people bow down before the King four times in the שְׁמוֹנֶה עֶשְׂרֵה. People who might find it more difficult than most to subjugate themselves to anyone must remind themselves that even they too must subjugate themselves to God. That is why the כֹּהֵן גָּדוֹל must bow for each blessing, and the Jewish king must remain bowed until the end of the שְׁמוֹנֶה עֶשְׂרֵה.[20]

---

17. See מדרש תנחומא, פרשת וירא סימן א; ספר המנהיג, הלכות שבת סימן יא. The Mordechai (מרדכי מסכת ברכות פרק שלושה שאכלו רמז קע״ה) writes that not pleading for our needs on Shabbat is based on a Yerushalmi (ירושלמי פרק אלו קשרים, שבת פרק טו) that says אָסוּר לִתְבֹּעַ צְרָכָיו בְּשַׁבָּת.

18. שולחן ערוך אורח חיים סימן קיג סעיף א

19. לבוש אורח חיים סימן קיג

20. רמב״ם הלכות תפילה פרק ה הלכה י; ברכות דף לד עמוד ב

We should bow by bending[21] until all the vertebrae of our spine protrude.[22] When bowing, one should not merely bend at the waist but take care to bend one's head down as well.[23] This bending brings to mind the verse in Psalms,[24] כָּל עַצְמוֹתַי תֹּאמַרְנָה יְיָ מִי כָמוֹךָ ("All my bones will say, 'God! Who is like You!'").

THE AMIDAH: BERACHOT OF PRAISE

When we begin the שְׁמוֹנֶה עֶשְׂרֵה, we take three steps forward to enter the presence of God. We approach God hesitantly, just as we would hesitatingly approach an important person who has our fate in his or her hands. The Torah uses three expressions for the realm of God: עָנָן (cloud), עֲרָפֶל (fog), and רָקִיעַ (firmament). We enter the presence of God by taking a step forward for each one of the realms of God.

The First Berachah: אָבוֹת

Why was the berachah of אָבוֹת (Patriarchs) chosen to be the first berachah? If you were asked to arrange the order of the first three berachot, it might seem like a good idea to start with the second or third berachah, which acknowledge God's power and holiness. Why start with a berachah about human beings?

The answer is that without the Patriarchs, we could not daven. Abraham, Isaac and Jacob set the precedent of prayer for us, so we may imitate them. They established our right to pray, to stand before God, to praise God, and to make requests of Him. They also dictated the pattern of our daily prayer services: Abraham established Shacharit, Isaac established Minchah, and Jacob established Ma'ariv.[25]

When we look at the first berachah of the שְׁמוֹנֶה עֶשְׂרֵה, we notice

---

21. שולחן ערוך אורח חיים סימן קיג סעיף ד: רמב"ם הלכות תפילה פרק ה הלכה יב: רש"י ברכות דף כח ע"ב
22. ברכות דף כח עמוד ב
23. שולחן ערוך אורח חיים סימן קיג סעיף ד
24. תהלים לה:י
25. ברכות דף כו עמוד ב

a few problems. Normally a berachah begins with בָּרוּךְ אַתָּה ה׳ אֱלֹקֵינוּ מֶלֶךְ הָעוֹלָם and finishes with a specific ending. The proper beginning of a berachah must contain two essential parts: the name of the One to whom we are praying ("Blessed are You, Hashem our God") and an acknowledgment of God's sovereignty ("King of the universe").

The first berachah of the Amidah, which is the only one that opens with בָּרוּךְ אַתָּה ה׳, seemingly leaves out the sovereignty aspect. It begins, בָּרוּךְ אַתָּה ה׳ אֱלֹקֵינוּ וֵאלֹקֵי אֲבוֹתֵינוּ אֱלֹקֵי אַבְרָהָם אֱלֹקֵי יִצְחָק וֵאלֹקֵי יַעֲקֹב ("Blessed are You, Hashem our God and God of our ancestors, God of Abraham, God of Isaac, and God of Jacob") and does not mention "King of the universe." This is because saying "God of Abraham" is akin to saying "King of the universe." Before Abraham, there were no people who believed in one God, only people who believed in many gods. Abraham, by his philosophical speculation and his keen mind, discovered the existence of God. He "crowned" God, so to speak, because ever since Abraham there have always been people who believe in God.[26]

Another issue is that this berachah does not follow a chronological order. We begin by saying, אֱלֹקֵינוּ וֵאלֹקֵי אֲבוֹתֵינוּ ("our God and God of our ancestors"). Our ancestors preceded us, so why don't we say it in the proper order – אֱלֹקֵי אֲבוֹתֵינוּ וֵאלֹקֵינוּ (God of our ancestors and our God)? Although it is true that we know of God because of patriarchs' insights and teachings, we should also try to discover God ourselves. We should be a little philosophically independent, as was Abraham, and discover God for ourselves. To whom do we owe this beautiful world and all the pleasures that we have? Whatever we cannot discover on our own, for that we should rely on our ancestors.[27]

Stylistically, this berachah is also quite redundant. Usually we avoid saying any name of God too often; here, we repeat it as much as possible. Wouldn't it be sufficient to say, "God of Abraham, Isaac, and Jacob," instead of "God of Abraham, God of Isaac, and God of Jacob"? When we speak about God, our relationship to God should be like

---

26. טור אורח חיים סימן קיג

27. *Dover Shalom* in *Otzar Hatefillot*, p. 308.

the relationship of Abraham to God, the relationship of Isaac to God, and the relationship of Jacob to God. Each one of the patriarchs had a different relationship with God, and we should try on our own to incorporate them all and even develop our own individual relationship with God.[28]

Abraham's relationship to God was founded upon his philosophical speculations. Abraham wondered who created this universe with everything coordinated so beautifully. He looked heavenward, saw the sun, and could scarcely look at it, so he thought the sun must be the creator of the universe. Then evening came, and the sun disappeared. Abraham concluded from this, "The Creator could not be the sun; it disappeared, and God would not disappear. The Creator must be the moon." Then the moon disappeared. Abraham continued his quest until he realized that the sun and moon are only creations of God and that God, who is invisible, called them into being.[29] Similarly, our relationship to God should be like Abraham's, one of philosophical speculation. Through our mental capacities we should understand the existence of God.

Isaac's relationship to God consisted of being willing to give up his life when Abraham bound him on the altar as a sacrifice. Our relationship to God must be one in which we are willing to give up our lives if that is demanded. Sometimes we are not called upon to make that supreme sacrifice, but only to make other, lesser sacrifices. Observing Shabbat is sometimes a sacrifice. Eating only kosher food is another type of sacrifice.

Jacob's relationship to God was never losing faith even though his life was a chain of misfortunes. His father favored his brother Esau who hated him. His uncle Laban persecuted him. His daughter was abducted. His favored wife died in childbirth. Then his favorite son disappeared. He never had a moment's peace in his life. Nobody suffered as much as Jacob, yet he never lost his faith in God.

---

28. *Eitz Yosef* and *Dover Shalom* in *Otzar Hatefillot*, p. 308. See also ספר בעל שם טוב, פרשת ויצא, ו ד"ה אני ה' אלקי אברהם אביך ואלקי יצחק.

29. נדרים דף לב עמוד א.

The next line of the first berachah is הָאֵ־ל הַגָּדוֹל הַגִּבּוֹר וְהַנּוֹרָא ("The Lord who is great, mighty, and awesome"). The Gemara[30] tells us that the terms used here to describe God were chosen carefully. Rabbi Chaninah was teaching his students, and it was time to daven, so he appointed one of the students to lead the davening. When the student came to the words describing God, he added a list of other adjectives as well. When he was through Rabbi Chaninah said to him, "Did you finish enumerating all the attributes of your Creator?" Rabbi Chaninah explained to his student that we cannot attempt to enumerate all of God's attributes because there are so many, and we cannot understand His greatness. So, we mention only the three that Moses already taught us: הַגָּדוֹל הַגִּבּוֹר וְהַנּוֹרָא (great, mighty, and awesome).[31] Here again we follow in the footsteps of our ancestors. We cannot fathom God's attributes, but Moses set a precedent for us.

In recent decades it has become very popular to compose one's own prayers. We should not do this casually. Today we have no prophets in our midst. Among the Men of the Great Assembly, there were several prophets. No ordinary person wrote the text of our prayers. There is much wisdom in our prayers that seems to have been inspired by God. We therefore should be very careful not to add to or subtract from the text.[32]

The expression אֵ־ל עֶלְיוֹן ("the highest God"), which is the next phrase in the berachah, was coined by מַלְכִּי־צֶדֶק (Melchitzedek), the king to whom Abraham brought a tithe.[33] Since Melchitzedek called God "אֵ־ל עֶלְיוֹן" and it was such an apt phrase, the Rabbis followed Melchitzedek's precedent.[34]

The next phrase, גּוֹמֵל חֲסָדִים טוֹבִים ("who performs good acts of

30. ברכות דף לג עמוד ב
31. דברים י:יז
32. יד המלך הלכות תפילה פרק א הלכה ד on the Rambam, citing ברכות מ, ב.
33. בראשית יד:כ
34. רמב"ן בראשית פרק יד, פסוק יח explains that all the nations served angels that were called אֵלִים (powerful beings), so referring to Hashem as the extreme powerful being (קֵל עֶלְיוֹן) indicates that God is the Supreme Being.

kindness") seems redundant. Aren't all acts of kindness good? If a kindness is not good, then it isn't a kindness. The trouble, however, is that although human beings intend to be kind and helpful, they are not always successful. A physician who wants the best for you may prescribe a medication that has terrible side effects. The doctor may have meant well, but you suffered. When God performs an act of kindness, however, it never goes wrong. It always helps you. It can only be a good kindness, not like fallible, human kindnesses.[35]

Then we say וְקוֹנֵה הַכֹּל, which literally means that God "acquires everything." This is another way of saying that God is the Creator of everything, so everything in the world belongs to God. In the weekday שְׁמוֹנֶה עֶשְׂרֵה we say גּוֹמֵל חֲסָדִים טוֹבִים וְקוֹנֵה הַכֹּל, but in the abbreviated repetition of the Amidah that the chazzan says on Friday night, it says קוֹנֵה שָׁמַיִם וָאָרֶץ ("who acquires heaven and earth") instead. Why do we specify on Friday night but not on weekdays that "everything" means the heavens above and the earth below? Shabbat celebrates the creation of heavens and the earth; therefore, on Shabbat we specify God's ownership of heaven and earth.[36]

The next phrase, וּמֵבִיא גוֹאֵל לִבְנֵי בְנֵיהֶם לְמַעַן שְׁמוֹ בְּאַהֲבָה ("And God lovingly brings a redeemer to their children's children for His name's sake"), says that no matter what happens or how many generations pass, the redeemer, or Messiah, will come one day, to redeem God's children because of God's name, because He loves the Jewish people. We Jews have strayed a lot. Our ancestors did many good deeds and earned great merit. Their merit helps us, since our actions do not measure up to theirs, and God has treated us kindly because of their merit. What happens if we "use up" this merit of our ancestors over the millennia?

The Tosafot raised this question because they believed that the זְכוּת אָבוֹת (merit of our ancestors) had been used up. Thus, when it says in our prayers, וּמֵבִיא גוֹאֵל לִבְנֵי בְנֵיהֶם לְמַעַן שְׁמוֹ בְּאַהֲבָה, it does not refer to our ancestors' merit, but to something else. God and the Jewish

35. *Iyun Tefillah* in *Otzar Hatefillot,* p. 310.

36. *Seder Avodat Yisrael,* pp. 190–191.

people made a covenant (בְּרִית אָבוֹת). When two partners make a covenant, each is obliged to keep it. We are obliged to keep it, and God is obliged to keep it. The covenant can never come to an end. As long as the covenant exists for all eternity, God will have to redeem the Jewish people. This is not because of our own merit or the merit of our ancestors, which we may have used up, but because the covenant between God and the Jewish people exists forever.[37]

We say מֶלֶךְ עוֹזֵר וּמוֹשִׁיעַ וּמָגֵן ("the King who helps and saves and shields"). עוֹזֵר and מוֹשִׁיעַ are almost synonyms. עוֹזֵר means that God helps you if you are going to fall down by giving you support so you won't fall. מוֹשִׁיעַ, on the other hand, means that if you have already fallen down or are completely lost, God picks you up. Thus, עוֹזֵר means who helps save you before you have fallen, and מוֹשִׁיעַ means to lift up a person who has already fallen.[38]

This ending, בָּרוּךְ אַתָּה ה׳, מָגֵן אַבְרָהָם ("Blessed are You, Hashem, the Shield of Abraham") follows the rule of long berachot, that we must end a berachah with the same theme as its opening.[39] However, we repeat only Abraham; why are the other Patriarchs omitted? At the beginning of Parshat Lech Lecha,[40] God tells Avram, וְאֶעֶשְׂךָ לְגוֹי גָּדוֹל וַאֲבָרֶכְךָ וַאֲגַדְּלָה שְׁמֶךָ וֶהְיֵה בְּרָכָה ("I shall make you a great nation, and I shall bless you and I will make your name great and you will be a blessing"). The Gemara explains[41] that the first phrase וְאֶעֶשְׂךָ לְגוֹי גָּדוֹל ("I shall make you a great nation") parallels the phrase אֱלֹקֵי אַבְרָהָם. The next phrase, וַאֲבָרֶכְךָ ("and I will bless you"), parallels אֱלֹקֵי יִצְחָק. The phrase וַאֲגַדְּלָה שְׁמֶךָ ("and I will make your name great") parallels the phrase וֵאלֹקֵי יַעֲקֹב. Then the Gemara raises our question. Shouldn't we

---

37. Regarding the concept of זְכוּת אָבוֹת (the merit of our ancestors, i.e., that Hashem protects us because of the good deeds that our ancestors did, see במדבר רבה פרשת נשא פרשה יא. As to whether or not זְכוּת אָבוֹת is unlimited, see שבת דף נה עמוד א. Tosafot (שם ד״ה ושמואל) introduces the idea of בְּרִית אָבוֹת.

38. *Iyun Tefillah* in *Otzar Hatefillot,* p. 312.

39. חידושי הרשב״א מסכת ברכות דף י עמוד א, פתח באשרי וסיים באשרי

40. בראשית פרק יב, ב

41. פסחים דף קיז עמוד ב: אמר רבי שמעון בן לקיש

end the berachah by referring to all three? The Gemara then explains that the last phrase of our verse, וֶהְיֵה בְּרָכָה ("and you will be a blessing"),[42] means that you, Abraham, alone are mentioned at the end of the berachah. In other words, this verse is the reason why Abraham alone is mentioned at the end, rather than all three Patriarchs. We could argue logically that since Abraham started everything, being the first to discover God, he therefore deserves more mention than the others. Another explanation is found in Chasidic lore. Abraham, Isaac, and Jacob represent the three pillars of Judaism: acts of kindness, worship/service, and the study of Torah.[43] Abraham represents acts of kindness. He gave food to the angels when he thought they were just men. He prayed for the people of Sodom and Amorah. Isaac represents worship/service because he was nearly offered as a sacrifice. Jacob represents the study of Torah since, according to the Rabbis, he studied in the academies of Shem and Eber for fourteen years.[44]

Today, when we want to serve God, is it easier for us to do so as Jacob did, by learning Torah? How many people today study Torah sufficiently? How many even commit themselves to give some time every day for the study of Torah? In our modern world it is very difficult to say that we serve God with Torah. Similarly, with worship/service, do we really serve God as we should in this way? Do we pray with the proper devotion and concentration? One thing that Jews can do in the modern age is acts of kindness. We are a smart and capable nation, thanks to God. If we know how to make money, for instance, we can share our income with others and give to charity. This is why the emphasis here is the shield of Abraham. What Isaac and Jacob did, we cannot so easily do, but we can and should do what Abraham did.

42. See Ramban on this verse.

43. See רבינו בחיי בראשית פרק לב, י and זוהר, סתרי תורה, ויצא דף קמו עמוד ב; בראשית רבה פרשת וישב פרשה פד, [ג ד]: וישראל אהב את יוסף מכל בניו.

44. אברבנאל בראשית פרק כה פסוק כד

עֲשֶׂרֶת יְמֵי תְּשׁוּבָה

The main body of the שְׁמוֹנֶה עֶשְׂרֵה was introduced in Talmudic times, from the time of the אַנְשֵׁי כְּנֶסֶת הַגְּדוֹלָה at the beginning of the Second Temple period, through the Tannaim of the Mishnah to the Amoraim of the Gemara. If any of the prayers that they authored are omitted, the davener must go back and say these parts.[45]

The Gemara[46] discusses the changes to the third berachah in the שְׁמוֹנֶה עֶשְׂרֵה during the days between Rosh Hashanah and Yom Kippur, where we change הָאֵ־ל הַקָּדוֹשׁ to הַמֶּלֶךְ הַקָּדוֹשׁ ("the holy King"), and to the eleventh berachah, where we change מֶלֶךְ אוֹהֵב צְדָקָה וּמִשְׁפָּט to הַמֶּלֶךְ הַמִּשְׁפָּט ("the King of justice"). What happens if you did not make these changes to the שְׁמוֹנֶה עֶשְׂרֵה? If you forgot the phrase הַמֶּלֶךְ הַקָּדוֹשׁ and you have already started the next berachah, you must go back to the beginning of the שְׁמוֹנֶה עֶשְׂרֵה. If you remember right away, before beginning the next berachah, you may recite הַמֶּלֶךְ הַקָּדוֹשׁ then, and continue.[47] If you forgot הַמֶּלֶךְ הַמִּשְׁפָּט, R. Yosef Karo[48] rules that if you have not yet completed the שְׁמוֹנֶה עֶשְׂרֵה, you go back to that berachah and recite it again from there. If you already took three steps back you repeat the שְׁמוֹנֶה עֶשְׂרֵה. The Rama,[49] however, holds that since the original phrase, מֶלֶךְ אוֹהֵב צְדָקָה וּמִשְׁפָּט, also mentions that God is a king of justice, if we forgot הַמֶּלֶךְ הַמִּשְׁפָּט we do not have to go back.

If the chazzan forgets to say הַמֶּלֶךְ הַקָּדוֹשׁ on Friday night in the modified repetition of the שְׁמוֹנֶה עֶשְׂרֵה, if we correct him immediately, the chazzan can make the change. But if he continued the tefillah without making the correction, we let it pass because this is not really a repetition of the שְׁמוֹנֶה עֶשְׂרֵה.[50]

---

45. See שולחן ערוך אורח חיים סימן קט סעיף ג וביאור הלכה שם.
46. ברכות דף יב עמוד ב
47. שולחן ערוך אורח חיים סימן תקפב סעיף א–ב
48. שולחן ערוך אורח חיים סימן תקפב סעיף א
49. רמ"א אורח חיים סימן קיח סעיף א
50. פרי חדש אורח חיים סימן תקפב סעיף ג

There are other additions made in the first two berachot and in the last two berachot of the שְׁמוֹנֶה עֶשְׂרֵה:[51]

- זָכְרֵנוּ לְחַיִּים מֶלֶךְ חָפֵץ בַּחַיִּים וְכָתְבֵנוּ בְּסֵפֶר הַחַיִּים לְמַעַנְךָ אֱלֹקִים חַיִּים to the end of the first berachah.
- מִי כָמוֹךָ אַב הָרַחֲמִים זוֹכֵר יְצוּרָיו לְחַיִּים בְּרַחֲמִים to the end of the second berachah.
- וּכְתֹב לְחַיִּים טוֹבִים כָּל בְּנֵי בְרִיתֶךָ to the end of the berachah of Modim (the eighteenth berachah), and
- בְּסֵפֶר חַיִּים בְּרָכָה וְשָׁלוֹם וּפַרְנָסָה טוֹבָה נִזָּכֵר וְנִכָּתֵב לְפָנֶיךָ אֲנַחְנוּ וְכָל עַמְּךָ בֵּית יִשְׂרָאֵל לְחַיִּים טוֹבִים וּלְשָׁלוֹם to the end of the last berachah.

If you forgot to include the four phrases, the Rosh says[52] you don't repeat the berachot in order to say the skipped phrases because they are not mentioned in the Gemara. The Shulchan Aruch too rules that if you forgot to recite these phrases, you don't have to go back to recite them.[53]

When the chazzan recites these four phrases during the Ten Days of Repentance, many people recite them out loud with him. According to Rav Soloveitchik, only the last two phrases are recited aloud with the chazzan.

These insertions raise a problem. The Gemara tells us that in the first three and last three berachot we should make no requests.[54] The rest of the שְׁמוֹנֶה עֶשְׂרֵה is for that purpose. However, the Geonim added these phrases in the first two berachot and the last two berachot because they maintained that the Gemara's prohibition was referring to a request added on behalf of an individual. We are not making requests here for an individual. We are making requests for the benefit of the whole community.[55]

---

51. טור אורח חיים סימן תקפב
52. רא"ש מסכת ברכות פרק א סימן טז
53. שלחן ערוך אורח חיים סימן תקפב סעיף ה, הגהות מיימוניות הלכות תפילה ונשיאת כפים פרק ב הלכה יט
54. ברכות דף לד עמוד א
55. מחזור ויטרי סימן שכו

Second Berachah: גְבוּרוֹת

The second berachah of the Amidah is difficult to understand. אַתָּה גִּבּוֹר means "You are mighty." But what do we know about God's strength? We can interpret "You are mighty" in the sense of "You are powerful in overcoming Your anger and ignoring our shortcomings and our sins; You let us live by giving us another chance in spite of our shortcomings." Later on, when we say מִי כָמוֹךָ בַּעַל גְּבוּרוֹת ("Who is mighty like You?"), we mean, "I am a sinful person and I really don't deserve Your kindness, but I know You overcome Your anger and give me another chance."

Others say that אַתָּה גִּבּוֹר means that God does mighty deeds: He feeds human beings, clothes them, and heals them. When we say אַתָּה גִּבּוֹר, we should try to imitate God.[56] When the Torah informs us of God's good deeds, we should do likewise. As the Rabbis say, the Torah too starts with God's acts of kindness. When Adam and Eve were driven from the Garden of Eden, they had no clothes, so God made them clothes. The Torah also ends with God's acts of kindness. When Moshe died, God buried him. Just as God provides clothing for those in need, so should we provide for those in need. Just as God is compassionate and buries the dead, so should we be compassionate and bury the dead.[57]

In other words, "You are mighty" could be interpreted to mean that God does mighty deeds to guide us. We don't try to fathom all the mighty deeds of God, but the blessing is simply a challenge for us to imitate His qualities and good deeds to the best of our understanding.

I, myself, prefer the first interpretation, that God is strong in ignoring our sinfulness and our shortcomings.

The next words, מְחַיֵּה מֵתִים ("You revive the dead"), are also difficult to understand. This idea is emphasized here because it is an important doctrine and one of the basic tenets of Judaism.

---

56. This philosophical doctrine is called *imitatio Dei*, or, imitation of God.

57. סוטה דף יד עמוד א

The berachah begins: אַתָּה גִּבּוֹר לְעוֹלָם ה׳ ("You are mighty forever, Hashem"), מְחַיֵּה מֵתִים אַתָּה ("You revive the dead"), רַב לְהוֹשִׁיעַ ("great in salvation"). Note how this statement should be divided. Not everybody breaks it up into the proper phrases.

The words מְחַיֵּה הַמֵּתִים are repeated a number of times in this berachah. Sometimes we repeat it exactly in this form and sometimes we change the words slightly. It is mentioned this way (מְחַיֵּה מֵתִים) at the beginning and we use the same form at the end of the berachah, בָּרוּךְ אַתָּה ה׳, מְחַיֵּה הַמֵּתִים ("Blessed are You, Hashem, who revives the dead"). In the middle of the berachah we also say מְחַיֶּה מֵתִים בְּרַחֲמִים רַבִּים ("who revives the dead with great mercy"), so this same grammatical form appears three times. We also express this idea in a slightly different form in the middle of the berachah an additional two times. We say מֶלֶךְ מֵמִית וּמְחַיֶּה ("the King who takes away life and brings to life") and וְנֶאֱמָן אַתָּה לְהַחֲיוֹת מֵתִים ("You are faithful in bringing the dead to life") in the middle of the berachah. These phrases have slightly altered grammatical forms. So, we find three instances of the form מְחַיֵּה מֵתִים (who revives the dead) and five times the concept of תְּחִיַּת הַמֵּתִים (the revival of the dead) in this berachah.

The three or five repetitions of this idea reflect different aspects of God's kindness to us. The three repetitions hint at the understanding that in human life there are three such revivals: The first is in the morning when we wake up, because at night we are almost like dead. The second is the great resurrection of the dead at the end of time. The third is the rain, because without rain there is no life. These are very broad, basic areas in which God provides salvation.[58]

Another explanation of this berachah relates the expressions of revival of the dead to the Talmud's categories of people who are compared to the dead because of a misfortune in their lives.[59] God brings them back to life, too. These categories are people who are in such a difficult position that they can lose all hope: the childless, lepers (who are quarantined from the community), the blind, and the poor.

---

58. אבודרהם שמונה עשרה אתה גבור לעולם ה׳

59. נדרים סד עמוד ב

These four misfortunes in human life were compared by the Rabbis to a living death. These four "living deaths," plus the ultimate death after which God gives us a new life, explain the five allusions to the revival of the dead. This is a profound expression of God's intimate participation in the troubles of a person, no matter how desperate a person's condition might be.

מַשִּׁיב הָרוּחַ וּמוֹרִיד הַגֶּשֶׁם

In this berachah we mention other mighty deeds of God. We say סוֹמֵךְ נוֹפְלִים ("who supports those who have fallen"), רוֹפֵא חוֹלִים ("who heals the sick"), מַתִּיר אֲסוּרִים ("who frees the imprisoned"). Why were these particular details chosen when there are so many other things that God does for us? Why do we only point out these few things that God does? The answer is that we are only mentioning those deeds that in some way resemble reviving the dead.

Another phrase in the berachah of מְחַיֵּה הַמֵּתִים is מַשִּׁיב הָרוּחַ וּמוֹרִיד הַגֶּשֶׁם ("He causes the wind to blow and the rain to fall"). It refers to God providing rain without which people cannot survive. There are two phrases in the שְׁמוֹנֶה עֶשְׂרֵה that refer to God providing life sustaining rain: the phrase מַשִּׁיב הָרוּחַ וּמוֹרִיד הַגֶּשֶׁם which is found in the berachah of מְחַיֵּה הַמֵּתִים, and the phrase וְתֵן טַל וּמָטָר לִבְרָכָה ("Grant dew and rain as a blessing") which is found in the ninth berachah of the שְׁמוֹנֶה עֶשְׂרֵה (בָּרֵךְ עָלֵינוּ, the berachah for a bountiful year). The berachah of מְחַיֵּה הַמֵּתִים is found in the section of the שְׁמוֹנֶה עֶשְׂרֵה that is devoted to praising God, and as such it is phrased as an expression of praise, not as a request. The phrase וְתֵן טַל וּמָטָר לִבְרָכָה is a request of God that He give us enough rain and dew, and it is in the part of the שְׁמוֹנֶה עֶשְׂרֵה that deals with petitions to God to fulfill our needs.

Both of these phrases are said only during parts of the year. If you forget the phrase מַשִּׁיב הָרוּחַ וּמוֹרִיד הַגֶּשֶׁם during the season when it is supposed to be said, what should you do? Since מַשִּׁיב הָרוּחַ וּמוֹרִיד הַגֶּשֶׁם in the second berachah of מְחַיֵּה הַמֵּתִים is a statement of praise, it can only be mentioned in a section of praise.[60] If you catch yourself while

60. עולת תמיד סימן קיד ס״ק ז

you are still in the middle of the berachah of מְחַיֵּה הַמֵּתִים and have not yet pronounced God's name, you merely go back to that part of the berachah and repeat it. If you remember it only after you finished the second berachah and have started the next berachah, then you must go back and start the שְׁמוֹנֶה עֶשְׂרֵה over again. But if your remember after completing the second berachah but before beginning the third, you should recite the phrase מַשִּׁיב הָרוּחַ וּמוֹרִיד הַגֶּשֶׁם by itself and then continue.[61]

There is a verse in Tehillim (119:12) that begins like a berachah. It says, בָּרוּךְ אַתָּה ה׳ לַמְּדֵנִי חֻקֶּיךָ ("Blessed are You, Hashem; teach me Your laws"). If you are reciting the second berachah of שְׁמוֹנֶה עֶשְׂרֵה and you have already said בָּרוּךְ אַתָּה ה׳, and then you remember that you forgot to say מַשִּׁיב הָרוּחַ וּמוֹרִיד הַגֶּשֶׁם, you can turn the beginning of the berachah into the verse from Tehillim by ending with the words לַמְּדֵנִי חֻקֶּיךָ. This makes your berachah a recitation of a verse, and you have not yet finished the berachah, so you can still say מַשִּׁיב הָרוּחַ וּמוֹרִיד הַגֶּשֶׁם. Some say that this is better than finishing the berachah and then reciting מַשִּׁיב הָרוּחַ וּמוֹרִיד הַגֶּשֶׁם immediately afterward.[62]

However, if you forget to say the phrase וְתֵן טַל וּמָטָר לִבְרָכָה in the ninth berachah of the שְׁמוֹנֶה עֶשְׂרֵה (בָּרֵךְ עָלֵינוּ), there is a way of including it without having to go back to that berachah.[63] You may continue with the שְׁמוֹנֶה עֶשְׂרֵה and add this phrase that you forgot to the berachah of שְׁמַע קוֹלֵנוּ ("Hear our voice").[64] Since וְתֵן טַל וּמָטָר לִבְרָכָה is a request, unlike מַשִּׁיב הָרוּחַ וּמוֹרִיד הַגֶּשֶׁם which is just an expression of praise, it can be inserted into שְׁמַע קוֹלֵנוּ, which is the berachah for God to listen to our prayers and where we can insert special requests.[65]

Although the first two sections of the שְׁמוֹנֶה עֶשְׂרֵה consist of praise and petition, there is another way of addressing God that is something

---

61. שולחן ערוך אורח חיים הלכות תפילה סימן קיד סעיף ו

62. See ביאור הלכה סימן קיד סעיף ו ד"ה בלא חתימה; משנה ברורה סימן קיד ס"ק כ; אגרות משה אורח חיים חלק ד סימן צג.

63. אורח חיים סימן קיז סעיף ה

64. ברכות כט עמוד א

65. רש"י, ברכות כט עמוד א ד"ה גבורות גשמים

in between. We call this רִצּוּי. "Who causes the wind to blow and the rain to fall" is not completely praise, yet it is certainly not making a request of God. It is an in-between case. It doesn't fit in one exact category in this berachah.

There is also a Sephardic custom to say the phrase מוֹרִיד הַטָּל ("He causes the dew to fall") in place of מַשִּׁיב הָרוּחַ וּמוֹרִיד הַגֶּשֶׁם from Pesach to Sukkot, when מַשִּׁיב הָרוּחַ וּמוֹרִיד הַגֶּשֶׁם is not said.[66] Dew also brings needed moisture that enables plants to survive. When we mention that God provides dew, we are still making a statement about God's life-enabling gifts which is the theme of this blessing. Reciting this phrase is the commonly accepted practice in Israel as well. There is one advantage in doing this. According to Ashkenazic custom, in which מוֹרִיד הַטָּל is not said, it is easy to forget to begin saying מַשִּׁיב הָרוּחַ וּמוֹרִיד הַגֶּשֶׁם on Shemini Atzeret. If we can't remember if we said it, we have to repeat the שְׁמוֹנֶה עֶשְׂרֵה. For those who say מוֹרִיד הַטָּל, however, even if one has forgotten to say מַשִּׁיב הָרוּחַ וּמוֹרִיד הַגֶּשֶׁם, the mention of dew is sufficient for one not to have to repeat the שְׁמוֹנֶה עֶשְׂרֵה.[67]

We start saying the phrase מַשִּׁיב הָרוּחַ וּמוֹרִיד הַגֶּשֶׁם on Shemini Atzeret, when the rainy season begins in Israel, and continue saying it until the first day of Pesach.[68] More specifically, we start saying מַשִּׁיב הָרוּחַ וּמוֹרִיד הַגֶּשֶׁם on Shemini Atzeret during Musaf. This is very strange. If it is to be said on a particular day, one would think that it should be said during all the prayer services of the day, beginning with Ma'ariv, continuing in Shacharit, and then recited again at Musaf. Why do we not say it before Musaf?

According to one opinion in the Talmud Yerushalmi,[69] the answer is that we cannot recite this phrase until the שְׁלִיחַ צִבּוּר has recited it first. In other words, מַשִּׁיב הָרוּחַ וּמוֹרִיד הַגֶּשֶׁם is such a holy phrase that

---

66. See מחצית השקל אורח חיים סימן קיד ס"ק ג. The Rav said that the phrase in the prayer for dew that says: *שָׁאַתָּה הוּא ה׳ אֱלֹקֵינוּ מַשִּׁיב הָרוּחַ וּמוֹרִיד הַטָּל* is an indication that the original version of the phrase was מַשִּׁיב הָרוּחַ וּמוֹרִיד הַטָּל.

67. שולחן ערוך אורח חיים סימן קיד סעיף ה

68. שולחן ערוך אורח חיים סימן קיד סעיף א

69. שולחן ערוך אורח חיים סימן קיד סעיף ב and ירושלמי תענית פרק א הלכה א.

we have no right to say it on our own; we have to be given permission to say it. The extent of the holiness of this phrase is explained in the Gemara: The Rabbis say, God kept the key to rain for Himself.[70] The Gemara explains: "Rabbi Yochanan said, 'There are three keys in the hands of the Holy One, blessed be He, that He didn't turn over to the control of a representative. They are: the key to rain, the key to birth and the key to the resurrection of the dead.' In Israel they added the key of livelihood. And Rabbi Yochanan did not include the key to livelihood because it is included in the key to rain."

While other things depend on natural law, whether there is rain in Israel is directly God's business. God provides rain according to what we deserve. Since this is such a sensitive matter, this phrase relating to God providing rain cannot be said unless we are first given permission to say it.

In this case, "permission" means that it is announced first in shul. In Talmudic times, many people did not go to shul for Ma'ariv.[71] If we would have announced the saying of מַשִּׁיב הָרוּחַ וּמוֹרִיד הַגֶּשֶׁם then, not many people would have heard it. So that was not a good place to announce it.

In Shacharit, there may be no interruption before the beginning of the שְׁמוֹנֶה עֶשְׂרֵה, so it cannot be announced then. We therefore have no choice but to wait for Musaf. Before Musaf begins, we can make the announcement to begin saying מַשִּׁיב הָרוּחַ וּמוֹרִיד הַגֶּשֶׁם.

Because there must be an announcement to begin saying מַשִּׁיב הָרוּחַ וּמוֹרִיד הַגֶּשֶׁם, if nobody announces it before the silent שְׁמוֹנֶה עֶשְׂרֵה of Musaf, then you have to wait for תְּפִילַּת גֶּשֶׁם (the Prayer for Rain), which serves as the announcement.

Third Berachah: קְדֻשַּׁת ה׳

The third berachah of the שְׁמוֹנֶה עֶשְׂרֵה is that of קְדֻשַּׁת ה׳ (Holiness of God). From Psalm 29 we derive both the number of berachot in the weekday שְׁמוֹנֶה עֶשְׂרֵה as well as the sequence of the first three berachot.[72]

---

70. תענית ב עמוד א

71. ירושלמי תענית פרק א הלכה א

72. מגילה דף יז עמוד ב

The fact that the third berachah deals with God's holiness is alluded to in Psalm 29, which begins מִזְמוֹר לְדָוִד הָבוּ לַה׳ בְּנֵי אֵלִים הָבוּ לַה׳ כָּבוֹד וָעֹז. הָבוּ לַה׳ כְּבוֹד שְׁמוֹ הִשְׁתַּחֲווּ לַה׳ בְּהַדְרַת קֹדֶשׁ ("A Psalm of David: Praise Hashem, O powerful ones; praise God for His mighty deeds. Praise God and say that His glory fills the world. Bow to God while telling of His splendor and holiness").

The first phrase, בְּנֵי אֵלִים (literally, "children of powerful ones"), is the source for the Amidah's first berachah referring to our powerful ones (the patriarchs). The second phrase, הָבוּ לה׳ כָּבוֹד וָעֹז ("Praise God for His mighty deeds"), reflects the same idea as the second berachah of the שְׁמוֹנֶה עֶשְׂרֵה (עֹז and גְּבוּרָה both refer to God's mighty acts or qualities). The third phrase, הִשְׁתַּחֲווּ לַה׳ בְּהַדְרַת קֹדֶשׁ, refers to the berachah of God's holiness.

This in itself would suffice for us to establish the order of the berachot in the שְׁמוֹנֶה עֶשְׂרֵה, but relying on logic would bring us to the same result. We start with the patriarchs, since it is they who gave us the precedent of praying to God. Then we recite the berachah about the powers of God, where we are thankful to God for His mighty deeds and for the acts of kindness that He extends to us. From this it seems that we have a special relationship with God. But then we must ask ourselves if it is proper to do so. Isn't God too holy, or different from all that we know, for us to approach Him in prayer? So, almost in awe, we exclaim, "What chutzpah of us to act as if we understand God and as if we can address Him whenever we want. His holiness is so great that not even the angels understand Him." Therefore, by saying the third berachah, we rectify the implication of our carelessly addressing God.

The Kedushah, which we recite in the chazzan's repetition of this berachah, is the song of the angels. We imitate their praises of God in His heavenly abode. Indeed, we could say that in the Kedushah of Musaf on Shabbat and Yom Tov we raise ourselves to the level of angels and sing together with them.[73] Since we cannot outdo the angels, at

---

73. Tosafot (Sanhedrin 37b ד״ה מכנף הארץ) cite the Teshuvot HaGeonim which states that in Eretz Yisrael, Kedushah was only recited on Shabbat. R. Yosef Rosen, the "Rogatchover Gaon" (שו״ת צפנת פענח [ורשא] סימן קמ), explains

best we imitate them when we quote their song, the Kedushah, and raise ourselves to their level.

The Kedushah belongs to a category of prayers in which we sanctify God's name. This category of prayer is known as דְּבָרִים שֶׁבִּקְדוּשָּׁה (matters of holiness). These prayers must be said with great respect and special concentration. The daily prayers that fall into this category are the קְדוּשָּׁה, בָּרְכוּ, and קַדִּישׁ. To recite these prayers, we must observe certain rules: The first rule is recorded in the Talmud, which states that דְּבָרִים שֶׁבִּקְדוּשָּׁה may be recited only in the presence of ten men (a minyan).[74] The second rule is contested: According to the Rama,[75] we must stand for דְּבָרִים שֶׁבִּקְדוּשָּׁה. Sephardic Jews do not accept this opinion, and accordingly they do not stand for Kaddish, unless it is a Kaddish following a prayer that is said standing. The third rule was observed by R. Soloveitchik. דְּבָרִים שֶׁבִּקְדוּשָּׁה are only recited with a summons, in other words, only when the leader calls upon the congregation to respond. The requirement of being summoned to respond is derived from the angels themselves. Isaiah 6:3 (וְקָרָא זֶה אֶל־זֶה וְאָמַר, "and each one called to the other and said") shows us that each angel had to be encouraged and summoned by his fellow angels to recite the Kedushah; we must do the same.

We learn the requirement of ten men from Leviticus 22:32, וְנִקְדַּשְׁתִּי בְּתוֹךְ בְּנֵי יִשְׂרָאֵל ("I shall be sanctified among Israel"). The Gemara explains that the word בְּתוֹךְ, "among," refers to a minimum of ten adult

---

that during the week we merely quote the Kedushah of the angels, but on Shabbat we recite Kedushah ourselves like the angels.

Rabbi Wohlgemuth discussed the concepts of דָּבָר שֶׁבִּקְדוּשָּׁה with Rav Soloveitchik extensively. Excellent summaries of the Rav's presentation can be found in the following:

רשימות שיעורים ברכות דף כא עמוד ב; שיעורי הרב על עניני תפלה וקריאת שמע, עמ' קצא-ריג. The Nefesh Hachaim discusses the Kedushah of the angels and of the Jewish people in נפש החיים, שער א פרק ו בהערה ד"ה וגם שלפי and נפש החיים שער א פרק יא. See also Chullin 91b: דאמר רב חננאל אמר רב.

74. Megillah 23b.

75. רמ"א אורח חיים סימן נו סעיף א

male Jews, based on a גְּזֵרָה שָׁוָה (an associative principle of traditional biblical exegesis).[76]

The Rama derives the requirement to stand from Judges 3:20, where Ehud informed Eglon, the king of Moab, that he had a message for him from God. Respectfully, Eglon stood up to honor God's name. This gave Ehud a chance to assassinate the king, who had cruelly oppressed Israel. If Eglon, the evil king of Moab, showed such respect to God's name, we certainly should.[77]

There is another opinion, however, that we do not derive laws applicable to Jews from gentiles, especially our persecutors. This is the reason that some people remain seated for these prayers. Even so, there is one prayer of sanctification during which standing is, without question, a requirement: this is the Kedushah of the angels. We derive this from Ezekiel 1:7, וְרַגְלֵיהֶם רֶגֶל יְשָׁרָה ("and their legs were as one straight leg"). As to whether all three of the קְדוּשּׁוֹת that we recite in Shacharit are considered the kind of Kedushah that we call a prayer of sanctification is something we have to explore.

Kedushot of Shacharit

In Shacharit we say three קְדוּשּׁוֹת: (1) in the first berachah preceding the Shema, called קְדוּשַּׁת יוֹצֵר; (2) in the repetition of the שְׁמוֹנֶה עֶשְׂרֵה; and (3) in the prayer of, וּבָא לְצִיּוֹן גּוֹאֵל at the end of the service. Why do we need three קְדוּשּׁוֹת? Shouldn't one be enough?

The main Kedushah in the third berachah of the שְׁמוֹנֶה עֶשְׂרֵה quotes the recitation of the Kedushah of the angels. Before we can refer to the angels sanctifying God in the Kedushah, however, we must understand what we are talking about. That is what the קְדוּשַּׁת יוֹצֵר accomplishes. It explains the nature of the Kedushah in general. The third Kedushah, in the prayer of וּבָא לְצִיּוֹן גּוֹאֵל, functions as a Torah study session.

The question arises as to how are we allowed to say the Kedushah in the Shema and the Kedushah at the end of the service while sitting

---

76. ברכות כא עמוד ב, מגילה כג עמוד ב

77. שופטים ג:כ. And see מגן אברהם סימן נו ס"ק ד.

and often without a minyan. Standing and the presence of a minyan are requirements of the Kedushah. The Rambam actually advises us to skip the Kedushah in the berachot of the Shema if there is no minyan.[78] The Shulchan Aruch cites two opinions about whether this Kedushah should be recited without a minyan. The first opinion maintains that this is not considered Kedushah but is merely a recounting of the angels' Kedushah. The second opinion is that this too is Kedushah and therefore shouldn't be recited without a minyan. The Shulchan Aruch argues that one shouldn't reject the second, more stringent opinion. Therefore, he maintains, one praying alone should recite the verses of this Kedushah with their cantillation notes to make it clear that one is merely reading them as verses from the Torah. The Rama, however, tells us that one may say the Kedushah in the Shema even without a minyan.[79] He maintains that the Kedushah in the berachot of the Shema is not a "real" Kedushah, but only informs us what the angels do.[80] If it were a real Kedushah, he too would feel that an individual praying without a minyan would have to skip it.

The differences between Ashkenazic and Sephardic prayer rites are minimal, and it would be easy to switch from one to the other. The Rabbis, however, emphasized that one should retain the custom in which one's family has prayed for generations, because the differences often express a completely different philosophical outlook.

In the Kedushah of the שְׁמוֹנֶה עֶשְׂרֵה, the Ashkenazim introduce the congregational response with the words לְעֻמָּתָם בָּרוּךְ יֹאמֵרוּ ("Those facing them say, 'Blessed'"), while the Sephardim say לְעֻמָּתָם מְשַׁבְּחִים וְאוֹמְרִים ("Those facing them praise by saying"). In Jewish philosophy, we often wonder how any human being can truly understand the greatness of God and praise Him. Our praises are worthless if we cannot fully appreciate what we are praising. Yet we do praise God. We rely on the great prophets and leaders of our people to teach us how. The Ashkenazim do not say לְעֻמָּתָם מְשַׁבְּחִים וְאוֹמְרִים in the Kedushah

78. רמב"ם הלכות תפילה פרק ז הלכה יז
79. רמ"א אורח חיים סימן נט סעיף ג
80. מגן גיבורים אלף המגן סימן נט ס"ק ד

because they believe that it is impossible for us to praise God properly. However, in the Kedushah of the Shema, the Ashkenazim do say this phrase, because it is not a description of what we do but of what the angels do. The angels can praise God since they have a better understanding of His omnipotence than human beings do. According to the Sephardic version, there is no difference between the Kedushah of the Shema and of the שְׁמוֹנֶה עֶשְׂרֵה; in both, we are reciting Kedushah ourselves. It therefore would not make sense to differentiate between the two.

As we have noted, the Kedushah consists primarily of two verses, one from Isaiah and one from Ezekiel. The first verse, which repeats the word קָדוֹשׁ ("holy") three times, indicates a superlative (i.e., holiest). The Hebrew language does not have a superlative form, so emphasizing a word three times is the Hebrew way to express a superlative.[81] By saying קָדוֹשׁ three times, we proclaim that no human being can ever understand the Almighty. His greatness is beyond our capacity to understand.

ה׳ צְבָקוֹת is translated in many prayer books as the "Lord of Hosts," which we have already stated is incorrect. The word[82] צְבָקוֹת by itself is one of the seven names of God that cannot be erased. The Divine name צְבָקוֹת indicates that God is the creator of the multitudes that inhabit heaven and earth. The "heavenly hosts" include the planets, the constellations and the angels.[83]

The phrase מְלֹא כָל הָאָרֶץ כְּבוֹדוֹ ("the whole earth is filled with His glory") may refer to the situation in the time of Isaiah. When Isaiah started prophesying, the land of Judea was still an independent political power. The שְׁכִינָה (Divine Presence) was felt in the Temple; God's protecting hand was spread over the land of Judea, and nobody dared to raise a hand against it. But things changed rapidly. During

81. See מלבי״ם ישעיהו פרק ו פסוק ג. and *Etz Yosef* in *Otzar Hatefillot*, עמ׳ קלא.

82. רמב״ם הלכות יסודי התורה פרק ו הל׳ ב.

83. See, for example, רד״ק ישעיהו פרק א: נקרא על שם צבאות מעלה ועל צבאות מטה. Also see מלבי״ם ישעיהו פרק א: שכל צבאות מעלה ומטה בידו. This includes all the heavenly bodies and angels as well as us in our world below.

the period of the prophecies of Ezekiel and Jeremiah, the Babylonians destroyed Jerusalem and the Temple. The שְׁכִינָה, if we are permitted to say so, was chased out of the Temple.

The prophet Ezekiel had a prophetic vision in which he saw the Divine chariot flying through the heavens to the true abode of the Divine majesty. Ezekiel could not say that the earth was full of the glory of God, because the Temple no longer existed. The enemy had dared to raise his hand against the Almighty; the human race vilified the God of Israel. The angelic song described by Isaiah, קָדוֹשׁ קָדוֹשׁ קָדוֹשׁ ה׳ צְבָקוֹת מְלֹא כָל הָאָרֶץ כְּבוֹדוֹ, describes the Jewish people at its height, protected by God, and the song described by Ezekiel, בָּרוּךְ כְּבוֹד ה׳ מִמְּקוֹמוֹ, describes the Jewish people at the low point of its history, during the desecration of the sanctity of Jerusalem and the Temple.[84]

To solve this discrepancy between past and present, we recite a third verse in our Kedushah that is not found in the angels' Kedushah. We quote King David, who in the last words of Psalm 146, envisioned God's return to Jerusalem (Zion) in the future: יִמְלֹךְ ה׳ לְעוֹלָם אֱלֹקַיִךְ צִיּוֹן לְדֹר וָדֹר הַלְלוּקָהּ ("Hashem shall reign forever, your God, O Zion, for all generations, praise Hashem"). In the future, nobody will dare to attack the Jewish people because everyone will know that they are under the protective hand of the Almighty.[85] There is an old Talmudic rule[86] that when two verses contradict each another, a third verse will balance their points of view. Isaiah and Ezekiel appear to contradict one another, but King David explains that there is truly no contradiction.

The various parts of the Kedushah are linked in the weekday שְׁמוֹנֶה עֶשְׂרֵה by short statements such as לְעֻמָּתָם בָּרוּךְ יֹאמֵרוּ ("those facing them say, 'Baruch'"). On Shabbat and Yom Tov, we expand those connecting links to pay respect to the sanctity of these days. In addition, in Musaf, we emphasize God's characteristic of mercy, because Musaf usually

84. See R. Soloveitchik's *Yemei Zikaron*, pp. 55–57; *And From There You Shall Seek*, p. 72.

85. This is the sentiment expressed by Alshich (Tehillim 146:10): עוד יש לכם משכון גדול.

86. ספרא ברייתא דרבי ישמעאל שלוש עשרה מידות

takes place during the time of day during which God judges the world, and we pray that He do so from a place of mercy.[87] Therefore, during the Kedushah of Musaf, we appeal to God's mercy to usher in the Messianic Age and put an end to our suffering. The Kedushah of Musaf expresses this concept in the phrase וְהוּא יַשְׁמִיעֵנוּ בְּרַחֲמָיו שֵׁנִית ("and He with His mercy will announce that He is our God").

In the Kedushah of Musaf, we include the beginning and the end of the Shema. This was inserted here because the early Christian Church, especially the Eastern Ottoman Empire, had its own interpretation for the threefold repetition of the verse from Isaiah. They said it referred to the Christian doctrine of the trinity. To say, as Jews do, that this verse refers to the unity of God as expressed in Shema was anathema to them. They even posted soldiers in the synagogues to prevent the recital of the Shema. Since the soldiers were instructed that Jews sit down during the recitation of the Shema, when people would stand during the repetition of the שְׁמוֹנֶה עֶשְׂרֵה, the soldiers were less alert, and the Jews could get away with proclaiming the unity of God at that point.[88]

The third Kedushah, which is recited in the prayer of וּבָא לְצִיּוֹן, is called the קְדוּשָּׁא דְסִדְרָא (Kedushah of the Order of the Day). Rav Samson Raphael Hirsch says it has this name because after reciting it we leave shul and become engaged in the mundane, daily routine. The term "order of the day" indicates the transition from our worship activities in the morning to our daily activities.[89]

It has been said that this Kedushah was introduced as a minor service for latecomers to shul.[90] Nevertheless, many of the commentators think that this Kedushah was also a result of censorship, as with the Shema.[91]

---

87. See תוספות עבודה זרה דף ג עמוד ב ד"ה שניות, and *Dover Shalom* in *Otzar Hatefillot*.

88. *Tikkun Tefillah* in *Otzar Hatefillot*, עמ' סח-סט.

89. *The Hirsch Siddur* (Feldheim Publishers, Jerusalem and New York, 2018), pp. 214–217.

90. Avudraham, in the section dealing with וּבָא לְצִיּוֹן גּוֹאֵל

91. See מחזור ויטרי סימן קלח:...ונראה לר' דסבר קדושה עצמה בשעת השמד תקנוה

The question is raised, of course, as to how the Jews could say the Kedushah in a seated position when the law clearly requires one to stand. This Kedushah can also be recited by individuals without a minyan. In order not to violate the laws connected with the recital of the Kedushah, the Rabbis turned its recital into a Torah study session. This is why we quote the Aramaic version immediately after the Hebrew. We try to understand the Kedushah better, so for this purpose we quote its translation from the commentary of Jonathan ben Uzziel.[92]

We are almost never permitted to recite half a verse, but in a דָּבָר שֶׁבִּקְדוּשָּׁה we make an exception. In the regular Kedushah we recite the second half of the verse from Ezekiel, בָּרוּךְ כְּבוֹד ה׳ מִמְּקוֹמוֹ, and omit the first half. In the קְדוּשָּׁה דְסִדְרָא, we quote the verse in its entirety. Since this a Torah learning session and we quote the verses in their entirety, this Kedushah can be recited while sitting and without a minyan.

The main Kedushah, we have noted, consists of three verses from Isaiah, Ezekiel, and Psalms. The third verse, Psalm 146:10, has been changed in the קְדוּשָּׁה דְסִדְרָא. Instead of the verse from Psalms, we quote a verse from the Torah (Ex. 15:18) from the אָז יָשִׁיר. Why do we use a different verse?

Logically, we should have always quoted Torah verses for the Kedushah, since the sanctity of the Torah is superior to the sanctity of the books of Psalms or the Prophets. So the question is why we do we ignore a verse of greater holiness and substitute a verse of lesser holiness in the regular Kedushah?

On every joyous occasion, we should remember Zion, the site of the Temple. Our joy is not complete unless Zion/Jerusalem has been restored to its former glory.[93] The Kedushah is a joyous event; we can, after all, join the angels in praising the Almighty. There is no greater

---

שגזרו שמד על ישראל שלא לענות קדושה בשמונה עשרה. ולאחר שהולכין האורבים משם היו אומרים מקראות הללו של קדושה.

92. See רש״י סוטה דף מט עמוד א ד״ה אקדושה דסידרא, and *Tikkun Tefillah* in *Otzar Hatefillot*, p. 424, who quotes a *teshuvah* of Rav Natronai Gaon which elaborates on this idea.

93. בבא בתרא דף ס עמוד ב: וכל המתאבל על ירושלים and שולחן ערוך אורח חיים סימן תקנד סעיף כה: כל האוכל ושותה

happiness for a Jew. Mentioning Zion is therefore essential. The Torah verse does not mention Zion, but the words from Psalms refers to God as the "God of Zion." Our love for Jerusalem led us to prefer this verse over a Torah verse. Once we have mentioned Jerusalem in the third verse of the main Kedushah, then we can choose a verse with greater holiness from the Torah, even though it has no reference to Jerusalem, for the third verse of the קְדוּשָּׁה דְסִדְרָא.[94]

In addition, we could not use the verse from Psalms in the קְדוּשָּׁה דְסִדְרָא for another reason. In order to make the קְדוּשָּׁה דְסִדְרָא into a learning session, we quote a Torah verse that was translated into Aramaic. Aramaic was the spoken language of the Jews for a long period in history. In the Kedushah of the Shema and the Kedushah of the Amidah, we do not need an Aramaic translation of the verses since we recite, rather than study, the Kedushah. In the קְדוּשָּׁה דְסִדְרָא, the Aramaic translation is crucial: Part of the study is translating the verses into the language that every Jew understood. Jonathan ben Uzziel wrote an Aramaic Targum for the books of the Prophets. However, there was no officially recognized translation available for Psalms, so we substituted a verse from the Torah that proclaims God's eternal sovereignty. Targum Onkelos was recognized by the Rabbis of the Talmud as an accepted Torah translation in Aramaic,[95] and we use his translation of this final verse.

There are various conclusions to the text of the Kedushah. Sephardim conclude with אַתָּה קָדוֹשׁ וְשִׁמְךָ קָדוֹשׁ ("You are holy and Your name is holy"), which is the usual text of the third berachah of שְׁמוֹנֶה עֶשְׂרֵה when the Kedushah is not said. Ashkenazim conclude with

---

94. Siddur Otzar Hatefillot, ימלך ה׳ לעולם - עיון תפלה עמ׳ קס.

95. Onkelos (possibly Achilles) lived during the second century C.E. and was a contemporary of Rabban Gamliel of Yavneh, with whom he was very close. He was also a colleague and pupil of Rabbi Eliezer ben Hyrcanus and Rabbi Joshua ben Chananiah. Onkelos is said by the Babylonian Talmud to have been the son of the sister of the emperor Titus; he converted to Judaism to the great displeasure of the emperor. The Talmud (Megillah 3a) states that Onkelos translated the Torah into Aramaic under the guidance of Rabbi Eliezer and Rabbi Joshua.

לְדוֹר וָדוֹר נַגִּיד גָּדְלֶךָ ("From generation to generation we will tell of Your greatness"). The last sentence of the berachah according to both versions, however, is בָּרוּךְ אַתָּה ה׳ הָקֵל הַקָּדוֹשׁ ("Blessed are You, Hashem, Holy God"), and during the Ten Days of Repentance, הַמֶּלֶךְ הַקָּדוֹשׁ ("the Holy King"). The emphasis on the kingship of God is so important at this time that if one mistakenly forgets to recite this conclusion instead of the one used for the rest of the year, one has to repeat the Amidah.[96]

The Kedushah of Musaf is referred to as קְדוּשָׁה רַבָּה (Major Kedushah).[97] The Sephardic text of this Kedushah begins, כֶּתֶר יִתְּנוּ לְךָ ה׳ אֱלֹקֵינוּ מַלְאָכִים הֲמוֹנֵי מַעְלָה עִם עַמְּךָ יִשְׂרָאֵל קְבוּצֵי מַטָּה ("The crowds of angels above and the assemblies of Your people Israel below will crown You, Hashem our God"), while the Ashkenazic text begins, נַעֲרִיצְךָ וְנַקְדִּישְׁךָ כְּסוֹד שִׂיחַ שַׂרְפֵי קֹדֶשׁ ("We will extol You and sanctify You in the words of the assembly of the holy angels"). According to the Ashkenazic text, human beings on earth sing a song just as the angels in the heavens above, כְּסוֹד שִׂיחַ שַׂרְפֵי קֹדֶשׁ ("in the words of the assembly of the holy angels"). We imitate the multitudes of angels above, even though we can never reach their greatness. The Sephardic version, however, suggests that human beings can raise themselves to the level of the angels. We do not just imitate the heavenly hosts, we raise ourselves to their level of understanding and, therefore sing together with them, יַחַד כֻּלָּם קְדֻשָּׁה לְךָ יְשַׁלֵּשׁוּ ("Together they recite the triple holy praise"). The Sephardic version, no doubt, envisions a higher achievement in the relationship between human beings and God.[98]

---

96. שולחן ערוך אורח חיים סימן תקפב סעיף א

97. It is called Kedushah Rabbah because it contains two verses from the Shema; the complete first verse and the ending words of the last verse (אבודרהם שחרית של שבת). The Avudraham says this was established by the Geonim because there was a time when the rulers forbade Jews from reciting Shema, so we said it in the Kedushah where our oppressors wouldn't look for it. The people fulfilled their obligation to recite Shema by the Chazzan's recital. Later it was kept in the Musaf, because Musaf has no recitation of Shema otherwise, and it serves to remind us of God's causing the decree to be voided.

98. See Teshuvot Tzofnat Paneach (Warsaw), no. 140 and the discussion by

What is the כֶּתֶר (crown) with which humans and angels together sanctify God? The gematria of the word כתר is 620 (כ=20 + ת=400 + ר=200); this number can refer to the 613 commandments of the Torah plus the seven additional mitzvot derabbanan. Each time we perform a mitzvah, we are "crowning" God and coming closer to Him.

THE AMIDAH: BERACHOT OF PETITION

The first three berachot of the שְׁמוֹנֶה עֶשְׂרֵה almost never change. The same is true with the last three berachot. The middle berachot, however, do change depending on the occasion. The weekday Amidah has thirteen berachot in the middle section, while the Amidah for Shabbat and for Yom Tov has only one middle berachah, known as קְדוּשַּׁת הַיּוֹם (the holiness of the day). The Amidah for Musaf of Rosh Hashanah has three middle blessings, unlike any other Amidah of the year.

It is actually wrong to speak about a "weekday" שְׁמוֹנֶה עֶשְׂרֵה, for the standard שְׁמוֹנֶה עֶשְׂרֵה is really a שְׁמוֹנֶה עֶשְׂרֵה for every day of the year. If an additional phrase were added to point out the special character of the day, one could fulfill one's obligation to recite the שְׁמוֹנֶה עֶשְׂרֵה with the weekday שְׁמוֹנֶה עֶשְׂרֵה on holidays and Shabbat as well.[99]

Berachot of Petition

The thirteen middle berachot (from אַתָּה חוֹנֵן to שְׁמַע קוֹלֵנוּ) are arranged in a specific order. This order, according to the Talmud,[100] is based on the sequence of verses in the Bible. But we can also understand a logical sequence in the order of the berachot. The fourth (אַתָּה חוֹנֵן) through ninth (בָּרֵךְ עָלֵינוּ) berachot are petitions of a personal nature: three deal with spiritual needs, and three deal with physical needs. The tenth (תְּקַע בְּשׁוֹפָר גָּדוֹל) through fifteenth (אֶת צֶמַח דָּוִד) berachot deal with the national needs of the Jewish people, such

R. Soloveitchik in רשימות שיעורים, ברכות דף כא עמוד ב, ד"ה אך קדושת כתר דמוסף.

99. שולחן ערוך אורח חיים סימן רסח סעיף ד

100. מגילה דף יז עמוד ב

as the ingathering of the exiles, the coming of the Messiah, and the complete redemption.[101]

The sixteenth, שְׁמַע קוֹלֵנוּ ("Hear our voice"), is a general prayer that gives us the opportunity to implore the Almighty to help us in any way that is not mentioned by the other middle berachot.[102] In addition, if you omitted something from a previous berachah, such as וְתֵן טַל וּמָטָר לִבְרָכָה ("Give us dew and rain as a blessing") in the berachah of בָּרֵךְ עָלֵינוּ, you have a chance to add it in this berachah of שְׁמַע קוֹלֵנוּ.[103]

On a fast day, an individual adds the request עֲנֵנוּ ("Answer us") to שְׁמַע קוֹלֵנוּ in Minchah, asking God to answer our prayers even before we have articulated them. Concerns that fit into other berachot, like for a seriously ill relative, can be inserted in the berachah of that theme. Many siddurim include a special addition in the berachah for health, רְפָאֵנוּ ("Heal us"), for this reason. If, however, there is a special need that is not reflected in any of the other specific berachot, it can be added in שְׁמַע קוֹלֵנוּ.[104]

However, according to the Tur, each of the middle berachot has a specific number of words or letters that is very meaningful. For instance, the berachah of אַתָּה חוֹנֵן לְאָדָם דַּעַת ("You grant humanity knowledge") has seventeen words, corresponding to the number of words in the verse (Exodus 28:3) וְאַתָּה תְּדַבֵּר אֶל כָּל חַכְמֵי לֵב אֲשֶׁר מִלֵּאתִיו רוּחַ חָכְמָה ("And you shall speak to all that are wise-hearted, whom I have filled with the spirit of wisdom").[105] The number 17 is also the gematria of the word טוֹב (good). This implies that דַּעַת (knowledge) is the greatest good that God can bestow upon a human being. The Sephardic version of the berachot often has more words than the Ashkenazic version, as it does not follow the Tur's opinion in this matter. While the Ashkenazic version more closely follows the Tur's

---

101. ספר אבודרהם שמונה עשרה ד"ה וכתב עוד כי י"ג ברכות אמצעיות וכו'

102. שולחן ערוך אורח חיים הלכות תפילה סימן קיט סעיף א

103. שולחן ערוך אורח חיים סימן קיט, סעיף א. Also שולחן ערוך אורח חיים סימן קיז סעיף ה.

104. See: עבודה זרה דף ח עמוד א.

105. טור אורח חיים סימן קטו

text, individuals nevertheless often add personal petitions to the berachot.

Fourth Berachah: אַתָּה חוֹנֵן

The text of the berachah is אַתָּה חוֹנֵן לְאָדָם דַּעַת, וּמְלַמֵּד לֶאֱנוֹשׁ בִּינָה, meaning, "You bestow innate understanding on people and enable mankind to use faculties of understanding." חָנֵּנוּ מֵאִתְּךָ דֵּעָה בִּינָה וְהַשְׂכֵּל, "Grant us the capability to use our innate abilities of discernment to explore and probe matters and arrive at true perceptions." בָּרוּךְ אַתָּה ה׳, חוֹנֵן הַדָּעַת, "Blessed are You who grants innate understanding."

Why is knowledge the first thing that we ask for? When Solomon became king, the Almighty encouraged him to ask for something of great value. King Solomon immediately asked for wisdom. The Almighty was very pleased with his request and said, "Since you asked Me for truly the greatest gift that I can give humanity, I will also bestow upon you many other gifts as well."[106] In our asking for knowledge first, we are following in the footsteps of King Solomon.

Looking at the berachah of אַתָּה חוֹנֵן, we notice that, unlike all the other berachot of petition, it starts with praising God. That is because this berachah is the transition from praise to petition.[107]

At the end of Shabbat or Yom Tov, we must add Havdalah[108] to the שְׁמוֹנֶה עֶשְׂרֵה. In fact, we say two Havdalahs: one in the שְׁמוֹנֶה עֶשְׂרֵה itself and one over a cup of wine.[109] These Havdalahs may be recited either in shul or at home. Before the Havdalah in the שְׁמוֹנֶה עֶשְׂרֵה, we are not permitted to do any type of creative work that is forbidden on Shabbat

---

106. מלכים א פרק ג: ג-יד

107. *Iyun Tefillah* in *Otzar Hatefillot*, p. 320.

108. See משנה ברורה סימן רצו ס"ק א: Havdalah means "separation." It is the prayer that separates, or distinguishes between, Shabbat or Yom Tov and the rest of the days of the week. Havdalah is the opposite and the parallel of Kiddush, which means "sanctification," and which serves to establish the beginning of Shabbat or Yom Tov. Both Kiddush and Havdalah are recited over a cup of wine.

109. שולחן ערוך אורח חיים סימן רצד סעיף א

or holidays.[110] Before the Havdalah over wine, we are not permitted to partake of food or drink other than water.[111] If we forget to recite Havdalah in the שְׁמוֹנֶה עֶשְׂרֵה, we can rely on the second Havdalah to also release us from the prohibition of performing Shabbat-forbidden work.[112]

The Talmud asks why Havdalah was added to the berachah of אַתָּה חוֹנֵן rather than to any other berachah, and it gives two answers. Rav Yosef explains that the ability to distinguish between what is holy and what is not is a basic form of wisdom, so Havdalah belongs in the berachah for wisdom. The Sages explain that the most appropriate place for Havdalah is in the first berachah that we say in the weekday unit of the שְׁמוֹנֶה עֶשְׂרֵה, as we usher in the beginning of the week.[113]

When we say Havdalah in the berachah of אַתָּה חוֹנֵן לְאָדָם דַּעַת, we add, אַתָּה חוֹנַנְתָּנוּ לְמַדַּע תּוֹרָתֶךָ ("You grant us the ability to know Your Torah"). That seems redundant. Indeed, there are opinions that suggest that at the conclusion of Shabbat, we should start this berachah with אַתָּה חוֹנַנְתָּנוּ לְמַדַּע תּוֹרָתֶךָ and leave out אַתָּה חוֹנֵן לְאָדָם דַּעַת. However, they aren't really redundant. These two statements express two independent ideas. In אַתָּה חוֹנֵן לְאָדָם דַּעַת, we ask for universal wisdom, whereas in אַתָּה חוֹנַנְתָּנוּ לְמַדַּע תּוֹרָתֶךָ we refer specifically to Torah wisdom; therefore, we should say both phrases.[114]

How many separations does this berachah contain? וַתַּבְדֵּל ה׳ אֱלֹקֵינוּ ("And You, Hashem our God, separated"): (1) בֵּין קֹדֶשׁ לְחֹל ("between the sacred and the secular"), (2) בֵּין אוֹר לְחֹשֶׁךְ ("between light and darkness"), and (3) בֵּין יִשְׂרָאֵל לָעַמִּים ("between Israel and the nations"). The next phrase, בֵּין יוֹם הַשְּׁבִיעִי לְשֵׁשֶׁת יְמֵי הַמַּעֲשֶׂה ("between the seventh day and the six days of creation") is not counted as one of the separations since it is simply a recapitulation of "between the sacred and

---

110. שולחן ערוך אורח חיים סימן רצט, סעיף י

111. שולחן ערוך אורח חיים סימן רצט, סעיף א

112. ברכות דף לג עמוד א

113. ברכות דף לג עמוד א

114. See לבוש וב"ח אורח חיים סימן רצד סעיף א; R. Soloveitchik, *Blessings and Thanksgiving: Reflections on the Siddur and Synagogue*, pp. 86–87.

the secular."[115] There is a difference of opinion in the Gemara about how many forms of separation are necessary to mention in Havdalah. Rabbi Yehudah HaNasi says one suffices, but the Gemara cites another opinion which maintains that either three or seven should be recited. The source for seven types of separation is the seven times that God made distinctions between two categories in the Torah. Three is the minimum number to establish the presence of the weekday by changing the status quo, and it is based on three being necessary to establish a חֲזָקָה (legal status of setting a precedent) in Jewish law. On most occasions, we mention three types of separation in Havdalah.

A special Havdalah is recited when Yom Tov immediately follows Shabbat. In Israel, the need for this special Havdalah is rare. Outside of Israel, however, each Yom Tov consists of two days, and the second day often begins on Motza'ei Shabbat. Rav and Shmuel, the great leaders of Babylonian Jewry (third century C.E.), were the authors of much of our liturgy. They composed the Havdalah that is recited between Shabbat and Yom Tov.[116] This Havdalah contains the seven maximum number of separations. The Talmud refers to this Havdalah as a pearl. The seven categories of differentiations of Havdalah in this berachah are: (1) בֵּין קוֹדֶשׁ לְחוֹל ("between the sacred and the secular"). (2) בֵּין אוֹר לְחֹשֶׁךְ ("between light and darkness"). (3) בֵּין יִשְׂרָאֵל לָעַמִּים ("between Israel and the nations"). These three phrases are the ones we use all year round. The next phrase, בֵּין יוֹם הַשְּׁבִיעִי לְשֵׁשֶׁת יְמֵי הַמַּעֲשֶׂה ("between the seventh day and the six days of creation") is not counted because it is a restatement of בֵּין קוֹדֶשׁ לְחוֹל. It is included in the regular Havdalah because a summary is necessary before the conclusion of a בְּרָכָה אֲרִיכְתָּא (a long berachah). Although in this version of Havdalah, this does not serve as a restatement before the conclusion, we nevertheless retain this phrase. We continue to add four more differentiations that reflect the changes in kedushah (holiness) that occur between the Shabbat and the festival: (4) בֵּין קְדֻשַּׁת שַׁבָּת לִקְדֻשַּׁת יוֹם טוֹב הִבְדַּלְתָּ ("You have distinguished between the sanctity of Shabbat and the sanctity of

115. See פסחים דף קג עמוד ב-דף קד עמוד א.

116. ברכות לג עמוד ב.

Yom Tov"). This is a reference to a category of actions referred to as צוֹרֶךְ אוֹכֶל נֶפֶשׁ that permits performing acts related to food preparation for Yom Tov that would not be allowed on Shabbat. (5) וְאֶת יוֹם הַשְּׁבִיעִי מִשֵּׁשֶׁת יְמֵי הַמַּעֲשֶׂה קִדַּשְׁתָּ ("and You sanctified the seventh day from the six days of Creation"). This refers to the difference between the intermediary days of Sukkot and Pesach where, unlike on Shabbat or Yom Tov itself, work is permissible for the sake of the holiday or to prevent financial loss. (6) הִבְדַּלְתָּ ("You have differentiated") and (7) וְקִדַּשְׁתָּ ("and You have hallowed") אֶת עַמְּךָ יִשְׂרָאֵל בִּקְדֻשָּׁתֶךָ ("Your people of Israel with Your holiness"). These last refer to the differences between the Kohanim and the Levi'im in the one case, and between the Kohanim and Levi'im together as opposed to the rest of the Jewish people on the other.[117]

Fifth Berachah: הֲשִׁיבֵנוּ

The second of the middle berachot is הֲשִׁיבֵנוּ אָבִינוּ לְתוֹרָתֶךָ ("Bring us back, our Father, to Your Torah"), וְקָרְבֵנוּ מַלְכֵּנוּ לַעֲבוֹדָתֶךָ ("and bring us near, our King, to Your service"), וְהַחֲזִירֵנוּ בִּתְשׁוּבָה שְׁלֵמָה לְפָנֶיךָ ("and bring us back in full repentance before You"); בָּרוּךְ אַתָּה ה׳ הָרוֹצֶה בִּתְשׁוּבָה ("Blessed are You, Hashem, Who desires repentance").

In this berachah we ask God to help us stay away from sin and become better Jews. Why do we ask God to help us in this matter? We have a basic philosophical concept in Judaism: that many things are predetermined: how long a person will live, whether a person has a certain innate talent, whether a person is tall or short. We have no say in these things really. But there is one thing that is totally up to us: to be good human beings or to be evil human beings. The choice between good and evil is all ours. This relates to what we call the "fear of Heaven." God will never interfere with whether we observe the commandments or live up to the tenets of Judaism.[118]

This berachah is a little difficult. What do we mean when we say,

117. רא״ש מסכת פסחים פרק י סימן יא, תוספות פסחים דף קד עמוד א ד״ה בעי

118. הכל בידי שמים - חוץ מיראת שמים :ברכות דף לג עמוד ב

"Bring us back to Your Torah"? It's not God's business; it's our business. We have to do it on our own.

This problem appears in other parts of the prayer book as well. For instance, every morning in the daily berachot we say, וְכֹף אֶת יִצְרֵנוּ לְהִשְׁתַּעְבֶּד לָךְ ("and force our inclination to be subservient to You"). How can we say "force"? We must fight the evil inclination ourselves. In these cases, we don't really take this literally. We mean that it's up to us to return to God, but we want God's help.[119]

The same issue is found in the Torah. We find first that Pharaoh was stubborn, but later it says that God made Pharaoh stubborn.[120] Why then should Pharaoh have been punished? Why should he suffer if God caused him to be stubborn? After a person has been given many chances, God may deprive him or her of the opportunity to return to Him. Pharaoh was given plenty of opportunities and finally had no more free choice.[121] Again, we cannot say this literally, because a human being always has free choice. Pharaoh had free choice, but it became much more difficult for him. God put obstacles in his way so it was not easy for him.

We explain this berachah in light of the precedents in the Torah. We

119. See מהרש"א חידושי אגדות ברכות דף י עמוד א ד"ה חטאים; רמב"ם הלכות תשובה פרק ו הלכה ד-ה. This sentiment is expressed by the Ramban in his explanation of the verse in Deuteronomy 30:6 (דברים פרק ל, פסוק ו), "And God will circumcise your hearts and the hearts of your descendants to love the Lord your God with all your hearts and all your souls." The Ramban cites a Gemara in Shabbat (104a) that if someone wants to purify himself, God helps him. The Ramban says that this is a promise that if you return to God with your whole heart, God will help you to do so.

120. See, e.g., שמות ז:ג.

121. See רמב"ן שמות ז:ג; רמב"ם הלכות תשובה פרק ו הלכה ג. Ramban (citing a Midrash) brings two views that he says are correct. According to one opinion, Pharaoh first hardened his own heart, and then Hashem punished him for those actions. The other opinion that the Ramban cites is that Hashem told Moshe that he knew what Pharaoh would do in the future. After Pharaoh would reject God's offers, God would use Pharaoh as an example to teach the world a lesson and demonstrate God's greatness.

ask God to remove temptation and obstacles from our way to make it easier for us to come back to Him. We cannot ask God to do it for us. It's still up to us. If we make the first effort, we ask God to help us somewhat. A person who is very hungry and passes a non-kosher restaurant will be tempted to eat there. But if he does not go near this restaurant, the temptation does not arise. Sometimes we might need a little help from God, and our prayerbook deals with this philosophical problem.

There are only two berachot, this one and the one that follows, where we refer to God as אָבִינוּ ("our Father") and מַלְכֵּנוּ ("our King"). We could have used these terms in any of the berachot, but since we didn't there must be a special reason for using these terms when we do.

In this berachah we say הֲשִׁיבֵנוּ אָבִינוּ לְתוֹרָתֶךָ וְקָרְבֵנוּ מַלְכֵּנוּ לַעֲבוֹדָתֶךָ ("Bring us back, our Father, to Your Torah, and bring us near, our King, to Your service"). Here God is referred to as our Father and our King because we, as God's children, receive from Him an inheritance which consists of the Torah and the Divine commandments. In that context we say "our Father." Bring us back to Your Torah, which we inherited from you. Give us our inheritance. Let us study Your Torah.[122] As far as referring to God as our King, once a person accepts upon himself the Divine yoke (in other words, accepts to keep the commandments), then he is freed from the yoke of other kingdoms. By accepting God's rule, we are removed from the rule of other kings. That is why we call God "our King."[123]

This berachah is structured along three parallel lines:

- הֲשִׁיבֵנוּ אָבִינוּ לְתוֹרָתֶךָ ("Bring us back, our Father, to Your Torah");
- וְקָרְבֵנוּ מַלְכֵּנוּ לַעֲבוֹדָתֶךָ ("and bring us near, our King, to Your service");

---

122. The טור אורח חיים סימן קטו states this idea: that as children vis-à-vis God, we can claim our right that He teach us the Torah because a father is obligated to teach his children Torah. See *Etz Yosef* in *Otzar Hatefillot*, ד"ה השיבנו לתורתך אבינו and ד"ה וקרבנו מלכנו לעבודתך.

123. See *Etz Yosef* in *Otzar Hatefillot*, ד"ה השיבנו אבינו לתורתך and ד"ה וקרבנו מלכנו לעבודתך.

- וְהַחֲזִירֵנוּ בִּתְשׁוּבָה שְׁלֵמָה לְפָנֶיךָ ("and bring us back in perfect repentance before You").

The first idea refers to the faculty of speech. The activity of Torah study involves speech. When you open the Bible and read the verses, or when you open the Shulchan Aruch to study the laws, you read them aloud. The second idea refers to deeds, while the third idea refers to our thought. Returning to God, or repentance, happens in our hearts.[124]

Thus, this berachah suggests that we want to serve God in those three areas that make human beings different from animals: speech, deeds, and thoughts. We ask God's help to do it properly.

It is interesting to note that this berachah starts and ends with the same letter, a heh (ה). No other berachah has this characteristic. Why is this berachah so structured?

The numerical value of ה is 5, so we have 2 × 5 = 10. We do תְּשׁוּבָה (the process of returning to God and repenting from our past misdeeds), primarily during the Ten Days of Repentance (between Rosh Hashanah and Yom Kippur).[125] This berachah, therefore, refers to the idea that even though the process of returning to God is important year-round, it is especially important during the Ten Days of Repentance, when God is more willing to accept our repentance and let us come close to Him. A verse from Isaiah,[126] דִּרְשׁוּ יְיָ בְּהִמָּצְאוֹ קְרָאֻהוּ בִּהְיוֹתוֹ קָרוֹב ("Seek God where He can be found, call to Him when He is near"), refers to the process of repentance during this time.

Sixth Berachah: סְלַח לָנוּ

The next berachah, the third of the middle berachot, is the berachah of סְלַח לָנוּ אָבִינוּ כִּי חָטָאנוּ מְחַל לָנוּ מַלְכֵּנוּ כִּי פָשָׁעְנוּ ("Forgive us, our Father, because we have sinned; pardon us, our King, because we have done iniquities"), כִּי מוֹחֵל וְסוֹלֵחַ אָתָּה ("because You are a forgiver and a

---

124. See *Dover Shalom* in *Otzar Hatefillot*, ד"ה השיבנו אבינו לתותך.

125. טור אורח חיים סימן קטו: והברכה מתחלת בה"י ומסיימת בה"י הרי י' כנגד י' ימים שבין ר"ה ליה"כ שמזומנים לבעלי תשובה.

126. ישעיהו פרק נה:ו

pardoner"); בָּרוּךְ אַתָּה ה׳, חַנּוּן הַמַּרְבֶּה לִסְלֹחַ ("Blessed are You, Hashem, who is gracious and forgives readily").

When we look carefully at this berachah, we find a number of difficulties. First of all, it refers to God as אָבִינוּ מַלְכֵּנוּ (our Father, our King), making it the second berachah in which we address God in this way. We then have two expressions in which we ask God's forgiveness: סְלַח, forgive, and מְחַל, pardon. First, we say "forgive" and then "pardon"; later we reverse this order.

What is the difference between סְלַח and מְחַל? סְלַח means to forgive our sins, but מְחַל has a slightly different meaning. When we use this term in Yiddish, it means to forgive a debt. If someone owes me money, I may say, "Ich bin dir moychel," meaning "you don't have to pay." This helps us to understand the difference between סְלַח and מְחַל. סְלַח involves Divine grace. If we sin, we have done something wrong, and we cannot retract it. But God in His Divine grace can elevate us above our sins and treat us as if they had never happened. It is a complete forgiveness by Divine grace. מְחַל, however, means canceling the debt. It means that you really did sin, but God will not collect the "payment" for the sin by punishing you.[127]

When we say סְלַח, we call God our Father because a father (theoretically or ideally) doesn't find fault with his children; he forgives them completely. Some parents are completely blind to their children's faults. In this case we are asking God to be like a perfect parent to us.

On the other hand, if a person rebels against a king, the king knows it and may never forget it, but he can be generous and withhold punishment even though a crime was committed. When we say מְחַל, we say that "we rebelled against You, and we cannot deny that it took place, but please do not punish us for it."[128]

Then we reverse the order, putting מְחַל before סְלַח. In order to explain this change, we have to look at the thirteen attributes of God that are listed in the Torah: ה׳ ה׳ קֵל רַחוּם וְחַנּוּן אֶרֶךְ אַפַּיִם וְרַב־חֶסֶד וֶאֱמֶת[129]

127. See *Iyun Tefillah* in *Otzar Hatefillot*, ד"ה סלח לנו אבינו.

128. See *Etz Yosef* and *Iyun Tefillah* in *Otzar Hatefillot*.

129. שמות לד:ו-ז

נֹצֵר חֶסֶד לָאֲלָפִים נֹשֵׂא עָוֹן וָפֶשַׁע וְחַטָּאָה וְנַקֵּה ("Hashem, Hashem, merciful and gracious God, slow to anger and true, provider of kindness for thousands, forgiver of intentional sins and rebellion, and eraser of sin"). An עָוֹן is a sin committed intentionally. A פֶּשַׁע is a sin committed in rebellion. A חֵטְא is a sin committed by mistake.[130]

Logically, this verse should mention the sin committed by mistake, the least offensive of the sins, first, but instead it lists it last. The verse mentions the more serious types of sins first to emphasize that they are, in fact, terrible sins, but that we want God to deal with the sins that were committed with premeditation as though they had been committed by mistake. In the same way, we put מְחַל before סְלַח at the end of this berachah.[131]

These three berachot have asked God to fill our spiritual needs: knowledge, repentance, and forgiveness. Now we move on to petitions for our physical needs.

Seventh Berachah: רְאֵה בְעָנְיֵנוּ

The fourth of the middle berachot reads as follows: רְאֵה בְעָנְיֵנוּ ("See our troubles"), וְרִיבָה רִיבֵנוּ ("fight our battles"), וּגְאָלֵנוּ מְהֵרָה ("and redeem us quickly"), לְמַעַן שְׁמֶךָ ("for Your name's sake"), כִּי גּוֹאֵל חָזָק אָתָּה ("because You are a strong redeemer"); בָּרוּךְ אַתָּה ה׳, גּוֹאֵל יִשְׂרָאֵל ("Blessed are You, Hashem, who redeems Israel").

When we finish the Shema, we immediately recite a blessing that ends, בָּרוּךְ אַתָּה ה׳, גָּאַל יִשְׂרָאֵל ("Blessed are You, Hashem, who redeemed Israel"), in the past tense. Now we say גּוֹאֵל, "who redeems," in the present tense.

When we thank God for taking us out of Egypt, as we do in the Shema, we are thanking God for something that took place in the past. In this berachah of the Amidah, however, we are speaking about our present needs. Therefore, we say, גּוֹאֵל יִשְׂרָאֵל, who redeems Israel at this moment, and the next moment – today, tomorrow, and always.[132]

---

130. רש"י שמות לד:ו

131. See *Etz Yosef* in *Otzar Hatefillot*, ד"ה כי מוחל וסולח אתה.

132. See פסחים דף קיז עמוד ב.

In this context, the present tense stands not only for the present but also for the future. It is a continuous action. God is always ready to redeem us.

It is important to be precise in pronouncing the end of this berachah while praying. If you were to say גָּאַל here, it wouldn't make sense, because this is not a prayer of thanks for the past but a petition for the future. We are asking for redemption, for the Jewish people to be free, for our exile to end, for us to be in the Land of Israel, and for the Messiah to come.

The first six berachot of the middle section of the Amidah, we have said, deal with personal needs, whereas the next six deal with national needs. When we pray to God in this berachah, "see our troubles," רְאֵה בְעָנְיֵנוּ, isn't this a national need? It seems that this berachah has not been placed in the right position; it should come later. It must be that this berachah is, in fact, not speaking about national redemption. Redemption can also refer to a personal redemption,[133] God helping me to overcome any impediment in life, helping me understand an important topic in the Gemara.[134]

Thus, the primary theme of רְאֵה בְעָנְיֵנוּ refers not to the rebuilding of Jerusalem or to the coming of the Messiah, but to helping us individually, giving each of us whatever we need. Since we couldn't spell out all our personal needs in the first three of the middle berachot, this berachah refers to any need that has not yet been articulated.

Berachah for Fast Days: עֲנֵנוּ

At this point, if it is a fast day in the Jewish calendar, the chazzan inserts the berachah of עֲנֵנוּ ("Answer us"). When we fast, we ask God to have

---

133. The Gemara (מגילה דף יז עמ׳ ב) asks why we have this berachah of redemption as the seventh berachah. The Gemara explains that it is because there is a tradition that the beginning of the redemption will come in the seventh era. Placing the personal berachah of redemption from our personal hardships as the seventh berachah alludes to the national redemption that will come in the seventh era.

134. רש״י מגילה דף יז עמוד ב ד״ה אתחלתא דגאולה.

additional mercy on us. This generates a special berachah, but why is it placed here? Why is it not placed in the general berachah of שְׁמַע קוֹלֵנוּ? Actually, there are two places where עֲנֵנוּ can be said: an individual does insert עֲנֵנוּ into the berachah of שְׁמַע קוֹלֵנוּ, but the chazzan leading a minyan of people fasting recites it as a separate berachah after the berachah of רְאֵה בְעָנְיֵנוּ.[135]

We have a fixed number of berachot in the שְׁמוֹנֶה עֶשְׂרֵה. An individual has no right to add another berachah, so all I can do is include this special prayer in the already established berachah of שְׁמַע קוֹלֵנוּ, which covers any request, wish or hope.[136]

אַנְשֵׁי כְּנֶסֶת הַגְּדוֹלָה allowed the community to address certain needs and a chazzan, on behalf of a community, can make special requests, but not in just any congregation. Before the chazzan says עֲנֵנוּ, there must be a community of fasters. If there is no minyan fasting, he may not say it. A chazzan only has special permission to add this extra berachah if he is representing a community of fasters who, by fasting, have a stronger right to call on God.[137]

Why does the chazzan add the berachah here rather than after another berachah? Again, we are following a pattern that King David established. Psalm 19 ends with the words יִהְיוּ לְרָצוֹן אִמְרֵי פִי וְהֶגְיוֹן לִבִּי לְפָנֶיךָ ה׳ צוּרִי וְגוֹאֲלִי ("May the utterances of my mouth and the thoughts of my heart be acceptable to You, Hashem, my Rock and Redeemer"). We plead to God, who is צוּרִי ("my Rock," or Creator) וְגוֹאֲלִי ("and my Redeemer"). The next verse in Psalms, the beginning of Psalm 20, begins, לַמְנַצֵּחַ מִזְמוֹר לְדָוִד יַעַנְךָ ה׳ בְּיוֹם צָרָה ("A Psalm of David for the conductor [in the Temple service]: May God answer you on the day of need"). Thus King David put together the ideas of וְגוֹאֲלִי, "my Redeemer," and יַעַנְךָ ה׳ בְּיוֹם צָרָה, "May God answer you on the day of need."[138] Following this juxtaposition of ideas, on a fast day, which is a

---

135. שולחן ערוך אורח חיים סימן תקסה סעיף א; סימן תקסו סעיף א

136. See תענית דף יג עמוד ב רש״י ד״ה וכי יחיד.

137. שולחן ערוך אורח חיים סימן תקסו סעיף ג

138. בית יוסף אורח חיים סימן תקסו:א וכן כתב הרי״ף וכתב באורחות חיים. Also מאירי בית הבחירה מסכת מגילה דף יז עמ׳ ב.

day of need, we recite עֲנֵנוּ ה׳ עֲנֵנוּ בְּיוֹם צוֹם תַּעֲנִיתֵנוּ ("Answer us, Hashem, answer us, on the day of our fasting") immediately after the berachah that concludes with בָּרוּךְ אַתָּה ה׳, גּוֹאֵל יִשְׂרָאֵל ("Blessed are You, Hashem, who redeems Israel").[139]

In ancient Israel, when there was a drought or famine, there was a series of fast days that we no longer observe. If the rains didn't start to fall by the beginning of the month of Kislev, a series of public fasts would be declared.[140] These public fasts were twenty-four hours long, during the last seven of which the Ark containing the Torah was taken from the shul to the city square, and there was an outpouring of sincere prayer.[141] On those days, the שְׁמוֹנֶה עֶשְׂרֵה was expanded to twenty-four berachot.[142] The extra berachot were added after רְאֵה בְעָנְיֵנוּ... וּגְאָלֵנוּ, because after we praise God as our Redeemer, we can bring all our special requests before Him. Since we don't have those fasts anymore, we now say only the berachah of עֲנֵנוּ for the fast days that we have today.

Originally, עֲנֵנוּ was said in all three prayer services of the day. After all, on Rosh Chodesh, the first day of the new month, that we celebrate as a minor holiday, we say the prayer that refers to the special nature of the day, יַעֲלֶה וְיָבוֹא, in all three services. When we make an addition to the service, we generally do so in all three services of the day. However, today, the Ashkenazic custom is that individuals recite עֲנֵנוּ only in Minchah.[143] Why?

The idea developed that if I said עֲנֵנוּ ה׳ עֲנֵנוּ בְּיוֹם צוֹם תַּעֲנִיתֵנוּ in Ma'ariv and Shacharit, and then did not complete the fast, I would have said something untrue. Therefore, the Rabbis decided that we should not say עֲנֵנוּ in the Ma'ariv at the beginning of the fast or even in Shacharit, because who can be sure in the morning of fasting all day long? Only

139. בית יוסף אורח חיים סימן תקסו

140. משנה מסכת תענית א:ד-ז. Also see שולחן ערוך אורח חיים הלכות תענית סימן תקעה סעיף ד

141. רמב״ם הלכות תעניות פרק ג

142. משנה מסכת תענית ב:ב-ג

143. רמ״א אורח חיים סימן תקסה סעיף ג

in Minchah, which we say shortly before nightfall, do we feel confident that if we fasted this long, we will probably fast the rest of the day.

The chazzan, however, can recite עֲנֵנוּ in Shacharit, too because he prays for the congregation and we are quite sure that there will always be some fasters in the congregation. We are not worried that the chazzan will be uttering a lie. (At night, there is no repetition of the Amidah for the chazzan to recite עֲנֵנוּ.)

Eighth Berachah: רְפָאֵנוּ

רְפָאֵנוּ ה׳ וְנֵרָפֵא הוֹשִׁיעֵנוּ וְנִוָּשֵׁעָה כִּי תְהִלָּתֵנוּ אָתָּה. This means, "Heal us, Hashem, and we will truly be healed, save us and we will be saved, because our source of pride is that You save us." וְהַעֲלֵה רְפוּאָה שְׁלֵמָה לְכָל מַכּוֹתֵינוּ, "Bring us a total cure for all our ailments," כִּי אֵ־ל מֶלֶךְ רוֹפֵא נֶאֱמָן וְרַחֲמָן אָתָּה, "because You are the Lord King true, merciful healer." בָּרוּךְ אַתָּה ה׳, רוֹפֵא חוֹלֵי עַמּוֹ יִשְׂרָאֵל, "Blessed are You, the healer of the sick among His nation, Israel."

The words of this berachah are taken from the Book of Jeremiah 17:14, רְפָאֵנִי ה׳ וְאֵרָפֵא הוֹשִׁיעֵנִי וְאִוָּשֵׁעָה כִּי תְהִלָּתִי אָתָּה ("Heal me, Hashem, and I will be healed . . . "). We change its form from the singular (רְפָאֵנִי, Heal me . . .) to the plural (רְפָאֵנוּ). This raises the problem of whether we have the right to change specific verses from the Bible to use in our prayers. We use biblical verses in our prayers as much as possible because of our sense of inadequacy when we come before God to speak to Him. We view the language of our prophets as a precedent.

This license to change a verse of Tanach only applies to an individual verse, but we may not take an entire chapter from Psalms and change it from singular to plural or vice versa.[144]

יְהִי רָצוֹן *in the Berachah of* רְפָאֵנוּ

The Mishnah states,[145] רַבִּי אֱלִיעֶזֶר אוֹמֵר: הָעוֹשֶׂה תְּפִלָּתוֹ קֶבַע אֵין תְּפִלָּתוֹ תַּחֲנוּנִים ("Rabbi Eliezer says: Whoever prays in a set manner renders his prayer ineffective"). One of the interpretations of קֶבַע (set) is that

144. רמ״א אורח חיים סימן קט״ז

145. ברכות דף כח עמוד ב

if we don't say something new every time we pray, then our prayers are not worthy.[146] There should be some new thought, new idea, or new intention in our prayers each time we pray, but we are often afraid that if we do this, we will lose our train of thought, get mixed up and thereby not finish our prayers properly.

In the berachah of רְפָאֵנוּ, many people add the prayer יְהִי רָצוֹן ("May it be Your will") if a loved one is sick, to beseech God for a cure. This prayer is printed in most prayer books.

The option of adding our individual thoughts holds true for every berachah in the שְׁמוֹנֶה עֶשְׂרֵה.[147] For instance, when you recite the berachah of סְלַח לָנוּ ("Forgive us"), and you did something you regret, you can specify that in your prayers and add, "Forgive me for [the specific wrongful deed]." It seems, in fact, to be a requirement, according to the Gemara, and not merely an option.

When we say יְהִי רָצוֹן, there are a few words that seem to be superfluous: בְּתוֹךְ שְׁאָר חוֹלֵי יִשְׂרָאֵל ("among the rest of the sick people in Israel"). Why do we have to say that? If I want a specific person to be healed, why do I have to mention every other Jew who is sick?

From this we learn that we do not have the right to pray for just one person. All Jews are equal. There are no privileged characters before God. The moment I say, "Heal this specific person," and I don't mention anybody else, it means that this individual is somehow more important, and it seems that I do not really care about the rest of the Jewish people. Thus, we always have to add בְּתוֹךְ שְׁאָר חוֹלֵי יִשְׂרָאֵל to show that God extends His mercy equally to the entire nation.[148]

Ninth Berachah: בָּרֵךְ עָלֵינוּ

בָּרֵךְ עָלֵינוּ ה' אֱלֹקֵינוּ אֶת הַשָּׁנָה הַזֹּאת, "God bless us that this year," וְאֶת כָּל מִינֵי תְבוּאָתָהּ לְטוֹבָה, "and its bounties be good," וְתֵן בְּרָכָה, "and grant us blessing" (in the winter, וְתֵן טַל וּמָטָר לִבְרָכָה – "grant us rain and dew for a blessing") עַל פְּנֵי הָאֲדָמָה, "on the land," וְשַׂבְּעֵנוּ מִטּוּבָהּ, "that we may

---

146. ברכות דף כח עמוד ב: רבה ורב יוסף דאמרי תרוייהו, כל שאינו יכול לחדש בה דבר

147. שולחן ערוך אורח חיים סימן קיט סעיף א

148. See רש"י שבת דף יב עמוד ב ד"ה בתוך חולי ישראל.

enjoy its fullness," וּבָרֵךְ שְׁנָתֵנוּ כַּשָּׁנִים הַטּוֹבוֹת, "and bless our year as the good years." בָּרוּךְ אַתָּה ה׳, מְבָרֵךְ הַשָּׁנִים, "Blessed are You, Hashem, who blesses the years."

In רְפָאֵנוּ, we asked for physical health. In the next berachah of the שְׁמוֹנֶה עֶשְׂרֵה we ask for sustenance, or food. Logically, if a person is ill, his ability to earn an income is impaired as well. Once we have prayed for God to grant us good health, we continue and ask him next for a full and easy livelihood. If someone has any concerns about sustenance, this is the berachah in which to ask for help. The text of this berachah varies depending on the season. Outside of Israel, from Ma'ariv on December 4th through Minchah on Erev Pesach, we say וְתֵן טַל וּמָטָר לִבְרָכָה. In Israel, saying וְתֵן טַל וּמָטָר לִבְרָכָה begins on the 7th of Cheshvan. The rest of the year we say instead the phrase וְתֵן בְּרָכָה.[149]

This berachah is a prayer for rain. In order to have income and livelihood in the Land of Israel, rain is essential. It is more important in Israel than in most other countries. Egypt, for example, depends on the Nile River to irrigate the land, but Israel depends entirely on the rains that come from the heavens.[150] The Rabbis in the Gemara say that God has reserved for Himself certain keys, and one of these is the key for rain.[151] The prosperity of the land depends on sufficient rain, which is itself dependent on God and our personal relationship with Him.

In Israel it doesn't rain after Pesach. In other parts of the world, the climate is different. Boston, for instance, needs a great deal of rain after Pesach for a good year. Suppose that someone who lives in Boston were to say, "I have a garden, a field and a vineyard. I need rain in the summer, so I would like to say וְתֵן טַל וּמָטָר לִבְרָכָה for longer." Is such a person permitted to extend the request for rain beyond Pesach? The Rosh said that it depends: If the people in a certain city need rain, they should ask for it in the berachah of שְׁמַע קוֹלֵנוּ, but if an entire country needs rain, they may say וְתֵן טַל וּמָטָר לִבְרָכָה even after the time we would

149. שולחן ערוך אורח חיים הלכות תפילה סימן קיז סעיף א

150. See דברים יא:י-יא.

151. תענית דף ב עמוד א

normally stop saying this.[152] But subsequent authorities did not agree with him. They said that even if an entire country needs rain during the summer, they should say וְתֵן טַל וּמָטָר לִבְרָכָה in שְׁמַע קוֹלֵנוּ, which is reserved for individual requests. The berachah of בָּרֵךְ עָלֵינוּ is reserved exclusively for the need for rain in the Land of Israel and no other place. This is how we have established the law.[153]

The other phrase relating to rain, מַשִּׁיב הָרוּחַ וּמוֹרִיד הַגֶּשֶׁם, which we discussed in the previous chapter, is said beginning on Shemini Atzeret. In that phrase, we are praising God as the giver of rain. Here, in the ninth berachah for sustenance, we are asking God, as a supplication, to give us rain. Logically, we should begin to say both of these phrases on the same day. In Israel we do start saying both closer together. We begin saying מַשִּׁיב הָרוּחַ וּמוֹרִיד הַגֶּשֶׁם on Shemini Atzeret, and we begin saying וְתֵן טַל וּמָטָר לִבְרָכָה on the seventh day of the Hebrew month of Cheshvan. This date, 7 Cheshvan, is fifteen days after Shemini Atzeret. In ancient times, before the Temple in Jerusalem was destroyed, Jews would make a pilgrimage to Jerusalem for the three major festivals (Pesach, Shavuot, and Sukkot). In order for them to have a chance to get home before the rains came, we would hold back our request for rain for fifteen days, enabling those Jews who lived the farthest from Jerusalem to reach home without any difficulties.[154]

Why do we wait so much longer to begin saying וְתֵן טַל וּמָטָר in the diaspora? The explanation is that if the Jews in Israel need rain, they should pray for rain. But if Jews outside Israel do not need rain (and, in fact, could have too much rain), they don't have to pray for rain until it is necessary, which Chazal determined was the sixtieth day of the season, i.e., the night of December 4th.[155]

Until early December, a lack of rain is not too dangerous in Israel. At that time, however, rain becomes a real need, and the danger of drought or famine looms. In ancient times, Jews would have declared

---

152. טור אורח חיים סימן קיז בשם הרא"ש

153. שולחן ערוך אורח חיים סימן קיז סעיף ב

154. משנה תענית א:ג

155. תענית דף י עמוד א ורש"י שם ד"ה ובגולה ששים

a special fast day by then,[156] so it becomes everyone's responsibility to pray for them. Even though people might live in the diaspora, everyone prays for rain in the Land of Israel because our brothers and sisters there need it.

Another issue concerning the two phrases for rain is the word that we use for rain. In the second berachah, we use גֶּשֶׁם, but in this berachah we use מָטָר. Why not be consistent and use the same noun twice? In the second berachah of the שְׁמוֹנֶה עֶשְׂרֵה, we enumerate the mighty attributes of God in His complete rule over nature. גֶּשֶׁם is one of those attributes of God's might. In this berachah, however, there is a moral aspect to rain, as explained in the second paragraph of the Shema.[157] If we are deserving, God will give us rain, but if we do not live up to His expectations, He will withhold the rain. מָטָר indicates not just the natural phenomenon of rain, but its connection to Israel's obligation to observe God's commandments.[158] Therefore, we are asking for God's guidance to help us preserve the מָטָר, and maintain our obligation to study and carry out the Torah.

The next line of this berachah is עַל פְּנֵי הָאֲדָמָה. There are two versions for the next two words: וְשַׂבְּעֵנוּ מִטּוּבֶךָ ("and satisfy us with Your goodness"), referring to God, or וְשַׂבְּעֵנוּ מִטּוּבָהּ ("and satisfy us with its goodness"), referring to the land.

The Vilna Gaon said "וְשַׂבְּעֵנוּ מִטּוּבָהּ." The commentary *Iyun Tefillah* supported the Vilna Gaon's version from the berachah we say after eating from the seven species of Israel (i.e., wheat, barley, grapes, figs, pomegranates, olives and dates) or drinking wine. There we say וְלִשְׂבּוֹעַ מִטּוּבָהּ ("and to be satisfied from its good"). Therefore, the *Iyun Tefillah*

---

156. משנה מסכת תענית י, עמ׳ א. See שולחן ערוך אורח חיים הלכות תפילה סימן קיז סעיף א, and the בית יוסף אורח חיים סימן קיז.

157. דברים יא:יד

158. The Malbim (ויקרא פרק כו אות ג) explains that גֶּשֶׁם refers to the natural phenomenon of rain, while מָטָר refers to the spiritual element of rain which is dependent upon Divine Providence and in which God makes it rain in response to our prayers.

believed that this is the correct text.[159] Of course, a person should follow his or her own tradition.

Tenth Berachah: תְּקַע בְּשׁוֹפָר גָּדוֹל

Now we come to the berachot that deal with national needs or redemption. This section starts with the berachah of תְּקַע בְּשׁוֹפָר גָּדוֹל לְחֵרוּתֵנוּ ("Blow the great shofar for our freedom"), וְשָׂא נֵס ("and lift the banner"), לְקַבֵּץ גָּלֻיּוֹתֵינוּ ("to bring our exiles together"), וְקַבְּצֵנוּ יַחַד ("and gather us together"), מֵאַרְבַּע כַּנְפוֹת הָאָרֶץ ("from four corners of the earth"). Here, Sephardim add the word לְאַרְצֵנוּ ("to our land"). The berachah ends with, בָּרוּךְ אַתָּה ה׳ מְקַבֵּץ נִדְחֵי עַמּוֹ יִשְׂרָאֵל ("Blessed are You, Hashem, who gathers the dispersed of His people Israel").

Why do we say תְּקַע בְּשׁוֹפָר גָּדוֹל? This phrase is also borrowed from the Bible. The prophet Isaiah[160] states: וְהָיָה בַּיּוֹם הַהוּא יִתָּקַע בְּשׁוֹפָר גָּדוֹל וּבָאוּ הָאֹבְדִים בְּאֶרֶץ אַשּׁוּר וְהַנִּדָּחִים בְּאֶרֶץ מִצְרָיִם וְהִשְׁתַּחֲווּ לַה׳ בְּהַר הַקֹּדֶשׁ בִּירוּשָׁלָםִ ("It will come to pass that on that day a great shofar will be blown and the lost Jews in the land of Ashur and the dispersed in the land of Egypt will come and bow down to God on the holy mountain in Jerusalem"). We pray that now be the time, לְחֵרוּתֵנוּ, for our freedom, and ask God to blow the great shofar.

Why do we call it a "great" shofar? Does it have special symbolism? The Midrash[161] says that we are speaking about the ram that Abraham found on Mount Moriah and sacrificed in place of Isaac. A ram has two horns: a big one and a small one. The left horn is not as powerful, strong, or big as the right horn.

The Midrash tells us that the left horn was the shofar that God blew on Mount Sinai when the Torah was given to the Jewish people. The right horn will be blown when the Messiah comes, and there will be complete redemption. In this berachah we are not asking for the type of revelation that we had on Mount Sinai but for the final revelation, when redemption comes to the Jewish people.

---

159. *Iyun Tefillah* in *Otzar Hatefillot*, ד"ה ושבענו מטובה; see also R. Hershel Schachter, *MiPeninei HaRav*, p. 36.

160. ישעיהו כז:יג

161. ילקוט שמעוני תורה פרשת וירא רמז קא ד"ה וישא אברהם את עיניו וירא והנה איל

Eleventh Berachah: הָשִׁיבָה שׁוֹפְטֵינוּ

The next berachah of the שְׁמוֹנֶה עֶשְׂרֵה is הָשִׁיבָה שׁוֹפְטֵינוּ כְּבָרִאשׁוֹנָה ("Return to us our judges as in the beginning").[162] After the berachah for the ingathering of the exiles, the next berachah logically deals with the next step: establishing judges who can bring the returning Jews back to God. The berachah continues וְיוֹעֲצֵינוּ ("and our advisors"), כְּבַתְּחִלָּה ("as in former years"), וְהָסֵר מִמֶּנּוּ ("and remove from us") יָגוֹן וַאֲנָחָה ("sorrow and sighing"), וּמְלֹךְ עָלֵינוּ אַתָּה ה׳ לְבַדְּךָ ("and You, Hashem, alone rule over us"), בְּחֶסֶד וּבְרַחֲמִים וְצַדְּקֵנוּ בַּמִּשְׁפָּט ("with benevolence and mercy and please find us righteous in judgment"). This berachah could refer to God's daily judgment of us or to His judgment on Rosh Hashanah. It could also refer to the ultimate judgment that every person has to face when one's soul is called to the next world. The berachah ends with בָּרוּךְ אַתָּה ה׳ מֶלֶךְ אוֹהֵב צְדָקָה וּמִשְׁפָּט ("Blessed are You, Hashem ... who loves righteousness and judgment").

This is one of the sections that is changed during the Ten Days of Repentance. Instead of saying מֶלֶךְ אוֹהֵב צְדָקָה וּמִשְׁפָּט we say הַמֶּלֶךְ הַמִּשְׁפָּט ("the King of judgment"). During the Ten Days of Repentance we want to emphasize that God is our King and our Judge, and we hope that our judgment will be favorable.

If a person forgets to say this alternate conclusion during the Ten Days of Repentance, the Shulchan Aruch says to go back to the beginning of this berachah and then continue from there. If you took three steps back already, the Shulchan Aruch says that you must go back to beginning of the שְׁמוֹנֶה עֶשְׂרֵה and repeat it with the correct ending of this berachah.[163] The Rama says that you are not required to repeat the שְׁמוֹנֶה עֶשְׂרֵה or return to the berachah,[164] because "King" is mentioned even in the regular conclusion to the berachah.[165] Ashkenazic Jewry follows the Rama's opinion.

---

162. This text is based on a verse from Yeshayahu (1:26): וְאָשִׁיבָה שֹׁפְטַיִךְ כְּבָרִאשֹׁנָה וְיֹעֲצַיִךְ כְּבַתְּחִלָּה.

163. שולחן ערוך אורח חיים סימן תקפב סעיף א

164. שולחן ערוך אורח חיים סימן קיח

165. משנה ברורה סימן תקפב ס״ק ו

Twelfth Berachah: וְלַמַּלְשִׁינִים

וְלַמַּלְשִׁינִים, "And regarding the slanderers," אַל תְּהִי תִקְוָה, "do not let them succeed." וְכֹל הָרִשְׁעָה כְּרֶגַע תֹּאבֵד, "And all wickedness should immediately be erased," וְכֹל אוֹיְבֵי עַמְּךָ מְהֵרָה יִכָּרֵתוּ, "And all the evil that is directed at Your nation should quickly be eradicated." וְהַזֵּדִים מְהֵרָה תְעַקֵּר וּתְשַׁבֵּר וּתְמַגֵּר וְתַכְנִיעַ בִּמְהֵרָה בְיָמֵינוּ, "And uproot and break and overthrow and suppress wickedness speedily in our time." בָּרוּךְ אַתָּה ה׳, שׁוֹבֵר אוֹיְבִים וּמַכְנִיעַ זֵדִים, "Blessed are You, Hashem, who breaks the evil and represses the wicked."

After bringing the Jews back to Israel and establishing a just and fair community, the next step is to eliminate the evildoers. That is covered in this berachah. This berachah is unusual in that it and only one other, וְלִירוּשָׁלַיִם ("And to Jerusalem"), start with "וְ" (and). There must be a reason for it. The commentators say that since the previous berachah asks for judges to restore the rule of law and Torah observance, this berachah, concerning those who go against Torah law, is then recited for emphasis. There is a very close thematic connection between the two berachot.[166] Another explanation derives from its historical context. Breakaway sects have often caused us trouble by trying to convert us or to make us change our beliefs. One such group was the Sadducees, who denied the validity of the Oral Law. They only accepted the Written Law, the Torah without any of its traditional explanations.[167] The Saducees existed during the time of the Second Temple. In post-talmudic times, a similar movement, called the Karaites, also ignored the Oral Law's interpretation of the Torah. They became very popular and constituted a real threat to

---

166. See *Iyun Tefillah* in *Otzar Hatefillot*, (עמ׳ קע) ד״ה ולירושלים עירך.

167. For instance, the Written Torah says to put the tefillin "between your eyes." The Oral Law interprets "between your eyes" as on one's head, above the eyes. The Sadducees, however, tied their tefillin between their eyes. The Sadducees also rejected the belief in תְּחִיַּת הַמֵּתִים, the reawakening of the righteous dead to live another physical existence in this world, because they said it was not mentioned in the Torah.

the survival of traditional Judaism. The Rabbis of this period had to convince the Jews of that time of the correctness of the Oral Law.[168]

Another threat came from powerful groups who wanted to accept Greek culture and reject all Jewish practices. One more example of a breakaway sect was the new Christian movement. According to the Talmud,[169] the recital of the Shema consisted of four sections, the additional section being the Ten Commandments, but this practice had to be discontinued because of the heretical statements of the Christians. They claimed that the recital of the Ten Commandments proved that only those commandments needed to be observed. To avoid doing anything that made the Ten Commandments seem more important than the rest of the Torah, and to fight the neglect of the other commandments that was promoted by the Jewish Christians, this section was removed from the daily recital of the Shema and was no longer part of the service.[170]

The Talmud calls וְלַמַּלְשִׁינִים the berachah against the sects (מִינִים).[171] The word מִינִים usually means "kinds," as in אַרְבַּע מִינִים, the four kinds of plants (lulav, etrog, willow, and myrtle) that we take on Sukkot. In this

---

168. This is most likely the origin of the statement made in Kol Nidrei before Ma'ariv on Yom Kippur. The original Kol Nidrei was a formula for the annulment of vows that was based completely on the Oral Law. On Yom Kippur, when all the Jews were assembled in the synagogues, the Rabbis made a statement about the importance of Oral Law by having the opening statement of the service come from the Oral Law.

169. ברכות דף יב עמוד א

170. In light of this, the custom of standing during the reading of the Ten Commandments in the synagogue Torah reading is difficult to understand. Since the Rabbis of the Talmud wanted to show that the Ten Commandments were not more important than the other commandments, Rav Soloveitchik believed that if you stand for the Torah reading all year round, you should stand for the reading of the Ten Commandments, but if you sit for the reading of the Torah throughout the year, you should sit for the reading of the Ten Commandments.

171. ברכות דף כח ע"ב - כט ע"א (in many editions of the Talmud, Christian censorship changed this name of the berachah to "the berachah against the Sadducees.")

context it could mean Jews of a different kind. Ismar Elbogen[172] maintains that in this case it refers to the Jewish Christians. Christianity started out as a Jewish sect. These Jews went to shul every morning, put on tallit and tefillin, and prayed with the congregation. They believed in the Torah, but they also believed in Jesus as the messiah and mentioned him in their prayers. They functioned as spies, because the Jewish Christians sided with the Romans against the Jews, who had ambitions for an independent nation and wanted to rebuild the Temple in Jerusalem. The Jewish Christians did not want to rebuild the Temple. They were taught that they didn't need sacrifices because Jesus had died for them instead. When the Jewish Christians heard that the Jews planned to build the Temple in Jerusalem, they went to the Romans who then arrested the Jewish leaders. As the Christians increased in number, they became a real danger for the Jewish people. We had spies in our midst and nobody knew who they were, because they didn't advertise the fact that they believed in Christianity.

Rabban Yochanan ben Zakkai received permission from the Romans to establish a yeshivah in Yavneh[173] and to convene the Sanhedrin (the supreme Rabbinic legislative body) there. He was not a descendant of King David, but he was the only leader approved by the Romans. After his death, Rabban Gamliel II, who was a descendant of King David and held the office of *nasi* (prince) restored the leadership to his own family.

Rabban Gamliel II settled the problem of identifying the Jewish Christians in our midst. He added this berachah of וְלַמַּלְשִׁינִים, to expose the members of the Christian sect so the Jews could be careful not to reveal their plans to them. When the chazzan came to this berachah, if a person skipped it or did not answer Amen after it, it became clear that this person was a Christian.[174] When a chazzan refused to say this berachah, or showed other signs of accepting other religions,

---

172. *Hatefillah Be'Yisrael*, p. 40 (התפלה בישראל בהתפתחותה ההיסטורית, יצחק משה אלבוגן, הוצאת דביר, ירושלים).

173. גיטין דף נו עמוד ב

174. ברכות דף כט עמ׳ א and see רמב״ם הלכות תפילה פרק י הלכה ג.

they were not allowed to continue with leading the prayers; they were silenced.[175]

The censors did not like this berachah and forced the Jews to change it many times. We know, more or less, the original text for all the berachot except this one. It is likely that it starts with "and" because there were preceding words that were censored. Most likely the berachah started with the word לַמְּשֻׁמָּדִים. A מְשֻׁמָּד is an apostate, a Jew who changes his faith. The berachah probably began, לַמְּשֻׁמָּדִים וְלַמַּלְשִׁינִים ("As for the apostates and the slanderers"). The sentiment expressed in this berachah is that Jews who changed their faith and slandered the Jewish people should have no hope, and their plans should not come true.[176]

In some versions of this berachah, the text reads, וְכָל עוֹשֵׂי רִשְׁעָה כְּרֶגַע יֹאבֵדוּ ("and all the evildoers shall be destroyed suddenly"). In other versions it says, וְכָל הָרִשְׁעָה כְּרֶגַע תֹּאבֵד ("and all evil shall be destroyed suddenly"). The first version asks that evil human beings should be destroyed, whereas the second version asks that evil itself be destroyed. There is a story in the Talmud[177] about Rabbi Meir, the famous Talmudic scholar, in which some people in his neighborhood were causing him great distress. Rabbi Meir was frustrated. When he davened, he prayed for God to destroy them. His wife, Beruriah, a great woman in Jewish history, said, "Meir, one shouldn't pray for a person to die. The Bible says, יִתַּמּוּ חַטָּאִים מִן־הָאָרֶץ ('Sins shall disappear from the earth').[178] Why don't you pray that they repent, and your problem will be solved?" He prayed that they would repent, and they did. The problem was solved. The version of וְכָל הָרִשְׁעָה כְּרֶגַע תֹּאבֵד follows Beruriah's advice by praying that evil, not the evildoers, be destroyed.

We then read the phrase וְכָל אוֹיְבֵי עַמְּךָ מְהֵרָה יִכָּרֵתוּ ("and all the enemies of Your people should quickly be cut off") followed by two

---

175. ברכות דף כט ע"א; שולחן ערוך אורח חיים סימן קכו סעיף א

176. See R. David Zvi Hoffmann, *Al Hatefillah*, p. 148.

177. ברכות דף י עמוד א

178. תהלים קד:לה

alternate texts: וְהַזֵּדִים מְהֵרָה תְעַקֵּר וּתְשַׁבֵּר וּתְמַגֵּר וְתַכְנִיעַ בִּמְהֵרָה בְיָמֵינוּ ("and the evildoers[179] should be uprooted, smashed, forcibly removed and suppressed speedily in our time"), or: וּמַלְכוּת זָדוֹן וְהַמִּינִים מְהֵרָה תְּעַקֵּר וּתְשַׁבֵּר וכו׳ ("and the evil kingdom and the sects should be uprooted, smashed," etc.). Here too, the second version asks for the "evil kingdom" to disappear, not its people.[180] This berachah teaches us that we have to protect ourselves from our enemies, but we prefer to pray for their repentance. In spite of the danger that was in our midst, it was still difficult for the psyche of our people to request that God punish human beings.

After the destruction of the Temple, around 70 C.E., the enemy from within tried to destroy Judaism. The survival of the Jewish people depended on the Sanhedrin in Yavneh. By exhibiting strength, Rabban Gamliel made the Sanhedrin in Yavneh the unchallenged authority of the Jewish people all over the world. To remain the unchallenged authority, Rabban Gamliel had to be firm and strict. He appeared at times to have been autocratic. In reality he was a kind and loving person, but he had to exert strength and stamina to preserve the unity of the Jewish people. He was greatly troubled by the influence of the Jewish Christians and decided once and for all to eliminate them from the Jewish people. This berachah was part of his plan.

If Rabban Gamliel had introduced this berachah by himself, however, his enemies would have come out against it and impugned his motives. So, very cleverly, he asked Shmuel HaKatan to compose this blessing.[181] Shmuel is most likely called "the Small" because of his

---

179. Rav Soloveitchik pointed out that the term זֵדִים (evildoers) is found in the prayer עַל הַנִּסִּים ("For the miracles") recited on Chanukah. There the term is used in parallel and as an antonym for the phrase עוֹסְקֵי תוֹרָתֶךָ ("those who are involved in Your Torah").

180. Since this berachah is referred to as the berachah of the sects, the word "sects" should occur in the text, although it does not in the Ashkenazi printed text of the siddur because of censorship. The destruction of the sects, together with the enemies of the Jewish people, is included in this berachah, albeit reluctantly.

181. ברכות דף כט עמוד א

humility. Everybody knew his noble character. Every Jew understood that Shmuel the Small acted out of love for his people and not out of hatred for his enemies, so his berachah was universally accepted by the people of Israel and introduced into the text of the שְׁמוֹנֶה עֶשְׂרֵה, making the "Eighteen berachot" into nineteen.

Thirteenth Berachah: עַל הַצַּדִּיקִים

After asking God to remove our enemies, we ask Him to have mercy on the righteous: עַל הַצַּדִּיקִים וְעַל הַחֲסִידִים וְעַל זִקְנֵי עַמְּךָ בֵּית יִשְׂרָאֵל וְעַל פְּלֵיטַת סוֹפְרֵיהֶם וְעַל גֵּרֵי הַצֶּדֶק וְעָלֵינוּ יֶהֱמוּ נָא רַחֲמֶיךָ ה׳ אֱלֹקֵינוּ, "Regarding the righteous and pious people, the elders of Your people Israel, the remnant of the teachers, the righteous converts, and on us, awaken Your mercy, Hashem our God."

All the terms used in this berachah are similar, but each one has a different nuance. A צַדִּיק fulfills the commandments properly, whereas a חֲסִיד goes beyond what is required by the law. The זִקְנֵי עַמְּךָ בֵּית יִשְׂרָאֵל are the members of the Sanhedrin. פְּלֵיטַת סוֹפְרֵיהֶם, the remnant of the teachers, refers to those who organized and categorized the laws. For instance, they said that there are thirty-nine categories of creative work that are forbidden on Shabbat. Another interpretation is that they protected the text of the Torah by telling us the number of words or number of letters in it,[182] which we call the מְסוֹרָה (tradition). This was necessary so that nobody could add to or subtract from it. In other words, the remnants of the teachers are the Talmudic scholars.[183]

We mention the גֵּרֵי הַצֶּדֶק (righteous converts), those who were born as non-Jews and converted. In the previous berachah of וְלַמַּלְשִׁינִים, we had to reject people. So, therefore, when we have the opportunity, we open our hearts to righteous converts to show that this is really our preference.[184] We wish for this always to be the case. We ask for God's mercy and for Him to grant that our lot should always be with them, that we should benefit from their spiritual greatness.

---

182. חגיגה דף טו עמוד ב. See *Iyun Tefillah* in *Otzar Hatefillot*, ד"ה ועל פליטת סופריהם.

183. See *Iyun Tefillah* in *Otzar Hatefillot*, ד"ה ועל פליטת סופריהם.

184. See R. Yissachar Yaakovson, *Netiv Binah* (Sinai: Tel Aviv, 1973), p. 324.

Fourteenth and Fifteenth Berachot

The fourteenth berachah begins, וְלִירוּשָׁלַיִם עִירְךָ בְּרַחֲמִים תָּשׁוּב, "And with mercy return to Your city Jerusalem." וְתִשְׁכֹּן בְּתוֹכָהּ כַּאֲשֶׁר דִּבַּרְתָּ, "Dwell in its midst as You said You would." וּבְנֵה אוֹתָהּ בְּקָרוֹב בְּיָמֵינוּ בִּנְיַן עוֹלָם. וְכִסֵּא דָוִד מְהֵרָה לְתוֹכָהּ תָּכִין, "And rebuild it as an eternal structure soon and in in our time." בָּרוּךְ אַתָּה ה׳, בּוֹנֵה יְרוּשָׁלַיִם, "Blessed are You, Hashem, Builder of Jerusalem."

The fifteenth berachah begins, אֶת צֶמַח דָּוִד עַבְדְּךָ מְהֵרָה תַצְמִיחַ, "May the descendant of David, Your servant, soon flourish," וְקַרְנוֹ תָּרוּם בִּישׁוּעָתֶךָ, "and may his kingdom be raised through Your salvation," כִּי לִישׁוּעָתְךָ קִוִּינוּ כׇּל הַיּוֹם, "because we long for Your salvation all day long." בָּרוּךְ אַתָּה ה׳. מַצְמִיחַ קֶרֶן יְשׁוּעָה, "Blessed are You, Hashem, who brings to fulfillment the kingdom of salvation."

When Rabban Gamliel added the nineteenth berachah, as we noted earlier, why was the name of the prayer (שְׁמוֹנֶה עֶשְׂרֵה) not changed to reflect this? Many scholars believe that the שְׁמוֹנֶה עֶשְׂרֵה of the Jews in Israel originally had only seventeen, not eighteen, berachot. In their opinion the two berachot of וְלִירוּשָׁלַיִם and אֶת צֶמַח דָּוִד were one berachah, ending with the words בָּרוּךְ אַתָּה ה׳ אֱלֹקֵי דָוִד וּבוֹנֵה יְרוּשָׁלַיִם ("Blessed are You, Hashem, God of David and Builder of Jerusalem"). Thus, the berachah added by Rabban Gamliel made a total of eighteen berachot.[185]

Our ancestors in Babylonia, however, recited them as two separate berachot. There had always been one more berachah in Babylonia than in Israel. Why did the Jews of Babylonia do this? In the diaspora, Christians claimed that the Messiah had already come. Jews felt a great deal of pressure from the Christians around them and wanted to emphasize that the Messiah hasn't yet come. Rav Soloveitchik explained that the Jews in Babylonia were concerned about their survival in exile until the coming of the Messiah, so they split the berachah in two. The berachah of אֶת צֶמַח דָּוִד עַבְדְּךָ מְהֵרָה תַצְמִיחַ ("May the descendant of David, Your servant, soon flourish") is a plea for keeping our identity even in the diaspora.

---

185. See Rabbi David Zvi Hoffman, *Al Hatefillah*, pp. 159–160.

One proof that the Amidah in Israel had only seventeen berachot can be found in the poetry of Rabbi Elazar Hakalir. We know very little about Rabbi Elazar Hakalir. Most scholars seem to agree that he lived in Israel about 600 years after the destruction of the Second Temple. He composed a poem to be added to the repetition of the שְׁמוֹנֶה עֶשְׂרֵה on Purim morning, in which he included a special verse for each berachah.[186] In this poem, there is no additional verse for the berachah of אֶת צֶמַח דָּוִד. This seems to indicate that there was no separate berachah of אֶת צֶמַח דָּוִד in his time and place. That the two berachot were only one unit may also explain why the berachah for Jerusalem begins with "and." (In our siddur today, however, the Jerusalem berachah precedes the Davidic berachah.)

The Davidic berachah emphasizes that the Messiah has not yet come and that we eagerly look forward every day to his coming. The Jews living in exile worried that they might not survive until the Messianic era, so they carved out of the berachah for Jerusalem a second berachah, which is a fervent plea that we may survive to that great era. The exile brings new dangers each day of our lives. Therefore, we emphasize that we need the strength and stamina to endure the hardships of life in exile.

Sixteenth Berachah: שְׁמַע קוֹלֵנוּ

שְׁמַע קוֹלֵנוּ ה׳ אֱלֹקֵינוּ חוּס וְרַחֵם עָלֵינוּ, "Hear our voices, Hashem our God, have pity and mercy on us, וְקַבֵּל בְּרַחֲמִים וּבְרָצוֹן אֶת תְּפִלָּתֵנוּ, "and accept our prayers mercifully and willingly, כִּי קֵל שׁוֹמֵעַ תְּפִלּוֹת וְתַחֲנוּנִים אָתָּה, "because You are a God who listens to prayers and pleas. וּמִלְּפָנֶיךָ מַלְכֵּנוּ רֵיקָם אַל תְּשִׁיבֵנוּ, "Do not answer us, our King, by sending us away empty handed, כִּי אַתָּה שׁוֹמֵעַ תְּפִלַּת עַמְּךָ יִשְׂרָאֵל בְּרַחֲמִים, "because You do listen to the prayers of Your people Israel with mercy." בָּרוּךְ אַתָּה ה׳ שׁוֹמֵעַ תְּפִלָּה, "Blessed are You, Hashem, who listens to prayers."

שְׁמַע קוֹלֵנוּ is a berachah that is a catch-all that gives us the opportunity to add any requests that might not have fit in elsewhere in the שְׁמוֹנֶה עֶשְׂרֵה.

---

186. In many siddurim, this is referred to as קְרוֹבֶץ לְפוּרִים.

שְׁמַע קוֹלֵנוּ can be used to add petitions from any of the requests left out of the middle section of the שְׁמוֹנֶה עֶשְׂרֵה (as in a case where a request or phrase was forgotten in an earlier berachah), or to add petitions for any additional matter not covered earlier.[187] It is an important berachah because of the idea that we mentioned earlier that we should not allow our prayers to become fixed and routine.[188]

In some prayer books the phrase before the conclusion of the berachah reads, כִּי אַתָּה שׁוֹמֵעַ תְּפִלַּת כָּל פֶּה ("because You hear the prayers of every mouth"). Other prayer books read כִּי אַתָּה שׁוֹמֵעַ תְּפִלַּת עַמְּךָ יִשְׂרָאֵל בְּרַחֲמִים ("because You hear the prayers of Your people, Israel, with mercy"). Rav Soloveitchik used to say both versions together when he recited the Amidah: כִּי אַתָּה שׁוֹמֵעַ תְּפִלַּת עַמְּךָ יִשְׂרָאֵל בְּרַחֲמִים. כִּי אַתָּה שׁוֹמֵעַ תְּפִלַּת כָּל פֶּה. בָּרוּךְ אַתָּה ה׳. שׁוֹמֵעַ תְּפִלָּה.

THE AMIDAH: BERACHOT OF THANKS

After we finish making our requests in the middle section of the שְׁמוֹנֶה עֶשְׂרֵה, we express our gratitude to God in the last three berachot. In the words of the Tur,[189] אַחֲרוֹנוֹת לְמָה הֵם דוֹמִים לְעֶבֶד שֶׁקִּבֵּל פְּרָס מֵרַבּוֹ שֶׁמְּשַׁבְּחוֹ ("The last berachot resemble a servant who has received a reward from his master and praises him"). But is that really true? The berachah of רְצֵה ("Accept") sounds more like a petition than thanks. Doesn't this berachah duplicate the idea of שְׁמַע קוֹלֵנוּ? The next berachah, called מוֹדִים ("We thank"), is indeed a berachah of thanks. But the final one, שִׂים שָׁלוֹם ("Grant peace") is certainly a request. In fact, the Tur's statement is based on the Talmud, but is slightly different from it. The Talmud[190] states that the final three berachot "one is like a servant who already received a reward from his master and is taking his leave and departing," but it does not say that they are all praise. They are a mix of praise and requests, but since they are the berachot

187. שולחן ערוך אורח חיים סימן קיט סעיף א; עבודה זרה דף ח עמוד א

188. See the section on יְהִי רָצוֹן in the berachah of רְפָאֵנוּ.

189. טור אורח חיים סימן קיב

190. ברכות דף לד עמוד א

in which we are taking leave from our master, they are not the place for personal requests.[191]

Seventeenth Berachah: רְצֵה

The berachah of רְצֵה[192] starts with: רְצֵה ה׳ אֱלֹקֵינוּ בְּעַמְּךָ יִשְׂרָאֵל וּבִתְפִלָּתָם ("Accept, Hashem, our God, Your people Israel and their prayers").

The next phrase, וְהָשֵׁב אֶת הָעֲבוֹדָה לִדְבִיר בֵּיתֶךָ וְאִשֵּׁי יִשְׂרָאֵל וּתְפִלָּתָם בְּאַהֲבָה תְקַבֵּל בְּרָצוֹן, presents a difficulty with regard to the placement of the words וְאִשֵּׁי יִשְׂרָאֵל ("and the fire offerings of Israel"). Does it belong to the phrase before it, וְהָשֵׁב אֶת הָעֲבוֹדָה לִדְבִיר בֵּיתֶךָ וְאִשֵּׁי יִשְׂרָאֵל ("and return the worship service and the fire offerings of Israel to the sanctuary of Your abode")? If so, then it is referring to the worship service and should be read as a part of that phrase.[193] Perhaps it belongs to the phrase following it: וְאִשֵּׁי יִשְׂרָאֵל וּתְפִלָּתָם בְּאַהֲבָה תְקַבֵּל בְּרָצוֹן ("Accept with goodwill and love the fire offerings of Israel and their prayers"). But today, there are no "fire offerings of Israel." Why would we ask God to accept them? The Tur[194] cites the Midrash which states that the archangel Michael offers up the souls of the righteous on the heavenly altar, and therefore the "fire offerings of Israel" means the souls of the righteous: the many personal sacrifices of time, money, and strength that God should accept along with the prayers of the Jewish people.

This berachah, which discusses the Temple service, concludes, וְתֶחֱזֶינָה עֵינֵינוּ בְּשׁוּבְךָ לְצִיּוֹן בְּרַחֲמִים בָּרוּךְ אַתָּה ה׳ הַמַּחֲזִיר שְׁכִינָתוֹ לְצִיּוֹן ("Let our eyes see Your return to Zion in mercy. Blessed are You, Hashem, who returns His presence to Zion").

After the destruction of the Temple, the berachah of רְצֵה had to be changed from a berachah for the acceptance of the Temple service to a request for the rebuilding of the Temple. The daily conclusion of the berachah is הַמַּחֲזִיר שְׁכִינָתוֹ לְצִיּוֹן ("who returns His presence to Zion"). During the time that the Temple existed, this ending would

191. See also שו"ת רדב"ז חלק ח׳ סימן ט"ו.

192. It is sometimes referred to as the berachah of עֲבוֹדָה (worship).

193. טור, בית יוסף ופרישה, אורח חיים סימן קכ

194. טור אורח חיים סימן קכ; תוספות מנחות דף קי עמוד א ד"ה ומיכאל שר הגדול

not have made sense. While the Temple was still standing, the conclusion to the berachah was שֶׁאוֹתְךָ לְבַדְּךָ בְּיִרְאָה נַעֲבֹד ("whom we will worship exclusively in awe").[195] This latter conclusion is still used in most congregations in the diaspora on the days that we say בִּרְכַּת כֹּהֲנִים (the Priestly Blessing). We forget our humiliations and suffering for a moment and imagine that we still have the Temple in our midst. It is worth noting that Rav Soloveitchik abolished this custom in his congregation, because we are not permitted to change the text of a berachah.[196]

יַעֲלֶה וְיָבוֹא

On special days that have greater holiness, we mention the character of the day (מֵעֵין הַמְּאֹרָע) by including the prayer יַעֲלֶה וְיָבוֹא in the berachah of רְצֵה in the שְׁמוֹנֶה עֶשְׂרֵה in Shacharit, in Minchah and in Ma'ariv.[197] On Yom Tov itself, there is no need to mention the holiday in רְצֵה because the entire middle berachah of the Amidah is devoted to the holiday. Thus, the only days on which we add יַעֲלֶה וְיָבוֹא to רְצֵה are days on which we recite the weekday שְׁמוֹנֶה עֶשְׂרֵה, but which nonetheless have additional holiness: Rosh Chodesh and the intermediate days of a festival. On all Yamim Tovim and Rosh Chodesh, we add יַעֲלֶה וְיָבוֹא to the third berachah of בִּרְכַּת הַמָּזוֹן.[198]

Originally, in the time of the Temple, the special character of Shabbat and Yom Tov was expressed by the specific sacrifices of that day. In רְצֵה and the בִּרְכַּת הַמָּזוֹן, we ask for the restoration of the sacrificial service. Logically, the special character of the day expressed by the sacrifices belongs in the berachah that speaks about the sacrifices.[199] When Shabbat fell on a day that יַעֲלֶה וְיָבוֹא is recited, Rav Soloveitchik

195. See רש"י ברכות דף יא עמוד ב ד"ה ועבודה; *Seder Avodat Yisrael*, ד"ה רצה; R. David Zvi Hoffmann, *Al Hatefillah*, p. 157.

196. As in many of his customs, R. Soloveitchik was following the practice of the Vilna Gaon. See *Pe'at Hashulchan* (הלכות ארץ ישראל, סימן ב ס"ק כד).

197. שבת דף כד עמוד א

198. שולחן ערוך אורח חיים סימן תכד סעיף א; סימן תצ סעיף ב

199. See also Tosafot (תוספות שבת דף כד עמוד א ד"ה בבונה ירושלים) who explain that יַעֲלֶה וְיָבוֹא was placed in the berachah of the Avodah (רְצֵה) in the Amidah

would add the phrase בְּיוֹם הַשַּׁבָּת הַזֶּה ("on this Sabbath day") to יַעֲלֶה וְיָבוֹא in order to mention the full nature of the holiness of the day.

Eighteenth Berachah: מוֹדִים

The next berachah is the berachah of thanks to God, מוֹדִים ("We thank").

Earlier in Pesukei D'Zimrah, we said the מִזְמוֹר לְתוֹדָה for all the miracles of which we are not aware.[200] In מוֹדִים we thank God for all the miracles of which we are aware.

In מוֹדִים we say the phrase נוֹדֶה לְּךָ וּנְסַפֵּר תְּהִלָּתֶךָ ("We will thank You and tell of Your praises"). The word מוֹדִים actually means both "thank" and "acknowledge." The גִּימַטְרִיָּא of מוֹדִים is 100. This is a reminder to us that one way to show our gratitude to God is not by just standing up at מוֹדִים and bowing down in appreciation, but by saying 100 berachot each day.[201]

The last section of מוֹדִים begins וְכָל הַחַיִּים יוֹדוּךָ סֶּלָה ("And all the living shall thank You"). Of course, it is the living who thank God – if we are dead, we can't thank God anymore. It seems to be an obvious statement.

One possible answer is that the word חַיִּים ("the living") can be understood as an acronym for the four situations which require a person to give thanks to God. The "ח" stands for חָבוּשׁ בְּבֵית הָאֲסוּרִים (one who was imprisoned and has now been released); the first "י" stands for יִסּוּרִין (one who was afflicted with disease and has now been healed); the second "י" yud stands for יָם (one who safely crossed the ocean); and the "מ" mem stands for מִדְבָּרוֹת (one who safely crossed the desert). When a person survives one of these experiences, the Gemara says that it is apprpopriate to publicly thank God for being delivered from a great danger.[202] The public expression of this gratitude is the

---

because that is a prayer for the return of Israel to Jerusalem. It was placed in the berachah of בּוֹנֵה יְרוּשָׁלַיִם in בִּרְכַּת הַמָּזוֹן for the same reason.

200. Seder Avodat Yisrael on Mizmor L'todah, p. 61.

201. Seder Avodat Yisrael, pp. 99–100.

202. ברכות דף נד עמוד ב and תהלים קז.

berachah called בִּרְכַּת הַגּוֹמֵל (the berachah to the Benefactor) that is recited in the presence of a minyan.[203]

In the berachah of מוֹדִים we thank God for all the miracles which might not warrant בִּרְכַּת הַגּוֹמֵל. As the berachah sets forth: נוֹדֶה לְּךָ וּנְסַפֵּר תְּהִלָּתֶךָ עַל חַיֵּינוּ הַמְּסוּרִים בְּיָדֶךָ וְעַל נִשְׁמוֹתֵינוּ הַפְּקוּדוֹת לָךְ וְעַל נִסֶּיךָ שֶׁבְּכָל יוֹם עִמָּנוּ וְעַל נִפְלְאוֹתֶיךָ וְטוֹבוֹתֶיךָ שֶׁבְּכָל עֵת עֶרֶב וָבֹקֶר וְצָהֳרָיִם ("We thank You and speak Your praise for our lives which are in Your hands and for our souls which are entrusted to You, and for the miracles You perform for us each day, and for the wonders and kindnesses that You do at all times, evening, morning and afternoon"). We publicly say בִּרְכַּת הַגּוֹמֵל for being saved on four specific occasions, but for all other occasions, we thank God in this berachah of מוֹדִים.

During the repetition of the Amidah, we usually just listen to the chazzan's recitation of the berachot and answer "Amen." In the berachah of מוֹדִים, however, we recite the alternate version that was instituted by the Rabbis, known as מוֹדִים דְּרַבָּנָן.[204] Generally, someone else can say prayers for me, such as a father making Kiddush for his family or the *ba'al koreh* reading the Torah for the whole shul. This is the halacha of שׁוֹמֵעַ כְּעוֹנֶה (listening is like reciting). When you listen with the intention of fulfilling the berachah, and when the person who recites the berachah has the intention of including you in the recitation, it is as though you yourself recited the berachah. With respect to giving thanks to God and accepting His sovereignty, we are reluctant to invoke this rule; we want to speak the words ourselves. Thus, when the chazzan recites מוֹדִים, each person recites the version that was instituted by the Rabbis.[205]

עַל הַנִּסִּים

Chanukah and Purim have no special holiness (קְדֻשַּׁת הַיּוֹם) since they were instituted after the Torah was given. It is the Torah, after all, that established the degree of holiness of the days. Nevertheless, we have

---

203. שולחן ערוך אורח חיים סימן ריט סעיף א

204. סוטה דף מ עמוד א; שולחן ערוך אורח חיים סימן קכז סעיף א

205. See Avudraham, ד"ה וכשיגיע ש"ץ למודים.

to mention the special character of Chanukah and Purim in the שְׁמוֹנֶה עֶשְׂרֵה as they were occasions when Judaism or the Jews were saved from destruction. We add עַל הַנִּסִּים in the berachah of מוֹדִים to thank God for our salvation.[206]

What do we do if we neglected to say עַל הַנִּסִּים? If we remember within the berachah of מוֹדִים, we can still recite it, but if we forgot until after we completed that berachah, we don't repeat it.[207] If we forget to say עַל הַנִּסִּים in בִּרְכַּת הַמָּזוֹן, when we reach the section of the הָרַחֲמָן verses, we can say הָרַחֲמָן יַעֲשֶׂה לָנוּ נִסִּים וְנִפְלָאוֹת כְּשֵׁם שֶׁעָשִׂיתָ לַאֲבוֹתֵינוּ בַּיָּמִים הָהֵם בַּזְּמַן הַזֶּה בִּימֵי מַתִּתְיָהוּ כו׳ ("Merciful One, grant us wonders and miracles as You did to our ancestors in this season in previous times").[208]

בִּרְכַּת כֹּהֲנִים

בִּרְכַּת כֹּהֲנִים is supposed to be recited daily during Shacharit and, on those days that it is said, in Musaf. It is also said in Ne'ilah and on other fast days in Minchah when Minchah is said close to sunset.[209] Minchah on a fast day close to sunset has a status of Ne'ilah.

Today, the Ashkenazic custom is that Kohanim ("priests," or descendants of Aharon) outside of Israel do not recite the בִּרְכַּת כֹּהֲנִים every morning. They only recite this berachah on Yamim Tovim, and even then, only in Musaf. It is very difficult to understand why we do not say בִּרְכַּת כֹּהֲנִים daily as the commandment actually requires.

The reason offered by the Rama[210] is that in order to bless a person, one has to be happy. In exile, life has been very hard for the Jew. It was almost a miracle that Jews could survive each day, especially in the Middle Ages. They simply did not have that extra feeling of joy to be able to convey it to the community. Therefore, the Kohanim abandoned the practice of their daily blessing.

Rav Soloveitchik used to say that the Vilna Gaon didn't see any

---

206. תוספות שבת דף כד עמוד א; שולחן ערוך אורח חיים סימן תרפב סעיף א

207. שולחן ערוך אורח חיים סימן תרפב סעיף ב

208. שולחן ערוך אורח חיים סימן קפז סעיף ד

209. שלחן ערוך אורח חיים סימן קכט סעיף א

210. רמ"א אורח חיים סימן קכח סעיף מד

logic in skipping בִּרְכַּת כֹּהֲנִים. One day the Gaon said to his people, "Tomorrow morning we will say בִּרְכַּת כֹּהֲנִים. There is no reason why we shouldn't say it." That night, on a false accusation, the Gaon was arrested by the czar's secret police. After this happened the Gaon said he would not again try to introduce a daily בִּרְכַּת כֹּהֲנִים. Rav Chaim Volozhin also thought the Vilna Gaon's reasoning was correct and Rav Chaim one day announced, "Tomorrow we will say the בִּרְכַּת כֹּהֲנִים." That night a fire started in the shul. Vilna had mostly wooden buildings, so the shul and half the town were destroyed. The Kohanim could not carry out the request. The shul was rebuilt, but he decided that these were signs that Heaven did not want it to be said.[211]

In the course of time, we introduced a "substitute" for בִּרְכַּת כֹּהֲנִים. It is recited by the chazzan on those occasions when we should say בִּרְכַּת כֹּהֲנִים but don't. Since we should recite the בִּרְכַּת כֹּהֲנִים during Shacharit, the chazzan says the substitute berachah there.[212] It is also recited in Shabbat Musaf when a Kohen does not recite the berachah, or even in Yom Tov Musaf when a Kohen would recite the berachah, but no Kohen is present.

Once נְשִׂיאַת כַּפַּיִם was recited during Minchah as well, but that custom has been abolished, because there is a law that a Kohen cannot recite this blessing if he has had any wine.[213] If he drinks even a small amount of wine, he is disqualified from saying the בִּרְכַּת כֹּהֲנִים. It used to be that people would drink wine with their meals. In many places they still do so today. Like everybody else, the Kohen would have had wine with his lunch. When he went to shul for Minchah, he would not have been able to say the בִּרְכַּת כֹּהֲנִים. Perhaps not being able to drink wine with his lunch would have spoiled his day. Perhaps he would have been embarrassed to admit that he had been drinking. In any case, the rabbis decreed: no more נְשִׂיאַת כַּפַּיִם at Minchah.[214]

On Simchat Torah, we have a similar problem because it is

---

211. See R. Naftali Tzvi Yehudah Berlin (Netziv), שו"ת משיב דבר חלק ב סימן קד.
212. רמ"א אורח חיים סימן קכז סעיף ב
213. תענית דף כו עמוד ב
214. שולחן ערוך אורח חיים סימן קכט סעיף א

customary to drink as part of the service. Most shuls have, therefore, instituted the practice of reciting the בִּרְכַּת כֹּהֲנִים during Shacharit, before the Torah service. Rav Soloveitchik disagreed with changing the custom from its norm, however, so the Kohanim in his shul did not drink on Simchat Torah until after Musaf.

Why do we say the בִּרְכַּת כֹּהֲנִים before the last berachah of the שְׁמוֹנֶה עֶשְׂרֵה? Parshat Shemini[215] talks about the dedication of the Mishkan in the desert. After all the sacrifices had been offered, the Torah says, וַיִּשָּׂא אַהֲרֹן אֶת־יָדָו אֶל־הָעָם וַיְבָרְכֵם וַיֵּרֶד מֵעֲשֹׂת הַחַטָּאת וְהָעֹלָה וְהַשְּׁלָמִים ("Aharon raised his hands over the people and blessed them; he descended from having sacrificed the sin offering, the burnt offering, and the peace offering"). Aharon offered all the sacrifices, and afterward he said the בִּרְכַּת כֹּהֲנִים. From this verse we derive that the בִּרְכַּת כֹּהֲנִים always follows the עֲבוֹדָה, which in its original meaning refers to the Temple worship. It has been expanded in the sense of worship of the heart to mean the שְׁמוֹנֶה עֶשְׂרֵה.[216] Thus, the Kohanim bless us here.

Is the בִּרְכַּת כֹּהֲנִים a Torah commandment or a Rabbinic practice? The Torah states it clearly, so it seems unequivocal that it is a Biblical commandment.[217] But it also says that Aharon recited the berachah right after the sacrifices were offered in the Temple. The question is whether or not בִּרְכַּת כֹּהֲנִים is still a Torah commandment even when there are no sacrifices.

The answer may depend on the status of the prayer service. If our prayer service is considered a "worship service" (*avodah*) on a Torah level, then the בִּרְכַּת כֹּהֲנִים still has the status of a Torah commandment. But if prayer is only considered to be *avodah* on a Rabbinic level, and the Torah commandment of בִּרְכַּת כֹּהֲנִים requires *avodah*, then

215. ויקרא ט:כב

216. The Gemara (Megillah 18a) says that the Priestly Blessing follows the berachah of Modim based on this verse (ויקרא ט:כב). The Torah Temimah (ויקרא פרק ט הערה יח) explains that you can't separate the berachah of Modim from the berachah of sacrifice (Retzeh) so נְשִׂיאַת כַּפַּיִם comes after the the berachah of Modim.

217. במדבר ו:כג

בִּרְכַּת כֹּהֲנִים today can no longer be viewed as a Torah commandment. However, almost all halachic authorities agree that even today בִּרְכַּת כֹּהֲנִים is a Torah commandment.[218] This may be because on a Torah level, בִּרְכַּת כֹּהֲנִים does not require *avodah* at all.[219] Alternatively, even according to the view that prayer is only a Rabbinic *requirement*, if one does pray it may be considered *avodah* on a Torah level.[220]

The verse in Numbers[221] states, כֹּה תְבָרֲכוּ אֶת־בְּנֵי יִשְׂרָאֵל אָמוֹר לָהֶם יְבָרֶכְךָ ה׳ וְיִשְׁמְרֶךָ... וְשָׂמוּ אֶת־שְׁמִי עַל־בְּנֵי יִשְׂרָאֵל וַאֲנִי אֲבָרְכֵם ("Bless the children of Israel like this. Say to them, 'May Hashem bless you…' They shall link My name with the people of Israel, and I will bless them"). We can interpret the word "אֲבָרְכֵם, I [God] will bless them" in two different ways. It could mean that God will bless the Kohanim; that is, the Kohanim bless the people and God blesses the Kohanim for doing His will. Or it could mean that God will bless the children of Israel, in which case the Kohanim are instrumental in conveying the words of the berachah, while the berachah itself comes from God.[222]

And what does the word כֹּה, "in this way," mean? The written Torah does not elaborate; we have to look to the Oral Torah for an explanation. The Gemara in Sotah[223] lists a number of requirements that we learn from this one word:

- בִּרְכַּת כֹּהֲנִים must be recited in Hebrew. It cannot be said in any other language.

---

218. See משנה ברורה סימן קכח סעיף מד, in a note, where he cites the Sifra and Sifrei, as well as other sources, to prove that בִּרְכַּת כֹּהֲנִים is not limited to the Beit Hamikdash. See also ערוך השולחן סימן קכח סעיף א.

219. See ביאור הלכה סימן קכח סעיף א ד"ה דזר עובר בעשה.

220. See R. Aryeh Pomeranchik, עמק ברכה, נשיאת כפים אות א, citing R. Chaim Soloveitchik.

221. במדבר פרק ו:כג-כז

222. Rashi on this verse offers both explanations as possible alternatives. Ibn Ezra suggests that both meanings are true: The verse means that God will bless the people and the Kohanim. The Rambam (הלכות תפילה וברכת כהנים פרק טו הלכה ז) clearly believes that the verse means that God will bless the people as a result of the Kohanim fulfilling the mitzvah.

223. סוטה דף לח עמוד א

- בִּרְכַּת כֹּהֲנִים must be recited while standing. If a Kohen cannot stand, he may not bless the people.
- בִּרְכַּת כֹּהֲנִים must be performed with outstretched hands.
- בִּרְכַּת כֹּהֲנִים is recited using the שֵׁם הַמְּפֹרָשׁ. This was true in the Temple. However, even in ancient times, when we recited the בִּרְכַּת כֹּהֲנִים outside the Temple, we did not pronounce the שֵׁם הַמְּפֹרָשׁ. The pronunciation that was used outside of the Temple, and which we use for this purpose today, is the name that refers to God as our Lord (*A-donai*).
- בִּרְכַּת כֹּהֲנִים is recited face to face. In many shuls the congregants don't face the Kohanim; they turn around, which is incorrect. The Kohanim stand in the front of the shul, and we are supposed to face them. There should be a direct interaction between the congregation and the Kohanim. However, we should not look at the Kohanim when they recite the blessing, nor should the Kohanim look at the people. The Kohanim should look down and focus on the blessing they are reciting, and the people should face the Kohanim without looking at them and focus on the blessing they are receiving.[224] But turning away makes it look as though you are rejecting the berachah. Someone who purposefully stands behind the Kohanim is also not included in the berachah, because that too is an act of rejection.
- בִּרְכַּת כֹּהֲנִים must be recited out loud. The Kohanim must say the berachah so that everybody can hear it.

Another halachah is derived from the words אָמוֹר לָהֶם ("Say to them"). Abaye understands these words to mean that you call on the Kohanim to recite בִּרְכַּת כֹּהֲנִים only if there is more than one Kohen present. If there is only one Kohen, you don't call on him. He would have to go up on his own without being called.[225]

---

224. רמב"ם הלכות תפילה וברכת כהנים פרק יד הלכה ז; שולחן ערוך אורח חיים סימן קכח סעיף כג.

225. סוטה דף לח עמוד א

There was an additional rule that was mentioned in this source. כֹּה תְבָרֲכוּ – "Bless in this way" – also means that this בְּרָכָה is intended as a בְּרָכָה exclusively between the Kohanim and the Jews. This is, however, a precondition for the בְּרָכָה, rather than a description of the way the בְּרָכָה must be performed.

The Priestly Blessing is related to תַּחֲנוּן (the Prayer of Supplication). This helps us to understand why תַּחֲנוּן is said (on a weekday) right after the שְׁמוֹנֶה עֶשְׂרֵה.

Ismar Elbogen makes this connection between prostrating ourselves when we hear God's name, as when the Kohanim recited the בִּרְכַּת כֹּהֲנִים in the Temple, and prostrating ourselves during תַּחֲנוּן. He says that after the sacrifices, the Kohanim arose and said the Priestly Blessing.[226] When the people heard the name of God in the Temple, they prostrated themselves. We still do this today on Yom Kippur when we invoke the worship service of the Temple. As the people were falling on their faces before God, each one poured out his heart to God. This is the precedent for saying תַּחֲנוּן in a prone position after the Amidah.

It is a great privilege to be blessed by the Kohanim, and such a privilege should not be taken for granted.[227] The Kohanim have to wait until the congregational leader gives them permission to pronounce the words of the berachah.[228] This is one explanation of why each word is recited by the chazzan before the Kohanim utter it. The Beit Yosef gives[229] another explanation, that this ensures the Kohanim will not make a mistake during the berachah. How do we call on the Kohanim? Rabbenu Tam was one of the Ba'alei Tosafot (and Rashi's grandson). He didn't think the chazzan saying "Kohanim" was a good idea.[230] When the Chazzan says "Kohanim," he means, "Come on. You have a job to do. Go up. We are waiting for you." Since the chazzan is

226. משנה מסכת תמיד פרק ז משנה ב. See יצחק משה אלבוגן, התפלה בישראל בהתפתחותה ההיסטורית, עמ' 59.

227. סוטה דף מ עמ' א

228. סוטה דף לט עמ' ב

229. בית יוסף אורח חיים סימן קכח, יג

230. תוספות ברכות לד עמוד א ד"ה לא יענה אמן

in the middle of the Amidah, and one is not permitted to interrupt in the middle of the Amidah, Rabbenu Tam says someone else, like the gabbai or congregational leader should call out, "Kohanim." In Israel, after the chazzan concludes the berachah of Modim, someone from the congregation (usually the gabbai or congregational leader) calls out, "Kohanim," and the Kohanim start their berachah.[231]

However, most Ashkenazic Jews outside Israel don't follow Rabbenu Tam. Outside of Israel, among Ashkenazic Jews, after concluding Modim the chazzan says, אֱלֹקֵינוּ וֵאלֹקֵי אֲבוֹתֵינוּ בָּרְכֵנוּ בַּבְּרָכָה הַמְשֻׁלֶּשֶׁת (the "substitute" Priestly Blessing). On those occasions when בִּרְכַּת כֹּהֲנִים is actually recited, the chazzan says this in an undertone, and when he comes to the word "Kohanim," he shouts it out loud, and then says in an undertone, עַם קְדוֹשֶׁךָ. כָּאָמוּר ("Your holy people, as it is said"). The Kohanim then begin their berachah.[232] Their rationale is that today, even Rabbenu Tam would agree that it is not an interruption. Nowadays, the "substitute Priestly Blessing" is usually said. It has become a part of the regular text of the prayer book. In this case the chazzan isn't actually interrupting anything. He says what he always says, only this time he says most of it quietly, and one word, "Kohanim," a little louder.[233]

The same problem arises with the chazzan saying the words of the berachah of the בִּרְכַּת כֹּהֲנִים before the Kohanim respond. Is the chazzan permitted to announce them? Again, we say that it is not considered an interruption, because reciting every word to the Kohanim is part of the prayer.[234]

A Kohen is obligated to perform the requirements of his office. If a Kohen does not go up to bless the people, unless he is not capable, the Gemara states that he violates three mitzvot:[235] כֹּה תְבָרֲכוּ אֶת בְּנֵי יִשְׂרָאֵל אָמוֹר לָהֶם וְשָׂמוּ אֶת שְׁמִי ("In this manner you should bless the

---

231. See בית יוסף אורח חיים קכח ס"ק יד בשם רבינו תם; ביאור הגר"א שם ס"ק כ; מעשה רב סימן קסח. See also רש"י מסכת סוטה דף לט עמוד ב: לעקור רגליהם.

232. See רמ"א שולחן ערוך אורח חיים סי׳ קכח סעיף י.

233. See תוספות ברכות דף לד עמוד א ד"ה לא יענה.

234. See בית יוסף אורח חיים סימן קכח ס"ק יד.

235. סוטה דף לח עמוד ב. The Rambam (הלכות תפילה וברכת כהנים פרק טו הלכה יב)

children of Israel"; "Say to them"; "And place my name upon them"). Moreover, a Kohen who blesses the people receives a blessing, as God promised Avraham and his descendants,[236] וַאֲבָרְכָה מְבָרְכֶיךָ ("and I will bless those who bless you"). If a Kohen does not bless the people, he does not receive this blessing.[237]

The Talmud[238] states that one of the nine enactments (תַּקָּנוֹת) of Rabbi Elazar ben Azariah was that the Kohanim must bless the people without their shoes on. The reasoning is that maybe the Kohen's shoelace will untie when he was on the way to give the blessing. He might stop to tie it and miss giving the blessing. People might think that he is not a valid Kohen, and that is what prevented him from giving the blessing. This ruling which requires blessing the people without shoes prevents that possibility.

The halachah is that the Kohanim must leave their seats during the berachah of רְצֵה.[239] If the chazzan has already reached Modim, and one of the Kohanim has not yet begun to move toward the front of the shul to recite the בִּרְכַּת כֹּהֲנִים, he forfeits the right to say the בִּרְכַּת כֹּהֲנִים. This is because the berachah of רְצֵה is about the Temple worship (the sacrifices that we hope to be able to offer again). This connects the בִּרְכַּת כֹּהֲנִים with the Temple worship. As we noted earlier, the בִּרְכַּת כֹּהֲנִים should immediately follow the worship service.

Outside Israel, the practice is to say the prayer רִבּוֹנוֹ שֶׁל עוֹלָם ("Master of the universe") after the first and second verses of the Priestly Blessing. This is a fervent prayer to God to prevent evil dreams from coming true. The Gemara tells us[240] that a person who had a bad dream and is afraid it may come true, should say a special prayer while the Kohanim recite their berachah. רִבּוֹנוֹ שֶׁל עוֹלָם is that prayer. If you are not afraid of a bad dream, you don't have to say it. Our ancestors

---

explains that the Kohen in fact only violates one commandment, but it is as if he violates three because the Torah repeats the command three times.

236. בראשית יב:ג

237. רמב"ם הלכות תפילה וברכת כהנים פרק טו הלכה יב; סוטה דף לח עמוד ב

238. סוטה דף מ עמוד א

239. סוטה דף לח עמוד ב

240. ברכות דף נה עמ׳ ב

were very afraid of evil dreams. The last chapter of Berachot is full of interpretations of dreams, which were considered to be part-prophecy that might come true. When our ancestors had a bad dream, they would fast on that day. There are many laws that deal with this kind of fast day. On Shabbat, for example, you are not usually permitted to fast, but if you had a bad dream you are permitted to fast, because otherwise your Shabbat might be spoiled by the fear of the bad dream.[241]

After the third verse of the berachah, there is a different prayer to recite instead of the רִבּוֹנוֹ שֶׁל עוֹלָם. This prayer, יְהִי רָצוֹן מִלְּפָנֶיךָ, is attributed to Rabbi Nathan Hanover. He believed that saying רִבּוֹנוֹ שֶׁל עוֹלָם twice was sufficient, and that we could add a different prayer for the third verse.

The רִבּוֹנוֹ שֶׁל עוֹלָם prayer states, וּכְשֵׁם שֶׁהֲפַכְתָּ אֶת קִלְלַת בִּלְעָם הָרָשָׁע מִקְּלָלָה לִבְרָכָה כֵּן תַּהֲפֹךְ כָּל חֲלוֹמוֹתַי עָלַי וְעַל כָּל יִשְׂרָאֵל לְטוֹבָה וְתִשְׁמְרֵנִי וּתְחָנֵּנִי וְתִרְצֵנִי ("Just as You turned the curse of the evil Bilaam into a blessing, so, too, may You turn all my dreams into good about myself and about all Israel and guard me and grant me grace and favor me"). The last three verbs, וְתִשְׁמְרֵנִי וּתְחָנֵּנִי וְתִרְצֵנִי, seem superfluous. We use them because each verb stands for a different verse of the Priestly Blessing: for the verse of the berachah that ends וְיִשְׁמְרֶךָ ("and guard you"), you say וְתִשְׁמְרֵנִי ("and guard me"). For the verse of the berachah that ends וִיחֻנֶּךָּ ("and give you grace"), you say וּתְחָנֵּנִי ("and grant me grace"). For the verse of the berachah that begins with יִשָּׂא ה' פָּנָיו אֵלֶיךָ ("May Hashem turn His face toward you"), you say וְתִרְצֵנִי ("and favor me"). This shows the connection between this prayer and the Priestly Blessing.[242]

In most prayer books, there are Biblical verses printed alongside each word of the בִּרְכַּת כֹּהֲנִים. Each verse begins with the parallel word of the בִּרְכַּת כֹּהֲנִים. There is a difference of opinion about whether congregants should recite these verses. The verses are printed in the prayer book because they are discussed in the Midrash. My opinion, based on the Shulchan Aruch,[243] is that one should not say them but

---

241. שולחן ערוך אורח חיים סי' רמט סעי' ד,ה.
242. *Tikkun Tefillah* in *Otzar Hatefillot*, עמ' תסט.
243. שולחן ערוך אורח חיים סימן קכח סעיף כו.

just listen to the Kohanim. By saying them when we are supposed to be listening to the בִּרְכַּת כֹּהֲנִים, we act as though we are turning our backs on the Kohanim and having a conversation with somebody else. During the בִּרְכַּת כֹּהֲנִים, we expect the Kohanim to be the instrument through which God's berachah is channeled to us, so we should just concentrate on the words of the berachah as we receive them and not recite them ourselves.

If a person lives longer than the average human life span, Judaism believes that God gave that person a long life. In Talmudic times, there were a number of rabbis who outlived their generation. In the yeshiva they asked Rabbi Elazar ben Shamua, "What did you do to deserve a long life?"[244] He replied, "There are three very special things I did that helped me. I never used a shul for a shortcut." Often a shul had two doors, one on each side, and people would cut through the shul instead of going around the block. This is abusing the shul. Simply using the shul as a shortcut is not permitted. There is a question about whether it is permissible to have a wedding in a shul. Rav Soloveitchik told me that though many times he does not fight it, he does not approve of it, because it means using a shul for private purposes. The only purpose of a shul is communal prayer.

The second reason that Rabbi Elazar lived so long, he claimed, is, "I did not step over the heads of the holy people." In those days, when a rabbi taught Torah, the students would sit on the ground in a circle, and the rabbi sat in the middle. If the rabbi came late, the students would all be sitting around waiting for him, so the rabbi would have to step over their heads. Rabbi Elazar said that was disrespectful. He either arrived first or asked them to make a space for him.

Third, he said, "I never raised my hands for the Priestly Blessing without first reciting a berachah." Rabbi Elazar, who was a Kohen, apparently introduced the berachah of בָּרוּךְ אַתָּה... אֲשֶׁר קִדְּשָׁנוּ בִּקְדֻשָּׁתוֹ שֶׁל אַהֲרֹן, וְצִוָּנוּ לְבָרֵךְ אֶת עַמּוֹ יִשְׂרָאֵל בְּאַהֲבָה ("Blessed are You... who sanctified us with the holiness of Aharon and commanded us to bless His people Israel with love"). Before he instituted this berachah, the Kohanim went up to bless the people without reciting a preceding berachah.

244. סוטה דף לט עמ׳ א.

Rav Soloveitchik explained that Rabbi Elazar coined the berachah with the added word בְּאַהֲבָה ("with love"). There was no arrogance when he said the berachah. It's easy for a person who does something special, such as blessing the people, to develop an exaggerated sense of self-importance. Rabbi Elazar was saying that he didn't have that feeling, that he was blessing the people out of love.

Nineteenth Berachah: שִׂים שָׁלוֹם

The prayer שִׂים שָׁלוֹם ("Grant peace") is actually an integral part of the Priestly Blessing, even though we also say it on the days that the Kohanim do not bless us. The Priestly Blessing is the first part and שִׂים שָׁלוֹם is the second part, in which we accept their berachah. We say to God, "Please, God, carry it out. Give us all the things with which the Kohanim blessed us." There are six nouns used here, שָׁלוֹם טוֹבָה וּבְרָכָה חֵן וָחֶסֶד וְרַחֲמִים ("peace, goodness, blessing, grace, kindness, and mercy"), because the Priestly Blessing has six verbs: **יְבָרֶכְךָ** ה׳ **וְיִשְׁמְרֶךָ** ("May God bless you and guard you"). **יָאֵר** ה׳ פָּנָיו אֵלֶיךָ **וִיחֻנֶּךָּ** ("May God shine His face toward you and give you grace"). **יִשָּׂא** ה׳ פָּנָיו אֵלֶיךָ **וְיָשֵׂם** לְךָ שָׁלוֹם ("May God turn His face toward you and give you peace").[245]

There is a difference between the customs of Ashkenazi and Sephardi Jews in reciting this berachah. Both Ashkenazim and Sephardim recite שִׂים שָׁלוֹם in Shacharit and on other occasions when בִּרְכַּת כֹּהֲנִים is said. However, Ashkenazic Jews say שָׁלוֹם רָב ("Great peace") as the basic text of the berachah when the Priestly Blessing is not recited, such as for Minchah and Ma'ariv. Sephardic Jews recite שִׂים שָׁלוֹם at Minchah as well, even though the Priestly Blessing is not said then. Sephardic Jews are following the original custom, which required the Priestly Blessing during the afternoon service as well. There is also an Ashkenazic sub-custom. Many Ashkenazic communities who say שָׁלוֹם רָב during the week recite שִׂים שָׁלוֹם in Minchah on Shabbat because שִׂים שָׁלוֹם also mentions the giving of the Torah,[246] and the Torah reading is an important part of that service.

---

245. מטה משה עמוד העבודה דיני תפילה סימן קעו.

246. כִּי בְאוֹר פָּנֶיךָ נָתַתָּ לָּנוּ ה׳ אֱלֹקֵינוּ תּוֹרַת חַיִּים וְאַהֲבַת חֶסֶד ("for by the light of Your face, You gave us the Torah of life and love of kindness").

שִׂים שָׁלוֹם is mentioned in the Talmud,[247] whereas שָׁלוֹם רָב is not. Rav Soloveitchik preferred to use the text provided by the Talmud. Therefore, he introduced the saying of שִׂים שָׁלוֹם in all Minchah services. I believe that the Rav never said שָׁלוֹם רָב even in Ma'ariv, for it was his practice not to say anything that was not mentioned in the Talmud.

Ending Meditation

With the berachah of שִׂים שָׁלוֹם, we end the berachot of שְׁמוֹנֶה עֶשְׂרֵה. Rabbi Yochanan added the verse, יִהְיוּ לְרָצוֹן אִמְרֵי פִי וְהֶגְיוֹן לִבִּי לְפָנֶיךָ. ה׳ צוּרִי וְגוֹאֲלִי ("May the words of my mouth and the intention of my heart come before You, Hashem, my Rock and Redeemer")[248] to the Amidah, and this has become a part of it.[249] Therefore, when we end the שְׁמוֹנֶה עֶשְׂרֵה, we step back to signify the conclusion of our prayers only *after* this verse. Rav Soloveitchik was very particular that the chazzan should say this verse out loud, since he maintained that it is indeed a part of the Amidah prayer.

Many of the Rabbis of the Talmud added a private meditation at the end of the Amidah after they finished the body of the berachot and before they stepped back to end the prayer. Mar the son of Ravina added:[250] אֱלֹקַי. נְצֹר לְשׁוֹנִי מֵרָע וּשְׂפָתַי מִדַּבֵּר מִרְמָה. וְלִמְקַלְלַי נַפְשִׁי תִדֹּם. וְנַפְשִׁי כֶּעָפָר לַכֹּל תִּהְיֶה. פְּתַח לִבִּי בְּתוֹרָתֶךָ. וּבְמִצְוֹתֶיךָ תִּרְדֹּף נַפְשִׁי. וְתַצִּילֵנִי מִפֶּגַע רַע מִיֵּצֶר הָרָע וּמֵאִשָּׁה רָעָה וּמִכָּל רָעוֹת הַמִּתְרַגְּשׁוֹת לָבֹא בָּעוֹלָם. וְכָל הַחוֹשְׁבִים עָלַי רָעָה מְהֵרָה הָפֵר עֲצָתָם וְקַלְקֵל מַחֲשַׁבְתָּם ("My God, guard my tongue from evil and my lips from speaking falsehood. May my soul be silent to them who curse me and may my soul be as the dust to all. Open my heart with Your Torah, and may my soul pursue Your commandments. Deliver me from evil happenings, from the evil impulse and from an evil woman and from all evils that threaten to come upon the world. As for all who design evil against me, speedily annul their counsel and frustrate their designs!") as his private meditation. Jews liked this prayer, and

247. מגילה דף יח עמוד א
248. תהלים יט:טו
249. ברכות דף ט עמ׳ ב
250. ברכות דף יז עמ׳ א

much of it was soon universally accepted. We say it before the verse יִהְיוּ לְרָצוֹן אִמְרֵי פִי וְהֶגְיוֹן לִבִּי לְפָנֶיךָ. ה׳ צוּרִי וְגוֹאֲלִי.

In Mar the son of Ravina's prayer it says, וְלִמְקַלְלַי נַפְשִׁי תִדֹּם וְנַפְשִׁי כֶּעָפָר לַכֹּל תִּהְיֶה ("May my soul be silent to those who curse me; may my soul be as the dust to all"). We should be humble, but why like dust? What does this comparison imply? The Tosafot[251] explain that we are saying, "Let me be like dust compared to those who curse me." When you step on dust, it stays there. It will never disappear. "Let the people who step over me perish. But I shall be like the dust; I shall outlive them all." God has fulfilled it. We are still here in spite of all the persecution we have faced.

In this supplication we ask for two things in particular: that we should be humble and that we should study Torah. The main thrust of this prayer is that we not gossip. How do we prevent ourselves from gossiping? It is, after all, a strong desire in every person. There are only two ways to stop oneself from gossiping: by being humble and by studying Torah.[252]

Finally, we step back.[253] The procedure to end the שְׁמוֹנֶה עֶשְׂרֵה parallels the way that we began it. To end the שְׁמוֹנֶה עֶשְׂרֵה, we first bow down and take three steps backward, because it is disrespectful to turn our backs to royalty. We begin with the left foot first, to show our reluctance to leave the presence of God, then after we have taken three steps we turn to the left and say, עֹשֶׂה שָׁלוֹם בִּמְרוֹמָיו ("He who makes peace in His heights above"), then turn to the right and say, הוּא יַעֲשֶׂה שָׁלוֹם עָלֵינוּ ("shall make peace for us"), then bow forward and say וְעַל כָּל יִשְׂרָאֵל ("and for all of Israel").[254] Thus we leave the three realms of God.

Why do we bow to the left side and then to the right? When we confront God, we imagine Him to be flanked by two angels: Michael on His right side and Gabriel on His left side. Gabriel is the angel of

251. תוספות ברכות דף יז עמוד א ד״ה ונפשי.
252. *Iyun Tefillah* in *Otzar Hatefillot*, ד״ה ולמקללי.
253. See יומא דף נג עמוד ב.
254. See שולחן ערוך אורח חיים סימן קכג סעיף א; לבוש שם.

strictness and judgment who carries out God's punishment in the world. Michael is the angel of kindness and mercy.[255] The right side represents God's mercy, and the left side represents God's strictness. When I bow down to the left side and then to the right side, I am acknowledging God's attributes. Sometimes God judges the world with full strictness and no mercy; sometimes God is thoroughly merciful. When to be strict and when to be merciful, when to punish and when to forgive, is a Divine secret. God mixes the traits of strictness and mercy according to what is right in His eyes, and we have to accept it.

We have a commandment to walk in God's ways (וְהָלַכְתָּ בִּדְרָכָיו, Devarim 28:9). Whatever God does, we should imitate. This means that we should also attempt to mix these attributes of mercy and strictness when appropriate. Parents know this better than anybody else. If parents do not possess the correct mixture of mercy and strictness in dealing with their children, then the children will be spoiled (too much mercy) or will rebel (too much strictness). To get the right balance, we need God's assistance. This is why we bow to one side and then the other. It is not the angels *per se* who are strict or kind; it is God who sends them to do His missions of strictness or kindness. We hope that God will give us the ability to deal with people in the proper way, with the proper mixture of the appropriate qualities.

We end this prayer by saying, וְאִמְרוּ אָמֵן ("and you shall say Amen"). Whom are we addressing in our silent שְׁמוֹנֶה עֶשְׂרֵה? Some suggest that we are addressing the angels. On the other hand, we should never address the angels in prayer; we should address only God.[256] Most likely the word וְאִמְרוּ entered by mistake. When the chazzan says Kaddish, he concludes with עוֹשֶׂה שָׁלוֹם בִּמְרוֹמָיו הוּא יַעֲשֶׂה שָׁלוֹם עָלֵינוּ וְעַל כָּל יִשְׂרָאֵל וְאִמְרוּ אָמֵן ("May He who makes peace in His heights make

255. See שיר השירים רבה פרשה ב.

256. There are some beautiful poetic additions in Selichot in which we appeal directly to the (personified) attributes of God; based on the fifth of Maimonides' Thirteen Articles of Faith, it seems that he would have been very much against them for this reason.

peace for us and for all Israel, and you shall say Amen") as the last line of Kaddish. In that case, he is addressing the congregation, so that they should say Amen. Since it is the same verse with which we end the שְׁמוֹנֶה עֶשְׂרֵה, it crept in here. But since we are not addressing anyone here, perhaps we shouldn't say the word וְאִמְרוּ.[257]

After we step back, we should remain in that place before we step forward. The Shulchan Aruch writes that one who is praying together with a congregation should remain in place at least until the chazzan begins his repetition of the Amidah. The Rama adds that one who is praying alone, and the chazzan himself, should remain in place for the amount of time that it takes to walk four steps.[258]

After we have taken the three steps back, we also say, יְהִי רָצוֹן מִלְּפָנֶיךָ... שֶׁיִּבָּנֶה בֵּית הַמִּקְדָּשׁ בִּמְהֵרָה בְיָמֵינוּ ("May it be Your will... that the holy Temple be speedily rebuilt in our days"), וְתֵן חֶלְקֵנוּ בְּתוֹרָתֶךָ ("and grant us a share in Your Torah"). וְשָׁם נַעֲבָדְךָ בְּיִרְאָה כִּימֵי עוֹלָם וּכְשָׁנִים קַדְמוֹנִיּוֹת ("There we shall worship You in awe as in the olden days and in former years").[259]

Finally, we quote a verse that says, וְעָרְבָה לַה׳ מִנְחַת יְהוּדָה וִירוּשָׁלָיִם כִּימֵי עוֹלָם וּכְשָׁנִים קַדְמוֹנִיּוֹת ("May the offerings of Judah and Jerusalem be pleasant to God as they were in the days of old").[260] With this we finish. We add this because there are two ways of serving God: the sacrificial service in the Temple and the service of our hearts, prayer. We can still carry out the prayer service, but we cannot carry out the Temple service. So, we indicate, "I serve God, but not completely, because I cannot offer the sacrifices." We pray the Temple will be restored so that we can again serve God completely.[261]

---

257. See *Siddur Otzar Hatefillot, Iyun Tefillah,* ד"ה ואמרו אמן.

258. שולחן ערוך אורח חיים סימן קכג סעיף ב

259. רמ"א אורח חיים סי׳ קכג סעי׳ א

260. מלאכי ג:ד

261. רמ"א שם

מֵעֵין י״ח — בִּרְכַּת וַהֲבִינֵנוּ

Sometimes it happens that you want to daven on time, but because of circumstances beyond your control, you cannot. Chazal composed a prayer that is a shortened version of the שְׁמוֹנֶה עֶשְׂרֵה.[262] It contains an abbreviated form of all the middle berachot of the regular שְׁמוֹנֶה עֶשְׂרֵה. In an emergency a person can say it and fulfill his obligations to recite the שְׁמוֹנֶה עֶשְׂרֵה[263] on time. When the person gets back to his regular routine, he would not need to say a make-up שְׁמוֹנֶה עֶשְׂרֵה.

To use this backup prayer, a person says the first three berachot of the regular שְׁמוֹנֶה עֶשְׂרֵה, then recites the middle section, called the מֵעֵין י״ח or abbreviated[264] שְׁמוֹנֶה עֶשְׂרֵה. Finally, the person says the last three berachot of the שְׁמוֹנֶה עֶשְׂרֵה. Sometimes this prayer is known by the beginning of its text: הֲבִינֵנוּ. The הֲבִינֵנוּ must be recited while standing, just like a regular שְׁמוֹנֶה עֶשְׂרֵה.[265]

This option should only be used as a last resort. The text of the מֵעֵין י״ח is as follows[266]:

הֲבִינֵנוּ יי אֱלֹקֵינוּ לָדַעַת דְּרָכֶיךָ וּמוֹל אֶת לְבָבֵנוּ לְיִרְאָתֶךָ וְתִסְלַח לָנוּ לִהְיוֹת גְּאוּלִים וְרַחֲקֵנוּ מִמַּכְאוֹב וְדַשְּׁנֵנוּ בִּנְאוֹת אַרְצֶךָ וּנְפוּצוֹתֵינוּ מֵאַרְבַּע תְּקַבֵּץ וְהַתּוֹעִים עַל דַּעְתְּךָ יִשָּׁפֵטוּ וְעַל הָרְשָׁעִים תָּנִיף יָדֶךָ וְיִשְׂמְחוּ צַדִּיקִים בְּבִנְיַן עִירֶךָ וּבְתִקּוּן הֵיכָלֶךָ וּבִצְמִיחַת קֶרֶן לְדָוִד עַבְדֶּךָ וּבַעֲרִיכַת נֵר לְבֶן יִשַׁי מְשִׁיחֶךָ. טֶרֶם נִקְרָא אַתָּה תַעֲנֶה. בָּרוּךְ אַתָּה יי, שׁוֹמֵעַ תְּפִלָּה.

262. ברכות דף טז עמוד א
263. ברכות דף כח עמוד ב
264. רמב״ם הלכות תפילה ונשיאת כפים פרק ב הלכה ב
265. שולחן ערוך אורח חיים סימן קי סעיף א
266. לבוש אורח חיים סימן קי סעיף א

Conclusion of Shacharit

After the chazzan's repetition of the שְׁמוֹנֶה עֶשְׂרֵה of Shacharit, we add the following prayers to our service:

- Tachanun (the supplication prayer); this is recited on a regular, non-festive weekday.
- וְהוּא רַחוּם ("He who is merciful"); this is usually recited on Monday and Thursday as an extension of Tachanun.
- קְרִיאַת הַתּוֹרָה (the Torah reading); this is recited on Monday and Thursday as well as other special occasions.
- אַשְׁרֵי (Psalm 145); this is recited every day at this point in the service.
- לַמְנַצֵּחַ (Psalm 20); this is recited every day except for Shabbat, Yom Tov, Rosh Chodesh, Chanukah, Purim, Erev Pesach, Erev Yom Kippur and Tisha B'Av.[1]
- וּבָא לְצִיּוֹן גּוֹאֵל ("A Redeemer will come to Zion"); this is recited on weekdays, followed by קַדִּישׁ תִּתְקַבֵּל.
- עָלֵינוּ לְשַׁבֵּחַ ("It is for us to praise"); this is recited as a closure for almost all services. It may be followed by a Mourner's Kaddish.
- The respective שִׁיר שֶׁל יוֹם (Psalms recited by the Levites in the Temple on the various days of the week); this is recited each day. It may be followed by a Mourner's Kaddish.

1. שולחן ערוך אורח חיים סימן קלא סעיף א

TACHANUN

Tachanun is a set of prayers following the שְׁמוֹנֶה עֶשְׂרֵה in which we beseech God for mercy and appeal to His grace rather than our merit.

וְהוּא רַחוּם

Is וְהוּא רַחוּם (He who is merciful) a part of Tachanun? Tachanun is said sitting down,[2] but we say וְהוּא רַחוּם standing. This would seem to indicate that it is not part of Tachanun but a kind of prayer known as Selichot (prayers for forgiveness).[3] Selichot must be said while standing. As a matter of fact, Selichot can be considered an addition to the שְׁמוֹנֶה עֶשְׂרֵה.[4] In ancient times, on fast days, Selichot were included as part of the שְׁמוֹנֶה עֶשְׂרֵה by integrating them into the berachah of סְלַח לָנוּ.[5] Nowadays, we say Selichot immediately following the שְׁמוֹנֶה עֶשְׂרֵה in order to connect the two prayers.[6]

וְהוּא רַחוּם is not said every day, but only on Monday and Thursday. The Gemara tells us[7] that Ezra introduced ten decrees. One of them was to read the Torah every Monday and Thursday. Court sessions also took place on these days. The Tosafot asked[8] why specifically Monday and Thursday? It could just as easily have been Tuesday or Friday or any other combination, as long as not more than three days passed without public Torah readings. Tosafot answer this by quoting the Midrash Tanchuma which states that the second time Moshe ascended

---

2. שולחן ערוך אורח חיים סימן קלא סעיף ב

3. However, in the Rambam's סדר התפילה, some of the verses which we recite as part of וְהוּא רַחוּם are included in the Tachanun that is recited with one's head down.

4. The Levush (אורח חיים סימן קלד סעיף א) writes that וְהוּא רַחוּם was composed in three parts, and each one mentions God's name eighteen times. Therefore, we say it silently while standing, as it is intended to parallel the שְׁמוֹנֶה עֶשְׂרֵה. Regarding the status of Selichot as connected to the Amidah, see: רשימות שיעורים ברכות דף ד עמוד ב, אות ג: ביסוד הדין דתפלה בעי מתיר.

5. סדר רב עמרם גאון סדר תענית. Also see שולחן ערוך אורח חיים סימן תקסו סעיף ד.

6. שולחן ערוך אורח חיים סימן תקסו סעיף ד

7. בבא קמא דף פב עמוד א

8. תוספות בבא קמא דף פב עמ׳ א ד״ה כדי שלא ילינו

Mount Sinai, it was on a Thursday, and the day he descended was a Monday. During the time he was on the mountain, he was able to appease God's anger. Thus, Monday and Thursday became associated with Divine goodwill.[9] In the course of time, a custom developed to fast and recite Selichot on Mondays and Thursdays. Most people do not fast every Monday and Thursday, but we find consolation and encouragement in saying the special Selichot prayers on these days.

What do we know about the text of וְהוּא רַחוּם? According to legend, it was written by outstanding people at the time of the Roman exile. Emperor Vespasian ordered a group of Jewish leaders to be put into three boats without a captain and set adrift. They were beset by storms and landed in different ports. One group landed in Lepanto, Greece, another landed in Arles, France, and the third group landed either in Bordeaux, France, or in Portugal. The last group was accepted in a very friendly manner by the leader of the city and given fields and vineyards. They prospered until that ruler died and another ruler took his place. The new ruler took away everything that the first one had given them, and he made their lives miserable, issuing many evil decrees against them. Among the Rabbis on this boat were two brothers, Yosef and Binyamin, and their cousin Shmuel. Their response to these troubles was to pray, fast, and put on sackcloth. They wrote וְהוּא רַחוּם.[10]

Yosef composed the part of the prayer from the beginning until אָנָּא מֶלֶךְ חַנּוּן וְרַחוּם ("Please, gracious and merciful King"). Binyamin composed the lines from there until אֵין כָּמוֹךָ ("There is none like You"), and Shmuel composed the lines from there to the end. Their prayers were heard. The evil ruler died a terrible death, and the Jews in the country were free again. The three men made their prayers known to all Israel, and Jews took it upon themselves to say this prayer every Monday and Thursday.[11]

Obviously, this prayer originated in days of persecution, when Jews

9. טור אורח חיים סי' קלד

10. *Seder Avodat Yisrael* deals with this issue thoroughly. This story is found in the Sefer Avudraham (דיני קריאת התורה) and in the Kol Bo (סימן יח).

11. טור אורח חיים סימן קלד

were constantly threatened with expulsion and death. וְהוּא רַחוּם excels in simple classical Hebrew that everybody can understand and use to pour out his or her heart to God. Who can count the many miracles that happened to Jews in those days, the greatest of which was just to survive? We can very well imagine how this prayer lifted their spirits and filled them with hope for the future. No wonder וְהוּא רַחוּם was so widely accepted as part of the prayer book.

Historians tell us that Monday and Thursday became prominent because they were the market days on which the farmers brought their produce to the city for sale. Once they were in the city, they could participate in communal life, which they could not do on their farms where they had no minyan. In the city they could hear the Megillah, they could hear the Torah reading, and they could say special prayers. Monday and Thursday thus became special days in Jewish life.

However, from our point of view, the development of the importance of Monday and Thursday did not come from their being market days but days of mercy, as the Tosafot explained. Therefore, the Jews of the villages went to the city to join a minyan and pour out their hearts to God. Many congregations, to this day, have special prayer services and fast days twice a year after Pesach and Sukkot in case we overdid the celebrations of those holidays and committed some sin. These are observed as a series of three days on the Monday, Thursday and the following Monday after the month of Nissan and after the month of Tishrei. They are called תַּעֲנִיּוֹת בה״ב (the Fasts of Monday, Thursday and Monday).[12]

Whether or not the story of the three rabbis was the exact origin of וְהוּא רַחוּם, we probably will never know. The legend of the three authors of the וְהוּא רַחוּם throws light on the historical background and issues concerning our people at the time.

In telling the legend of the origin of וְהוּא רַחוּם, we should digress a moment and talk about legends. Are legends true? Did the events really happen or are they just fictional stories? There is a legend about

12. שולחן ערוך אורח חיים סי׳ תצב סע׳ א

Rashi's birth which points to the importance of these stories, even when they are not historically accurate.[13]

Rashi was the son of Rabbi Yitzchak, a great rabbi in Troyes, France. Rabbi Yitzchak was one of those scholars whose business interests would take him to faraway countries. On those business trips he would acquire rare objects and sell them in France for a great profit. This gave him an opportunity to have undisturbed time for studying Torah.

On one occasion, he brought a precious stone, the size and brilliance of which nobody had ever seen. The bishop of the city heard about it and wanted to purchase the diamond to decorate one of the statues in the church. When the bishop made his offer to Rabbi Yitzchak, Rabbi Yitzchak decided not to sell it to the bishop because he did not want to derive any monetary gain from idolatry.

But the bishop insisted that he had to have the diamond. Rabbi Yitzchak was forcibly brought to the river and put on a boat that carried him across to the other side, where the bishop's palace was located. Rabbi Yitzchak asked the soldiers who guarded him if they would like to see the diamond, and they were very eager to do so. Rabbi Yitzchak put his hand in his pocket and took out the box with the diamond in it. The soldiers were excited about the spectacle offered to them. As they admired the diamond, Rabbi Yitzchak carefully started rocking the boat until the diamond fell out of his hand into the river. Then he suddenly cried out, "My diamond! My fortune! I am wiped out!" What could they do? He was inconsolable. The soldiers comforted him and said, "It's only money. You'll buy another one." There was then no point in taking him to the bishop.

That night, the legend tells us, Rabbi Yitzchak had a dream. An angel of God appeared to him and said, "Since you have abandoned your fortune by letting the diamond fall into the water in order not to serve other gods, God will give you another diamond to make up for it: a human diamond, a diamond that will light up the words of

---

13. See *Rashi* by Maurice Liber, translated from the French by Adele Szold (Hermon Press, New York, 1970), pp. 37–40.

the Torah for every Jew." In due time Rashi was born and he turned out to be the human diamond.

Did all of this happen? Perhaps, or perhaps not. Either way, the story is significant because it gives us a picture of Jewish thinking at the time, which centered on one idea: improving the world for the kingdom of God. To this end, anything reminding us of foreign worship was rejected, and the Torah had to be studied by every Jew. The highest good for a Jew was Torah knowledge. By embellishing the story of Rashi's birth, those concepts became models for every Jew.

In the case of the three authors of וְהוּא רַחוּם, we really don't know whether they were sent away in a rudderless boat, but the story depicts the lives of the Jews in those days: always in danger of extinction or exile. Our lesson is that the Jews will survive no matter what our enemies have in store for us. Legends are a way of teaching history to generations of Jews in an interesting way and making clear the basic philosophy of Judaism.

נְפִילַת אַפַּיִם

Is Tachanun an independent prayer or is it connected to the שְׁמוֹנֶה עֶשְׂרֵה? According to the Rambam, it is connected to the שְׁמוֹנֶה עֶשְׂרֵה. He enumerates[14] eight conditions that should ideally be observed when reciting the שְׁמוֹנֶה עֶשְׂרֵה, but under extreme circumstances the omission of these conditions would not render the prayer invalid. The eighth condition is bowing down, by which he is referring to Tachanun.[15] The שְׁמוֹנֶה עֶשְׂרֵה is said while standing, but the Tachanun, which we call נְפִילַת אַפַּיִם (falling on one's face),[16] is said in a fallen or bowing position.

In the שְׁמוֹנֶה עֶשְׂרֵה we stand before God. Logically, we should

---

14. רמב"ם הלכות תפילה ונשיאת כפים פרק ה הלכה א

15. רמב"ם הלכות תפילה פרק ה הל' א והל' יג

16. תַּחֲנוּן is traditionally also called נְפִילַת אַפַּיִם (falling on one's face) and derived from Moshe who said "and I fell down before God" (וָאֶתְנַפַּל לִפְנֵי יְיָ, דברים ט:יח), and from Joshua who also "fell on his face to the ground before the ark of Hashem" (וַיִּפֹּל עַל־פָּנָיו אַרְצָה לִפְנֵי אֲרוֹן יְיָ, יהושע ז:ו).

prostrate ourselves before God in a posture of total subjugation, but we have the nerve to stand erect before God, face to face. This is an enormous privilege. Since Abraham stood during his prayers, we take this as a precedent and pretend to be on the same level as him, as we argue with God about our fate and the fate of all Israel.[17]

When we come to the end of the שְׁמוֹנֶה עֶשְׂרֵה, we suddenly realize the magnitude of what we have done, standing and arguing before God. In great embarrassment we fall on the ground and surrender ourselves to Him.[18] In Tachanun we are more realistic about our status in this world.

Tachanun originally had no set text, but merely requires us to pour out our hearts before God, tell Him our problems, and ask Him to extend His kindness to us. The שְׁמוֹנֶה עֶשְׂרֵה and Tachanun both have the same goal. If in the שְׁמוֹנֶה עֶשְׂרֵה we emphasize the potential greatness of humanity as a true partner with God in Creation, in Tachanun we reveal the truth about ourselves: how dependent we are on God's mercy and grace.[19]

The *Tikkun Tefillah*[20] points out that in the time and place of Rav Amram Gaon and in the time and place of the Tur, there was no set text for Tachanun. The Avudraham remarks that "each one chose the psalm of one's choice until Tachanun became standardized as it is today." [21] In the Rambam's time and place there was a set version, and in the course of time our text was formulated. During that period there was much trouble from external enemies, which the selected texts reflect. The customs of this text have varied over time and in different communites,[22] but the practice of reciting Tachanun is quite old.[23]

---

17. ברכות דף ו עמוד ב
18. Rav Soloveitchik expressed this idea, and it is summarized in: רשימות שיעורים ברכות דף כא עמוד ב: ביאור הדין שאין לחלוץ התפילין עד לאחר ובא לציון.
19. ספר כלבו סימן יט
20. *Tikkun Tefillah* in *Otzar Hatefillot*, ד"ה ויאמר דוד.
21. *Avodat Yisrael*, p. 116.
22. See ערוך השולחן אורח חיים סימן קלא סעיף ט, which states ולאחר שיגביה ראשו אחר נפילת אפים יתחנן מעט כל מקום ומקום לפי מנהגו
23. שולחן ערוך הרב אורח חיים סימן קלא סעיף א

Today we have a fixed text for Tachanun. We say a mixture of Piyyutim and Psalms as a substitute for the free prayer that our ancestors said.

To the basic Psalm that makes up the body of Tachanun, we add a special prayer of penance beforehand. Among Sephardim and those who follow the Ari *z"l*'s nusach, Tachanun is said before וְהוּא רַחוּם and the י״ג מִדּוֹת שֶׁל רַחֲמִים before Tachanun.[24] Some add the verse וַיֹּאמֶר דָּוִד אֶל־גָּד צַר־לִי מְאֹד נִפְּלָה־נָּא בְיַד־יְיָ כִּי־רַבִּים רַחֲמָיו וּבְיַד־אָדָם אַל־אֶפֹּלָה ("David said to Gad, 'I am in great distress. Let us fall into the hand of God because His mercy is great; let me not fall into the hands of man'")[25] before Tachanun, probably because נִפְּלָה־נָּא ("Let us fall") is understood to be a reference to Tachanun. In the Ashkenazi text, it has become customary to build Tachanun around Psalm 6, preceded by a short prayer requesting God's mercy.[26] Then we recite Psalm 6, beginning with the second verse and continuing to the end. The Sephardim chose a different text: Psalm 25,[27] "I will lift up my soul to You."

To show the unity of Tachanun with the rest of the שְׁמוֹנֶה עֶשְׂרֵה, we have to be aware of the role of Kaddish. We recite Kaddish following Tachanun to unite the Tachanun and שְׁמוֹנֶה עֶשְׂרֵה into one unit. The Kaddish after Tachanun is known as a חֲצִי קַדִּישׁ, whose role is to separate one section (the שְׁמוֹנֶה עֶשְׂרֵה) from another section (that which follows the שְׁמוֹנֶה עֶשְׂרֵה). Since this Kaddish is recited after Tachanun, this indicates that Tachanun and the שְׁמוֹנֶה עֶשְׂרֵה are considered as part of the same section. The Kaddish after וּבָא לְצִיּוֹן גּוֹאֵל is a concluding Kaddish, indicating the conclusion of the entire service.

The connection of Tachanun to the שְׁמוֹנֶה עֶשְׂרֵה is very important. The Kol Bo explains[28] that we derive the most effective way of

---

24. פסקי תשובות אורח חיים סימן קלא, ט

25. שמואל ב פרק כד פסוק יד

26. רַחוּם וְחַנּוּן חָטָאתִי לְפָנֶיךָ. ה׳ מָלֵא רַחֲמִים. רַחֵם עָלַי וְקַבֵּל תַּחֲנוּנָי ("Merciful and gracious One, I have sinned before You. Hashem, who is full of mercy, have mercy on me and accept my pleas").

27. תהלים פרק כה, which was favored by the Zohar (end of Bamidbar).

28. ספר כלבו סימן יט

approaching God in prayer from Moshe. Just as Moshe is described as having "sat" atop Mount Sinai for forty days,[29] we sit when we say Shema. Just as Moshe is described as having "stood,"[30] we stand when we say the שְׁמוֹנֶה עֶשְׂרֵה. Just as Moshe "fell before God,"[31] we fall before God when we recite Tachanun.

There is a story in the Gemara[32] that shows how important it is not to interrupt between the שְׁמוֹנֶה עֶשְׂרֵה and Tachanun for Tachanun to have its full effect. Rabbi Eliezer ben Hyrcanus was excommunicated by his brother-in-law, Rabban Gamliel, because Rabbi Eliezer would not accede to Rabban Gamliel's opinion. Ima Shalom was Rabbi Eliezer's wife and Rabban Gamliel's sister. She understood the power of prayer and was afraid that if her husband were to pour out his heart during Tachanun, God might listen to his plea for mercy and punish or even kill her brother. Ima Shalom always watched her husband and interrupted him before he could say Tachanun, so his concentration would be broken and his prayers would lose their impact. One day she had no opportunity to stop him, because she was giving bread to a poor Jew who knocked at her door. When she came back and realized that her husband had said Tachanun, she said, "You killed my brother!" Sure enough, a little while later, the blast of a shofar announced the death of Rabban Gamliel.

From this story we see that one should not have any interruption between the שְׁמוֹנֶה עֶשְׂרֵה and Tachanun. Rabbi Yosef Karo[33] rules that one should not speak between the שְׁמוֹנֶה עֶשְׂרֵה and Tachanun because they are considered one unit of prayer.

One of the primary sources for Tachanun is in the following Gemara[34]: "Rav arrived in Babylonia on a fast day... When everyone else fell on their faces, Rav did not fall on his face."[35] The Gemara

---

29. דברים ט:ט
30. דברים י:י
31. דברים ט:יח
32. בבא מציעא דף נט עמוד ב
33. בית יוסף טור אורח חיים סימן קלא:א
34. מגילה דף כב עמ׳ ב
35. See רש״י מגילה דף כג עמ׳ א דמצלי אצלויי.

explains that Rav did not "fall on his face" (i.e., recite Tachanun) because there was a stone floor in that synagogue beneath the seat of Rav. There is a law forbidding a Jew to prostrate oneself on a stone floor.[36] The Gemara asks why only Rav was concerned about this prohibition and explains that only Rav was standing over a stone section of the synagogue floor. Why did Rav not leave his seat and go to where there was no stone? First, the Gemara explains that he did not want to inconvenience the congregation by forcing everybody to stand up when he passed by. The rules of not disturbing the congregation and of standing when a great rabbi passes by are ones we observe today as well.[37]

Another view in the Gemara is that Rav's practice was to prostrate himself completely on the floor. The other people merely bowed down with their heads parallel to the ground, which is permitted where there is a stone floor. Why didn't Rav follow their practice? The Gemara explains that Rav did not want to change his manner of bowing, so he omitted Tachanun on that occasion. This shows us the importance of observing one's accepted customs.

What sort of bowing down do we practice today? Do we prostrate ourselves totally on the floor or bow down with our head parallel to the ground? Our practice is a combination of both. As far as נְפִילַת אַפַּיִם, we bend over with our heads parallel to the ground.[38] There are only two times of year when we actually get down on our knees and bow on the ground: on Rosh Hashanah and Yom Kippur during the Musaf repetition. In the Temple Service, during the Avodah, the high priest would pronounce God's name, and the entire people would prostrate

---

36. רמב"ם הלכות עבודה זרה פרק ו הל' ז

37. The issue of טִירְחָא דְּצִבּוּרָא (inconveniencing the congregation) is found in a number of places in the Gemara and halachic authorities. See, for example, שולחן ערוך יורה דעה סימן רמד סעיף ו. Standing before one's rabbi is also a halachah. See שולחן ערוך יורה דעה הלכות כבוד רבו ותלמיד חכם סימן רמב סעיף טז.

38. ערוך השולחן אורח חיים סימן קלא סעיף ד. Also see משנה ברורה סימן קלא ס"ק ג. Originally we used to prostrate ourselves, but today we bend our head and cover our face instead.

themselves.[39] Today when we reenact the Temple service, we prostrate ourselves on the floor. Even if it is not a stone floor, it is forbidden to prostrate oneself entirely unless we put something, such as paper or a mat, between our faces and the floor or we turn to the side. [40]

Should you bow down anyplace besides a shul? When the Book of Joshua discusses "falling on your face," it mentions that the Ark was nearby[41]; therefore, we usually perform נְפִילַת אַפַּיִם only when there is a Torah scroll in the room.[42] However, some authorities make no mention of the Ark or Torah scroll as a condition for נְפִילַת אַפַּיִם,[43] and they would maintain that you should always bow down while saying it.[44] Other authorities permit bowing down if there is no Torah present, if there are other holy books present.[45]

The Shulchan Aruch then remarks that Tachanun should be recited while sitting[46] and adds that when we bow down, we should do so to the left side.[47] The Rama[48] writes that during Shacharit, if he has tefillin on his left arm, a man should bend down on the right side out

---

39. משנה יומא ו:ב

40. רמ"א שולחן ערוך אורח חיים סי' קלא סע' ח. Also see רמב"ם הלכות עבודה זרה פרק ו הלכה ז.

41. וַיִּפֹּל עַל־פָּנָיו אַרְצָה לִפְנֵי אֲרוֹן יְיָ: יהושע ז:ו ("and he fell on his face to the ground before the ark of Hashem").

42. רמ"א אורח חיים סימן קלא סעיף ב

43. See בית יוסף אורח חיים סימן קלא ס"ק ג. The Rama cites the view that a Sefer Torah is necessary, but R. Yosef Karo does not. See also כף החיים סימן קלא ס"ק מ.

44. משנה ברורה סימן קלא ס"ק יא. See also ערוך השולחן אורח חיים סימן קלא סעיף י.

45. באר היטב אורח חיים סימן קלא ס"ק ו

46. שולחן ערוך אורח חיים סי' קלא סעי' ב

47. שולחן ערוך אורח חיים סי' קלא סעי' א. The Aruch Hashulchan (אורח חיים קלא:ו) quotes the Beit Yosef who writes that an important person should do Tachanun leaning on the left, because the korban tamid was turned on the left before being slaughtered. Another reason he cites for leaning to the left (in the name of Rav Hai Gaon) is that it is a sign of being free (as it is at the Pesach Seder). One should give up his freedom and subjugate himself to God. Another reason is that the Shechinah is on the right, so falling on the left arm means that one's face is directed toward the Shechinah.

48. רמ"א אורח חיים סי' קלא סעי' א

of respect for the tefillin, but when there are no tefillin on his arm, such as at Minchah, he should bow down on the left side.

Rav Soloveitchik always used to say Tachanun while leaning on his left side, even at Shacharit. He said it was not disrespectful to the tefillin to lean on the left arm while wearing tefillin. His practice was the same as that of the Vilna Gaon.[49] Even so, most people have adopted the custom of the Rama.

The Shelah adds that when we reach the verse וַאֲנַחְנוּ לֹא נֵדַע מַה נַּעֲשֶׂה ("And we don't know what to do"), we stand, indicating that we have nothing else left to do. We have prayed to God seated, standing, and falling on our faces; now it is up to God to help us, for what else can we do?[50]

Our custom is not to say Tachanun during Ma'ariv. According to the Rambam you can,[51] but the Shulchan Aruch accepts the opinion that Tachanun is not said at night.[52] The Levush explains that this is for the same reason as why we don't say Tachanun at the home of a mourner. When someone mourns a close relative, it is a sign that God's judgment has been aroused. We are afraid that saying Tachanun under such circumstances would just increase God's wrath.[53] Similarly, night is said to be a time of judgment. In Tachanun we proclaim that we have no merit of our own; at a time of judgment we do not need to bring this up.[54]

We do not say Tachanun on joyous occasions, either, because it would cast a shadow on our celebration. We extend this approach so far as to say that by omitting תַּחֲנוּן on a specific occasion, we are sharing in the joy of our fellow Jews. If a bridegroom or a member of the immediate family of a boy having a brit milah (or even the mohel on the day of a brit milah) comes to shul, no one in shul says

---

49. מעשה רב אות נ
50. של"ה מסכת תמיד פרק נר מצוה צא
51. רמב"ם הלכות תפילה פרק ה הלכה טו
52. שולחן ערוך אורח חיים סימן קלא סעיף ג
53. עטרת זקנים סימן קלא ס"ק ג
54. לבוש אורח חיים סימן קלא סעיף ד

Tachanun during that service.[55] In this way we all celebrate that happy occasion.

Similarly, since nobody says Tachanun in the house of a mourner, we also identify ourselves with the calamities that a fellow Jew has endured.

אַשְׁרֵי, לַמְנַצֵּחַ, וּבָא לְצִיּוֹן

The Avudraham says that the conclusion of Shacharit, which consists of a second recitation of Ashrei, followed by לַמְנַצֵּחַ (Psalm 20) and וּבָא לְצִיּוֹן גּוֹאֵל, is in itself a miniature service for the latecomers and unlearned people.[56] At first, we must ask ourselves, why is Ashrei recited again at the end of the service? In פְּסוּקֵי דְזִמְרָא, it functions as an anchor to inspire greater concentration. Here it prompts us to end our davening with a high level of concentration as well. Ashrei is recited before the שְׁמוֹנֶה עֶשְׂרֵה of Minchah for the same reason. As we mentioned in the section on פְּסוּקֵי דְזִמְרָא, the חֲסִידִים הָרִאשׁוֹנִים (early pious ones) used to wait an hour before their prayers in order to pray with concentration, and remained an hour afterward before they took up their daily activities. Saying Ashrei in פְּסוּקֵי דְזִמְרָא and again together with לַמְנַצֵּחַ and וּבָא לְצִיּוֹן גּוֹאֵל after the end of Tachanun serve the same purpose.[57]

לַמְנַצֵּחַ מִזְמוֹר לְדָוִד and וּבָא לְצִיּוֹן גּוֹאֵל actually play several roles. We shall discuss one at a time. If one were to ask the average davener where in Shacharit does Tachanun end, he would say that it ends with the section וַאֲנַחְנוּ לֹא נֵדַע מַה נַּעֲשֶׂה ("And we do not know what to do"). That is perhaps not true. לַמְנַצֵּחַ and וּבָא לְצִיּוֹן גּוֹאֵל may also be part of the Tachanunim.[58]

---

55. שולחן ערוך אורח חיים סי׳ קלא סעי׳ ד

56. אבודרהם נפילת אפים אשרי למנצח ובא לציון

57. See the Rav's explanation of the function of Ashrei and why it is recited three times a day in רשימות שיעורים ברכות דף ד עמוד ב.

58. The Rav explained, based on the Rambam, that וּבָא לְצִיּוֹן גּוֹאֵל has a status of Tachanun as well. See רשימות שיעורים ברכות דף כא עמוד ב.

לַמְנַצֵּחַ, which is recited after Tachanun and Ashrei, certainly has the characteristics of Tachanun even though it may be recited on many days when Tachanun is not said. (The Sephardim are more consistent by treating Tachanun and לַמְנַצֵּחַ equally.) We recite לַמְנַצֵּחַ to implore God to extricate us from difficult situations, as we see from its opening line: "May Hashem answer you in time of trouble."

There are a number of verses in וּבָא לְצִיּוֹן גּוֹאֵל that contain elements of Tachanun, for instance: ה׳ צְבָקוֹת עִמָּנוּ מִשְׂגָּב לָנוּ ("Hashem, Creator of the heavenly and earthly hosts, be a fortress for us and protect us"). Furthermore, at the conclusion of our daily service, after the וּבָא לְצִיּוֹן גּוֹאֵל, we say a full Kaddish, with תִּתְקַבֵּל צְלוֹתְהוֹן וּבְעוּתְהוֹן ("May the prayers and requests[59] be accepted"). This refers to the Amidah and to Tachanun. Ending our prayers with this Kaddish may demonstrate that וּבָא לְצִיּוֹן גּוֹאֵל is considered a part of Tachanun.

Why do we break up Tachanun into two sections, the first portion ending before the Torah reading and the second section ending with וּבָא לְצִיּוֹן גּוֹאֵל? It seems clear that we want to include the Torah reading in the midst of Tachanun. [60] Perhaps the interruption of Tachanun by the Torah reading tells us that if we read, study and carry out the words of the Torah, God will show His mercy and respond to our pleas.[61]

Usually the term קְדֻשָּׁה דְסִדְרָא refers to the part of the prayer וּבָא לְצִיּוֹן גּוֹאֵל that contains the קְדֻשָּׁה with its Aramaic translation. The word סִדְרָא comes from the word סֵדֶר which means something that is organized, planned or a program. It applies to the prayer of וּבָא לְצִיּוֹן גּוֹאֵל because the Kedushah that was installed within it with its explanation of

---

59. Targum Onkelos on בראשית מח:כב explains that when Yaakov referred to his "sword and bow" he meant his prayers and requests, using the same words as the Kaddish. R. Soloveitchik explained that there are two types of prayer, which can be compared to a sword and a bow: A prayer for a short-term need, and a prayer for the long-term destiny of our people.

60. Rashi in Sotah 49a, ד"ה אקדושה דסידרא, explains that וּבָא לְצִיּוֹן גּוֹאֵל consists of Torah study as well as sanctification of God's name. See *Tikkun Tefillah* in *Otzar Hatefillot*, p. 424.

61. Rav Netronai Gaon quoted by Rav Soloveitchik: רשימות שיעורים [רי"ד סולובייצ'יק] מסכת ברכות דף כא עמוד ב ביאור שיטת הרמב"ם בקדושה דסידרא.

those verses qualifies as a Torah study session as far as the mitzvah of studying Torah is concerned. Rashi explains that since many people were too busy to set up regular Torah study periods, by including the Kedushah in this prayer, there would be public Torah study as well as a sanctification of God's name. The Gemara states that the world continues to exist after the destruction of the Temple by the merit of the קְדֻשָּׁה דְסִדְרָא and the יְהֵא שְׁמֵהּ רַבָּא, the line from the Kaddish where we accept God as our king. The Kaddish to which the Gemara is referring is the one recited after studying the Oral Law, אַגַּדְתָּא.

Rashi explains that there used to be a custom where a teacher would give a public class every Shabbat afternoon. All the people would come to study with him because they didn't have to go to work, and this is how they chose to spend their time. The teacher would teach the Oral Law, and after the study session, they would recite the Kaddish. This Kaddish, recited after learning the Oral Law, is what we know as the קַדִּישׁ דְּרַבָּנָן. Rashi is telling us that God sustains the world because of the people who, whenever they have the opportunity, get together to study Torah and then say Kaddish, accepting God as our King (קַבָּלַת עֹל מַלְכוּת שָׁמַיִם).

Generally we are only permitted to quote biblical verses in their entirety.[62] However, in the Kedushah of the שְׁמוֹנֶה עֶשְׂרֵה, we recite partial verses. Prayers that contain special holiness (דָּבָר שֶׁבִּקְדֻשָּׁה), such as Kedushah, are an exception,[63] and can include partial verses. In the קְדֻשָּׁה דְסִדְרָא we avoid this problem by reciting the entire verses from which the Kedushah texts are taken. This further strengthens the opinion that this Kedushah might not be an official Kedushah that can only be recited with a minyan.

---

62. כָּל פְּסוּקָא דְּלָא פַּסְקֵהּ מֹשֶׁה אֲנַן לֹא פָּסְקִינַן לֵיהּ (Any verse that Moshe did not divide, we likewise should not divide) ברכות דף יב עמ׳ ב.

63. Many of these concepts can be found in Rav Soloveitchik's explanations of the nature of דָּבָר שֶׁבִּקְדוּשָּׁה (prayer of sanctification). These were expressed in רשימות שיעורים (רי״ד סולובייצ׳יק) מסכת ברכות דף כא עמוד ב, Section 12, בדין ביסוד גדר, 13 and קריאת שמע ביחיד ובדין אמירת קדושת יוצר ביחיד ואמירת י״ג מדות קדושת יוצר, קדושת העמידה, וקדושה דסידרא.

According to some, this Kedushah was introduced during a time of persecution, when the hostility of our enemies made it impossible for us to say the regular Kedushah in its proper place (in the repetition of the שְׁמוֹנֶה עֶשְׂרֵה). In those days the land of Israel belonged to the Eastern Roman Empire (Byzantium), whose religion was Orthodox Christianity. Emperor Justinian (known for his animosity to Jews) and the Christians were outraged by Jews rejecting Christian teachings in favor of observing their own faith in their own traditional manner. Justinian was especially vexed by the Jews' interpretation of the verse קָדוֹשׁ קָדוֹשׁ קָדוֹשׁ ה' צְבָקוֹת מְלֹא כָל־הָאָרֶץ כְּבוֹדוֹ.[64] According to Christian doctrine this is a reference to the trinity, but Jews, long before Christianity, explained this verse as referring to one God. Byzantine soldiers were stationed in the synagogues to stop the "sacrilege" of interpreting this verse in the Jewish way. The soldiers knew when to expect the Kedushah and they were very alert, but after Kedushah they relaxed and did not pay such close attention. The Jews thought that after the שְׁמוֹנֶה עֶשְׂרֵה, in this concluding section of the service, they could recite Kedushah without being caught by the Emperor's soldiers. To escape danger, they recited it while sitting down, since the soldiers expected the Kedushah to be recited while standing.[65]

But here we encounter halachic problems. Prayers such as Kedushah can only be recited when the following three conditions are met: (1) the chazzan must summon the congregation to recite the specific prayer;[66] (2) there must be a minyan; and (3) according to the Rama, it must be recited while standing (the latter is true only according to Ashkenazic custom).[67] The Rama writes that this Kedushah has the

64. ישעיהו ו:ג.

65. See אור זרוע חלק ב סימן נ, citing ספר המקצועות. See also מחזור ויטרי סימן קלח.

66. The requirement of being summoned to respond is derived from the angels themselves. Isaiah 6:3, וְקָרָא זֶה אֶל־זֶה וְאָמַר קָדוֹשׁ ("and each one called to the other and said"), shows us that each angel had to be encouraged and summoned by his fellow angels to recite the Kedushah and teaches us to do the same. רשימות שיעורים (רי"ד סולובייצ'יק) מסכת ברכות דף כא עמוד ב ביסוד גדר קדושת יוצר, קדושת העמידה, וקדושה דסידרא.

67. רמ"א אורח חיים סימן קלב סעיף א.

same rules as the Kedushah recited during the first berachah of Keriat Shema. There is a question about that Kedushah as well. The Rama says the Kedushah of Keriat Shema is a description of what the angels do, but we are not really reciting Kedushah ourselves. According to the Rama, therefore, the Kedushah of ובא לציון is also not a real Kedushah. However, the Rambam feels that Kedushah of Keriat Shema should be omitted if there is no minyan to recite it. The Shulchan Aruch agrees with the Rambam, but accepts that there is a custom for individuals to recite it without a minyan. If there is no minyan, the Shulchan Aruch prefers chanting it with the Torah cantillation (trop) to indicate that you are saying it as verses from the Bible. The Rama believes we can follow the custom that an individual can recite it without a minyan.

There is another alternative that allows us to recite Kedushah without a minyan and not violate any conditions mentioned above. This becomes possible by viewing the recital of the Kedushah not as a special prayer, but as a learning session. In this case, we interpret the verses of Kedushah by explaining them with the commentary of Jonathan ben Uzziel. When studying we do not need a minyan, so even an individual can read it. Rashi explains that the reason that this Kedushah was established was to involve all the Jewish people in the study of Torah every day.[68]

The third verse in the Kedushah of the Shacharit Amidah, יִמְלֹךְ ה׳ לְעוֹלָם אֱלֹקַיִךְ צִיּוֹן לְדֹר וָדֹר הַלְלוּ־קָהּ ("May Hashem reign forever, the God of Zion throughout the generations, praise Him"), is taken from Psalms,[69] and is not, strictly speaking, part of Kedushah because it was not recited by the angels.[70] In this prayer of וּבָא לְצִיּוֹן גּוֹאֵל, we substitute

68. רש״י סוטה דף מט עמ׳ א ד״ה אקדושה דסידרא

69. תהלים קמו:י

70. For this reason, if you are reciting the section of Shema and its accompanying berachot while the congregation is saying Kedushah, you may interrupt the recitation of Shema and its berachot to join with the congregation in saying the first two verses of Kedushah. However, this does not apply to the third verse since, strictly speaking, it is not part of Kedushah, the angels' song (עטרת צבי אורח חיים סימן סו ס״ק ה).

the third verse of the regular Kedushah for another verse, ה׳ יִמְלֹךְ לְעֹלָם וָעֶד ("Hashem will reign forever").[71]

If we are treating this Kedushah as a full דָּבָר שֶׁבִּקְדֻשָּׁה, the leader should call out to the congregation to respond with a statement accepting God, but according to most customs, the congregation says the entire וּבָא לְצִיּוֹן גּוֹאֵל including the Kedushah as one unit, without the leader's call and the congregation's response.

All these things seem to be leading us to believe that this is not a דָּבָר שֶׁבִּקְדֻשָּׁה. However, according to the Rama, it is the same as the Kedushah said in the berachot of Keriat Shema, which according to the Rambam cannot be said without a minyan. That is why many yeshivot recite the Kedushah in וּבָא לְצִיּוֹן גּוֹאֵל responsively, as we do with any other bona fide Kedushah. The correct way of saying this Kedushah, if it is to be considered a דָּבָר שֶׁבִּקְדֻשָּׁה, is for the chazzan to request the congregation's response of accepting the sovereignty of God. The chazzan says out loud, וְאַתָּה קָדוֹשׁ יוֹשֵׁב תְּהִלּוֹת יִשְׂרָאֵל וְקָרָא זֶה אֶל זֶה וְאָמַר. Then the congregation responds קָדוֹשׁ קָדוֹשׁ קָדוֹשׁ ה׳ צְבָקוֹת etc. The chazzan then repeats this phrase. Next the chazzan does the same with the second verse, reciting aloud וַתִּשָּׂאֵנִי רוּחַ וָאֶשְׁמַע אַחֲרַי קוֹל רַעַשׁ גָּדוֹל, after which the congregation responds בָּרוּךְ כְּבוֹד ה׳ מִמְּקוֹמוֹ. Then the chazzan repeats this part of the verse as well.

Since the verse from Exodus, ה׳ יִמְלֹךְ לְעֹלָם וָעֶד, is used here as a part of this Kedushah, the chazzan must also introduce it as a responsive recitation. He says out loud the preceding words, בְּרִיךְ יְקָרָא דַה׳ מֵאֲתַר בֵּית שְׁכִינְתֵּהּ ("Blessed be the glory of God in His place") and the congregation responds, ה׳ יִמְלֹךְ לְעֹלָם וָעֶד ("Hashem will reign forever"). The chazzan then repeats the same phrase out loud so that he does not exclude himself from the people who are accepting God's sovereignty.

וּבָא לְצִיּוֹן גּוֹאֵל is always recited in the same format except for one instance.[72] Since the first two verses refer to the redemption, meaning the coming of the Messiah, we leave out these first two verses at

---

71. שמות טו:יח

72. אבודרהם סדר שחרית של חול ופירושיה ובא לציון

times we know the the Messiah will not come (for example, during nighttime). The exception to the exception is Shabbat afternoon. We know that the Messiah probably won't come on Shabbat, but the rabbis would customarily give a class every Shabbat afternoon which all the people would attend. At the end of this class, the rabbi would deliver some words of inspiration and comfort, relating to the coming of the Messiah. In deference to this, we include those two verses of redemption at the beginning of וּבָא לְצִיּוֹן on Shabbat afternoon. Because of its importance as a multi-themed prayer, we even say it at times when Kedushah would normally not be recited, such as in the Saturday night service.

We must yet explain why the third verse in the Kedushah of the שְׁמוֹנֶה עֶשְׂרֵה is from Psalms, while the third verse in the קְדֻשָּׁה דְסִדְרָא (וּבָא לְצִיּוֹן גּוֹאֵל) has been changed to the verse from Exodus.

One explanation is based on the verse אִם־לֹא אַעֲלֶה אֶת־יְרוּשָׁלַםִ עַל רֹאשׁ שִׂמְחָתִי ("...if I don't remember Jerusalem even at my happiest hour").[73] On any happy occasion we must make mention of Jerusalem, meaning first and foremost that we pray for the rebuilding of the Holy City.[74] Certainly, Kedushah is a happy occasion. Through it we join hands with the angels to sing God's praises. On such a glorious occasion we must think about Jerusalem. In the regular Kedushah we refer to Jerusalem when we say אֱלֹקַיִךְ צִיּוֹן ("God of Zion"). Since we have already remembered Jerusalem during Shacharit, we have the right to choose a different verse here. We prefer the verse from Exodus to the verse from Psalms, because the verse from Exodus is a verse from the Five Books of Moses and thus has greater sanctity.

Iyun Tefillah suggests[75] that since the קְדֻשָּׁה דְסִדְרָא is a learning session, and therefore requires commentary, we ought to use the verse from the Torah.

In the קְדוּשָּׁה דְסִדְרָא, the Aramaic translation is crucial: we translated the verses into the language that every Jew understood. Jonathan

---

73. תהלים פרק קלז פסוק ו

74. אבודרהם שמונה עשרה ואומר שליח צבור בסוף ברכת אתה גבור

75. *Iyun Tefillah* in *Otzar Hatefillot*, ובא לציון, עמ׳ רי״ג.

ben Uzziel wrote an Aramaic Targum for the books of the Prophets. There was no officially recognized translation available for Psalms, however, so we substituted a verse from the Torah that proclaims God's sovereignty. תַּרְגּוּם אוּנְקְלוֹס (Onkelos) had been recognized by the Rabbis of the Talmud as an accepted Torah translation in Aramaic and we used his translation of this final verse.

Why is this Kedushah called קְדֻשָּׁה דְסִדְרָא? Rabbi Samson Raphael Hirsch suggests that this name is appropriate since we are reaching the end of the service and it is a transition from our religious activities to the world of mundane living.[76]

Rav Soloveitchik once explained[77] that the Kedushah of וּבָא לְצִיּוֹן גּוֹאֵל is called קְדֻשָּׁה דְסִדְרָא because all the sanctities of creation are alluded to in this prayer: the sanctity of the Jewish people in the world, the sanctity of the angels in heaven above, and the sanctity of both worlds combined. In this case, סִדְרָא means the order of the sanctities or the list of the kinds of sanctity.

Rav Soloveitchik explained further: We usually recite our Kedushah separately from the Kedushah of the angels. The first Kedushah of Shacharit recited in the berachot of Shema is the Kedushah of the angels. We only recount the fact that they recite Kedushah, and we do not participate with them.

The Kedushah of the שְׁמוֹנֶה עֶשְׂרֵה of Shacharit is the second Kedushah of the day. It begins: נְקַדֵּשׁ אֶת שִׁמְךָ בָּעוֹלָם כְּשֵׁם שֶׁמַּקְדִּישִׁים אוֹתוֹ בִּשְׁמֵי מָרוֹם ("Let us sanctify God's name in the world just as the angels do in the heavens above"). This means that we are reciting this Kedushah on our own and not reciting this Kedushah together with the angels.

When Musaf is recited, it is the third Kedushah that we recite. The Kedushah of that עֶשְׂרֵה שְׁמוֹנֶה, according to the Sephardic custom, begins: כֶּתֶר יִתְּנוּ לְךָ ה׳ אֱלֹקֵינוּ מַלְאָכִים הֲמוֹנֵי מַעְלָה עִם עַמְּךָ יִשְׂרָאֵל קְבוּצֵי מַטָּה. יַחַד כֻּלָּם קְדֻשָּׁה לְךָ יְשַׁלֵּשׁוּ ("A crown is presented to You... by the angels who dwell in throngs above *together* with Your nation Israel gathered

---

76. *Hirsch Siddur*, p. 220.

77. This was conveyed to Rabbi Wohlgemuth directly by the Rav. See also Rabbi Reichman's רשימות שיעורים ברכות דף כא עמוד ב ד"ה ולפי"ז נראה לבאר ענין ג׳ הקדושות של שחרית.

below. *Together* they recited the threefold Kedushah to You"). The קְדוּשָּׁה דְסִדְרָא of the וּבָא לְצִיּוֹן גּוֹאֵל also reflects this idea of the angels and the Jewish people joining together to sing God's praise, as expressed in the phrase קַדִּישׁ לְעָלַם וּלְעָלְמֵי עָלְמַיָּא ("holy in this world and for all eternity"). This refers to the name that people call God in this world[78] as well as the name used for eternity, which is the name used by the angels.

According to the Sephardic version, in this Kedushah, as opposed to the others, humanity and the angels stand shoulder to shoulder to bring honor to their Creator. As we have seen, by saying וּבָא לְצִיּוֹן we fulfill various obligations. We conclude Tachanun and enable the latecomers to join in the Kedushah. In addition to those two aspects, וּבָא לְצִיּוֹן emphaizes the importance of Torah study. In days of old, the rabbis would gather the worshippers at the end of the service and teach them verses from Tanach, primarily selected verses that would encourage the Jewish people and give them hope for a brilliant future.

Today because of the lack of time we skip the learning session and just recite a few verses culminating in the Kedushah. Now we can understand why throughout the וּבָא לְצִיּוֹן there are so many verses in praise of the Torah. Toward the end, we ask for God's help in observing the mitzvot by saying יְהִי רָצוֹן מִלְּפָנֶיךָ...שֶׁנִּשְׁמֹר חֻקֶּיךָ בָּעוֹלָם הַזֶּה וְנִזְכֶּה וְנִחְיֶה וְנִרְאֶה וְנִירַשׁ טוֹבָה וּבְרָכָה לִשְׁנֵי יְמוֹת הַמָּשִׁיחַ וּלְחַיֵּי הָעוֹלָם הַבָּא ("May it be Your will that we observe Your statutes in this world, and may we be entitled to live, to see and to inherit good and blessing of the time of the Messiah and of the life of world to come"). These words were chosen carefully.

In the time of the Gemara, the people of the land of Israel recited a berachah when removing their tefillin before nightfall, because they followed the view that tefillin may not be worn at night.[79] We do not recite that berachah.[80] However, the text of that berachah

---

78. רש"י דברי הימים א פרק טז (כט) הבו לה' כבוד שמו
79. ברכות דף מד עמוד ב
80. שולחן ערוך אורח חיים סימן כט

was: בָּרוּךְ אַתָּה...אֲשֶׁר קִדְּשָׁנוּ בְּמִצְוֹתָיו וְצִוָּנוּ לִשְׁמוֹר חֻקָּיו. Even though we do not observe their custom, the use of the words שֶׁנִּשְׁמֹר חֻקֶּיךָ בָּעוֹלָם הַזֶּה implies a connection to the mitzvah of tefillin. In וּבָא לְצִיּוֹן we are asking God's help in observing mitzvot, such as the mitzvah of tefillin, as well as other mitzvot that we can aspire to fulfill in their most complete fashion.

The prayer וּבָא לְצִיּוֹן גּוֹאֵל was added to the service of Minchah on Shabbat and Saturday night Ma'ariv as well. On Saturday night, it was introduced together with וִיהִי נֹעַם ("May the favor of the Lord, our God, be upon us")[81] to prolong Shabbat. From a mystical point of view, on Shabbat the souls in purgatory get a respite from their suffering, and they don't have to continue with their punishment until after Shabbat is over. We prolong Shabbat for their benefit as well as our own.[82]

שִׁיר שֶׁל יוֹם AND עָלֵינוּ לְשַׁבֵּחַ

Returning to the weekday Shacharit, after the concluding קַדִּישׁ תִּתְקַבַּל we finish the service by saying עָלֵינוּ לְשַׁבֵּחַ. This practice to conclude all our services with עָלֵינוּ is of rather recent origin, dating from around the 12th century.[83] What is the origin of עָלֵינוּ?

Rav, the founder of the yeshivah in Sura, Babylonia, and Shmuel, the leader of the yeshivah in Nehardea, Babylonia (the two major Torah study academies in the world at the time) were the leading scholars of the first generation of the Babylonian Talmud. They established a community of dedicated Jews who made Torah study the center of their lives. Rav and Shmuel were the authors of many prayers. One of their contributions was the text of the three middle berachot of the Musaf on Rosh Hashanah. Their text is written in the most elegant Hebrew, in classical language. עָלֵינוּ לְשַׁבֵּחַ is the introduction to Rav and Shmuel's blessings. At the beginning we recognize the Creator and at the end we express our hope that all humanity will

81. תהלים פרק צ פסוק יז, ופרק צא פסוקים א-טז

82. סדר רב עמרם גאון סדר מוצאי שבת

83. The Machzor Vitri (written by a student of Rashi in the twelfth century) includes the עָלֵינוּ לְשַׁבֵּחַ (מחזור ויטרי סימן צט).

also do so. The Jewish people were so moved by this prayer that they decided to make it part of each religious service. This is the historical background of עָלֵינוּ לְשַׁבֵּחַ.

There is a conflicting tradition saying that עָלֵינוּ dates back to the time of Joshua.[84] This tradition developed because עָלֵינוּ describes with disgust the idolatrous practices of the Canaanites. When the Jews crossed the Jordan River, they were shocked to see the abominable rites of the Canaanites. עָלֵינוּ expresses the feeling of the Jews at this time. Most likely, Rav is the author of עָלֵינוּ. He describes our shock at observing the morally corrupt ritual of the Canaanites; in other words, Rav expressed the feelings experienced by Joshua.

About two centuries after the introduction of עָלֵינוּ to the daily service, opposition arose to this prayer.[85] Christian religious leaders claimed that it mocked the Church and the founders of Christianity through the line שֶׁהֵם מִשְׁתַּחֲוִים לְהֶבֶל וָרִיק וּמִתְפַּלְלִים אֶל אֵל לֹא יוֹשִׁיעַ "they bow down to nothingness and emptiness and worship a god that cannot help [יוֹשִׁיעַ] them"). They decided that this phrase referred to Yeshu, the founder of their religion. There was so much pressure that Ashkenazic Jews dropped the sentence completely and skipped these words. Only in our age have many congregations dared to restore the ancient text. It is important to read the original text especially in Musaf of Rosh Hashanah.

One of the reasons given for the institution of the prayer services was to parallel the Temple service. Every day the Levites used to sing a Psalm for the day. The last Mishnah in Tamid lists exactly which ones were recited. We continue the analogy to the Temple service by including these Psalms at the end of the daily service. Before we say the daily psalm, we announce the day of the week in relation to Shabbat: הַיּוֹם יוֹם רִאשׁוֹן בְּשַׁבָּת ("Today is the first day of the week since Shabbat") and so on, שֶׁבּוֹ הָיוּ הַלְוִיִּם אוֹמְרִים בְּבֵית הַמִּקְדָּשׁ ("on which the Levites used to recite the following psalm in the Temple"). Aside from commemorating the song of the Levites, this fulfills another mitzvah

84. תשובות הגאונים - שערי תשובה סימן מג

85. ליפמן מילהויזן, ספר נצחון, סימן שמ"ז

as well. There is a mitzvah to count the days in terms of Shabbat.[86] The names of the days of the week in Hebrew count from Shabbat. A Jew's existence is always based on the cycle of weekdays and waiting for Shabbat. We include this phrase here to fulfill the additional mitzvah. This recitation is one of the daily mitzvot, not necessarily a morning practice. If you miss saying this during Shacharit, you can, and should, say it later in the day when you are able to do so.

תְּפִלַּת הַדֶּרֶךְ

The Gemara[87] discusses prayers that are said for special circumstances. תְּפִלַּת הַדֶּרֶךְ is a prayer that you say when you are going on a dangerous journey. Following the practice of including others in our requests when we pray, it is recited in the plural.[88] If possible, it should be recited while standing, but if that is not practical, it can be recited while sitting. תְּפִלַּת הַדֶּרֶךְ is usually recited only one time in a day, even if the trip is broken up by layovers, but if the person intended to stop travelling for the day, and then changed his mind, he should recite the תְּפִלַּת הַדֶּרֶךְ a second time when he begins his journey again.

תְּפִלַּת הַדֶּרֶךְ should be recited soon after you start a journey, but not on a short trip, even if it a dangerous one. If you forgot to say it at the beginning of the trip, you can say it as long as you are still in transit and not too close to the destination.

תְּפִלַּת הַדֶּרֶךְ is a berachah which ends with בָּרוּךְ אַתָּה ה׳ and a closing, just like a בְּרָכָה אֲרֻכָּה does, but it strangely has no typical beginning that starts with בָּרוּךְ אַתָּה ה׳ אֱלֹקֵינוּ מֶלֶךְ הָעוֹלָם. For that reason, if he was traveling in the morning, the Maharam of Rottenberg used to say תְּפִלַּת הַדֶּרֶךְ together with the berachah of בָּרוּךְ אַתָּה ה׳ הַגּוֹמֵל חֲסָדִים טוֹבִים לְעַמּוֹ יִשְׂרָאֵל so it could be recited as a בְּרָכָה הַסְּמוּכָה לַחֲבֶרְתָּהּ.[89]

There are a few versions of this prayer, but they are all relatively similar.

---

86. רמב"ן שמות פרק כ פסוק ח
87. ברכות דף כט עמוד ב - דף ל עמ׳ א
88. שולחן ערוך אורח חיים סימן קי סעיף ד-ז
89. שולחן ערוך אורח חיים סימן קי סעיף ו

בִּרְכַּת הַמָּזוֹן

The usual medium for expressing our love for Hashem, our gratitude to Him, and our admiration of His creative powers is a benediction, a berachah. David Hamelech uses this formula in Psalms: בָּרוּךְ אַתָּה ה׳ לַמְּדֵנִי חֻקֶּיךָ ("Blessed are You, Hashem, teach me Your ways").[1]

The Rambam[2] explains that there are three categories of berachot:

> All the blessings can be divided into three categories: blessings over benefit (בִּרְכוֹת הֲנָאָה);[3] blessings over mitzvot (בִּרְכוֹת הַמִּצְוֹת);[4] and blessings of thanksgiving (בִּרְכוֹת הוֹדָאָה)[5] which consist of praise, thanks and petition, so that we will always remember the Creator and fear Him.

Chazal established many rules for berachot, and it is our task to carry them out. The recitation of all these berachot is a מִצְוָה דְרַבָּנָן, a mitzvah introduced by the authority of the Rabbis.[6] The only berachot that definitely are ordained by the Torah (מִצְוָה דְאוֹרָיְיתָא) is בִּרְכַּת הַמָּזוֹן.[7]

The commandment to thank God after we satisfy our appetite is

---

1. תהלים קיט:יב
2. הלכות ברכות פרק א הלכה ד
3. ברכות לה עמ׳ א׳
4. פסחים דף ז עמ׳ ב
5. For the Rav's explanation of this concept, see רשימות שיעורים ברכות דף מו עמוד א ביאור דברי תוס׳ ד״ה כל.
6. ברכות דף לג עמ׳ א
7. If you eat bread and feel full you are obligated from the Torah to say בִּרְכַּת

found in Parshat Ekev:[8] וְאָכַלְתָּ וְשָׂבָעְתָּ וּבֵרַכְתָּ אֶת ה׳ אֱלֹקֶיךָ עַל־הָאָרֶץ הַטֹּבָה אֲשֶׁר נָתַן־לָךְ ("You will eat and be satiated and bless the Lord your God for the good earth that He gave you"). The Rabbis analyzed this verse and found in it an obligation to say several berachot.[9] Eating even a volume of bread the size of an olive within a specified amount of time[10] also obliges us to say the בִּרְכַּת הַמָּזוֹן.[11]

וּבֵרַכְתָּ is the source for the first of the four berachot in בִּרְכַּת הַמָּזוֹן: בִּרְכַּת הַזָּן ("Who feeds"). אֶת ה׳ אֱלֹקֶיךָ ("Hashem your God") is the source for the introductory berachah of בִּרְכַּת הַזִּימּוּן or the invitation to recite בִּרְכַּת הַמָּזוֹן. עַל־הָאָרֶץ ("for the land") is the source for saying the berachah of בִּרְכַּת הָאָרֶץ (the blessing of the land, also referred to by its beginning words, נוֹדֶה לְּךָ, "We thank You"), the second of the berachot, which thanks God for giving us the Land of Israel. הַטֹּבָה ("the good [land]") is the source for our reciting the berachah of בּוֹנֵה יְרוּשָׁלָיִם ("Builder of Jerusalem"), the third of the berachot,[12] which expresses our wish for the rebuilding of the Temple in Jerusalem. The word הַטֹּבָה refers to the best part of the Land of Israel, namely Jerusalem and the Temple. אֲשֶׁר נָתַן־לָךְ ("that He gave you") refers to the berachah of הַטּוֹב וְהַמֵּטִיב, which is the fourth and final blessing of the בִּרְכַּת הַמָּזוֹן.[13]

We have a rule that we cannot put more than one idea in the conclusion of a berachah. This raises a problem. The בִּרְכַּת הַמָּזוֹן seems

---

הַמָּזוֹן; if you have eaten even a *kezayit* (olive-sized piece) of bread and are not full, you still have to say birkat hamazon, but it is a rabbinic obligation. Birkat Kohanim is also a Torah obligation, but in that case, the mitzvah is for the Kohanim to bless the people, not to bless God.

8. דברים ח:י

9. ברכות דף מח עמוד ב

10. The amount of time that it takes to eat either three or four eggs. This is known as כְּדֵי אֲכִילַת פְּרָס (see משנה ברורה סימן רח ס״ק מג).

11. שולחן ערוך אורח חיים סי׳ קסח סעי׳ ט

12. Incidentally, the Rav, following the Vilna Gaon, omitted the word בְּרַחֲמָיו (with mercy) from the חֲתִימָה of this berachah (בּוֹנֵה יְרוּשָׁלָיִם: אָמֵן).

13. The Gemara (ברכות דף מו עמ׳ א) tells us that this berachah is required only as a Rabbinic obligation.

to end the second blessing, עַל הָאָרֶץ וְעַל הַמָּזוֹן ("for the land and the food") with more than one idea. Although it appears to be two ideas, the berachah is simply stating that the land produces the food; it is really one idea.[14]

It is strange that our בִּרְכַּת הַמָּזוֹן contains not only our gratitude for the food we consumed, but also for Eretz Yisrael which produces the food and for Jerusalem which becomes our spiritual nourishment. In ancient times the third berachah did not start with the request רַחֵם ("Have mercy"), asking God to rebuild Jerusalem, but rather with words of gratitude that Jerusalem is ours.

The great leaders of the Jewish people composed the berachot we say today. The Gemara states that Moshe Rabbenu established בִּרְכַּת הַזָּן, the first berachah of בִּרְכַּת הַמָּזוֹן, when the manna came down. Yehoshua established בִּרְכַּת הָאָרֶץ, the second berachah thanking God for the gift of the land, when they entered the land of Israel. David and Shlomo established בּוֹנֵה יְרוּשָׁלָיִם, the third berachah of בִּרְכַּת הַמָּזוֹן: David Hamelech included עַל יִשְׂרָאֵל עַמֶּךָ, וְעַל יְרוּשָׁלַיִם עִירֶךָ about Israel and Jerusalem. Shlomo added עַל הַבַּיִת הַגָּדוֹל וְהַקָּדוֹשׁ, about the great and holy Temple.[15]

The Rabbis added the fourth berachah to בִּרְכַּת הַמָּזוֹן after the massacre of the Jews in the city of Beitar.[16] After the destruction of the Second Temple, the Jews in Israel rebelled against Roman rule and wanted to rebuild the Temple. The Romans would not give them their permission or reneged on their promise to do so. With a group of patriotic Jews, Bar Kochba almost succeeded in bringing the Roman Empire to its knees. Rabbi Akiva himself believed Bar Kochba to be the Messiah. The Romans rushed their most powerful legions to Judea and with great losses, succeeded to crush the rebellion. They were so upset by coming so close to defeat, that they decided to destroy the Jewish people. The corpses of the Jewish defenders of Beitar were

---

14. ברכות דף מט עמוד א
15. פסיקתא זוטרתא (לקח טוב) דברים פרשת עקב דף יג עמוד ב
16. ברכות דף מח עמוד ב

thrown all over the countryside. There did not seem to be a future for the Jewish people.

Miraculously, the Romans had a change of heart and permitted the burial of the heroes of Beitar. The Rabbis saw in this a double miracle. The first miracle was that the Jews received permission to bury their dead. The second miracle was that the bodies did not decompose in the summer heat before burial. The berachah established to thank God in commemoration of these miracles is called הַטּוֹב וְהַמֵּטִיב ("who is good and who does good"): הַטּוֹב because of the first miracle and הַמֵּיטִיב because of the second miracle.[17]

As we have seen, the berachah of הַטּוֹב וְהַמֵּטִיב deals with Jewish history and has no bearing on the food we are eating. Why did the Rabbis ordain to mention the miracles of Beitar in בִּרְכַּת הַמָּזוֹן? Each time when we partake of our food, we are reminded that God guides the fate of His people in a mysterious way. We are the Jews who enjoy their meal and life today, while yesterday we almost were exterminated.

There is a grammatical switch in בִּרְכַּת הַמָּזוֹן. As we said previously, when we switch from addressing God in second person to addressing God in third person it indicates a change in relationship between God and the Jewish people. In the first blessing, בִּרְכַּת הַזָּן, we address God in the third person, הוּא נֹתֵן לֶחֶם לְכָל בָּשָׂר, כִּי לְעוֹלָם חַסְדּוֹ. In the fourth berachah, we similarly speak about God in the third person: הוּא הֵטִיב הוּא מֵטִיב הוּא יֵיטִיב לָנוּ. On the other hand, the second blessing – בִּרְכַּת הָאָרֶץ – speaks to God directly in the second person, for example, נוֹדֶה לְּךָ ה׳ אֱלֹקֵינוּ. The third blessing – בּוֹנֵה יְרוּשָׁלָיִם – also addresses God in the second person – אָבִינוּ, רְעֵנוּ, זוּנֵנוּ, פַּרְנְסֵנוּ וְכַלְכְּלֵנוּ וְהַרְוִיחֵנוּ, וְהַרְוַח לָנוּ.

In the first berachah, which was instituted when the Jews were in the desert, they missed the opportunity to be with God on holy ground. In בִּרְכַּת הַטּוֹב וְהַמֵּטִיב, we think of the massacre of Beitar. These two berachot therefore express a limited relationship between God and Israel by the grammatic use of the third person. God is not so close to us, and we must search for Him until the ideal relationship has been reestablished.

---

17. ברכות דף מח עמוד ב

In the second and third blessings, בִּרְכַּת הָאָרֶץ and בִּרְכַּת בּוֹנֵה יְרוּשָׁלָיִם, we are literally in God's country; we enter the land of Israel, and we build Jerusalem and the בֵּית הַמִּקְדָּשׁ; God is very close to us. We stand in His presence, and have a very personal relationship with Him.

בִּרְכַּת הַזִּימּוּן

In addition to the mitzvah of בִּרְכַּת הַמָּזוֹן, there is an additional requirement to begin with בִּרְכַּת הַזִּימּוּן, popularly known as a מְזוּמָּן (invitation). When three or more adults eat a meal together, they are also obligated to recite the בִּרְכַּת הַמָּזוֹן together.[18] According to Ashkenazic custom, the מְבָרֵךְ (leader) addresses the group by saying, רַבּוֹתַי, נְבָרֵךְ ("Gentlemen, let us recite the blessings"). The reply of the group is יְהִי שֵׁם ה׳ מְבֹרָךְ מֵעַתָּה וְעַד עוֹלָם ("May the name of God be blessed forever"). The leader then repeats that statement so as not to be excluded from praising God. The core of בִּרְכַּת הַזִּימּוּן is the next part. The leader once more turns to the group and asks their permission to procede: בִּרְשׁוּת מָרָנָן וְרַבָּנָן וְרַבּוֹתַי, נְבָרֵךְ שֶׁאָכַלְנוּ מִשֶּׁלּוֹ ("With the permission of the respected company let us bless Him whose food we have eaten"). The group replies, בָּרוּךְ שֶׁאָכַלְנוּ מִשֶּׁלּוֹ וּבְטוּבוֹ חָיִינוּ ("Blessed is the One whose bounty we have eaten and whose goodness has sustained us"). The leader then repeats this line as well.

When ten men eat together and combine for a מְזוּמָּן, God's name (אֱלֹקֵינוּ) is added to the בִּרְכַּת הַזִּימּוּן (נְבָרֵךְ אֱלֹקֵינוּ שֶׁאָכַלְנוּ מִשֶּׁלּוֹ and בָּרוּךְ אֱלֹקֵינוּ שֶׁאָכַלְנוּ מִשֶּׁלּוֹ וּבְטוּבוֹ חָיִינוּ).

The leader then recites the בִּרְכַּת הַמָּזוֹן aloud, word by word. Originally, in the time of the Gemara, the leader alone recited בִּרְכַּת הַמָּזוֹן, while the rest of the group listened to the leader's recitation and responded Amen after each berachah.[19] Thanking God together in a

---

18. ברכות מה עמוד א

19. רמב"ם הלכות ברכות פרק ה, הלכה ב-ג. Each member of the group had to listen to the leader's every word intently and understand that the leader was saying every word on his behalf. Based on this concept of only one person reciting בִּרְכַּת הַמָּזוֹן, it is also the practice for a guest to lead the בִּרְכַּת הַזִּימּוּן, so that he

group is a higher level of thanks than having people recite the berachot individually. Unfortulately, it did not work out too well; people's minds would wander and they would lack the proper concentration. Therefore, today everybody says every single word even when there is a מְזוּמָן.

When there is a מְזוּמָן, the group should try to finish each berachah ahead of the leader so that each person can answer Amen after the leader concludes each berachah.

Complex Berachot: בְּרָכָה אֲרוּכָּה

The first berachah of בִּרְכַּת הַמָּזוֹן is a בְּרָכָה אֲרוּכָּה (a long, or complex berachah). This kind of berachah contains different thoughts or ideas. It begins with a פְּתִיחָה (opening sentence) and ends with a חֲתִימָה (concluding sentence) that contain the same major theme. The פְּתִיחָה usually starts with a berachah in the form of בָּרוּךְ אַתָּה ה׳ אֱלֹקֵינוּ מֶלֶךְ הָעוֹלָם and the חֲתִימָה starts with a berachah in the form of בָּרוּךְ אַתָּה ה׳ together with a restatement of the theme.[20]

As we learned, when we have a string of בְּרָכוֹת אֲרוּכּוֹת, especially if they continue the topic of the first berachah, only the first one needs to begin with the signature בָּרוּךְ אַתָּה ה׳ אֱלֹקֵינוּ.[21] The second berachah, בִּרְכַּת הָאָרֶץ, which begins נוֹדֶה לְךָ (We give thanks to You), and the third berachah, בּוֹנֵה יְרוּשָׁלָיִם (Builder of Jerusalem), are all part of this series. They are referred to as הַסְּמוּכָה לַחֲבֶרְתָּהּ (in proximity to another) and all rely on the opening of the first berachah.

In that case, what about the fourth berachah, הַטּוֹב וְהַמֵּטִיב? If it continues the theme of the previous berachot, it should not open with בָּרוּךְ אַתָּה ה׳ אֱלֹקֵינוּ מֶלֶךְ הָעוֹלָם. But it does start that way! The reason for this is that the fourth berachah is distinct from the ones that precede it. While the previous berachot are part of the Torah obligation, this berachah is only a Rabbinic requirement.[22]

---

could include a blessing for his host in בִּרְכַּת הַמָּזוֹן. See ערוך השולחן אורח חיים סימן רא סעיף ג.

20. ברכות דף מו עמוד א-ב

21. ברכות דף מו עמוד א-ב

22. ברכות דף מו עמוד ב

יַעֲלֶה וְיָבֹא AND רְצֵה

On special days we must mention the special nature of the day in בִּרְכַּת הַמָּזוֹן. For instance, on Shabbat we add to the berachah of בּוֹנֵה יְרוּשָׁלָיִם to the paragraph of רְצֵה וְהַחֲלִיצֵנוּ ("Favor us and strengthen us") that explains the sanctity of Shabbat. On Rosh Chodesh and Yamim Tovim, we include the prayer יַעֲלֶה וְיָבֹא ("May our remembrance arise and come before You") in the same berachah to mention each day's special character.[23]

What is the law if we forget to include this addition? It depends on our obligation to eat bread on that day. If we omit these on days when we are supposed to eat bread, we have to repeat the whole בִּרְכַּת הַמָּזוֹן. On Shabbat and on Yamim Tovim, there is a requirement to eat bread. On Rosh Chodesh, however, there is no requirement to have a festive meal, though fasting is fobidden. Omitting יַעֲלֶה וְיָבֹא on Rosh Chodesh therefore does not require us to repeat the בִּרְכַּת הַמָּזוֹן, since Rosh Chodesh can be celebrated without eating bread.[24]

אָמֵן

In Parshat Haazinu, Moshe tells the people, "When I proclaim the name of the Lord, give glory to our God!"[25] One of the laws the Sages derive from this verse is that when I recite a berachah in your presence, you must respond with "Amen," affirming God's praise.[26] It is usually a response to somebody else's berachah. We almost never find an instance where where we follow up our own statement by saying Amen.

In בִּרְכַּת הַמָּזוֹן, though, we have a strange phenomenon. After the

23. שולחן ערוך אורח חיים סימן קפח סעיף ה; שבת דף כד עמוד א

24. See שולחן ערוך אורח חיים סי׳ קפח סעי׳ ז. If you remember that you didn't say רְצֵה or יַעֲלֶה וְיָבֹא on Shabbat, Yom Tov or Rosh Chodesh, the Shulchan Aruch (ibid.) provides a substitute to say as long as you haven't yet started the next berachah.

25. דברים לב:ג

26. ספרי האזינו פיסקא שו

conclusion of the first three berachot (after בּוֹנֵה יְרוּשָׁלָיִם), we actually do answer Amen after our own berachah. The Rishonim explain it in the following way: Since the fourth berachah is only a Rabbinic requirement, while the first three berachot are Biblical requirements, we need a visible sign to show where the Torah obligation stops, and the Rabbinic obligation begins. Amen is the sign.[27]

עַל הַנִּסִּים

On Chanukah and Purim we express our gratitude to God by adding עַל הַנִּסִּים ("For the miracles") in the second berachah, נוֹדֶה לְּךָ. The additions to בִּרְכַּת הַמָּזוֹן for Shabbat and Yom Tov, however, are recited in the third berachah of רַחֵם which ends with בּוֹנֵה יְרוּשָׁלָיִם. Those additions deal with the sanctity of those days, which, in turn, is connected to the Temple service. Since Chanukah and Purim stress thanking God rather than the Temple service, which is the subject of יַעֲלֶה וְיָבֹא, we place עַל הַנִּסִּים in the berachah that expresses our gratitude to God for non-food related matters, נוֹדֶה לְּךָ.

If one forgets to say עַל הַנִּסִּים on Chanukah or Purim, we don't require that the person repeat בִּרְכַּת הַמָּזוֹן.[28] The Rama recommends adding עַל הַנִּסִּים in the form of a הָרַחֲמָן in that section of בִּרְכַּת הַמָּזוֹן.[29]

THE END OF בִּרְכַּת הַמָּזוֹן

The official ending of בִּרְכַּת הַמָּזוֹן are the last words of the berachah of הַטּוֹב וְהַמֵּטִיב, the words לְעוֹלָם אַל יְחַסְּרֵנוּ ("may He never cause us to be lacking"). Even though this berachah does not seem to have a חֲתִימָה, nevertheless, when we hear someone conclude לְעוֹלָם אַל יְחַסְּרֵנוּ, we must respond with Amen.[30]

---

27. שולחן ערוך אורח חיים סי׳ קפח סעי׳ א

28. שולחן ערוך אורח חיים סימן תרפב, סעיף א; משנה ברורה סימן תרצה ס״ק טו

29. רמ״א, שולחן ערוך אורח חיים סי׳ תרפב סעי׳ א

30. The Gemara (ברכות דף מו עמוד א-ב) mentions that this berachah is an exception to the rule of a long berachah ending with בָּרוּךְ אַתָּה ה׳. The Piskei

The הָרַחֲמָן verses following the berachah of הַטּוֹב וְהַמֵּטִיב were added in the Geonic times.[31] Though we fulfill our obligation if we stop bentching after reciting לְעוֹלָם אַל יְחַסְּרֵנוּ, it is recommended to recite the הָרַחֲמָן verses as well.[32]

I recall Rav Soloveitchik explaining to us that one should recite Amen after the הָרַחֲמָן verses because they are each considered one חֲתִימָה of the berachah of הַטּוֹב וְהַמֵּטִיב. In other words, הַטּוֹב וְהַמֵּטִיב is a berachah that has many endings.[33]

Rabbi Yochanan in the name of Rabbi Shimon bar Yochai instituted a method for guests to show appreciation to their host in the בִּרְכַּת הַמָּזוֹן. A special prayer was coined to express the good wishes to the host. The exact words of the blessing, now known as בִּרְכַּת הָאוֹרֵחַ, are mentioned in the Gemara.[34] Today many versions of the text of the בִּרְכַּת הַמָּזוֹן include this text.

We conclude בִּרְכַּת הַמָּזוֹן by reciting appropriate verses from the Bible. One of these verses says:[35] נַעַר הָיִיתִי גַּם־זָקַנְתִּי וְלֹא־רָאִיתִי צַדִּיק נֶעֱזָב וְזַרְעוֹ מְבַקֶּשׁ־לָחֶם ("I was a youth and also have aged, and I have not seen a righteous person forsaken and whose children were begging for bread"). This verse is strange. After all, even in wealthy America, there

---

Rid explains that even though it looks like a long berachah, since it is all of one theme it does not end with בָּרוּךְ אַתָּה ה׳.

31. See Seder Rav Amram Gaon. The Tur (אורח חיים קפ"ט) relates them to an expansion of the berachah that the guests recite for the host (based on a Gemara in ברכות מו עמוד א).

32. The verses beginning with the word הָרַחֲמָן ("The Merciful One") were added on to the end of בִּרְכַּת הַמָּזוֹן either as requests (for example, הָרַחֲמָן הוּא יְפַרְנְסֵנוּ בְּכָבוֹד, "May the Merciful One grant us an honorable income"), or to praise God in addition to what already was included in the body of בִּרְכַּת הַמָּזוֹן (for example, הָרַחֲמָן הוּא יִתְבָּרַךְ בַּשָּׁמַיִם וּבָאָרֶץ, "May the merciful One be blessed in the heavens and on the earth"). They are found in the earliest siddurim that we have.

33. The Machatzit Hashekel (אורח חיים סימן קפט ס"ק א ד"ה יש לענות אמן) gives a different reason for saying Amen: Even though הָרַחֲמָן is not a formal berachah, it is appropriate to recite Amen to any prayer of a Jew.

34. ברכות דף מו עמוד א

35. תהלים לז:כה

are many poor people. Many commentators struggle to explain this difficulty. I have seen it interpreted in the following way: King David, the author of the Book of Psalms, said: "Indeed, there are people who are poor and forsaken. I have never seen them *without doing something about it.*" King David was indicating that he would never let a destitute person perish. David's words, then, are intended as an inspiration for us. In our age that produced so many refugees, many Jews have risen to the challenge and made sure that no family would miss the traditional Shabbat meals or go without basic necessitites. There have been many communal aide societies formed, and we as individuals give charity in great measure.[36]

36. It is so built into our psyches that we, as individuals and as communities, cannot abide standing aside and not helping those who need help. We have traditionally set up private and public free loan funds and social organizations to provide for the physical, educational, vocational and emotional needs of those members of our society who are in need.

Tefillot of Shabbat and Yom Tov

On Shabbat and Yom Tov there are changes in the davening to express the nature of the holiness of each of these days. The most striking changes were those made to the עֲמִידוֹת of Shabbat and Yom Tov. Usually all three עֲמִידוֹת in a day are identical, with only slight variations. On Shabbat, however, we have a different שְׁמוֹנֶה עֶשְׂרֵה for each service. On Friday night we say אַתָּה קִדַּשְׁתָּ ("You sanctified"), in the morning we say יִשְׂמַח מֹשֶׁה ("Moshe rejoiced"), and in the afternoon we say אַתָּה אֶחָד ("You are One").

Furthermore, the Rabbis thought that the recital of the ordinary שְׁמוֹנֶה עֶשְׂרֵה on Shabbat or a holiday might deprive the worshipper of the special enjoyment that he is supposed to experience on these sacred days. Petitions that would sadden us are omitted, but we do retain petitions that bring us closer to God, such as the paragraph אֱלֹקֵינוּ וֵאלֹקֵי אֲבוֹתֵינוּ רְצֵה בִמְנוּחָתֵנוּ ("Our God and God of our ancestors, accept our rest"), which is included in the middle berachah of the Shabbat Amidah.

קַבָּלַת שַׁבָּת

During the First Temple period in Israel, there were no standardized prayers. In the period of the אַנְשֵׁי כְּנֶסֶת הַגְּדוֹלָה, our prayers became more formal. By the end of the Talmudic period, most prayers were standardized, and very little was added to the main prayers during the

Geonic period. But in the sixteenth century, the קַבָּלַת שַׁבָּת service was added to the Siddur.

קַבָּלַת שַׁבָּת is actually a halachic term. It defines the way we take upon ourselves the sanctity of Shabbat. For instance, once the woman of the house kindles the Shabbat candles, it is almost universally accepted that she is also accepting Shabbat. It means she is forbidden to do any more work.[1] In our case, however, קַבָּלַת שַׁבָּת is a liturgical term. It connotes the psalms, songs, and learning sessions that precede Ma'ariv of Shabbat.

How did this come about? By the end of the 15th century, the edict of King Ferdinand and Queen Isabella of Spain put an end to the largest and most influential Jewish community in the world. Suddenly, thousands of Jews became homeless. The expulsion of the Jews from Spain was a traumatic experience of catastrophic proportions. Nobody will ever know how many Jews perished in this tragedy. Most of the refugees settled in the Mediterranean countries. A number of Jews settled in Palestine, as it was then called, which was part of the Ottoman Empire.

The most influential community in Palestine was in the city of Safed. In the sixteenth century, Safed had attracted an accumulation of the greatest scholars of that age. Ordinary Jews who were engaged in the textile industry made it possible for the scholars to pursue their studies. The expulsion of the Jews from Spain was on everybody's minds. The people of Safed, lay people and scholars alike, frantically wanted to bring about the Messianic Age so that Jews would never again have the tragic experience of persecution and homelessness.

Toward that end the people of Safed engaged in three major activities. First of all, they studied Halachah. A meticulous observance of the laws would certainly hasten the redemption of the Jews. It is no wonder that Rabbi Joseph Karo was among the scholars of Safed.

Actually, Rabbi Karo had no intention of authoring a legal guide for every Jew. His intention was merely to write a commentary on the Turim of Rabbi Yaakov ben Asher. This commentary was called Beit

---

1. ערוך השולחן אורח חיים סימן רסג סעי׳ יג-טו

Yosef. Because it was very long, he made a short outline of it, which he called the Shulchan Aruch, or "set table." To look up a law is just like helping yourself from a prepared table of food.

A second way that the people of Safed tried to speed up the redemption was through the establishment of a new Sanhedrin. The Rambam maintains that it is possible to restore the original סְמִיכָה (Rabbinic ordination). All members of the Sanhedrin had to be ordained by the scholars whose ordination went back in an unbroken chain to Moshe. Naturally, the exile broke this chain, since the סְמִיכָה had to be performed in Israel. The Rambam suggests that the leading scholars of Israel could agree on one of their group to be ordained, and he, in turn, could ordain the other scholars.[2]

The Rabbis of Safed wanted Rabbi Yaakov Berab to play the role of the restorer of סְמִיכָה. A reconstituted Sanhedrin could legislate all the laws that would bring about the unity of Israel and lay the groundwork for the coming of the Messiah. Rabbi Levi ibn Chaviv opposed this plan. As a resident of Jerusalem, he believed that a scholar of Jerusalem should be chosen rather than a resident of Safed. The resulting disagreement foiled the renewal of the Sanhedrin.

The third activity in which the people of Safed engaged was mysticism, or Kabbalah. The greatest Kabbalists of this age were the Ari[3] – Rav Isaac Luria – and his student, Rabbi Chaim Vital, who popularized the teachings of the Ari. The Kabbalists believed that the performance of the commandments has cosmic significance. They felt that a kabbalistic interpretation of the commandments could force a speedy materialization of the Divine promise.

Shabbat is called מֵעֵין עוֹלָם הַבָּא (a miniature version of the next world). The people of Safed eagerly awaited the coming of the Messiah. On Friday they engaged in feverish activities to welcome the Shabbat. Perhaps it was their hope that a miniature messianic age would develop into the true Messianic Age, and their welcoming of the Shabbat would be the beginning of the Redemption.

---

2. רמב"ם הלכות סנהדרין פרק ד הלכה יא
3. This is the acronym for Rabbi Isaac Luria Ashkenazi (1534–1572).

The Talmud[4] tells us that Rabbi Chaninah dressed up and said, "Let us go and greet the Sabbath Queen." Rabbi Yannai would say, "Come, O Bride; come, O Bride." The people of Safed developed those short greetings into a lengthy ceremony. They would get dressed in their good Shabbat clothes and go to the outskirts of the city, singing psalms and other songs in honor of the Sabbath Queen. These ceremonies developed in Safed but soon became part of the Friday night services throughout the Jewish world.

During the hymn לְכָה דוֹדִי ("Come, Beloved"), the whole congregation turns around, symbolizing their march toward the Sabbath Queen, who is considered to come from the west. (In our shuls we face east, toward Israel. In the Temple itself, the holiest part, the *Kodesh Hakodashim*, was on the western side.) Some people actually walk a few steps toward the Sabbath Queen.

In many congregations, the chazzan leads the קַבָּלַת שַׁבָּת service from the *bimah* (the podium where the Torah is read) rather than from his regular place before the Ark in order to signify that קַבָּלַת שַׁבָּת is an addition to, rather than an essential part of, the Friday night service. My late colleague, Rabbi Isaac Simon, suggested that the elevated position of the chazzan (in synagogues where the *bimah* is elevated) reflects the ancient tradition of announcing the coming of the Shabbat by blowing the shofar from a rooftop.[5]

The קַבָּלַת שַׁבָּת service contains the following sections: Psalms 95 through 99, Psalm 29, the hymn לְכָה דוֹדִי, Psalms 92 and 93, בַּמֶּה מַדְלִיקִין (the second chapter of Mishnayot Shabbat) and קַדִּישׁ דְּרַבָּנָן.

Rashi at the beginning of Psalm 90 tells us that Moshe Rabbenu wrote the eleven chapters in the book of Psalms, starting with Psalm 90. Four of them are included in the expanded פְּסוּקֵי דְזִמְרָה for Shabbat and other Yamim Tovim. Seven of them were included in the קַבָּלַת שַׁבָּת service (Psalm 92, מִזְמוֹר שִׁיר לְיוֹם הַשַּׁבָּת, Psalm 93, ה׳ מָלָךְ גֵּאוּת לָבֵשׁ, as well as Psalms 95–99).

Psalms 95 through 99 form a unit within the Book of Psalms which

4. שבת דף קיט עמ׳ א
5. שבת דף לה עמ׳ ב

describes the Messianic era. The Hebrew word for "joyful song of redemption" is שִׁיר. The masculine form is used to indicate that the Redemption will be permanent.[6]

The feminine form, שִׁירָה, suggests change.[7] After the miracle of the Red Sea, a שִׁירָה (in the feminine form) was sung because the situation was to change, the redemption was not permanent. Many periods of oppression would follow. Jewish history has been a constant cycle of change, from slavery to freedom. In the six Psalms that usher in Shabbat (95 through 99 and 29), the word used is always שִׁיר (masculine), to indicate the coming age of permanent Redemption. This was the desire of the people of Safed: that with the coming of Shabbat, the Messianic Age would commence.

A thorough study of these six Psalms reveals much repetition. It is only natural that the jubilation of Israel over the end of thousands of years of oppression would be repeated over and over. Yet each Psalm emphasizes a different point. Psalm 95, for example, declares that it is up to us to bring about the Redemption. If we listen to God, the Messianic Age could begin even today.

Why are there six Psalms? Many commentators feel that these six Psalms correspond to the six days of the week, which will be turned into days of closeness to God.[8] It has also been pointed out that the first letters of these six Psalms add up to the number 430. The number 430 is also the gematria of the word נֶפֶשׁ, "soul" (נ = 50; פ = 80; ש = 300).[9] In other words, the recitation of these joyful songs creates the "additional soul" that we receive on Shabbat.[10] It is difficult to define this concept. It means: our closeness to God; the absence of sins; the performance of additional commandments; the good spirit brought about by Shabbat songs and Shabbat food; the

6. רש"ר הירש בראשית פרק ט פסוק כ
7. מכילתא דרבי ישמעאל בשלח - מסכתא דשירה פרשה א
8. *Iyun Tefillah* in *Otzar Hatefillot*, ד"ה לכו נרננה.
9. See *Otzar Hatefillot* at the beginning of Kabbalat Shabbat.
10. The source for the concept of the "additional soul" of Shabbat is a statement of Resh Lakish in the Talmud (ביצה דף טז עמוד א).

sense of oblivion from our problems; and a sense of pride that Jews are privileged to experience the sanctity of the Shabbat.

The sixth psalm we recite, Psalm 29 (מִזְמוֹר לְדָוִד הָבוּ לַה׳ בְּנֵי אֵלִים), is usually recited while standing. The psalm describes a violent storm starting on the ocean and making its way to the mountains of Lebanon. From there it turns south, spreading fear and destruction. In other words, this psalm describes how we stand in awe of God's great power and control over nature. The commentators, however, see in this psalm a symbol of the giving of the Torah.[11] Indeed, the Revelation on Mount Sinai took place amid thunder and lightning. This psalm was chosen for קַבָּלַת שַׁבָּת, since the Torah was given on Shabbat. Since this psalm reenacts the Revelation on Mount Sinai, we stand in reverence of the Almighty.

Following Psalm 29, we recite לְכָה דוֹדִי, written by Rabbi Shlomo Halevi Alkabetz who lived in the 16th century.[12] Then we recite Psalm 92 and Psalm 93, which are the songs recited in the Beit Hamikdash for Shabbat and for Friday, respectively, followed by a mourners' Kaddish.

Originally the Shabbat service began with Ma'ariv, starting with בָּרְכוּ. Generally, a woman accepts Shabbat with lighting the candles if she has intention to do so.[13] Once the reciting the קַבָּלַת שַׁבָּת service became widespread, then acceptance of Shabbat began with saying the Psalms for the Shabbat and לְכָה דוֹדִי. There are those who say that when we recite Psalm 29, we are accepting Shabbat.[14]

There is no public mourning on Shabbat.[15] As a general rule, a mourner does not leave the house during shivah. A mourner may leave the house on Shabbat and come to shul. This might be the first time the community has an opportunity to comfort the mourner, so there is a custom for the mourner to wait outside the shul until

---

11. *Iyun Tefillah* in *Otzar Hatefillot*, מזמור לדוד בתוך סדר קבלת שבת.
12. *Iyun Tefillah*, *Otzar Hatefillot*, לכה דודי.
13. ערוך השולחן אורח חיים סימן רסג: סעיף יד
14. *Otzar Hatefillot*, סדר קבלת שבת.
15. שולחן ערוך יורה דעה סימן שצג, סעיף ג

the end of the קַבָּלַת שַׁבָּת service. At that time the gabbai announces that we should rise to comfort the mourner, and the congregation recites: הַמָּקוֹם יְנַחֵם אֶתְכֶם בְּתוֹךְ שְׁאָר אֲבֵלֵי צִיּוֹן וִירוּשָׁלָיִם ("May the Holy One's presence comfort you together with the other mourners of Zion and Jerusalem"). The practice of reciting a mourner's Kaddish[16] was established to be said after the עָלֵינוּ prayer. This Kaddish, recited after קַבָּלַת שַׁבָּת, was instituted for the mourner to recite when he first comes into the shul during the shivah mourning period. It has become common practice for people who are saying Kaddish but aren't in their initial mourning period to recite this Kaddish as well. Even if there is no mourner who is sitting shiva, any mourner present can still recite the mourners' Kaddish after Psalm 93.[17]

The last part of the קַבָּלַת שַׁבָּת service is בַּמֶּה מַדְלִיקִין, which is a chapter from the Mishnah about the obligation to light Shabbat candles. We then say a selection about how Torah scholars bring peace into the world. This fulfills the obligation to study Aggadah.

Why was בַּמֶּה מַדְלִיקִין chosen? Because we say, "There are three questions that a person should ask the members of one's household on Friday evening before dark: Did you give the מַעֲשֵׂר (tithe)[18] for the food we are to eat on the Shabbat?" This is only practical in the Land of Israel, where you are not allowed to eat the produce until you tithe it, and you are not allowed to do that on Shabbat. A person must ask the other members of the household whether they gave this tithe before Shabbat starts.

The next question is, "Did you make an עֵרוּב?" One neighbor cannot carry food (or anything else) from one apartment to another through the same courtyard on Shabbat unless there is an עֵרוּב חֲצֵרוֹת;

16. *Seder Avodat Yisrael*, p. 182.

17. R. Yitzchak ben Moshe (ספר אור זרוע חלק ב - הלכות שבת סימן נ) states that "the custom of the Rhine is that after the congregation says *Ein K'Elokeinu*, the mourner rises and says Kaddish, but in France, I saw that they aren't careful about whether someone who is a mourner or not [recites it]."

18. An obligatory tax on produce grown in Israel and required to be set aside for the Levites and the poor.

an עֵרוּב תְּחוּמִין[19] allows a person to walk outside the city beyond a certain distance on Shabbat. The third question is, "Did you light the Shabbat candles?" Lighting the Shabbat candles and עֵרוּב חֲצֵרוֹת are both Rabbinic commandments. The Rabbis established these two laws to foster peace among the Jewish people on Shabbat. The Talmud tells us[20] that there were once two neighbors who didn't get along. One Shabbat, one of the women said to her little girl, "This is a delicious kugel. Bring it to our neighbor so that she will have something good to eat on Shabbat." The neighbor was delighted and said, "I thought all along that she hated me, and now she is sending me such good food." So, we see, an עֵרוּב חֲצֵרוֹת, which allows you to carry between one apartment and another on Shabbat, fosters good will between neighbors.

In the time of the Mishnah, the candles were the primary source of light in the house. The Talmud addresses the benefit of having light in the home on Shabbat. It teaches that we kindle Shabbat candles for the sake of harmony in the household.[21] A person is less likely to hurt oneself in a lit room than in an unlit room. If the house is dark, you can stumble and fall and get hurt. On Shabbat, there should also be harmony and peace and friendship. If you sit in darkness, there is none of these. Because these Rabbinic decrees create peace among the Jewish people, we conclude with the Talmudic excerpt[22] "Torah scholars increase peace in the world" as the Aggadic section to close the learning session.

קַדִּישׁ דְּרַבָּנָן follows the study of Halachah and Aggadah. These requirements have now been satisfied, and קַדִּישׁ דְּרַבָּנָן is now recited. According to Rashi, קַדִּישׁ דְּרַבָּנָן is recited after studying an explanation of a Torah text that includes an element of consolation. Reciting this group of mishnayot generates a קַדִּישׁ דְּרַבָּנָן. This Kaddish is an

19. שולחן ערוך אורח חיים סימן תח
20. ירושלמי מסכת עירובין פרק ג הלכה ב
21. שבת דף כג עמוד ב
22. ברכות דף סד עמוד א: אָמַר רַבִּי אֶלְעָזָר אָמַר רַבִּי חֲנִינָא: תַּלְמִידֵי חֲכָמִים מַרְבִּים שָׁלוֹם בָּעוֹלָם

expression of faith and trust that God will bring the redemption. This is a fitting end of the קַבָּלַת שַׁבָּת service that was instituted by rabbis and lay people, mystics and scholars of Safed who frantically wanted to bring about the Messianic Age so that Jews would never again have the tragic experience of persecution and homelessness.

Repetition of the Amidah of Ma'ariv

On Friday night, after the Amidah, we say the paragraph beginning with וַיְכֻלּוּ הַשָּׁמַיִם וְהָאָרֶץ וְכָל־צְבָאָם ("And the heavens and the earth were completed").[23] The Tosafot[24] explain that whenever Shabbat and Yom Tov coincide, the Amidah does not contain this paragraph, and therefore we say it after the Amidah even on a regular Shabbat. In addition, the Rabbis introduced it as the beginning of Kiddush at home for the benefit of those who did not recite it in shul.

In Ma'ariv there is usually no repetition of the Amidah by the chazzan. However, we have an abbreviated repetition on Friday evening called בְּרָכָה אַחַת מֵעֵין שֶׁבַע (a single berachah that is an abbreviation of seven). It is not really a repetition. It was introduced for one purpose only: to extend the service to make sure that all the worshipers, including the latecomers, get home safely.[25] The shuls used to be outside the city, and it was dangerous for people to walk home alone. On weekdays we extend Ma'ariv to protect latecomers by reciting the extra verses beginning בָּרוּךְ ה׳ לְעוֹלָם אָמֵן וְאָמֵן.[26] We cannot use these verses on Friday night however, since they contain nineteen names of God which correspond to the nineteen berachot of the weekday שְׁמוֹנֶה עֶשְׂרֵה. Therefore, we have a different way of prolonging the services on Friday night. The Friday night repetition stands for the seven berachot of the Amidah of Shabbat. That is an appropriate substitute for the extra verses in the weekday service.

In many shuls the main part of this Friday night repetition is sung

---

23. בראשית ב: א-ג
24. תוספות פסחים דף קו עמ׳ א ד״ה זוכרהו על היין
25. משנה ברורה סימן רסח ס״ק כ
26. תוספות מסכת ברכות דף ב עמוד א מברך שתים לפניה

by the congregation and the chazzan does not repeat it. He should, however, recite every word because otherwise it is a berachah uttered in vain. The Shulchan Aruch even mentions that the latecomers fulfill their obligation to recite the שְׁמוֹנֶה עֶשְׂרֵה with this repetition.[27] In order for a congregant to fulfill an obligation to recite שְׁמוֹנֶה עֶשְׂרֵה, that congregant must hear every word of the replacement שְׁמוֹנֶה עֶשְׂרֵה. This means that the chazzan has to recite every word out loud.[28] The Rama says that if someone wants to be strict, he is allowed to say the middle part of this repetition, and this is customary,[29] but once an individual has completed reciting this section (מָגֵן אָבוֹת בִּדְבָרוֹ), he or she has to listen to the chazzan say every word.

The berachah of the Friday night repetition parallels the seven berachot of the Shabbat Amidah. In the first section, recited only by the chazzan, is the phrase קוֹנֵה שָׁמַיִם וָאָרֶץ ("Who possesses heaven and earth"), which stands for the phrase וְקוֹנֵה הַכֹּל of the weekday Amidah. The phrase מָגֵן אָבוֹת ("Shield of the patriarchs") stands for the berachah of מָגֵן אַבְרָהָם of the Amidah. The next phrase, מְחַיֵּה מֵתִים, is the same as the second berachah of the שְׁמוֹנֶה עֶשְׂרֵה. The third phrase, הָקֵל הַקָּדוֹשׁ שֶׁאֵין כָּמוֹהוּ ("the Holy God who has none like Him"), parallels the third berachah (אַתָּה קָדוֹשׁ) of the שְׁמוֹנֶה עֶשְׂרֵה, the Holiness of God. The fourth phrase, הַמֵּנִיחַ לְעַמּוֹ בְּיוֹם שַׁבַּת קָדְשׁוֹ ("Who gives His nation rest on His holy Shabbat day"), parallels the berachah in the Amidah of Kedushat Hayom (וְהַנְחִילֵנוּ ה׳ אֱלֹקֵינוּ בְּאַהֲבָה וּבְרָצוֹן שַׁבַּת קָדְשֶׁךָ). The fifth phrase, לְפָנָיו נַעֲבֹד בְּיִרְאָה וָפַחַד ("we will worship before Him in awe and fear"), parallels the berachah that mentions the Temple worship, רְצֵה. The sixth phrase, וְנוֹדֶה לִשְׁמוֹ בְּכָל יוֹם תָּמִיד ("And we will always give thanks to His name"), is parallel to the berachah of מוֹדִים אֲנַחְנוּ לָךְ. And the seventh phrase, אֲדוֹן הַשָּׁלוֹם ("Master of peace"), parallels the final berachah of the Amidah, שִׂים שָׁלוֹם.[30]

In Ashkenazi siddurim, the phrase מֵעֵין הַבְּרָכוֹת appears as part of

---

27. שולחן ערוך אורח חיים סימן רסח סעיף יג וביאור הגר"א שם
28. משנה ברורה סימן רסח ס"ק כב
29. רמ"א אורח חיים סימן רסח סעיף ח
30. סדר עבודת ישראל, עמ׳ 190

the short excerpt of מוֹדִים. The *Iyun Tefillah* and *Avodat Yisrael* explain it based on the Talmudic phrase, תֵּן לוֹ מֵעֵין בִּרְכוֹתָיו ("Give Him the appropriate blessings").[31] If so, it is the conclusion of the phrase וְנוֹדֶה לִשְׁמוֹ בְּכָל יוֹם תָּמִיד, meaning, "We will give thanks to him each day, with the appropriate blessings."[32] However, in Yemenite siddurim these words read instead מָעוֹן הַבְּרָכוֹת, meaning: "You are the home of blessings." Rav Soloveitchik said that the phrase should be read as מַעְיַן הַבְּרָכוֹת, which means "the wellspring of blessings," and he noted that this phrase is also found in the Ramban.[33] According to this reading, the sentence ends with וְנוֹדֶה לִשְׁמוֹ בְּכָל יוֹם תָּמִיד, and we continue to give three descriptions of God, the other two being קֵל הַהוֹדָאוֹת ("God who is worthy of thanks"), and אֲדוֹן הַשָּׁלוֹם ("Master of peace"). The repetition of בְּרָכָה אַחַת מֵעֵין שֶׁבַע is not a real repetition of the Amidah but merely a method of protecting people who come late to shul. If the members of the congregation had been obliged to stay after the service to say the שְׁמוֹנֶה עֶשְׂרֵה themselves, they would have had to walk home alone through the fields. In this context, we can understand the reason why the normal rule of long berachot, that the beginning and end must have the same theme, and the usual changes reflecting the nature of the day do not apply. These exceptions to the rules were allowed by the Rabbis in order to protect the people who went to shul on Friday night.[34]

---

31. ברכות דף מ עמוד א

32. Note that the word מֵעֵין, meaning "corresponding," is used with two different connotations in regard to this berachah. This berachah is called בְּרָכָה אַחַת מֵעֵין שֶׁבַע, meaning "one blessing corresponding to seven," because it is a condensed version of the seven berachot of the Shabbat Amidah. But the phrase תֵּן לוֹ מֵעֵין בִּרְכוֹתָיו means that we are to bless God in correspondence to the blessings that He has bestowed on us. The Gemara uses this expression to tell us that on Shabbat, we should praise God for Shabbat, and on Yom Tov, for Yom Tov, etc. Thus, the phrase מֵעֵין הַבְּרָכוֹת in this berachah does not mean that we give God "a condensed version of blessings," but that we bless Him appropriately, according to what He has provided us.

33. רמב"ן בראשית ב:ג

34. שבת דף כד עמ׳ ב

קִידּוּשׁ

The Torah tells us it is a mitzvah to remember the Shabbat and make it holy (זָכוֹר אֶת יוֹם הַשַּׁבָּת לְקַדְּשׁוֹ), and we observe that by announcing it in the prayers and in Kiddush.[35] We recite Kiddush over wine both on Friday night, at the beginning of Shabbat, and on Shabbat day, after davening. Tosafot quote two verses that connect the act of remembering with the pleasant qualities of wine.[36] Here too, we invoke the pleasant qualities of wine with remembering the holiness of Shabbat. The main observance of sanctifying the Shabbat occurs on Friday night.[37] The text of the Kiddush on Friday night spells out the special character of Shabbat very clearly.

By the time Shabbat morning comes, the nature of the day is clearly understood. The Kiddush for Shabbat during the day is different than on the previous night. It is referred to as קִדּוּשָׁא רַבָּא, which means the "Great Kiddush." Rashi tells us why. It is because it only needs to include the blessing over wine. The blessing over wine is called the "Great Kiddush" because it is part of every Kiddush.[38] Reciting a blessing over wine parallels the song of the Levi'im in the Temple, which was also sung when the wine was poured on the altar; adding this blessing at the beginning of the meal reflects the sanctity of the meals of Shabbat.[39]

Everyone, men and women alike, is required to hear Kiddush.[40] According to one opinion,[41] the wine is part of the Biblical mitzvah of Kiddush. According to most authorities, however, the wine is only a Rabbinic requirement of Kiddush. The Rambam explains that a person can fulfill the Torah requirement to sanctify the Shabbat

35. ברכות דף לג עמוד ב ; פסחים דף קו עמוד א
36. זִכְרוֹ כְּיֵין לְבָנוֹן - הושע יד:ח and נַזְכִּירָה דֹדֶיךָ מִיַּיִן – שיר השירים א:ד.
37. פסחים דף קו עמוד א
38. רש״י פסחים דף קו עמוד א ד״ה קידושא רבא
39. See רש״י פסחים דף קו עמוד א ד״ה אמר רב יהודה בפה״ג.
40. ברכות דף כ עמ׳ ב
41. רש״י נזיר דף ד עמוד א ד״ה והרי מושבע ועומד

by words alone.[42] According to this position, we fulfill the Biblical mitzvah by reciting the middle blessing in the Amidah which ends with מְקַדֵּשׁ הַשַּׁבָּת. That is a sanctification of the Shabbat, a Kiddush. If declaring the Shabbat a holy day in the Amidah is considered Kiddush from a Torah perspective, as the Rambam says, then the Kiddush that we say at home with wine is a fulfillment of a Rabbinic mitzvah.[43]

The בִּרְכַּת הַמָּזוֹן is the other time where we mention the special character of the day. We have the paragraph of רְצֵה וְהַחֲלִיצֵנוּ ("Desire and strengthen us") that describes the special nature of Shabbat. Now we see that we actually sanctify the Shabbat three separate times on Friday night: in the שְׁמוֹנֶה עֶשְׂרֵה, in the Kiddush and in the בִּרְכַּת הַמָּזוֹן.

The Gemara records Rabbi Hamenuna's statement that anyone who says the paragraph of וַיְכֻלּוּ ("And God completed") on Friday night becomes a partner with God in the creation of the world. Rav Chisda says that when one recites this paragraph, the two angels that accompany each person place their hands on his head and say to him, "Your sins have been forgiven."[44] By saying this paragraph, we attest to God's creation of the world, and we stand when doing so, just as we would stand while giving testimony in *beit din* (a Jewish court).[45]

In Kiddush on Friday night, the sentences starting with וַיְכֻלּוּ (or the previous verse with which many people begin Kiddush) are not really a part of the actual Kiddush.[46] The reason the paragraph of וַיְכֻלּוּ is said at the table Friday night is for the benefit of people who might not have gone to shul. They would not have had the opportunity to recite the paragraph of וַיְכֻלּוּ which is said in the synagogue. The recitation of וַיְכֻלּוּ was established at the Friday night table where everyone can participate.

On regular Friday nights, we say וַיְכֻלּוּ in the שְׁמוֹנֶה עֶשְׂרֵה, following the שְׁמוֹנֶה עֶשְׂרֵה and in Kiddush. When Friday night coincides with a

42. רמבם הלכות שבת פרק כט הלכה א
43. ערוך השולחן אורח חיים סימן רעא סעיף א
44. שבת דף קיט עמוד ב
45. ערוך השולחן אורח חיים סימן רסח סעיף טו
46. תוספות פסחים דף קו עמוד א ד"ה זוכרהו על היין

Yom Tov, we recite the paragraph of וַיְכֻלּוּ only twice because there is no וַיְכֻלּוּ in the שְׁמוֹנֶה עֶשְׂרֵה.

There used to be a widespread custom to recite Kiddush in shul on Friday night after the prayers before everyone went home.[47] Originally the custom began because Jewish travelers would often stay in a shul while on their travels. They would eat there, so if there were travelers in the shul over Shabbat, they would need to hear Kiddush before their meal. There might not have been wine for everyone. Kiddush was made by the chazzan at the end of davening for them.

Even though we no longer, in general, use shuls for lodging for Jewish travelers, we did not stop this custom that had developed of making Kiddush in the shul. The custom has a parallel to lighting the Chanukah candles in shul on Chanukah. It doesn't serve so much to help a person fulfill the core mitzvah, but it does display an aspect of פִּרְסוּם הַנֵּס, publicizing the miracle: In the case of Chanukah, it publicizes the miracle of God saving us from a nation that tried to obliterate our religion and our people. In the case of Shabbat, it publicizes that we acclaim God who created the world in six days and rested on the seventh. For that reason, people who hear this Kiddush in shul stand. They are acting as witnesses to the miracle of Shabbat, and witnesses stand.

The practice of saying Kiddush in shul does present some problems, however. There is a blessing over wine, which means that someone must drink the wine so that it is not a blessing in vain. Who should drink the wine? Usually, the one reciting Kiddush drinks the wine, but here there is another problem. Kiddush must be recited in the place where one is eating his meal, and the person reciting the Kiddush will not be eating in the shul, but at home. Since he will not fulfill the mitzvah with this Kiddush, he cannot yet drink because it is forbidden to eat or drink before Kiddush. The usual solution was to give some wine to a child, so that the blessing is not in vain, and the adult is not drinking before Kiddush. Because of this issue, the Levush says that if you are in a place where this custom is observed, you should not

47. לבוש אורח חיים סימן רסט סעיף א; שולחן ערוך אורח חיים סימן רסט

change an established custom, but if there is no such custom in that place, it is better not to institute it.

All that we have mentioned regarding Kiddush on Shabbat applies to Kiddush on Yom Tov as well.[48]

SHACHARIT OF SHABBAT

On Shabbat, the פְּסוּקֵי דְזִמְרָה is expanded. More psalms are added before אַשְׁרֵי, and נִשְׁמַת כָּל חַי ("The soul of every living being") is added to the beginning of יִשְׁתַּבַּח. Of the chapters of Psalms that Moshe Rabbenu wrote,[49] four are included in פְּסוּקֵי דְזִמְרָה of Shabbat. They are: Psalm 90, תְּפִלָּה לְמֹשֶׁה אִישׁ־הָאֱלֹקִים ("A prayer by Moshe, the man of God"); Psalm 91, יֹשֵׁב בְּסֵתֶר עֶלְיוֹן ("He who sits in the protection of the Almighty"); as well as Psalm 92, מִזְמוֹר שִׁיר לְיוֹם הַשַּׁבָּת, and Psalm 93, ה׳ מָלָךְ גֵּאוּת לָבֵשׁ, which were also included in קַבָּלַת שַׁבָּת.

There are three different texts that are called Hallel: הַלֵּל הַגָּדוֹל; הַמִּצְרִי and הַלֵּל דְּכָל יוֹם. Rashi explains[50] that הַלֵּל הַמִּצְרִי is the Hallel we say on holidays. It includes Psalms 113–118 and thanks God for the miracles that were done for the Jewish people when God saved us from destruction. The Gemara explains that הַלֵּל דְּכָל יוֹם is פְּסוּקֵי דְזִמְרָא.[51] They are the prayers we say in the morning from בָּרוּךְ שֶׁאָמַר until יִשְׁתַּבַּח in which we thank God for the miracles of Creation and for daily miracles. The Gemara defines[52] הַלֵּל הַגָּדוֹל as תהלים פרק קלו (Psalm 136). We recognize it as starting with הוֹדוּ לַיְיָ כִּי־טוֹב כִּי לְעוֹלָם חַסְדּוֹ.

It repeats כִּי לְעוֹלָם חַסְדּוֹ twenty-six times corresponding to the גִּימַטְרִיָּא (numerical value) of God's name (the שֵׁם הַמְּפֹרָשׁ). It is also the number of generations from the Creation of the world until the Revelation of the Torah on Mount Sinai. During this era, God directed the world with the attribute of חֶסֶד (kindness).[53] It is called הַלֵּל הַגָּדוֹל

48. רמב"ם הלכות שבת פרק כט הלכה יח
49. רש"י תהלים פרק צ פסוק א׳
50. רש"י ברכות דף נו עמ׳ א ד"ה הללא מצראה
51. שבת דף קיח עמ׳ ב
52. פסחים דף קיז עמוד ב
53. ספר אבודרהם שחרית של שבת

because it describes how Hashem provides food for those that need.[54] The purpose of both פְּסוּקֵי דְזִמְרָא and הַלֵּל הַגָּדוֹל is primarily to thank God for the creation of the world. On Shabbat, פְּסוּקֵי דְזִמְרָא ends with נִשְׁמַת כָּל חַי.

Many people sit for נִשְׁמַת כָּל חַי, and then they stand for יִשְׁתַּבַּח. This follows the instructions printed in many siddurim. However, according to some, נִשְׁמַת and יִשְׁתַּבַּח are one unit, part of the same berachah.[55] It is a very long berachah, and it was established that we don't say it on weekdays because we may not have the time to focus on it properly. On Shabbat, when we have more time because we don't go to work, we say the whole thing. So if we stand for יִשְׁתַּבַּח, we should stand for נִשְׁמַת.[56]

נִשְׁמַת has the same theme as Psalm 92, מִזְמוֹר שִׁיר לְיוֹם הַשַּׁבָּת. Psalm 92 says, טוֹב לְהוֹדוֹת לַה׳ וּלְזַמֵּר לְשִׁמְךָ עֶלְיוֹן ("It is good to thank Hashem and to sing praises to Your most high name"); לְהַגִּיד בַּבּוֹקֶר חַסְדֶּךָ. וֶאֱמוּנָתְךָ בַּלֵּילוֹת ("to speak of Your kindness each morning and of Your faithfulness each night"). What does this song have to do with Shabbat? Nothing. It speaks about righteous people getting their final reward, and it speaks about wicked people, but it doesn't speak about Shabbat. Some say it is called the Psalm for Shabbat simply because of the verse טוֹב לְהוֹדוֹת לַה׳.[57] Usually we do not have the time to thank God properly. On Shabbat we have more time, so we lengthen our praises in honor of God and recite נִשְׁמַת and many more Psalms in פְּסוּקֵי דְזִמְרָה.[58]

---

54. פסחים דף קיח עמוד א

55. The Chayei Adam (כלל יט סעיף ו) writes that you cannot skip נִשְׁמַת even if you arrived late to shul. Seemingly, he holds that נִשְׁמַת is part of יִשְׁתַּבַּח and therefore it is indispensable.

56. The Sephardic custom is to sit for יִשְׁתַּבַּח, while the Ashkenazic custom, recorded by Rama (Orach Chaim 51:7), is to stand. Regarding נִשְׁמַת, see R. Hershel Schachter, *Mipeninei Harav*, p. 80. See also Rabbi Yitzchak Lichtenstein, הגדה של פסח שיח הגרי״ד בענין ברכת השיר. Rav Soloveitchik explained that on Shabbat we conclude פְּסוּקֵי דְזִמְרָה with נִשְׁמַת and יִשְׁתַּבַּח because נִשְׁמַת is a part of יִשְׁתַּבַּח.

57. *Etz Yosef* in *Otzar Hatefillot*, p. 209.

58. טור אורח חיים הלכות שבת סימן רפא

The paragraph at the end of נִשְׁמַת following the phrase רַנְּנוּ צַדִּיקִים בַּה׳ has two versions. The common Ashkenazic version is:

בְּפִי יְשָׁרִים תִּתְהַלָּל.
וּבְדִבְרֵי צַדִּיקִים תִּתְבָּרֵךְ.
וּבִלְשׁוֹן חֲסִידִים תִּתְרוֹמָם.
וּבְקֶרֶב קְדוֹשִׁים תִּתְקַדָּשׁ

The other version, favored by some Ashkenazic congregations and among Sephardic congregations, is:

בְּפִי יְשָׁרִים תִּתְרוֹמָם.
וּבְשִׂפְתֵי צַדִּיקִים תִּתְבָּרֵךְ.
וּבִלְשׁוֹן חֲסִידִים תִּתְקַדָּשׁ.
וּבְקֶרֶב קְדוֹשִׁים תִּתְהַלָּל

The *Seder Avodat Yisrael* and *Iyun Tefillah* both write that this latter version is inaccurate. The acrostic of Yitzchak is based on a Midrash which explains the verse רַנְּנוּ צַדִּיקִים בַּה׳ as relating to יִצְחָק. In the latter version, both Yitzchak and Rivkah's names are embedded as acrostics. But this comes at the cost of the prayer's accuracy.[59]

The same way we expand פְּסוּקֵי דְזִמְרָה on Shabbat morning, we also expand the first berachah of קְרִיאַת שְׁמַע. During the daily service, the Rabbis used the first berachah of Shema as a polemic against paganism. On Shabbat, we use the acrostic hymn קֵל אָדוֹן to speak about the seven visible planets that the ancients used to symbolize the powers of nature. Most of this hymn speaks about the sun and the moon. In the last stanza, שֶׁבַח נוֹתְנִים לוֹ כָּל צְבָא מָרוֹם ("All the hosts above give Him praise"), we allude to the other visible planets: The *shin* of שֶׁבַח refers to Saturn (שַׁבְּתַאי), the *nun* of נוֹתְנִים refers to Venus (נוֹגַה), the *kaf* of כָּל refers to Mercury (כּוֹכָב), the *tzadi* of צְבָא stands for Jupiter (צֶדֶק), and the *mem* of מָרוֹם stands for Mars (מַאְדִים). In this hymn the poet points

59. See *Seder Avodat Yisrael* and *Iyun Tefillah* on בפי ישרים תתהלל, where they explain that the author of the prayer intended to echo the verse לישרים נאוה תהלה. Thus, they write that changing this to בפי ישרים תתברך in order to create the acrostic of רבקה deviates from the original version.

out that the planets have no power of their own, that their task is to carry out God's will and to strengthen our faith in the Almighty.[60]

THE AMIDOT OF SHABBAT

Why do we have a different Amidah for each service on Shabbat? The differences were introduced (probably in Geonic times, since the Talmud never mentions them) because Shabbat has three entirely different aspects, and we want to acknowledge each one in a separate service.[61]

The theme of Friday night is the creation of the world, so we say וַיִּשְׁבֹּת בַּיּוֹם הַשְּׁבִיעִי מִכָּל מְלַאכְתּוֹ אֲשֶׁר עָשָׂה ("And He rested on the seventh day from all the work that He had done"). According to the Rabbis, the Torah was given on Shabbat.[62] Therefore, on Shabbat morning we speak about receiving the Torah in the paragraph יִשְׂמַח מֹשֶׁה בְּמַתְּנַת חֶלְקוֹ ("Moshe rejoiced in the the gift that was his portion"). In the afternoon, we emphasize the Messianic Age, that there will be a time when everyone will accept God and carry out His will. In that שְׁמוֹנֶה עֶשְׂרֵה we recite אַתָּה אֶחָד וְשִׁמְךָ אֶחָד ("You are one and Your name is one"). In the Messianic Age, every day will be like Shabbat because we will be closer to God. There will be no war and no hatred.

In the Bible, the word Shabbat is a feminine noun. In the Friday night Amidah of Shabbat, the pronoun referring to Shabbat is in the correct grammatical feminine form (בָהּ). Originally, this was the case in all three Amidot. However, under the influence of Kabbalah (Jewish mysticism), the pronoun was changed to the masculine singular gender on Shabbat morning (בוֹ) and to the plural (בָם) on Shabbat afternoon. This was done to underscore the three different aspects of Shabbat. The *Iyun Tefillah*[63] points out that these changes

60. *Iyun Tefillah* in *Otzar Hatefillot*, pp. 263–264 and the explanation in the section of Shabbat about קֵל אָדוֹן ("Lord, Master").

61. מחזור ויטרי עמידה של שבת סימן קסב

62. שבת דף פו עמ׳ ב - פז עמ׳ א

63. *Iyun Tefillah*, מנחה של שבת.

ignore simple grammatical rules. He suggests that we modify the text to say יוֹם שַׁבָּת, "the day of Shabbat" (a masculine noun), in the morning and יְמֵי שַׁבָּת, "the days of Shabbat" (masculine plural), in the afternoon. Rav Soloveitchik used to say יוֹם שַׁבָּת in the morning and שַׁבָּתוֹת (feminine plural) in the afternoon. That wording is found as part of the Yemenite version of the text. Then the Rav would use a feminine plural pronoun to agree with the plural form, i.e., בָּהֶן. In this way the texts for each Amidah would be grammaticaly correct.

In the Friday night Amidah and the Amidah of Shabbat morning we emphasize the respective aspects of the Shabbat by quoting selections from the Torah, but on Shabbat afternoon, we do not. On Friday night we quote וַיְכֻלּוּ הַשָּׁמַיִם וְהָאָרֶץ וְכָל צְבָאָם,[64] which is the portion dealing with creation. On Shabbat morning we quote וְשָׁמְרוּ בְנֵי יִשְׂרָאֵל אֶת הַשַּׁבָּת ("the Children of Israel will observe Shabbat").[65] Shabbat afternoon reflects the aspect that refers to the Messianic Age. There is no section in the Torah, however, that has the Messianic Era as its theme, therefore this Amidah does not quote any Torah section.

In the Shabbat morning Amidah, we begin the berachah that describes the קְדֻשַּׁת הַיּוֹם with a description of how Moshe brought down two tablets of stone on which were inscribed the laws concerning the observance of Shabbat. One might expect that this would be followed by a quotation from the Torah about the Ten Commandments, with a specific mention of the fourth commandment, to keep Shabbat. But instead we quote an entirely different selection: וְשָׁמְרוּ בְנֵי יִשְׂרָאֵל אֶת הַשַּׁבָּת.[66]

Rav Soloveitchik explained that this verse is preferred because when Shabbat was created, it was meant to be a universal concept, for all of humanity to observe. When nation after nation rejected Shabbat, and only one small nation, the Jews, adopted it as its spiritual foundation, Shabbat changed from a universal day to a day particular to one nation. The Ten Commandments were also supposed to have

64. בראשית פרק ב פסוק א-ג
65. שמות פרק לא: פסוק טז-יז
66. שמות פרק לא פסוק טז

a universal appeal. There is a famous Midrash about how the nations of the world rejected the Ten Commandments and all of God's Torah.[67] If we quoted the Ten Commandments as our source, we would not distinguish between the universal aspect of the Shabbat of Creation and the Jewish nature of the Shabbat of the Giving of the Torah. The verse that we use in the Shabbat morning Amidah explains the transition from the universal aspect of Shabbat to the Jews' actual acceptance of Shabbat and the Torah. It specifically describes Shabbat as בֵּינִי וּבֵין בְּנֵי יִשְׂרָאֵל אוֹת הִיא לְעוֹלָם (the sign of the covenant between God and the Jewish people).

On Shabbat, after the Torah reading and before we recite אַשְׁרֵי, we recite אַב הָרַחֲמִים ("Merciful Father"). It is a prayer that implores God to remember the individuals and communities who were slaughtered in martyrdom. It is said after Shacharit but before Musaf. It also expresses a request for Divine revenge against those who spilled their blood.

אַב הָרַחֲמִים was originally instituted in the aftermath of the massacres on Tishah B'Av in the Crusades of 1096. It was also added as a reaction to the slaughter of the Jews of York just before Pesach in 1190 and the mass murder of Jews in the season just prior to the holiday of Shavuot.[68] The ancient custom of Ashkenaz (Germany) called for reciting this prayer only twice a year: on the Shabbat before Shavuot and on the Shabbat before Tishah B'Av.[69] Today, however, the custom is to say it on most Shabbatot. This is due to the never-ending persecution to which the Jews were exposed.

תְּפִלַּת מוּסָף לְשַׁבָּת

On all days on which an additional sacrifice was offered, we say the Musaf (additional) service. The Amidah of Musaf has seven berachot (except on Rosh Hashanah): the standard first three and last three berachot of any שְׁמוֹנֶה עֶשְׂרֵה, and one middle berachah of קְדֻשַּׁת הַיּוֹם. In the middle berachah of Musaf, we express our sorrow for the

67. איכה רבה פרשה ג אני הגבר.
68. *Iyyun Tefillah*, אב הרחמים.
69. *Seder Avodat Yisrael*, p. 233.

destruction of the Temple and our inability to serve God properly (with sacrifices as well as prayer). We fervently pray for the rebuilding of the Temple.[70]

In the other עֲמִידוֹת we petition God directly to fulfill all our wishes. It seems that Musaf is different in status from the other Amidot. Musaf might actually be a substitute for the Temple service. Interpreting the verse וּנְשַׁלְּמָה פָרִים שְׂפָתֵינוּ ("And the words of our lips [prayer] will take the place of the animal sacrifices"),[71] the Rabbis assured us that by mentioning the sacrifices God will consider it as though we actually offered them up on the altar.[72]

As an expression of the difference between Musaf and the other prayers, the Gemara notes[73] that one who accidentally missed a prayer service can make it up at the next service by saying the שְׁמוֹנֶה עֶשְׂרֵה a second time. When it comes to Musaf, however, the Rishonim maintain that this cannot be done. Musaf is a substitute sacrifice, and a sacrifice has only one time for its offering. Therefore, there is no make-up prayer for Musaf.[74]

This raises the question of how one can ever make up a prayer. After all, prayer takes the place of the daily sacrifice, and we have a principle that if you miss the time for offering the sacrifice, you cannot bring the sacrifice at another time. The Gemara suggests that prayer is more than a substitute for sacrifices; it is also a petition for God's mercy. We know that people always have the right to bring their problems before the Master of the Universe, so if one missed Minchah, we can have a substitute prayer at the time of the next service, the Ma'ariv of that

70. In recent years, some prayer books have been published in which the promise that we make to offer sacrifices in the (restored) Temple is changed to the past tense. This subtle change in the tense of the verb makes the whole prayer worthless and causes it to be a berachah uttered in vain as well as a denial of a basic tenet of Judaism.

71. הושע פרק יד פסוק ג

72. יומא דף פו עמוד ב

73. ברכות דף כו עמ׳ א

74. שולחן ערוך אורח חיים סימן קח סעיף ו; ט״ז שם ס״ק ד

evening. But Musaf only serves as a replacement for the sacrifice, and therefore if one misses reciting it in its time it cannot be made up.

The berachah of קְדֻשַּׁת הַיּוֹם in Musaf on Shabbat lists the sacrifices that were brought on that day. Yet before we come to this main theme of Musaf, we add a few lines praising Shabbat. This section, תִּכַּנְתָּ שַׁבָּת רָצִיתָ קָרְבְּנוֹתֶיהָ ("You established Shabbat and You willingly accept the sacrifices of that day"), begins with the Alef-Bet in reverse order and utilizes rhymes. The Sephardic version also adds on to the end of the reverse alphabetical order the אוֹתִיּוֹת סוֹפִיּוֹת – final letters. Both the reverse Alef-Bet and the rhymes are devices of medieval piyutim.[75] Thus, this phrase seems to date from that time.[76]

The rabbis of Provence and France explained how the reverse Alef-Bet was more than a poetic device. It connects these words to the prophesies of the redemption.[77]

The understanding of the lines that lead up to the recital of the Temple sacrificial service is mysterious. What is meant by מְעַנְּגֶיהָ לְעוֹלָם כָּבוֹד יִנְחָלוּ which literally means, "Those who enjoy Shabbat will always enjoy glory," or טוֹעֲמֶיהָ חַיִּים זָכוּ ("Those who taste Shabbat deserve life"), or וְגַם הָאוֹהֲבִים דְּבָרֶיהָ גְּדֻלָּה בָּחָרוּ ("and also those who love its words have chosen greatness")?

The Kol Bo[78] offered a solution to the meaning of מְעַנְּגֶיהָ לְעוֹלָם כָּבוֹד יִנְחָלוּ. He explains that it refers to the Midrash about Rabbi Yosef Mokir Shabbat, who found a lost jewel in the belly of a fish.[79] Rabbi Yosef

75. Paytanic literature, better known as פִּיּוּטִים, consists of compositions that express a more complete description of the significance of the day in halachic, historical, or spiritual terms. This development began in Israel when the Sages instituted fixed prayers, later spreading to Europe (southern Italy, Germany, France, Greece, and Spain), and peaking in the 11th century in North Africa, Yemen, and Babylonia.

76. *Seder Avodat Yisrael*, p. 238, traces the Ashkenazic version of this text to Rav Amram and Rav Saadia Gaon. He notes that the Sephardic text differs and follows the Rambam's version.

77. *Seder Avodat Yisrael*, p. 238.

78. ספר כלבו סימן לז

79. שבת דף קיט עמ׳ א

had a rich neighbor. A Chaldean prophesied that Rabbi Yosef would acquire all of the neighbor's property, so the neighbor sold his holdings and bought a large jewel that he placed in his hat. While crossing a bridge, the wind blew his hat off, and the jewel was swallowed by a fish. The fish was caught and brought to market just before Shabbat, and the merchant remembered that Rabbi Yosef always bought special foods in honor of Shabbat. He offered him the fish. Rabbi Yosef bought the fish and found the jewel inside. From this incident the Gemara derives that whoever spends money in honor of Shabbat will be repaid. This alludes to the belief of the Rabbis that the money that God allots to us each year does not include the special expenses for Shabbat and Yom Tov, which we get back as a gift from God.[80] טוֹעֲמֶיהָ חַיִּים זָכוּ refers to the Gemara on the same page where Rabbi Yehoshua explains to the emperor that Shabbat contains a special ingredient that is effective only for those who keep Shabbat. It even makes our food smell special. This fragrance is reserved for Shabbat observers alone. The third phrase, וְגַם הָאוֹהֲבִים דְּבָרֶיהָ גְּדֻלָּה בָּחָרוּ, can be explained with a verse from Isaiah (58:13): וְכִבַּדְתּוֹ מֵעֲשׂוֹת דְּרָכֶיךָ מִמְּצוֹא חֶפְצְךָ וְדַבֵּר דָּבָר ("and if you honor [Shabbat] and do not go your ways nor look to your affairs, nor speaking thereof"). The Gemara[81] explains that one's speech on Shabbat should not be like one's speech on weekdays. Rashi explains that this refers to discussions about business.[82] Our conversation on Shabbat should not deal with weekday concerns. When we say הָאוֹהֲבִים דְּבָרֶיהָ גְּדֻלָּה בָּחָרוּ, we mean one who observes the rules of speech on Shabbat, whose words on Shabbat are different from his words during the rest of the week.

In Musaf on Shabbat, after we mention the sacrifices, we say, יִשְׂמְחוּ בְמַלְכוּתְךָ שׁוֹמְרֵי שַׁבָּת וְקוֹרְאֵי עֹנֶג ("Those who keep the Shabbat and call it a delight will rejoice in Your kingship"). Unlike Yom Tov, there is no mitzvah to rejoice on Shabbat. Instead there are the commandments of כִּבּוּד (honor) and עֹנֶג (pleasure) on Shabbat, which the Rabbis

---

80. ביצה דף טז עמ׳ א

81. שבת דף קיג עמ׳ ב

82. רש״י שם ד״ה שלא יהא דבורך של שבת

derive from the verse in Isaiah (58:13), וְקָרָאתָ לַשַּׁבָּת עֹנֶג לִקְדוֹשׁ יְיָ מְכֻבָּד וְכִבַּדְתּוֹ מֵעֲשׂוֹת דְּרָכֶיךָ מִמְּצוֹא חֶפְצְךָ וְדַבֵּר דָּבָר ("and call the Sabbath a delight and Hashem's holy day honored, and honor it…").[83] Then why do we mention rejoicing in Musaf? The answer lies in the dual aspect of Shabbat: its nature within the Temple walls and its nature outside of them. Musaf reflects the celebration of Shabbat within the Temple, where there was rejoicing. Therefore, immediately after mentioning the sacrifices, we mention the rejoicing of Shabbat in the Temple. The glory of rejoicing in the presence of God elevates our feelings of true happiness.[84]

Similarly, on Rosh Chodesh, there is no commandment obliging us to rejoice outside of the Temple. In the Musaf prayer of Rosh Chodesh we recite: מִזְבֵּחַ חָדָשׁ בְּצִיּוֹן תָּכִין .... וּבַעֲבוֹדַת בֵּית הַמִּקְדָּשׁ נִשְׂמַח כֻּלָּנוּ ("You will establish a new altar in Zion…and all of us will rejoice in the sacrificial service of the Temple"). Rosh Chodesh is more or less an ordinary day, but there is an island of happiness in the Temple.[85]

The Sephardim add יִשְׂמְחוּ בְמַלְכוּתְךָ in all prayer services on Shabbat. They agree halachically with the Ashkenazim that "rejoicing" applies only in the Temple, but they maintain that since there is a place for happiness on Shabbat, it may be mentioned in every service of the day.

During Musaf, after mentioning the special sacrifices of the day, we add a small paragraph that explains the meal offerings and libations that accompanied the animal sacrifices. If Yom Tov coincides with Shabbat, we mention the sacrifices of Shabbat before the sacrifices of Yom Tov. In the subsequent paragraph, dealing with the Yom Tov sacrifices, meal offerings, and libations, if we include the words וּשְׁנֵי תְמִידִים כְּהִלְכָתָם ("and two tamid sacrifices, as is the law"), we will have included two sacrifices too many. There are only two a day, not four. This is why Rav Soloveitchik would ask the chazzan to skip those words.

---

83. Usually we explain "honor" as referring to the preparations for Shabbat, while "pleasure" represents the enjoyment that we have on Shabbat itself. See רמב"ם הלכות שבת פרק ל הל' ב and הלכה ז.

84. See R. Soloveitchik, *Shiurim Lezecher Aba Mari*, vol. 2, p. 88.

85. See R. Soloveitchik, *Divrei Hagut Veha'arachah*, pp. 167-168.

THE AMIDAH OF YOM TOV

When we compare the Amidah of Shabbat with the Amidah of Yom Tov, we notice a few differences. On Shabbat, when we come to the middle berachah, the berachah of the holiness of the day, we immediately speak about Shabbat. On Yom Tov, however, we first mention the chosenness of the Jewish people: אַתָּה בְחַרְתָּנוּ מִכָּל הָעַמִּים ("You chose us from among all the nations"). Then we approach the main subject, the holiness of the day.

This difference is based on the sequence of historical events that took place in the desert. Shabbat was given to the Jewish people before the Torah was given at Mount Sinai.[86] Therefore, when we speak about Shabbat, we cannot yet mention the chosenness of Israel. The laws of יום טוב were revealed during the giving of the Torah, after the Jews had been chosen by God. We reflect this in the Amidah of Yom Tov by starting with the mention of our chosenness and then mentioning the specifics of the holiday.

There is another difference between the Amidot of Shabbat and Yom Tov. At the end of the berachah of קְדֻשַּׁת הַיּוֹם on Shabbat, we say, וְהַנְחִילֵנוּ ה׳ אֱלֹקֵינוּ בְּאַהֲבָה וּבְרָצוֹן שַׁבַּת קָדְשֶׁךָ ("Hashem our God, bequeath to us, with love and favor, Your holy Shabbat"). In the parallel passage of the Yom Tov Amidah, we say, וְהַנְחִילֵנוּ ה׳ אֱלֹקֵינוּ בְּשִׂמְחָה וּבְשָׂשׂוֹן מוֹעֲדֵי קָדְשֶׁךָ ("Hashem our God, bequeath to us, with gladness and joy, Your holy days of assembly"). If Shabbat and Yom Tov happen to coincide, we must mention both of these characteristic aspects: וְהַנְחִילֵנוּ ה׳ אֱלֹהֵינוּ בְּאַהֲבָה וּבְרָצוֹן בְּשִׂמְחָה וּבְשָׂשׂוֹן שַׁבָּתוֹת וּמוֹעֲדֵי קָדְשֶׁךָ.

Happiness and joy are not connected with Shabbat because there is no commandment of *simchah* on Shabbat. There is a commandment to rejoice on Yom Tov: וְשָׂמַחְתָּ בְּחַגֶּךָ אַתָּה וּבִנְךָ וּבִתֶּךָ וְעַבְדְּךָ וַאֲמָתֶךָ וְהַלֵּוִי וְהַגֵּר וְהַיָּתוֹם וְהָאַלְמָנָה אֲשֶׁר בִּשְׁעָרֶיךָ ("And you shall rejoice on your festivals: you, your son, your daughter, your servant, your maid, the Levite, the convert, the orphan, and the widow who are within your

86. Shabbat was one of the mitzvot given to the Jewish people at the desert camp of Marah (Sanhedrin 56b).

gates").[87] Although the Torah does not mention rejoicing with respect to Shabbat, in the Book of Isaiah (58:14) it says that observing Shabbat properly leads to "delight in the Lord." On the other hand, בְּאַהֲבָה וּבְרָצוֹן ("with love and favor") is only said on Shabbat. Why is it not said on Yom Tov? Doesn't God love us or accept our worship on Yom Tov? Why should "love and favor" be limited to Shabbat only?

Rav Soloveitchik explained that if you study Parshat Pinchas[88] carefully, you will see that the additional sacrifices are always accompanied by a *chatat* (sin offering). Regarding Shabbat, however, we read nothing about the *chatat*. On Yom Tov the *chatat* was necessary because human beings always sin. On Shabbat no mention is made of sinning because Shabbat brings about such a close bond between God and the Jewish people that God's love erases all our sins and shortcomings. God's grace frees us on Shabbat from iniquities, and this is the meaning of the words בְּאַהֲבָה וּבְרָצוֹן that we recite only on Shabbat.

There is also an interesting difference between Shabbat and Yom Tov in the closing of the berachah of קְדֻשַּׁת הַיּוֹם. On Shabbat we say, בָּרוּךְ אַתָּה ה׳ מְקַדֵּשׁ הַשַּׁבָּת ("Blessed are You, Hashem, who sanctifies Shabbat"). On Yom Tov, we conclude, בָּרוּךְ אַתָּה ה׳, מְקַדֵּשׁ יִשְׂרָאֵל וְהַזְּמַנִּים ("Blessed are You, Hashem, who sanctifies Israel and the times"). The reason for this distinction is given by the Talmud.[89] The Talmud explains that fixing of the proper date for the beginning of Yom Tov is done through a cooperative effort of God and the Jewish people. God tells us the date of Yom Tov, but only the beit din (Jewish court) can proclaim when the new moon occurs, thus setting the date for all the holidays in that month. The conclusion for the Yom Tov blessing of the Amidah, בָּרוּךְ אַתָּה ה׳ מְקַדֵּשׁ יִשְׂרָאֵל וְהַזְּמַנִּים, and the conclusion for Musaf of Rosh Chodesh, בָּרוּךְ אַתָּה ה׳, מְקַדֵּשׁ יִשְׂרָאֵל וְרָאשֵׁי חֳדָשִׁים ("Blessed are You, Hashem, who sanctifies Israel and the new months"), reflect

87. דברים פרק טז פסוק יד

88. במדבר פרק כח-כט

89. רש״י ברכות דף מט עמוד א מקדש השבת וישראל והזמנים; פסחים דף קיז עמ׳ ב

the fact God sanctified the Jewish people, who in turn generate the sanctity of Yom Tov and Rosh Chodesh.

On the other hand, the Jewish people have nothing to say about the fixing of Shabbat. God did not have the Jews as partners in setting the day for Shabbat; God sanctified the day Himself. Thus, the conclusion of the berachah of the Amidah of Shabbat does not mention Israel.

In relation to the conclusion of the Yom Tov berachah, we can raise another issue. Why do we use a generic term, וְהַזְּמַנִּים ("and the times"), instead of mentioning the Yom Tov by its particular name? For example, on Pesach we could conclude, בָּרוּךְ אַתָּה ה׳, מְקַדֵּשׁ יִשְׂרָאֵל וְחַג הַמַּצּוֹת. After all, in the beginning of this berachah we do mention all the Yamim Tovim by their proper names, so why do we not do so at the end of the berachah?

Rav Soloveitchik pointed out that there are three Torah sections that discuss the Yamim Tovim: Emor,[90] Pinchas,[91] and Re'eh.[92] Whereas the portion in Emor acquaints us with the character and the dates of the holidays, in Pinchas we learn about the sacrifices of each day. Re'eh adds the element of the obligation to go to Jerusalem and spend the holiday there. The mitzvah of spending time at the Temple is not a distinct commandment for each individual Yom Tov, but one commandment that applies for all of them together.

The berachah of קְדֻשַּׁת הַיּוֹם in the Amidah of Yom Tov reflects three kinds of information about the holidays. At the beginning of this berachah we mention the Yom Tov in the way that Emor does, i.e., conveying the particular aspects of each Yom Tov. We mention חַג הַמַּצּוֹת (the holiday of matzot) and describes it as זְמַן חֵרוּתֵנוּ (the time of our freedom), חַג הַשָּׁבוּעוֹת (the holiday of weeks) and describes it as זְמַן מַתַּן תּוֹרָתֵנוּ (the time of the giving of the Torah). Likewise, it mentions חַג הַסֻּכּוֹת (the holiday of Sukkot) and describes it as זְמַן שִׂמְחָתֵנוּ (the time of our rejoicing).

In the beginning of the section of the berachah of קְדֻשַּׁת הַיּוֹם, we

---

90. ויקרא פרק כג

91. במדבר פרק כח-כט

92. דברים פרק טז

refer to the worship service and the sacrifices, וְקֵרַבְתָּנוּ מַלְכֵּנוּ לַעֲבוֹדָתֶךָ ("And You, our King, brought us close to Your worship"). This parallels the portion of Pinchas that outlines the sacrifices offered on each holiday.

In the middle section of this berachah, the paragraph of יַעֲלֶה וְיָבוֹא ("May our remembrance go ascend and reach You"), we mention וְזִכְרוֹן מָשִׁיחַ בֶּן דָּוִד עַבְדֶּךָ וְזִכְרוֹן יְרוּשָׁלַיִם עִיר קָדְשֶׁךָ ("the remembrance of the Messiah, the son of David, and the remembrance of Jerusalem, Your holy city"). This parallels the section from the portion of Re'eh, which connects the holidays to the place of the Temple: בַּמָּקוֹם אֲשֶׁר־יִבְחַר יְיָ לְשַׁכֵּן שְׁמוֹ שָׁם ("in the place that God will choose to establish His name there").

In the concluding paragraph of this berachah we explain the commandment of going to Jerusalem on the holiday. In Musaf we employ direct quotations on this theme, but even in the other prayers we ask God for complete joy on Yom Tov, which can only take place in Jerusalem. In other words, the conclusion of the berachah refers to the shared aspect of all three holidays, the pilgrimage to the Temple to bask in God's Presence. Therefore, we choose an expression that is applicable to every Yom Tov: וְהַזְּמַנִּים.

The Torah Reading

The study of Torah is a fundamental commandment, fulfilling the verses וְשִׁנַּנְתָּם לְבָנֶיךָ ("teach them well to your students") and וְהָגִיתָ בּוֹ יוֹמָם וָלַיְלָה ("delve into it day and night").[1] We start our day with berachot for the study of Torah.[2] In addition to the commandment to study Torah, we are also obliged to read the Torah publicly, although public reading of the Torah is not in itself a Torah commandment.

The Talmud[3] tells us how this added תַּקָּנָה (regulation) developed. It states that there were ten regulations that Ezra promulgated. One was that we publicly read the Torah on Shabbat at Minchah. Another was that we publicly read the Torah on Monday and Thursday mornings. The Gemara immediately raises a question: Did the regulation to publicly read the Torah on Monday and Thursday not originate much earlier, in the time of Moshe?

The Gemara then quotes a beraita. Interpreting the verse וַיֵּלְכוּ שְׁלֹשֶׁת־יָמִים בַּמִּדְבָּר וְלֹא־מָצְאוּ מָיִם ("and they went three days in the desert and didn't find water"),[4] our sages explained that they went three days without finding the life-giving sustenance of the Torah, because Torah is compared to water. After the Jews had wandered through the desert for three days without Torah, they became tired and rebellious. Then Moshe decreed that the Jews should read the Torah on Shabbat. There

---

1. יהושע א:ח; דברים פרק ו:ז
2. רמ"א שולחן ערוך אורח חיים סי' מו סעי' ט
3. בבא קמא דף פב עמ' א
4. שמות טו:כב

was no need to read the Torah again on Sunday, but Moshe instituted a public Torah reading again on Monday. There was no Torah reading established for Tuesday or Wednesday, but it was established again on Thursday, though not on Friday. In this way the Jews never went three days without hearing the words of Torah.

We stated, however, that Ezra introduced the public Torah reading, and now we see that this requirement dates back to Moshe. The Gemara solves this problem by telling us that originally one man was called up to the Torah to read three verses, or perhaps three men were called up to read three verses. Ezra elaborated on Moshe's directive by establishing the law that three people should be called up to read at least ten verses. Rav Asi said[5] that the three Aliyot were established to represent the whole of the written law: Torah, Nevi'im (Prophets) and Ketuvim (Scriptures). Rava said the three Aliyot represent the three categories of Jews: Kohanim, Levi'im and Israelites.[6] Our practice is for a Kohen to receive the first Aliyah, a Levi the second, and a Yisrael the third.[7] The ten verses correspond to the ten בַּטְלָנִים, ten Jews whose job was to ensure that there would always be a minyan present on time for prayer.[8] Another opinion is that we must read ten verses to correspond to the Ten Commandments. And still another opinion is that the ten verses correspond to the ten phrases God used to create the world.[9]

In other words, both Moshe and Ezra were responsible for the practice of public Torah reading in shul. Ezra elaborated upon Moshe's original decrees.

---

5. בבא קמא דף פב עמ׳ א
6. מגילה דף כא עמ׳ ב
7. שולחן ערוך אורח חיים סימן קלה, סעיף ג; גיטין דף נט עמ׳ א.
8. Usually we think of בַּטְלָנִים as people who are free of all responsibilities and waste their time by not studying Torah. This is clearly not the case here. Rashi explains that the ten בַּטְלָנִים were dedicated Jews who were free from all personal work so that they could devote themselves entirely to the needs of the community. They came to shul early, spending their time there so that there would always be a minyan. The klaus in prewar Germany was a similar institution, as is our modern day kollel.
9. מגילה דף כא עמ׳ ב

Rashi[10] explains that Ezra's תַּקָּנָה to read the Torah on Shabbat afternoon during Minchah was for the benefit of the people who did not have the opportunity to hear the Torah read on Monday and Thursday.

Originally, the one called to the Torah would read his own portion. This turned out to be very embarrassing for many who were called up to read the text publicly and did not know how to do so. Consequently, the Rabbis established that an appointed reader (בַּעַל קוֹרֵא) must read the Torah for the man who had the aliyah, whether the latter was learned or ignorant.[11] In this way, everyone was treated equally.[12]

Actually, there is a problem if only one person reads the Torah. When one person relies on another to read for him, we rely on the principle of שׁוֹמֵעַ כְּעוֹנֶה,[13] that the person reading is acting on behalf of the person getting the Aliyah. However, it is always better for a person who recites a blessing to perform the action over which he recites the berachah.[14] Therefore, the Shulchan Aruch advises[15] that if possible, the person getting the Aliyah should read along with the בַּעַל קוֹרֵא. That raises the issue of תְּרֵי קָלֵי לֹא מִשְׁתַּמְעִי, meaning that two people reading at the same time makes it difficult for the congregation to hear. The Shulchan Aruch qualifies his statement by saying the person getting the Aliyah should read along softly.[16]

---

10. רש״י בבא קמא דף פב עמ׳ א, ד״ה משום יושבי קרנות

11. רא״ש מגילה פרק ג סימן א

12. Since it is an important principle not to embarrass someone, there are many similar laws that demonstrate the same sensitivity. For instance, a bridegroom ought to recite the berachah upon marriage himself. It is, after all, his commandment that he is fulfilling. Since not every bridegroom was capable of saying the berachah, the Rabbis established that the person conducting the wedding ceremony should pronounce the berachah on behalf of every bridegroom. See שולחן ערוך אבן העזר הלכות קידושין סימן לד סעיף א and ט״ז אבן העזר סימן לד ס״ק א.

13. בית יוסף אורח חיים סימן קמא based on סוכה לח עמ׳ ב.

14. See ערוך השולחן אורח חיים סימן קמא סעיף ה.

15. שולחן ערוך אורח חיים סימן קמא סעיף ב

16. There are some mitzvot where we are not concerned that the congregation will not be able to hear two voices at the same time, because they are so

What is the function of the Torah reading in our service? Why did Moshe and Ezra establish it as a requirement and why is it placed in the middle of the prayer service? Rav Soloveitchik explained that reading the Torah in shul fulfills the commandment of קַבָּלַת עֹל מַלְכוּת שָׁמַיִם (accepting God's rule).[17] Since the public Torah reading is not merely about study but also about accepting God as our King, it is appropriate to place this Torah reading in the context of prayer, where accepting God as our King is a major theme.

If you look around the synagogue during the Torah reading, you will see that some people stand and some people sit during the reading.[18] Originally, everyone stood during the study of Torah, too. In the time of the Gemara it was already permitted to sit during the study of the Torah.[19] Some explain that reading the Torah in shul is a re-enactment of the experience at Sinai, when everyone was gathered together to hear God give the Torah. At that time, everyone stood. Rav Soloveitchik agreed with this opinion and stood during the Torah reading for this reason.[20]

When the man called to the Torah reaches the bimah, he must know which portion is allotted to him in order to recite a berachah. The reader must show him the beginning of his portion. Then the one called up must grasp the Torah handles, look inside, turn aside, and recite his berachah.[21] The laws of reciting "Amen" require the reader, as well as the congregation, to immediately answer, without any interruption.[22]

---

beloved that the congregants will overcome the difficulty and listen properly. For example, with regard to hearing the Megillah, the Shulchan Aruch rules that even if ten people are reading at the same time, those listening can fulfill their obligation. See שולחן ערוך אורח חיים סימן תרצ סעיף ב ומשנה ברורה שם ס"ק ד.

17. See Rabbi Reichman's רשימות שיעורים, ברכות דף יא עמוד ב, בענין חלות דין דבר שבקדושה בקרה"ת.

18. See שולחן ערוך אורח חיים סימן קמו סעיף ד.

19. See מגילה דף כא עמוד א.

20. Rav Soloveitchik expressed this idea many times. See *Shiurim Lezecher Abba Mari*, vol. 2, pp. 227–230.

21. שולחן ערוך אורח חיים סי' קלט סעי' ד

22. רמ"א אורח חיים סימן קכד סעיף ח

The berachah must be recited immediately before the reading. Many people close the Torah before their berachah so no one will mistakenly think the words of the berachah are written in the Torah. Rav Soloveitchik required people to recite the berachah while the Torah was held open, so the reader could immediately begin to read after the berachah. To make sure that people would not think the words of the berachah were found in the Torah, he suggested, following the Rama, that people look to the side when reciting the berachah.[23] After the Torah reading, the scroll is closed and the berachah is said while the one called to the Torah still holds on to the Torah handles.[24]

The בַּעַל קוֹרֵא should stand while he reads the Torah. This is derived from the verse in which God instructed Moshe, וְאַתָּה פֹּה עֲמֹד עִמָּדִי ("and as for you, stand here with Me").[25] In the case of Megillat Esther, however, the reader may choose whether to sit or stand.[26]

After the appropriate number of Aliyot are read, a half-Kaddish is recited. This half-Kaddish is like a punctuation mark in the service, indicating the end of a section. Here it indicates the end of the Torah reading.

On Shabbat, fast days and Yamim Tovim, we also have a מַפְטִיר (additional reading) and a הַפְטָרָה (reading from the Prophets). On Shabbat, we call up seven people in addition to the מַפְטִיר.[27] For מַפְטִיר, we re-read the last few verses (at least three) of the concluding aliyah. It is interesting how the מַפְטִיר is now sometimes considered the most important honor because the one who receives this Aliyah is able to recite the Haftarah. In the time of the Talmud, it was considered less important, because no new Torah verses are recited.[28]

Rav Soloveitchik used to encourage boys to read the Torah during the weekday minyan in the week before their bar mitzvah. This would help the boy, giving him courage to read well at the actual bar mitzvah.

---

23. רמ"א אורח חיים סי' קלט סעי' ד
24. משנה ברורה סימן קלט ס"ק יז
25. דברים, פרק ה, פס' כח
26. מגילה דף כא עמ' א
27. שולחן ערוך אורח חיים סימן רפב סעיף ד
28. מגילה דף כג עמוד א

We know that in order to fulfill one's obligation to hear the Torah reading, the person actually performing the reading must be similarly obligated to fulfill this commandment.[29] This criterion is not met in this instance, so it would seem that a minor should not be able to exempt an adult from performing this obligation. Rav Soloveitchik relied on the view that this rule need not be applied to Torah reading. A person is obliged not to read the Torah, but to hear it read publicly. Hence, anyone, including a minor, could read from the Torah. Rav Soloveitchik continued to encourage this practice as he felt that it was important to bring young students to love the Torah and to enjoy participating in the prayer service.

Ezra's decree was that we read ten verses during the week and that each Aliyah contain at least three sentences. The Gemara was concerned that latecomers or people leaving shul early might get a mistaken idea that we allowed an Aliyah of less than three sentences. That is why they directed that an Aliyah not start less than three senteces from the beginning, or end less than three sentences from the end of the Torah's paragraph.[30]

The requirement that we read at least three verses, but not less than three, impacts on where we start and end an Aliyah. The readings for Yamim Tovim and other special occasions always reflect the nature of the day on which they are read. Sometimes there were only a limited number of verses in the Torah which were relevant to a special day.[31] On these days, there was no option but to read less than three verses in an Aliyah unless we arrived at a creative solution.[32] As a result we arrived at different ways of repeating verses to enable the three sentence minimum for Aliyot.

---

29. Explained in detail in רשימות שיעורים (רי"ד סולובייצ'יק) מסכת ברכות דף טו עמוד א.

30. מגילה דף כב עמוד א

31. Rosh Chodesh, for example.

32. תוספות מגילה דף כא עמ' א ד"ה אין מתחילין explained that since these exceptions were so well known as exceptions to the rule, people would not be confused about their requirements.

There are two berachot for the public Torah reading. The first berachah of בָּרוּךְ...אֲשֶׁר בָּחַר בָּנוּ מִכָּל הָעַמִּים וְנָתַן לָנוּ אֶת תּוֹרָתוֹ ("Blessed is He...who chose us from among all the nations and gave us His Torah...") is recited before the reading. The second berachah of בָּרוּךְ...אֲשֶׁר נָתַן לָנוּ תּוֹרַת אֱמֶת וְחַיֵּי עוֹלָם נָטַע בְּתוֹכֵנוּ ("Blessed is He...who gave us the Torah of truth, thereby implanting in our midst eternal life...") is recited afterward. Originally, the first berachah was said by the first person to be called up to the Torah, and the second berachah was said by the last person after the completion of the reading. The Rabbis decided that since people sometimes came late to the service and might have mistakenly believed that there was only one berachah to be recited at the end of the reading, or that people who left early might believe there was only one berachah recited at the beginning of the reading, each person must recite a berachah both before and after each aliyah.[33]

In the morning berachot, we say the same berachah that is recited before the public Torah reading (אֲשֶׁר בָּחַר בָּנוּ). Even though we have already said this berachah, we can recite it again before the reading of the Torah, because the aliyah is a clearly defined segment of Torah reading. We do not need the berachah following the Torah reading (אֲשֶׁר נָתַן לָנוּ תּוֹרַת אֱמֶת) in the morning berachot, because we never end our Torah study for the day.

The two berachot for the public reading of the Torah are stylistically somewhat different. In the first berachah we say וְנָתַן לָנוּ אֶת תּוֹרָתוֹ ("and He gave us His Torah"), while in the second berachah we say, נָתַן לָנוּ תּוֹרַת אֱמֶת ("Who gave us the Torah of truth"). The reason for the difference is that in the first instance, we are reciting a berachah before we have read the Torah; we are still unfamiliar with it. It was given to us by God and it is His. The second berachah is recited after we have read the Torah. God gave us the Torah and through study we have acquired it and made it our own.[34]

Beyond obligating us to read the Torah at specific times, Moshe's

---

33. מגילה דף כא עמוד ב

34. The Hirsch Siddur, p. 204 – ברוך אשר נתן.

institution resulted in our completing the reading of the Torah periodically. The most common practice had us finish the reading of the entire Torah each year. According to Minhag Eretz Yisrael, the Torah was read in a triennial (three-year) cycle. Eventually the one-year cycle to read the entire Torah was universally adopted.[35]

One might think that since we read a section of the Torah in the proper order every week, that each portion falls out on that particular week by coincidence. Actually, the Rabbis arranged that certain specific sections of the Torah would be read on specific days because of the close connection of the Torah reading and that particular calendar week. Rav Amram Gaon offers us the following mnemonic device in his prayerbook: פקי״ד ופס״ח מנ״ה ועצ״ר צו״ם וצל״י קו״ם ותק״ע.[36] פקיד means "command." The reading of the weekly portion we call Tzav,[37] meaning "command," precedes Pesach (ופס״ח). מנה means "count." In the weekly portion at the beginning of the Book of Numbers (בְּמִדְבַּר),[38] we start with a census of Jewish males. ועצר is an allusion to Shavuot, which is called עֲצֶרֶת in Rabbinic literature. The Torah portion of counting, Bamidbar, precedes Shavuot (ועצר). צוֹם is a fast and refers to the Fast of Tishah B'Av. Parshat Va'etchanan[39] must immediately follow Tishah B'Av, referred to in this mnemonic as צְלִי. Both words mean "pray." קוּם means "stand up," and the parshah of Nitzavim means "standing." Nitzavim[40] must precede תְּקַע, which means "blow a shofar," referring to Rosh Hashanah. These mnemonic devices of Rav Amram Gaon demonstrated a strong connection between the established readings of the Torah and the particular season of the year. For example, Parshat Tzav, we have noted, always precedes Pesach. In this Torah portion we find the laws regarding the process by which a metal pot is able to be made kosher.[41] While these laws

35. רמב״ם הלכות תפילה פרק יג הלכה א
36. See רמב״ם הלכות תפילה פרק יג הלכה ב and the הגהות מיימוניות there.
37. ויקרא ו:א-ח:לו
38. במדבר א:א-ד:כ
39. דברים ג:כג-ז:יא
40. דברים כט:ט-ל:כ
41. ויקרא ו:כא

were relevant for the Kohanim with regard to the sacrifices, it is also the same process necessary to remove *chametz* for Pesach.

There is also a connection between the time we read the curses that will be visited upon the Jews if we stray from God and the seasons of the year.[42] The Gemara tells us[43] that Ezra established that the curses from Leviticus be read before Shavuot and the curses from Deuteronomy be read before Rosh Hashanah. The reason for Ezra's edict was so they would be completed in the old year, leaving the New Year to bring nothing but blessing. The Gemara then points out that this explanation applies to the curses from Deuteronomy, but it does not explain the need to complete the curses from Leviticus before Shavuot. The Gemara answers that Shavuot is also a new year, for the fruit of the trees. On Shavuot, God determines how many fruits the trees will produce that coming year, among other matters. Thus, we can clearly see the correlation between the Torah reading and the calendar.

SPECIAL TORAH READINGS

The Gemara also quotes the verse וַיְדַבֵּר מֹשֶׁה אֶת־מֹעֲדֵי יְיָ אֶל־בְּנֵי יִשְׂרָאֵל ("Moshe told the children of Israel about God's festivals")[44] and explains that from this we derive that we are obliged to read passages about the holiday from the Torah on each of the various holidays.[45]

The Mishnah[46] lists the number of aliyot we have on the days when we read the Torah. On weekdays and Minchah on Shabbat we have three aliyot, no more and no less. On Rosh Chodesh and Chol Hamoed we have four aliyot, no more and no less. On Yamim Tovim, we have five aliyot; on Yom Kippur, we have six and on Shabbat, we have seven. Then the Mishnah adds a phrase that causes some

---

42. פַּרְשַׁת כִּי־תָבוֹא: דְּבָרִים, פֶּרֶק כח, פְּסוּקִים טו-סט and פַּרְשַׁת בְּחֻקֹּתַי: ויקרא כו:יד-לט.
43. מגילה דף לא עמ׳ ב
44. ויקרא כג:מד
45. See רש״י מגילה דף לא עמ׳ א ד״ה שנאמר וידבר משה.
46. מגילה דף כא עמוד א

controversy: We cannot have fewer aliyot, but we can add to the number. The two questions we must answer are: Why can we add and to which days is the Mishnah referring when it says we can add?

The Ran has one approach.[47] He says that the reason for additional aliyot is to indicate higher levels of holiness of that day. In other words, the number of aliyot on each day reflects a different amount of innate holiness. A day that has six aliyot (Yom Kippur) is holier than a day that has five aliyot (Yom Tov), and they have more holiness than an intermediary day of the festival or Rosh Chodesh that each have four aliyot. Since Shabbat is the holiest day, adding aliyot does not reflect on any other day, and we are permitted to do so.

Rashi has a different approach. He explains[48] that the reason we should not add additional aliyot is because lengthening the service will cause a financial hardship on people. The Ran explains that according to Rashi we cannot add extra aliyot on any days when work is permitted, such as Rosh Chodesh and Chol Hamoed (when it is permitted to work to prevent financial loss), but we may add aliyot on days when work is forbidden, such as Yom Tov. The Rambam[49] allows adding to the number of aliyot on all יָמִים טוֹבִים when we don't perform מְלָאכָה. The Shulchan Aruch[50] rules in accordance with the Rambam, but the Rama adds that the Ashkenazic custom is to allow extra aliyot only on Shabbat, with the one exception of Simchat Torah when we add many extra aliyot.

קְרִיאוֹת הַתּוֹרָה לְרֹאשׁ הַשָּׁנָה וְיוֹם כִּפּוּר

On Rosh Hashanah we read[51] the section of וַה׳ פָּקַד אֶת־שָׂרָה כַּאֲשֶׁר אָמָר.[52] This section describes how God remembered that Sarah wanted to

47. ר״ן מגילה דף יב עמוד ב בדפי הרי״ף, quoted by בית יוסף אורח חיים סימן רפב ס״ק א.
48. רש״י מגילה דף כא עמ׳ א ד״ה ואין מוסיפין עליהן
49. רמב״ם הלכות תפילה פרק יב הלכה טז
50. שולחן ערוך ורמ״א אורח חיים סי׳ רפב סעי׳ א
51. מגילה דף לא עמ׳ א
52. בראשית פרק כא פס׳ א-כא

have a child. The הַפְטָרָה for that day, וַיְהִי אִישׁ אֶחָד מִן־הָרָמָתַיִם,[53] contains the same theme as the Torah reading: Chanah wanted children, she prayed and God answered her prayers. The reason for the selection of these two portions for this day[54] is that both Sarah and Chanah's prayers were answered on Rosh Hashanah.

On the second day of Rosh Hashanah we read[55] the description of the binding of Isaac, Abraham being prepared to make the extreme sacrifice to God, וַיְהִי אַחַר הַדְּבָרִים הָאֵלֶּה.[56] It became an example of the Jews' dedication to God ever since, and we call on it as a reminder both for God and for ourselves on the day when God begins judging the world.

The Torah reading[57] for Yom Kippur morning, וַיְדַבֵּר יְיָ אֶל־מֹשֶׁה אַחֲרֵי מוֹת שְׁנֵי בְּנֵי אַהֲרֹן,[58] and the הַפְטָרָה selection, וְאָמַר סֹלּוּ־סֹלּוּ,[59] have themes that are relevant to the nature of the day: The Torah reading describes the Temple service (Avodah) of Yom Kippur, and the הַפְטָרָה describes the penitential process, including a description of fasting as well as the behaviors God wants from us. The Torah portion describes the death of Aharon's sons. Their deaths were the result of an improper observance of the Temple service. That is sobering enough. On the one hand, there are those who use it as an example of how we should be very careful in ensuring what we do is proper.[60] On the other hand, many look to the story to develop a sense of empathy. The Zohar says that anyone who cries for the death of Aharon's sons is forgiven all his sins.[61]

For Minchah, the Torah reading lists[62] some of the most serious

---

53. שמואל א פרק א פס׳ א - פרק ב פס׳ י
54. פרי מגדים אשל אברהם על שולחן ערוך אורח חיים סי׳ תקפד סעי׳ ב
55. שולחן ערוך אורח חיים הלכות ראש השנה סימן תקפד סעיף ב
56. בראשית פרק כב פס׳ א–כד
57. שולחן ערוך אורח חיים סי׳ תרכא סעי׳ א - סי׳ תרכב סעי׳ ב
58. ויקרא פרק טז פס׳ א–לד
59. ישעיהו פרק נז פס׳ יד - פרק נח פס׳ יד
60. אליה רבה סימן תרכב סעי׳ ב
61. מגן אברהם סימן תרכא
62. ויקרא פרק יח פס׳ א–ל

sins in the Bible. This is to remind us that as we have just received forgiveness for our sins, it would be tragic to slip back to an undesirable way of living. The הַפְטָרָה is the Book of Jonah, whose message is that repentance helps in achieving forgiveness from God, and that a person can never escape Him.[63]

אַרְבַּע פַּרְשִׁיּוֹת

During the time between the beginning of the month of Adar through Pesach, there are some changes to the regular Torah reading cycle.

Over the course of six weeks, beginning with the Shabbat preceding Rosh Chodesh Adar (or on Shabbat Rosh Chodesh Adar), four weeks have special מַפְטִיר readings (אַרְבַּע פַּרְשִׁיּוֹת).[64] If there are two months of Adar, these changes occur starting with the second month of Adar.

פַּרְשַׁת שְׁקָלִים

In the time of the Temple,[65] it was publicly announced starting at Rosh Chodesh Adar that it was time to prepare the gift of a מַחֲצִית הַשֶּׁקֶל (half shekel) for the Temple. This gift was used for buying the public sacrifices.[66] On the fifteenth of the month, everybody gave their half shekel, and the money was brought to Jerusalem.

On the Shabbat before or on Rosh Chodesh Adar, after the regular Torah reading, we have a special מַפְטִיר.

The Gemara[67] debated which selection from the Torah is most suited for Parshat Shekalim. They considered two possibilities. The first is the selection from Parshat Ki Tisa,[68] which is the first instance of collecting the half shekel. The second emphasizes the use of the shekalim, the purchase of the new year's sacrifices, and is taken from

---

63. אליה זוטא סימן תרכב סע׳ ב
64. שולחן ערוך אורח חיים סימן תרפה
65. רמב״ם הלכות שקלים פרק א הלכה ט
66. ערוך השולחן העתיד הלכות שקלים סימן פב הל׳ א
67. מגילה דף כט עמוד ב
68. פרשת כי תשא שמות פרק ל פסוק יא-טז

Parshat Pinchas,[69] relating to the order of the sacrifices. The halachah follows the view that the reading is from Parshat Ki Tisa.[70]

The reading is called פַּרְשַׁת שְׁקָלִים because it is about collecting the half shekel donation from each person. The collection of money for the public sacrifices is mentioned before the month of Nisan because Nisan begins the year of sacrifices. The הַפְטָרָה for this Shabbat is בֶּן־שֶׁבַע שָׁנִים יְהוֹאָשׁ בְּמָלְכוֹ[71] which mentions these contributions.

Today, we commemorate this obligation by giving a symbolic half shekel to charity before Purim every year. The Rama spells out this halachah[72]: In addition to the mitzvah of giving charity on Purim, we make a donation of half of the unit of the currency of the country we live in on the eve of Purim before we read the megillah. Since the section in the Torah mentions the word תְּרוּמָה (donation) three times, we give three מַחֲצִיּוֹת הַשֶּׁקֶל (or three half units of the currency of the state).

פַּרְשַׁת זָכוֹר

The second special reading of this series is called פַּרְשַׁת זָכוֹר. It is read on the Shabbat before Purim. Here too, we read the regular portion of the week, and reserve the מַפְטִיר for a special text.[73] This reading is about what Amalek did to us in the desert and our obligation to fight them. Haman was from the nation of Amalek, and this ties in our reading to Purim. The הַפְטָרָה for פַּרְשַׁת זָכוֹר is about King Shaul's war with Amalek,[74] and contains the same theme as the מַפְטִיר. There are those who believe that this portion and the next portion (פַּרְשַׁת פָּרָה) are significant in that it is a מִצְוָה דְּאוֹרַיְיתָא to hear them read.[75]

---

69. במדבר פרק כח
70. שולחן ערוך אורח חיים סימן תרפה סעיף א
71. מלכים ב׳ פרק יב עד פסוק יז. Some start with פרק יא פסוק יז.
72. שולחן ערוך אורח חיים סימן תרצד סעיף א
73. פרשת זכור כי תצא דברים כה, יז-יט
74. שמואל א טו, ב-לד - כה אמר ה׳ צבקות פקדתי את אשר עשה עמלק
75. שולחן ערוך אורח חיים סימן תרפה אות ז

פַּרְשַׁת פָּרָה

The last two special weeks are called פַּרְשַׁת פָּרָה and פַּרְשַׁת הַחֹדֶשׁ. The week of פַּרְשַׁת פָּרָה always comes one week before פַּרְשַׁת הַחֹדֶשׁ. This could cause a skip in weeks of the special readings. The reading of פַּרְשַׁת פָּרָה is found in the book of Numbers.[76] It talks about the way to remove ritual impurity (טוּמְאָה) that would prevent a person from offering the sacrifices. The idea expressed in the reading moves our focus from Purim to Pesach, and reflects the preparation for the next holiday. The הַפְטָרָה describes[77] removing טוּמְאָה in a spiritual process of becoming closer with God.

פַּרְשַׁת הַחֹדֶשׁ

The last of these four weeks occurs on the Shabbat before the beginning of the month of Nissan, and is called פַּרְשַׁת הַחֹדֶשׁ.[78] The reading is found in Parshat Bo and the הַפְטָרָה is taken from Ezekiel.[79] The מַפְטִיר calls the month of Nissan the first month and describes the preparation for the first Pesach. The theme of the הַפְטָרָה also mentions the Pesach sacrifices.

Torah Readings for Rosh Chodesh

The Gemara tells us that we should read at least three verses for each person who gets an Aliyah. We should not begin an Aliyah less than three verses from the beginning of a paragraph or end with less than three verses from the end of a paragraph so as not to mislead people who come late or leave early from shul and miss a part of the Torah reading.

There is a difficulty with the Torah reading of Rosh Chodesh. The Rosh Chodesh reading has four aliyot because Rosh Chodesh is called a festival (מוֹעֵד), and a מוֹעֵד has more holiness than a regular

---

76. פרשת חקת, במדבר יט, א-כב
77. יחזקאל לו, טז-לח
78. שולחן ערוך אורח חיים סי׳ תרפה סעי׳ ד
79. פרשת בא (שמות יב, א-כ) החדש הזה לכם עד תאכלו מצות. ומפטיר ביחזקאל פרק מה, פסוק טז או יח עד פרק מו:יח

day. The Torah portion for Rosh Chodesh has fifteen verses spread over three paragraphs. The first paragraph contains eight sentences. The second paragraph contains two sentences, and the third paragraph contains five sentences. It is not possible to give each person an aliyah containing at least three sentences and still not start a paragraph with less than three sentences of its beginning or without leaving less than three sentences from the end.

We have to make a compromise. In order to fulfill the requirements of an aliyah, we are missing one verse. There are two approaches to adjusting for the missing verse. Both address the missing verse by doubling up and having one aliyah repeat a verse. The two views merely differ on which verse it is. These two opinions are very old, and the Shulchan Aruch tells us one version.[80] The other version was favored by the Vilna Gaon, and popularized by his students in Israel.[81]

Rosh Chodesh was always a happy occasion. To feel a sense of this excitement, we see that there was even a special הַפְטָרָה instituted when Rosh Chodesh falls out on the day after Shabbat. The הַפְטָרָה is referred to as מָחָר חֹדֶשׁ – "Tomorrow is Rosh Chodesh." The special הַפְטָרָה begins:[82] וַיֹּאמֶר־לוֹ יְהוֹנָתָן מָחָר חֹדֶשׁ. Similarly, when Rosh Chodesh occurs on Shabbat, the Maftir reflects the sacrifices brought on Rosh Chodesh and the הַפְטָרָה refers to Rosh Chodesh. The Maftir is וּבְיוֹם הַשַּׁבָּת, וּבְרָאשֵׁי חָדְשֵׁיכֶם[83] and the הַפְטָרָה for Shabbat Rosh Chodesh is כֹּה אָמַר יְיָ הַשָּׁמַיִם כִּסְאִי.[84]

Torah Readings for Regular Fast Days

The Gemara[85] instructs that on fast days we read the section of the curses found in Parshat Bechukotai.[86] Rashi explains that this is because

80. שולחן ערוך אורח חיים סימן תכג סעיף ב
81. משנה ברורה סימן תכג ס"ק ג
82. שמואל א פרק כ פס' יח-מב
83. במדבר פרק כח פס' ט-טו
84. ישעיהו פרק סו פס' א-כד
85. מגילה דף ל עמ' ב - לא עמ' א
86. ויקרא פרק כו

Chazal wanted to tell us that troubles come as a result of our sins and that we should repent. The Shulchan Aruch, however, has a different selection. It tells us[87] that we read from וַיְחַל מֹשֶׁה both during Shacharit and during Minchah. At Minchah, we also read a Haftarah. On fast days we do not have a Haftarah for Shacharit, but we do for Minchah.

Why do we read a different selection than what the Gemara says? The Aruch Hashulchan explains,[88] based on the Rambam,[89] that the reading that the Gemara mentions is for a fast of a special occasion that the community declares in response to a special hardship. However on the regular fast days, we have a different reading because they are for past events, mostly relating to the destruction of the Temple, not to current events for which we must take acute responsibility. He points to Masechet Sofrim[90] as the source for our alternate readings on the fixed fast days, and explains that וַיְחַל was chosen because it relates to God forgiving the sin of the golden calf, giving us the second set of tablets and to the hope that in the future God will rebuild the Temple, soon in our time.

Torah Readings for Purim

The Torah reading for Purim is וַיָּבֹא עֲמָלֵק. Three people are called up to the Torah for this reading. This selection has nine verses. The Gemara tells us[91] that we must read a minimum of ten verses for a whole reading. Tosafot say that we can be a bit lenient with the ten-verse requirement if it is one complete theme and we take into consideration the meaning and lesson presented there. That is why when we read the Torah portion on Purim of וַיָּבֹא עֲמָלֵק[92] we are satisfied with the nine verses that complete a whole idea.[93] This allows three verses to each person's Aliyah but falls short of a tenth verse. Interestingly,

87. שולחן ערוך אורח חיים סימן תקסו סעיף א
88. ערוך השולחן אורח חיים סימן תקסו סעיף ב
89. רמב"ם הלכות תפילה פרק יג הלכה יח
90. מס' סופרים פי"ז
91. מגילה דף כא עמ' ב
92. שמות פרק יז פס' ח-טז
93. שולחן ערוך אורח חיים סימן קלז סעי' ד

the Avudraham[94] says that even though it isn't strictly necessary, the readers have a custom to repeat the last verse of the portion on Purim to bring the number to ten.

Last Eight Verses

The last eight verses in the Torah have a special status. There is a disagreement between Rabbi Yehudah and Rabbi Shimon about whether they were written by Moshe or by Joshua, after Moshe's death. The Gemara says that one person should read these verses during the public Torah reading. There are many different interpretations of these words. Tosafot quote[95] Rabbenu Meshullam who explained this to mean that instead of having a בַּעַל קוֹרֵא and the one who gets the aliyah read them together, only the one who gets the aliyah should read them.[96]

Rabbenu Tam does not accept this interpretation. Instead, following Rashi, he explains that these eight verses should not be divided into two aliyot, as may be done with other sections of eight verses. These last eight verses must be read as only one aliyah.

HAFTAROT

The Haftarot were established because Antiochus, the Greek king, decreed that the Jews were no longer allowed to read publicly from the Torah. In response, the Rabbis established reading in the synagogue, selections from the prophets with the same theme as the weekly Torah portion, in place of the Torah readings.[97] After the decree was no longer in place, the practice had already become institutionalized.

There is another group of changes in the regular order of readings. These changes affect the הַפְטָרוֹת.

---

94. ספר אבודרהם פורים

95. תוספות בבא בתרא דף טו עמוד א: שמונה פסוקים שבתורה

96. תוספות מנחות דף ל עמוד א ד"ה שמונה פסוקים

97. תוספות יום טוב מסכת מגילה פרק ג

שֶׁבַע דְּנֶחָמְתָּא

After Tishah B'Av there is a series of seven הַפְטָרוֹת that bring us up to Rosh Hashanah. They are known as שֶׁבַע דְּנֶחָמְתָּא, "seven of comfort." The הַפְטָרוֹת are:

1. (ישעיהו פרק מ, פס׳ א-כו) נַחֲמוּ נַחֲמוּ עַמִּי יֹאמַר אֱלֹקֵיכֶם
2. (ישעיהו פרק מט פס׳ יד-כו, ישעיהו פרק נ פס׳ א-יא,) וַתֹּאמֶר צִיּוֹן עֲזָבַנִי יְיָ ישעיהו פרק נא פס׳ א-ג)
3. (ישעיהו פרק נד פס׳ יא-יז, ישעיהו פרק נה פס׳ א-ה) עֲנִיָּה סֹעֲרָה לֹא נֻחָמָה
4. (ישעיהו פרק נא פס׳ יב-כג, ישעיהו פרק נב פס׳ א-יב) אָנֹכִי אָנֹכִי הוּא מְנַחֶמְכֶם
5. (ישעיהו פרק נד פס׳ א-י) רָנִּי עֲקָרָה לֹא יָלָדָה
6. (ישעיהו פרק ס א-כב) קוּמִי אוֹרִי כִּי בָא אוֹרֵךְ
7. (ישעיהו פרק סא פס׳ י-יא, ישעיהו פרק סב) שׂוֹשׂ אָשִׂישׂ בַּייָ תָּגֵל נַפְשִׁי בֵּאלֹקַי פס׳ א-יב, ישעיהו פרק סג פס׳ א-ט)

These seven הַפְטָרוֹת were set up as a kind of conversation between God and the Jewish people[98] after their experiences of great distress.

God addresses the leaders of the people: נַחֲמוּ נַחֲמוּ עַמִּי, "Comfort, comfort, my people."

The people respond: וַתֹּאמֶר צִיּוֹן עֲזָבַנִי יְיָ, we feel like God has deserted us.

The next week we read עֲנִיָּה סֹעֲרָה לֹא נֻחָמָה: We are like a small ship in a violent storm. We cannot accept comforting.

God answers: אָנֹכִי אָנֹכִי הוּא מְנַחֶמְכֶם – I personally am here to comfort you.

The people still maintain: רָנִּי עֲקָרָה לֹא יָלָדָה. Our pain is like a barren woman all alone.

God answers: אוֹרִי כִּי בָא אוֹרֵךְ – Arise. The trouble you experienced in the darkness is past. Now comes the time of light.

Finally, the Jewish people accept God's comforting: שׂוֹשׂ אָשִׂישׂ בַּייָ תָּגֵל נַפְשִׁי בֵּאלֹקַי – I will rejoice in God, my soul will delight in my God.

98. ספר אבודרהם סדר הפרשיות וההפטרות

תְּלָת דְּפֻרְעָנוּתָא

The three weeks between י״ז בְּתַמּוּז and תִּשְׁעָה בְּאָב have special הַפְטָרוֹת known as תְּלָת דְּפֻרְעָנוּתָא, "three of calamity." The הַפְטָרוֹת are:

1. (ירמיהו פרק א פס׳ א–יט, ירמיהו פרק ב פס׳ א–ג) דִּבְרֵי יִרְמְיָהוּ בֶּן־חִלְקִיָּהוּ
2. (ירמיהו פרק ב פס׳ ד–לז, ירמיהו פרק ג פס׳ א–ד) שִׁמְעוּ דְבַר־יְיָ בֵּית יַעֲקֹב
3. (ישעיהו פרק א פס׳ א–כז) חֲזוֹן יְשַׁעְיָהוּ בֶן־אָמוֹץ אֲשֶׁר חָזָה עַל־יְהוּדָה וִירוּשָׁלָםִ

תַּרְתֵּי דִתְיוּבְתָּא

The pair of הַפְטָרוֹת known as תַּרְתֵּי דִּתְיוּבְתָּא, "two of repentance," are read during the time of the עֲשֶׂרֶת יְמֵי הַתְּשׁוּבָה, the ten days of repentance between Rosh Hashanah and Yom Kippur. Sometimes there are two הַפְטָרוֹת to be read, and only one Shabbat in these ten days. That has led to some complicated solutions. One suggestion is that the pleas for repentance are still forceful immediately after Yom Kippur, so they can be included in the Shabbat right afterward, when we read Parshat Ha'azinu.[99] The הַפְטָרוֹת are:

1. הושע פרק יד פס׳ ב–י, מיכה פרק ז פס׳ יח–כ, יואל פרק ב פס׳ יא–יד) שׁוּבָה יִשְׂרָאֵל
2. (ישעיהו פרק נה פס׳ ו–יג, ישעיהו פרק נו פס׳ א–ח) דִּרְשׁוּ יְיָ בְּהִמָּצְאוֹ

בִּרְכַּת הַגּוֹמֵל

There is a custom in many Chasidic shuls on Friday night before Minchah to say Psalm 107. There is a phrase that is repeated four times in this psalm: יוֹדוּ לַה׳ חַסְדּוֹ וְנִפְלְאוֹתָיו לִבְנֵי אָדָם ("They will thank God for His goodness and his miracles that He does for people"). This psalm describes the four categories of danger that would cause a person to give thanks to God for emerging safely. The four categories, in the words of King David, are, תָּעוּ בַמִּדְבָּר, those who wandered in the desert; אֲסִירֵי עֳנִי וּבַרְזֶל, those who were imprisoned and set free; וַיַּגִּיעוּ עַד שַׁעֲרֵי מָוֶת, those who recovered from a serious illness, and יוֹרְדֵי הַיָּם בָּאֳנִיּוֹת, those who crossed the ocean. Rav Yehudah said in the name of Rav[100]

---

99. ספר אבודרהם סדר הפרשיות וההפטרות
100. ברכות דף נד עמוד ב

that these four categories of people must thank Hashem by reciting the בִּרְכַּת הַגּוֹמֵל. In fact, there are two opinions in the Shulchan Aruch about whether בִּרְכַּת הַגּוֹמֵל is recited only when one is saved from these specific dangers or whether it is recited in any case when one is saved from a life-threatening danger. The Shulchan Aruch recommends that in cases other than these four, one recite a blessing without God's name.[101] However, Ashkenazic Jewry generally accepts the other view, that we must recite בִּרְכַּת הַגּוֹמֵל not only for these four things, but also when He saves us miraculously from any serious situation.[102]

We recite the blessing in the presence of a minyan, usually during the reading of the Torah. The one reciting the blessing says out-loud: בָּרוּךְ אַתָּה ה׳ אֱלֹקֵינוּ מֶלֶךְ הָעוֹלָם הַגּוֹמֵל לְחַיָּבִים טוֹבוֹת, שֶׁגְּמָלַנִי כָּל טוּב ("Blessed are You Hashem, our God, King of the universe, who grants good things to those who are unworthy and who has granted me all this good"). The congregation responds: אָמֵן. מִי שֶׁגְּמָלְךָ כָּל טוּב, הוּא יִגְמָלְךָ כָּל טוּב סֶלָה ("Amen. May the One who granted you all this good continue to grant you all good"). A woman can recite this blessing from the other side of a mechitzah. Alternatively, a man can recite it for her.

101. שולחן ערוך אורח חיים סימן רי״ט סעיף ט

102. משנה ברורה סימן רי״ט ס״ק לב; ערוך השולחן שם סעיף יב

Hallel

THE ESSENCE OF HALLEL

Hallel is an essential part of the prayers on special occasions. The Hallel that is recited on festivals consists of songs of thanksgiving to God.[1] The full Hallel, also known as הַלֵּל הַמִּצְרִי, is a collection of Psalms (Psalms 113–118). Rav S.R. Hirsch calls Hallel the national anthem of the people of Israel.

The Shulchan Aruch states[2] that הַלֵּל should be said while standing. The Mishnah Berurah explains why: Just as witnesses before a beit din (court of Jewish Law) must stand, we stand when reciting Hallel as we are testifying to the glorious miracles that God performed.[3]

Rav Soloveitchik explained that the structure of Hallel parallels the structure of the Amidah. We begin by praising God who cares for the welfare of the individual and the world as a whole. In the middle section of Hallel we implore God not to forsake us. And in the last part of Hallel we thank God for miracles past, present, and future.

The Themes of Hallel

The Gemara[4] tells us that Hallel includes five major themes:

- the Exodus from Egypt;[5]
- the splitting of the Red Sea;[6]

1. רש״י מגילה דף יד עמ׳ א ד״ה הלל נמי נימא שירה
2. שולחן ערוך אורח חיים סי׳ תכב סעיף ז
3. משנה ברורה סי׳ תכב ס״ק כח
4. פסחים דף קיח עמ׳ א
5. יְצִיאַת מִצְרַיִם דִּכְתִיב בְּצֵאת יִשְׂרָאֵל מִמִּצְרָיִם
6. וּקְרִיעַת יַם סוּף - דִּכְתִיב הַיָּם רָאָה וַיָּנֹס

- the giving of the Torah;[7]
- the revival of the dead;[8]
- the difficulties preceding the Messianic Age.[9]

In other words, Hallel deals with all of Jewish history, from the birth of our nation to the establishment of the Messianic Era. In Hallel we express our joy at past miracles and our faith in future miracles.

Is Hallel מִדְּאוֹרַיְיתָא or מִדְּרַבָּנָן?

In addition to the 613 commandments in the Torah,[10] there are also several מִצְווֹת דְּרַבָּנָן (commandments that the Rabbis introduced). For example, washing our hands before we eat bread, reciting berachot before eating food, lighting candles on Chanukah, and hearing the Megillah on Purim are all Rabbinic mitzvot.

The Rambam maintains that Hallel is also a Rabbinic mitzvah.[11] The Gemara explains that even if a mitzvah is from the Rabbis, we can say a berachah with the word וְצִוָּנוּ ("and God commanded us") because God authorized the Rabbis to create Rabbinic mitzvot.[12]

The Ramban[13] disagrees with the Rambam and maintains that Hallel on Yamim Tovim when we recite the full Hallel is a Torah requirement. The Ramban suggests that Hallel may be one of the halachot which were transmitted orally to Moshe, called a הֲלָכָה לְמֹשֶׁה מִסִּינַי. Alternatively, he suggests that Hallel on Yom Tov may be part of the mitzvah to rejoice on festivals; Hallel is one of the ways by which we express our joy. Even according to the Ramban, Hallel on Chanukah is only Rabbinic.

---

7. מַתַּן תּוֹרָה - דִּכְתִיב הֶהָרִים רָקְדוּ כְּאֵילִים
8. תְּחִיַּת הַמֵּתִים - דִּכְתִיב אֶתְהַלֵּךְ לִפְנֵי ה׳
9. חֶבְלוֹ שֶׁל מָשִׁיחַ - דִּכְתִיב לֹא לָנוּ ה׳ לֹא לָנוּ. Also, Rashi says כָּל גּוֹיִם סְבָבוּנִי refers to בְּמִלְחֲמוֹת גּוֹג וּמָגוֹג.
10. מכות דף כג-כד
11. רמב"ם הלכות חנוכה פרק ג הלכה ה-ו
12. שבת דף כג עמוד א
13. השגות הרמב"ן לספר המצוות שורש א

There is one case (at the seder on Pesach) where at least two chapters of the Hallel might very well be of a מִצְוָה דְּאוֹרַיְיתָא as part of סִפּוּר יְצִיאַת מִצְרַיִם.[14]

WHO WAS THE FIRST TO SAY HALLEL?

The Gemara in Pesachim[15] tells us that Moshe and the Jews leaving Egypt were the first ones to recite Hallel. Once Moshe and the Jewish people recited Hallel at the shores of the Red Sea, Jews ever after made a point of reciting Hallel on occasions when God saved us from trouble: Joshua recited Hallel when he defeated the kings of Canaan; Deborah and Barak recited Hallel when they destroyed the army of Sisera; Hezekiah recited Hallel when Jerusalem was liberated from the siege of Sancheriv; Hananiah, Mishael and Azariah recited Hallel when they were rescued from the ovens of Nebuchadnezzar; and Mordechai and Esther recited Hallel when they defeated Haman.

As a result, the prophets instituted the practice that we should recite Hallel as a song of thanks whenever we are faced with a terrible trouble and God saves us. Based on this, Rashi in Taanit 28b tells us that reciting Hallel on an occasion when God has saved us from destruction is "close to a Torah-level obligation."

HALLEL IN THE TIME OF CHAZAL

The Gemara[16] describes that Hallel was recited by the chazzan, with the congregation responding after each phrase by saying הַלְלוּקָהּ ("Praise God"). Only one person used to say Hallel.[17] The congregation fulfilled its requirement just by responding הַלְלוּקָהּ and not by reciting the entire Hallel themselves.

---

14. See רמב"ם ספר המצות מצות עשה קנז, where he writes that part of the mitzvah of סִפּוּר יְצִיאַת מִצְרַיִם is giving thanks to God.

15. פסחים דף קיז עמ׳ א and see Rashi, ד"ה יהושע.

16. סוכה דף לח עמוד א

17. רמב"ם הלכות מגילה וחנוכה פרק ג הלכה יב-יג

The Rambam notes that Hallel was divided into 123 phrases[18] and after each one, the congregation said הַלְלוּקָה.[19] In those days, when prayers were chanted from memory, this made it easy for everybody to fulfill their obligation of Hallel.

Rashi[20] explains that if we are able to, we each should recite the whole Hallel ourselves. When not everyone was familiar with the text, one person recited Hallel, and everyone else responded (שׁוֹמֵעַ כְּעוֹנֶה).[21] This format was important in a time when not everyone knew the text.

Today, when we all have printed prayer books, we do not have to rely on listening to another's recitation. However, by reciting it in our modern way, we also lose some of its force. The prayer of one individual can never equal the ecstasy of many prayers forged into one.

THE PARAGRAPHS OF HALLEL

Hallel begins with Psalm 113 (הַלְלוּקָה הַלְלוּ עַבְדֵי יְיָ), a psalm of praise, expressing thanks to God Who raises up the downtrodden and poor.

Psalm 114 (בְּצֵאת יִשְׂרָאֵל מִמִּצְרָיִם) praises God for miraculously freeing us from Egypt, making our survival possible. The Gemara explains that referring to the Exodus, the splitting of the Red Sea and giving the Torah are key reasons for this paragraph's inclusion in the Hallel.

In the first half of Psalm 115 (לֹא לָנוּ יְיָ לֹא לָנוּ) we appeal to God for assistance. This psalm contrasts our devotion to God and our knowledge of His power with the rejection of Him by our enemies. As we thanked God in the previous psalm for taking us out of the land of our slavery, now we ask God to continue to help us. The Gemara tells us that this paragraph is referring to asking for God's help in the difficult times preceding the coming of the Messiah.[22]

---

18. רמב"ם הלכות מגילה וחנוכה פרק ג הלכה יב
19. רמב"ם הלכות מגילה וחנוכה פרק ג הלכה יב
20. רש"י סוכה לח עמוד ב ד"ה ממנהגא דהלילא
21. מסכת סוכה דף לח עמוד ב
22. פסחים דף קיח עמ' א

The last part of Psalm 115 (יְיָ זְכָרָנוּ יְבָרֵךְ) is a prayer to God to bless us. We ask God who has always remembered us in our trouble to continue to bless us. Our role is to praise Him, and we can only do so if He keeps us alive.

The first part of Psalm 116 (אָהַבְתִּי כִּי־יִשְׁמַע יְיָ) describes a tormented soul's plea with God for survival. This plea comes from a knowledge that God listens to us when we are in trouble and emanates from a complete faith in God's mercy. The Gemara interprets the phrase אֶתְהַלֵּךְ לִפְנֵי ה׳ בְּאַרְצוֹת הַחַיִּים ("I will walk before God in the lands of the living") as a reference to our faith in תְּחִיַּת הַמֵּתִים, the revival of the dead that will occur after the coming of the Messiah.

The last part of Psalm 116 (מָה־אָשִׁיב לַייָ כָּל־תַּגְמוּלוֹהִי עָלָי) expresses our thanks to God for His saving us from death. The verse כּוֹס יְשׁוּעוֹת אֶשָּׂא וּבְשֵׁם ה׳ אֶקְרָא ("I raise the cup of salvation and I call upon God's name") thanks God for His salvation even before we ask.[23]

In Psalm 117 (הַלְלוּ אֶת־יְיָ כָּל־גּוֹיִם), the shortest of all the psalms, we invite the nations of the world to join our songs of thanksgiving for our redemption.

Psalm 118, the last psalm of Hallel, begins with הוֹדוּ לַייָ כִּי־טוֹב ("Give thanks to God, because His kindness endures forever"). It can be interpreted in two different ways. Perhaps King David is giving personal thanks to God for his survival, or perhaps it is the collective thanks of the entire nation of Israel.[24]

When we reach this last chapter of Hallel, we strangely start to repeat verses.[25] The first four verses are recited one at a time, responsively, with the chazzan. After the chazzan recites each verse, the congregation responds with הוֹדוּ לַייָ כִּי־טוֹב.

Then we read the next verses individually, from מִן הַמֵּצַר ("From the straits") until אוֹדְךָ כִּי עֲנִיתָנִי וַתְּהִי־לִי לִישׁוּעָה ("I thank You because You answered me, and were for me a salvation"). From that point, we continue to read and repeat each verse.

---

23. אוצר התפלות, פי׳ מעשה נסים, עמ׳ תנב

24. See רד"ק תהלים קיח:א.

25. סוכה דף לח עמ׳ א

Rashi on the Gemara[26] explains that in the first part of Psalm 118, the ideas in every verse are each repeated twice until אוֹדְךָ כִּי עֲנִיתָנִי וַתְּהִי־לִי לִישׁוּעָה. Therefore, we customarily repeat the remaining verses in the chapter so that these ideas will be repeated as well.

When we reach the verse אָנָּא יְיָ הוֹשִׁיעָה נָּא אָנָּא יְיָ הַצְלִיחָה נָּא ("Please, God, save us; please, God, grant us success") we split the verse in half. The chazzan says the first half, אָנָּא יְיָ הוֹשִׁיעָה נָּא, and then the congregation repeats that after him. The chazzan then repeats it again and the congregation repeats it after him. Then the chazzan recites the second half of the verse, אָנָּא יְיָ הַצְלִיחָה נָּא, and everyone repeats that after the chazzan. Then the chazzan repeats the second half of the verse and the congregation repeats it after him. After אָנָּא יְיָ הוֹשִׁיעָה נָּא אָנָּא יְיָ הַצְלִיחָה נָּא, we continue to read each whole verse twice.

We should properly recite the entire verse before saying it a second time, but with regard to אָנָּא יְיָ הוֹשִׁיעָה נָּא אָנָּא יְיָ הַצְלִיחָה נָּא, we do not. The general rule is that we must always quote a verse in its entirety. The only exception is made for teachers, since their students cannot understand a large block of text at one time.[27] Why then do we not follow that rule here?

According to the Talmud,[28] the verses that we double, from אוֹדְךָ כִּי עֲנִיתַנִי through אֱלֹקַי אֲרוֹמְמֶךָּ were part of a conversation between the prophet Shmuel; Yishai, the father of David; David himself; and his brothers, those present when David was told he would be king of Israel. The conversation as presented by the Talmud went as follows:

David: אוֹדְךָ כִּי עֲנִיתַנִי. וּתְהִי לִי לִישׁוּעָה.
Yishai: אֶבֶן מָאֲסוּ הַבּוֹנִים. הָיְתָה לְרֹאשׁ פִּנָּה.
David: מֵאֵת ה׳ הָיְתָה זֹּאת. הִיא נִפְלָאת בְּעֵינֵינוּ.
Shmuel: זֶה הַיּוֹם עָשָׂה ה׳. נָגִילָה וְנִשְׂמְחָה בוֹ.
David's brothers: אָנָּא ה׳ הוֹשִׁיעָה נָּא.
David: אָנָּא ה׳ הַצְלִיחָה נָּא.

---

26. רש"י סוכה דף לח עמ׳ א ד"ה לכפול
27. מגילה דף כב עמ׳ א
28. פסחים דף קיט עמ׳ א

Yishai: בָּרוּךְ הַבָּא בְּשֵׁם ה׳.
Shmuel: בֵּרַכְנוּכֶם מִבֵּית ה׳.
All of them together: אֵ־ל ה׳ וַיָּאֶר לָנוּ.
Shmuel: אִסְרוּ חַג בַּעֲבֹתִים עַד קַרְנוֹת הַמִּזְבֵּחַ
David: אֵ־לִי אַתָּה וְאוֹדֶךָּ:
All together: אֱלֹקַי אֲרוֹמְמֶךָּ

In other words, in this verse, אָנָּא יְיָ הוֹשִׁיעָה נָּא אָנָּא יְיָ הַצְלִיחָה נָּא, the first half, אָנָּא יְיָ הוֹשִׁיעָה נָּא, was said by the brothers. The second half, אָנָּא יְיָ הַצְלִיחָה נָּא, was said by David himself. Tosafot explain[29] that since these two requests were uttered by different people, we may stop in the middle of a verse.

The paragraph of יְהַלְלוּךָ is not a chapter of Psalms. It is the closing berachah of the Hallel and is called בִּרְכַּת הַשִּׁיר (the berachah of song). שִׁיר is another way of referring to Hallel. According to the Gemara some communities had the custom not to say the berachah at the end,[30] but today everyone says this berachah.

WHEN IS THE HALLEL RECITED?

Rabbi Shimon ben Yehotzadak gives a list of the special days on which Hallel must be chanted.[31] These are: the eight days of Sukkot, the eight days of Chanukah, the first day of Pesach, and the one day of Shavuot. He also notes the extra days celebrated by Jews outside of Israel. There is an alternative list of Rabbi Shimon ben Yehotzadak in Masechet Sofrim which adds the first night of Pesach, and outside of Israel, the first two nights.[32]

The Gemara[33] asks why Hallel is not said on Shabbat, and replies that Hallel is said only on a מוֹעֵד (holiday of assembly) and Shabbat is not a מוֹעֵד. On Shabbat we celebrate the natural miracles of Creation,

---

29. תוספות סוכה דף לח עמ׳ ב ד״ה הוא אומר אנא ה׳
30. סוכה לט עמ׳ א
31. תענית דף כח עמוד ב
32. מסכת סופרים פרק כ הלכה ז
33. ערכין דף י עמ׳ א

not an historic event. The Gemara continues with its inquiry: Why do we not recite Hallel on Rosh Hashanah and Yom Kippur? Rabbi Avahu solves the problem by reporting a conversation between God and the angels: "Is it possible that the King sits on the throne of judgment while the Book of Life is open before Him, and Israel should sing a song?" The answer of Rabbi Avahu is self-explanatory.

Pesach and Sukkot are both weeklong holidays; why do we say Hallel every day of Sukkot, whereas on Pesach we say the whole version only on the first day? The Talmud[34] answers that the sacrifices of Sukkot differ from day to day, whereas on Pesach the same sacrifices are offered each day. Evidently, on Sukkot the character of the sanctity of Yom Tov is different on each day; therefore, each day of Sukkot requires a new recitation of Hallel.[35] The character of Pesach does not change from day to day, so the full Hallel is recited only at the beginning.

The Midrash has another answer to this problem: Sukkot is a joyous holiday,[36] whereas on Pesach our joy is limited. The Rabbis tell us that the angels of heaven wanted to sing a joyous song at the deliverance of the Israelites from bondage and the destruction of our enemies. The Almighty rebuked the angels: "My creatures drowned in the waters of the sea and you want to sing a song?"[37] Our joy on Pesach cannot be complete since it is based on human suffering.[38]

This means that we should omit saying a full Hallel on the seventh day of Pesach, when the Egyptians drowned, but to do this alone would give the intermediary days of Pesach a higher status than the last day, which is a full Yom Tov. Therefore, we stop saying the full version of Hallel on the intermediary days as well.[39]

---

34. ערכין דף י עמ׳ א-ב
35. See רש״י תענית דף כח עמוד ב ד״ה יחיד.
36. בית הבחירה (מאירי) מסכת סוכה דף מב עמוד ב
37. סנהדרין דף לט עמוד ב
38. This Midrash is cited by the Beit Yosef (אורח חיים סימן תצ). See also ילקוט שמעוני משלי כד:יז.
39. לבוש אורח חיים סימן תצ סעיף ד

Hallel on Rosh Chodesh

The Gemara also inquires as to why we do not say Hallel on Rosh Chodesh, which is a semi-holiday; after all, in the Book of Lamentations,[40] Rosh Chodesh is called a מוֹעֵד. It replies that on Rosh Chodesh, מְלָאכָה (creative work) is not forbidden, and therefore it lacks the full sanctity of a holiday, which is a requirement for the recitation of Hallel. Why, then, do we say a partial Hallel on Rosh Chodesh?

The Levush[41] says that it is an ancient custom to recite Hallel on Rosh Chodesh. While it is not a day when מְלָאכָה is prohibited, since it is called a מוֹעֵד, we have the custom to recite Hallel.

The Gemara[42] says that Hallel on Rosh Chodesh is not a Torah-level requirement. The Gemara relates the following anecdote: Rav went from Israel to Babylonia and saw people saying Hallel on Rosh Chodesh, which was not one of the days that Chazal established for saying Hallel. In Israel they didn't recite Hallel on Rosh Chodesh, so he wanted to stop them. Then Rav saw that they were not reciting the whole Hallel, but were saying what we call Half Hallel.[43] He realized that these people were observing a custom and not going against Rabbi Shimon ben Yehotzadak's list for when Hallel is recited.

In one of his lectures, Rav Soloveitchik once reconstructed the development of this custom. He explained that Rosh Chodesh is a special day, but there is no way of celebrating it because work is permitted on this day. There is one exception: In the Temple in Jerusalem, there was great joy on Rosh Chodesh. The Kohanim offered special sacrifices in accordance with the laws of the Torah, the Levites sang beautiful songs, and the rest of the people experienced this atmosphere of joy. This is why we state in the Amidah of Musaf on Rosh Chodesh, וּבַעֲבוֹדַת בֵּית הַמִּקְדָּשׁ נִשְׂמַח כֻּלָּנוּ. וּבְשִׁירֵי דָוִד עַבְדֶּךָ הַנִּשְׁמָעִים בְּעִירֶךָ

40. איכה א:טו

41. לבוש אורח חיים סימן תכב

42. תענית דף כח עמוד ב

43. The term the Gemara used was קוֹרִין אוֹתוֹ בְּדִלּוּג, which means they "read it with skipping."

("We will all rejoice in the Temple service and in the songs by David, Your servant, which were heard in Your city").

After the fall of Jerusalem, Rosh Chodesh ceased to be a day of joy, and a real danger existed that it would be completely forgotten. Therefore, many Jews spontaneously started singing parts of Hallel in the synagogues. They could not sing all of it, since it was against Jewish law to do so on Rosh Chodesh. So, a few paragraphs were omitted but the rest was said to retain the joy of Rosh Chodesh. For the people of Israel, Rosh Chodesh remained a day of rejoicing.

There were different customs regarding which parts of Hallel ought to be skipped. Today we skip the paragraphs of לֹא לָנוּ ה׳ לֹא לָנוּ ("Not for our sake, Hashem") and אָהַבְתִּי כִּי יִשְׁמַע ה׳ אֶת קוֹלִי תַּחֲנוּנָי ("I loved that Hashem heard my voice, my pleas").

Why are these paragraphs the ones that are omitted? According to Rav Soloveitchik, Hallel parallels the שְׁמוֹנֶה עֶשְׂרֵה. It has the same three parts of praise, petition, and thanks. The two paragraphs we skip represent the petitions to God, so by eliminating them we are destroying its character as a שְׁמוֹנֶה עֶשְׂרֵה. That left just enough of the verses from Hallel to keep us from forgetting the importance of Rosh Chodesh.

The Talmud[44] states that there is no prohibition of working on Rosh Chodesh. However, women customarily abstain from work on this day. When the men in the desert wanted to build the golden calf, they demanded that the women contribute their jewelry for this effort. The women refused. Therefore, God promised a special holiday to reward them.[45] Rav Soloveitchik explained that the prohibition of work on Rosh Chodesh is the way that women maintain the memory of the day as it was celebrated in the Temple.

Since we do not fulfill any commandment by saying the abridged form of Hallel on Rosh Chodesh, another problem arises: Should we say the berachah before it? The Rambam clearly indicates that

---

44. ערכין דף י עמ׳ א

45. טור אורח חיים סימן תיז

we should not.[46] As a proof, commentators cite the Gemara which says[47] that we do not say a berachah on the minhag of the aravah on Hoshana Rabbah, since it is only a custom that was introduced by the prophets.

Ashkenazim do make a berachah on the abridged form of Hallel. Rabbenu Tam (one of the Tosafists) makes a distinction[48] between two types of customs: Taking the aravah is only a minhag, and does not have any other fulfillment of a mitzvah involved in its performance. On such a custom, one does not recite a berachah. But by reading the Hallel on Rosh Chodesh, in addition to fulfilling the minhag, one is also fulfilling the mitzvah of reading from the Torah. On such a minhag, which is related to the fulfillment of a mitzvah, one does recite a berachah.[49]

The Shulchan Aruch[50] agrees with the Rambam. The Rama accepts the view of Rabbenu Tam, and says that even an individual should say a berachah over Hallel, but in deference to the view which maintains that a berachah is only recited on Rosh Chodesh when Hallel is recited together with a minyan, we should try to do so.[51]

The custom to recite Hallel on Rosh Chodesh has become universally accepted, and among the Ashkenazim, the berachot have been accepted as well.

Do We Say Hallel on Purim?

Chanukah and Purim are very much alike. On both holidays we praise and thank God for a miracle that occurred. Why, then, do we

---

46. רמב״ם הלכות ברכות פרק יא הלכה טז; רמב״ם הלכות מגילה וחנוכה פרק ג הלכה ז

47. סוכה דף מד עמוד ב

48. תוספות סוכה דף מד עמוד ב ד״ה כאן במקדש כאן בגבולין; תוספות ברכות דף יד עמוד א ד״ה ימים שהיחיד גומר בהם את ההלל

49. תוספות ערכין דף י עמ׳ א ד״ה י״ח ימים שהיחיד גומר בהן את ההלל

50. שולחן ערוך אורח חיים סימן תכב סעיף ב

51. רמ״א אורח חיים סימן תכב סעיף ב. The Rif maintains that a berachah is recited for Hallel on Rosh Chodesh only when it is said with a minyan; see בית יוסף אורח חיים סימן תכב ס״ק י.

not say Hallel on Purim? The Gemara[52] describes a disagreement between Rabbi Yitzchak and Rav Nachman. Rabbi Yitzchak explains that we do not recite Hallel for a miracle that occurred outside of the Land of Israel, and the miracle of Purim took place outside of Israel. Rav Nachman points out that we say Hallel on Pesach and the miracles of the Exodus also took place outside of the Land of Israel. Rav Nachman, therefore, believes that Purim should have a Hallel to celebrate being saved from Haman and his plans. The recitation of the Megillah on Purim serves the same function as Hallel and takes its place. In Hallel proper we praise and thank God, and on Purim, when we relate the miracles of those days, our heart is also filled with joy and thanksgiving.

ARE WOMEN OBLIGED TO SAY HALLEL?

When Moshe first sang praise to God after God saved the Jewish people from the Egyptian army, Miriam and all the women also sang a similar praise.[53] We also know that the Jewish women suffered greatly during the slavery of Egypt and the righteous women specifically were largely responsible for the redemption.[54] You cannot separate the women from the events that led up to reciting the first Hallel or the women's recitation of the song on the shores of the Red Sea.

The Gemara that describes the people who were the first to recite Hallel includes the prophetess Devorah and Queen Esther.[55] The prophets decreed that when we are saved from destruction, we must recite Hallel. One cannot say that if women were among those that were saved, they should not recite Hallel.

There is, however, another halachah that impacts on women's obligation in mitzvot. Positive commandments that are tied to an observance at a specific time are called מִצְווֹת עֲשֵׂה שֶׁהַזְּמַן גְּרָמָא. Hallel

52. ערכין דף י עמ׳ א

53. שמות פרק טו פס׳ כ,כא

54. סוטה דף יא עמוד ב

55. פסחים דף קיז עמוד א

must be performed on certain specific occasions, so it falls into this category. Women are not obligated to perform these kinds of commandments, but if they do perform them, they receive the reward for doing so.

There is a list of such commandments that, nevertheless, women are obligated to perform. They are: שִׂמְחַת יוֹם טוֹב (rejoicing on Yom Tov); הַקְהֵל (gathering in Jerusalem once every seven years to hear the king read from the Torah); Kiddush; eating matzah on the first night of Pesach; hearing the reading of the Megillah on Purim; lighting the Chanukah candles; and drinking four cups of wine during the Pesach seder. The Avudraham citing Rabbenu Tam adds a few more commandments that women are required to perform: eating three meals on Shabbat, לֶחֶם מִשְׁנֶה (the two loaves of challah at a Shabbat meal), and reciting Havdalah at the end of Shabbat or Yom Tov. The Rambam adds slaughtering and eating the Pesach sacrifice. But reciting Hallel is not in this list.

That means that a woman who feels the urge to express praise to God on Yom Tov may do so and is credited with performing the mitzvah, but is not obligated to do so. One exception is the Hallel recited at the Pesach seder. In that case, women are required to recite Hallel, either because Hallel is connected to the four cups which women must drink,[56] or because Hallel is part of the mitzvah of recounting the story of the Exodus, and women are obligated in that mitzvah.[57]

56. תוספות סוכה דף לח עמוד א ד"ה מי שהיה

57. See ערוך השולחן אורח חיים סימן תעב סעיף טו.

סְלִיחוֹת

סְלִיחוֹת are a specific kind of prayer. The word לִסְלֹחַ means to forgive, and סְלִיחוֹת are prayers asking God for forgiveness. The סְלִיחוֹת are most often associated with prayers during times of trouble and with fast days. During the יָמִים נוֹרָאִים (High Holy Days), we say, וּתְשׁוּבָה וּתְפִלָּה וּצְדָקָה מַעֲבִירִין אֶת רֹעַ הַגְּזֵרָה, that repentance, prayer and charity nullify the bitter decree that might be ordered against us. The Rosh[1] tells us that at the time of the Purim story, the Jews gathered together to pray for their lives, לְהִקָּהֵל וְלַעֲמֹד עַל־נַפְשָׁם. The same occurred when the Jewish people had to fight against Amalek. Chazal explain that a fast was declared when Moshe, Aaron and Chur went up to the top of the hill above the battlefield to pray.[2] Fast days are associated with reciting סְלִיחוֹת and תַּחֲנוּנִים. There are many sources that reiterate that theme. The Midrash Tanchuma[3] goes one step beyond and says that the main aspects of a fast day are the סְלִיחוֹת and requests for mercy.

The Midrash Tehillim[4] brings us the final piece we need to understand fully the reason behind our recitations of סְלִיחוֹת. When the Temple was standing and a person committed a sin, he could bring a sacrifice and God would forgive him. But after the Temple was destroyed, we could no longer depend on that. All we can do is fast

---

1. רא"ש מסכת מגילה פרק א
2. מדרש תנחומא פרשת בשלח סימן כז
3. מדרש תנחומא פרשת בראשית: שעיקר תענית סליחות ורחמים הוא.
4. מדרש תהלים מזמור כה

and hope that the fast can take the place of the sacrifice. We must rely on God's mercy, and therefore we recite סְלִיחוֹת.

Nature of סְלִיחוֹת

סְלִיחוֹת is part of the piyut literature. Piyutim are religious poems dealing with our history, our philosophy of life, our relationship to God, and Halachic or Aggadic problems. At the time the Talmud was concluded, our prayers were more or less the standard prayers we say today. But our ancestors were very eager to demonstrate their love of God, so they added more prayers for many different occasions. The authors of these prayers, the Paytanim, included the spiritual leaders of Jewry, such as Yossi ben Yossi and Yannai in Israel; Shlomo ibn Gabirol, Avraham ibn Ezra, and Yehudah Halevi in Spain. Germany was also a very prolific area of the development of the piyutim. Additional authors of those piyutim were great Rabbis, such as Rabbenu Gershon Me'or Hagolah, Rashi, and others spiritual giants. Of some paytanim we know absolutely nothing, such as Rabbi Elazar Hakalir.

Outside Israel two days are observed for most Yamim Tovim. The Amidah of the first day usually contains piyutim of Rabbi Elazer Hakalir. These piyutim are very difficult to understand since Rabbi Elazer Hakalir utilized the Hebrew language in a remarkable way, constantly alluding to the Midrash. We are not even always aware of his sources since they are often very obscure. On the second day of the Yamim Tovim, many piyutim recited are those composed by some of the great rabbis of Germany. Those piyutim are much easier to understand as they are written in much simpler language. Rabbi Hakalir did not write piyutim for the second day of the Yamim Tovim because, as most historians have concluded, he lived in Israel, where there is only one day of Yom Tov.

Originally, סְלִיחוֹת were included in the sixth berachah of the Amidah, סְלַח לָנוּ ("Forgive us").[5] Today we say סְלִיחוֹת following the

5. סדר רב עמרם גאון סדר תענית. See also שולחן ערוך אורח חיים סימן תקסו סעיף ד.

שְׁמוֹנֶה עֶשְׂרֵה,[6] or we get up in the middle of the night and recite them before sunrise.

Another example of סְלִיחוֹת is the וְהוּא רַחוּם that we say on Monday and Thursday after the שְׁמוֹנֶה עֶשְׂרֵה and before Tachanun.[7] Mondays and Thursdays were days of mercy before God, so many of our ancestors used to fast almost every Monday and Thursday. We do not fast every Monday and Thursday today, but we still say the original סְלִיחוֹת that are associated with these days. The וְהוּא רַחוּם was composed in three parts, and each one mentions God's name eighteen times.[8] That means it was designed to parallel the שְׁמוֹנֶה עֶשְׂרֵה, just as the סְלִיחוֹת do. This would explain why we stand for וְהוּא רַחוּם and sit down only for Tachanun itself.

י״ג מִדּוֹת הָרַחֲמִים

The central part of the סְלִיחוֹת are the י״ג מִדּוֹת הָרַחֲמִים. Everything is structured as a vehicle to allow us to recite the plea of those י״ג מִדּוֹת הָרַחֲמִים to ask God for forgiveness. There are a number of different prayers and verses that are built around it.

The Gemara explains[9] that Hashem showed Moshe what to do if people sin and want Hashem to forgive them. It says that Hashem wrapped himself in a tallit like a שְׁלִיחַ צִבּוּר (chazzan) and then He told Moshe what prayers to say so that He would forgive them: God said, "Whenever Israel sins, recite the י״ג מִדּוֹת הָרַחֲמִים and I will forgive them." This is a strange Gemara. How can we talk about Hashem in such anthropomorphic terms? In fact, that very Gemara quotes Rabbi Yochanan as saying that if this wasn't written in a verse, we could never say such things.

The י״ג מִדּוֹת הָרַחֲמִים are a דָּבָר שֶׁבִּקְדֻשָּׁה, so we can only say them if

---

6. Rav Soloveitchik said the piyutim after the repetition of the Amidah, before the concluding Kaddish. This indicated that they were still considered within the Amidah framework.

7. See the section on וְהוּא רַחוּם.

8. לבוש אורח חיים סימן קלד, סעיף א

9. ראש השנה דף יז עמ׳ ב

summoned by the chazzan. We also must stand,[10] and we must have a minyan. סְלִיחוֹת can be said if one is praying alone, but without its most important part – the י״ג מִדּוֹת הָרַחֲמִים. Without a minyan, סְלִיחוֹת cannot have the same force as it does when recited with a minyan.

We say the י״ג מִדּוֹת הָרַחֲמִים more than once in the סְלִיחוֹת service. During the סְלִיחוֹת preceding Rosh Hashanah we usually say them once as part of the introductory prayers and three times during the body of סְלִיחוֹת. On Erev Rosh Hashanah we increase the number of סְלִיחוֹת recited, while on Erev Yom Kippur סְלִיחוֹת is almost eliminated, because Erev Yom Kippur is a somewhat celebratory day.

When the י״ג מִדּוֹת הָרַחֲמִים is recited in the סְלִיחוֹת service, it is preceded by a paragraph calling us to respond. Usually that paragraph begins with קֵל מֶלֶךְ יוֹשֵׁב ("Lord, King who sits on the throne of mercy"). The Ashkenazic custom is that for the first time the י״ג מִדּוֹת הָרַחֲמִים is recited in a סְלִיחוֹת service, a different paragraph beginning with the words קֵל אֶרֶךְ־אַפַּיִם ("Lord who is slow to anger") is said.

This paragraph ends with the reader invoking the congregation to accept God's sovereignty. In both cases, at the end of the paragraph the reader calls out to the congregation to respond. The reader and the congregation turn to God as the source of their help and cry out the י״ג מִדּוֹת הָרַחֲמִים.

It is interesting to know exactly what the י״ג מִדּוֹת הָרַחֲמִים are and what they mean.[11] As a prayer to God to implore His mercy, this prayer consists of thirteen phrases, begging God to forgive us in different ways:

וַיַּעֲבֹר יְיָ עַל־פָּנָיו וַיִּקְרָא יְיָ יְיָ אֵ־ל רַחוּם וְחַנּוּן אֶרֶךְ אַפַּיִם וְרַב־חֶסֶד וֶאֱמֶת: נֹצֵר חֶסֶד לָאֲלָפִים נֹשֵׂא עָוֹן וָפֶשַׁע וְחַטָּאָה וְנַקֵּה (לֹא יְנַקֶּה פֹּקֵד עֲוֹן אָבוֹת עַל־בָּנִים וְעַל־בְּנֵי בָנִים עַל־שִׁלֵּשִׁים וְעַל־רִבֵּעִים)[12]

1,2. The first two words, ה׳ ה׳, refer to God showing the attribute of mercy. It is repeated to indicate that God acts mercifully to a person

10. Following the opinion of the Rama, אורח חיים סי׳ נו סעיף א.
11. Generally following Rashi's explanation on the verses.
12. שמות לד:ו–ז

before the person commits a sin. The second time indicates that God acts mercifully to a person even after he has sinned.

3. קֵל is also an expression of God's mercy.
4. רַחוּם – God is merciful.
5. וְחַנּוּן – He helps people even when they do not deserve it.
6. אֶרֶךְ אַפַּיִם – God is slow to anger and gives people a chance to change for the better.
7. וְרַב חֶסֶד – God is full of kindness, even when the person really does not deserve it.
8. וֶאֱמֶת – The attribute of truth indicates that we can rely on Him to reward us when we perform His will.
9. נֹצֵר חֶסֶד – God keeps kindness, meaning that God preserves the good that a person does. לָאֲלָפִים – for thousands of generations, meaning that God preserves these acts of good far into the future. The next attribute begins a series of phrases of God's addressing different kinds of offenses.
10. נֹשֵׂא עָוֹן – God forgives sins committed on purpose.
11. וָפֶשַׁע – God forgives sins committed in rebellion.
12. וְחַטָּאָה – God forgives simple sins as well.
13. וְנַקֵּה – God erases the sin altogether.

This last attribute ends in the middle of the verse. We do not complete the verse because this is where the attributes of mercy end. The verse continues לֹא יְנַקֶּה פֹּקֵד עֲוֹן אָבוֹת עַל־בָּנִים וְעַל־בְּנֵי בָנִים עַל־שִׁלֵּשִׁים וְעַל־רִבֵּעִים. This means that erasing the sin might only be done gradually, or only for the people who reform, and God doesn't erase the sin for those who continue in the sinful ways of their forebears.

After we recite the י״ג מִדּוֹת הָרַחֲמִים, we continue saying a few verses of hope for forgiveness.

The last of the סְלִיחוֹת prayers before the וִדּוּי and תַּחֲנוּן section is a prayer called a פִּזְמוֹן, which means "beautiful poetry." Many פִּזְמוֹנִים rhyme and have beautiful melodies. They are recited responsively with the שְׁלִיחַ צִבּוּר (leader of the service) and can be recognized because they include a refrain.

סְלִיחוֹת BEFORE יָמִים נוֹרָאִים

Both Ashkenazim and Sephardim blow the shofar without a berachah every morning during the whole month of Elul until the day before Rosh Hashanah. This reflects the forty days during which Moshe implored God to forgive the Jewish people.[13]

There is a special group of סְלִיחוֹת that we say before Rosh Hashanah through Yom Kippur. The Sephardim say סְלִיחוֹת during the whole month of Elul until Yom Kippur, and they repeat the same סְלִיחוֹת every day.[14] Ashkenazic Jews say them for at least four days before Rosh Hashanah, and they are different every day.

What is the significance of four days? In the past, there was a custom to fast for the Ten Days of Repentance, except the two days of Rosh Hashanah, Shabbat, and Erev Yom Kippur.[15] Therefore, they declared four substitute fast days before Rosh Hashanah. Another explanation for the four days of סְלִיחוֹת can be found in the laws of sacrifices. The korban tamid offered as a sacrifice to God in the Temple in Jerusalem had to be examined thoroughly for any physical blemish for four days prior to being sacrificed. We therefore must examine ourselves for any spiritual defects for four days before facing the Divine judgment on Rosh Hashanah.[16]

We always start saying סְלִיחוֹת on Motzaei Shabbat, because we are still under the influence of the sanctity of the Shabbat, when the Shechinah is in our midst.[17]

The proper time for סְלִיחוֹת is shortly before daybreak. סְלִיחוֹת is to be followed immediately by Shacharit. In recent years the custom has developed to say the first סְלִיחוֹת service on the Saturday night before Rosh Hashanah right after midnight, when the holiness of Shabbat is still present and only gradually waning.

---

13. רש״י דברים פרק י פסוק א
14. שולחן ערוך אורח חיים סי׳ תקפא סעי׳ א
15. ט״ז אורח חיים סימן תקפא ס״ק ב
16. משנה ברורה סימן תקפא ס״ק ו
17. לקט יושר חלק א, אורח חיים, עמוד קיח ענין א

In order to evoke the proper concentration, we begin the סְלִיחוֹת with אַשְׁרֵי. Next, we say a half-Kaddish. We recite an introduction (לְךָ אֲ־דֹנָי הַצְּדָקָה) to the many verses of praise of God (שׁמֵעַ תְּפִלָּה) and the main body of סְלִיחוֹת, the actual piyutim, followed by the י״ג מִדּוֹת הָרַחֲמִים. It is followed by וִדּוּי (the confessional).

Within the וִדּוּי we say אָשַׁמְנוּ (the short, alphabetical וִדּוּי). It has become customary to to say it three times. The reason is not clear. Rav Soloveitchik believed, as did the Vilna Gaon, that we should recite it only once.[18]

In the שְׁמוֹנֶה עֶשְׂרֵה, after the petitions we thank God (הוֹדָאָה). No part of סְלִיחוֹת seems to correspond to this section of thanksgiving. Yom Kippur, with (hopefully) complete forgiveness, is still many days away, so perhaps the thanks is postponed until then.

Furthermore, just as the שְׁמוֹנֶה עֶשְׂרֵה is followed by Tachanun, the סְלִיחוֹת are followed by Tachanun as well. Preceding the Tachanun we have a number of paragraphs of special pleas, which probably go back to the days of the Temple in Jerusalem.[19] These are litanies which repeat the same refrain over and over again such as עֲנֵנוּ ("Answer us"). Like שְׁמוֹנֶה עֶשְׂרֵה, the סְלִיחוֹת are followed by the concluding Kaddish of תִּתְקַבֵּל ("Accept our prayers").

סְלִיחוֹת ON YOM KIPPUR

Because the סְלִיחוֹת are so integral to the nature of the day of Yom Kippur, many different customs arose as to how to best integrate them into the different prayers of the day. The Geonim had different customs for the number of times we recite the י״ג מִדּוֹת הָרַחֲמִים during the services for Yom Kippur. The Tur mentions[20] a number of such different customs.

---

18. מעשה רב אות רב

19. משנה מסכת תענית פרק ב משנה ד has a version of סְלִיחוֹת that includes elements of the עֲנֵנוּ that we recite.

20. טור אורח חיים סימן תרכ

Rav Amram Gaon's custom[21] was to recite the י״ג מִדּוֹת הָרַחֲמִים five times in Shacharit, seven times in Musaf, three times in Minchah and three times in Ne'ilah, or five times in Ne'ilah if possible. Rav Natronai Gaon wanted to recite them seven times for Shacharit, five times for Musaf, three times for Minchah. The Baal HaItur said them three times in Shacharit, Musaf and Minchah and once for Ne'ilah. Ten times reminds us of the ten times the Kohen Gadol would pronounce God's name on Yom Kippur. The Avi Haezri used to recite them thirteen times in the morning to parallel the י״ג מִדּוֹת הָרַחֲמִים.

Rav Soloveitchik said the י״ג מִדּוֹת הָרַחֲמִים seven times for each service except for Ne'ilah where he said the י״ג מִדּוֹת הָרַחֲמִים thirteen times.

When we say סְלִיחוֹת in the Amidot of Yom Kippur, we do not start with an introductory praise of God like אַשְׁרֵי. Since סְלִיחוֹת are already part of the שְׁמוֹנֶה עֶשְׂרֵה, they need no introduction.

סְלִיחוֹת before Rosh Hashanah has the status of custom. We say סְלִיחוֹת on Yom Kippur during the שְׁמוֹנֶה עֶשְׂרֵה for a very different reason. If we do not say סְלִיחוֹת before Rosh Hashanah, we are only not fulfilling a custom. But the סְלִיחוֹת of Yom Kippur are, in a sense, part of the sanctity of Yom Kippur itself, and any omission of these סְלִיחוֹת would render the prayer service incomplete.

The enigma is that in today's order of the services, there is a practice of reciting סְלִיחוֹת during the שְׁמוֹנֶה עֶשְׂרֵה of Ne'ilah, the ending service, but not in the Amidot of the other services. In ancient times we used to have two Yom Kippur books: one with the prayers of Yom Kippur and another with the סְלִיחוֹת of Yom Kippur. Somehow, we neglected the second book and were eventually left without סְלִיחוֹת. Rav Soloveitchik added סְלִיחוֹת to all the Amidot of Yom Kippur as he believed סְלִיחוֹת should be said even though the machzorim omitted them.

When we say the סְלִיחוֹת at the end of the Kol Nidrei service, most shuls recite יַעֲלֶה תַּחֲנוּנֵינוּ ("May our supplications ascend") immediately after the שְׁמוֹנֶה עֶשְׂרֵה. Rav Soloveitchik did not start with this but with the other verses of praise that follow it. The other סְלִיחוֹת services

---

21. סדר רב עמרם גאון תפילת מנחה של יום הכיפורים

of Yom Kippur include the סְלִיחוֹת in the repetition of the שְׁמוֹנֶה עֶשְׂרֵה, but since Ma'ariv has no repetition of the שְׁמוֹנֶה עֶשְׂרֵה, we want to connect them to the שְׁמוֹנֶה עֶשְׂרֵה.

The authors of the פִּיּוּטִים freely utilized the Scriptures, and in doing so have changed many verses from the singular to the plural. Rav Soloveitchik generally quoted the verses in the singular, the way they appear in the Bible. He did not wish to tamper with the words of God.

There are some sections in the סְלִיחוֹת where it seems that we address our prayers to the angels or to the Divine attributes. The Rambam vehemently opposed this. He believed that we must only pray to God directly and not any intermediary. Rav Soloveitchik always skipped these prayers or reworded them.

OTHER PIYUTIM: מַעֲרָבוֹת, יוֹצְרוֹת AND קְרוֹבֵץ

The other piyutim that some have the custom to say are called called מַעֲרָבוֹת (additions to the berachot of Shema in Ma'ariv for special occasions), יוֹצְרוֹת (additions to the berachot of the Shema in Shacharit for special occasions), and קְרוֹבֵץ (additions to the repetition of the שְׁמוֹנֶה עֶשְׂרֵה on Purim). The halachic authorities argued about whether it is proper to add these poetic compositions of piyutim to our standard prayers. In the Shulchan Aruch[22] we find an example of this basic argument. The author of the Shulchan Aruch, Rav Yosef Karo, mentions that some people have a custom to add piyutim to the middle of קְרִיאַת שְׁמַע. However, his opinion is that it is better not to interrupt the Shema with them. The Rama, commenting on this, says that there isn't anything wrong with this practice. Furthermore, it is an accepted custom to do so. The Rama adds that there is nothing wrong if one does not add the piyutim, but if one does say them, one should be careful not to make any other interruption.

Rav Soloveitchik introduced the following practice: In Ma'ariv of Yom Tov, מַעֲרָבוֹת were included. The exception was when Yom

---

22. שולחן ערוך אורח חיים סימן סח

Tov occurred on Shabbat. We were afraid that because of the many unfamiliar words, someone might forget it is Shabbat and adjust the light to see better. He also omitted them in Ma'ariv of Rosh Hashanah, when many Jews had the custom to fast during the day before Rosh Hashanah began. The addition of מַעֲרָבוֹת would have placed an undue hardship on the worshippers by prolonging the fast.

In any case, at the Maimonides School, the יוֹצְרוֹת were skipped while the מַעֲרָבוֹת were recited. This seems to be contradictory: Are we permitted to have additions in the berachot of the Shema or not? Rav Soloveitchik explained it in the following way: We want to add to the festive mood of Yom Tov by reciting special piyutim. In Ma'ariv we add those piyutim to the berachot of the Shema since there is no other location for them, as there is no reader's repetition of the שְׁמוֹנֶה עֶשְׂרֵה. Even though it is improper to interrupt the berachot of the Shema, we have no other choice. In Shacharit there is no need for these interruptions. We simply add the special Yom Tov prayers to the repetition of the שְׁמוֹנֶה עֶשְׂרֵה.

Rav Soloveitchik pointed out that all the piyutim that are added to the שְׁמוֹנֶה עֶשְׂרֵה are included before the Kedushah. The Kedushah is the song of the angels praising God's omnipotence, and the piyutim are Israel's praise of God. Thus, once the angels have had their say, we humans must keep quiet. Our song is no match for the song of the angels.

יָמִים נוֹרָאִים: The Days of Awe

ROSH HASHANAH: יוֹם הַזִּכָּרוֹן

Rosh Hashanah is known as יוֹם הַזִּכָּרוֹן, the Day of Remembrance, because it is the beginning of the period when God judges each person,[1] and we want God to remember the good we have done. We hope God will remember us together with the rest of the Jewish people and judge us mercifully.

There are many ways we try to show God that our intentions are for good. We spend the month before Rosh Hashanah, Elul, praying with special כַּוָּנָה, saying סְלִיחוֹת, and trying to observe the commandments at a higher level. We also recite Psalm 27, לְדָוִד ה׳ אוֹרִי וְיִשְׁעִי ("A Psalm of David: God is my light and my savior"), from the beginning of Elul through Shemini Atzeret (or Hoshanna Rabba in Israel) because of an opinion that the final judgement occurs at the end of Sukkot. Sephardim say this psalm at the end of Shacharit and Minchah. Ashkenazim recite it and the end of Shacharit and Ma'ariv. On Rosh Hashanah we ask God, in the davening, to remember us for good. We blow the shofar to remind Hashem about our devotion to Him since the time of Avraham Avinu.

אָבִינוּ מַלְכֵּנוּ

Once during a drought, after many remedies had been attempted, Rabbi Akiva, as chazzan, recited the prayer אָבִינוּ מַלְכֵּנוּ ("Our Father, our King") for rain.[2] His prayer was answered, and rain came. The

---

1. ערוך השולחן אורח חיים סימן תקפב סעיף יב
2. תענית דף כה עמוד ב

Gemara relates this incident in order to show us the power of that prayer. אָבִינוּ מַלְכֵּנוּ has been treated as a special prayer ever since. We say it on all fast days and during עֲשֶׂרֶת יְמֵי הַתְּשׁוּבָה (the Ten Days of Repentance) but we don't say it on Shabbat because we don't ask for things on Shabbat as that would spoil the atmosphere of the day.[3] There are exceptions to this rule. One of those exceptions is if there is a community emergency and we have to ask God to help the community.

אָבִינוּ מַלְכֵּנוּ was added to the Rosh Hashanah service at the end of Shacharit and Minchah and to every service of Yom Kippur because of its power as a prayer. When Yom Kippur falls out on Shabbat, we have a conflict between the requirements of Shabbat and the requirements of Yom Kippur. On the one hand, we want to say אָבִינוּ מַלְכֵּנוּ because it is Yom Kippur. We are, after all asking God's help on behalf of the community. This is a time of trouble – these are the last moments before God judges us, and if we can't say אָבִינוּ מַלְכֵּנוּ now, when could we say it?[4] On the other hand, Yom Kippur is called שַׁבַּת שַׁבָּתוֹן, the Sabbath of Sabbaths,[5] and maybe we should not say it.

As a result, we find a difference of opinion about how to treat אָבִינוּ מַלְכֵּנוּ on Shabbat. The Shulchan Aruch[6] says we do say it if Yom Kippur falls out on Shabbat. The Rama[7] says we do not say אָבִינוּ מַלְכֵּנוּ on Shabbat. The Mishnah Berurah provides[8] the Rama's rationale: we just don't ask for our specific needs on Shabbat. The Aruch Hashulchan[9] agrees, but makes a distinction between אָבִינוּ מַלְכֵּנוּ where we are asking for our personal needs, on the one hand, and the Selichot and י״ג מִדּוֹת הָרַחֲמִים which are an intrinsic part of the prayers of Yom Kippur. So, he says we should not say אָבִינוּ מַלְכֵּנוּ on Shabbat, but should say the Selichot and י״ג מִדּוֹת הָרַחֲמִים.

3. שלחן ערוך אורח חיים סימן תריט סעיף ח
4. משנה ברורה סימן תרכב ס״ק יא
5. ויקרא פרק טז פס׳ לא
6. שולחן ערוך אורח חיים סימן תרכב סעי׳ ג
7. שולחן ערוך אורח חיים סימן תרכב סעי׳ ג
8. משנה ברורה סימן תרכב ס״ק יג
9. ערוך השולחן אורח חיים סימן תריט סעיף ח

Blowing the Shofar

On every American coin it says *e pluribus unum* (from many [people], one [nation]). When we blow the shofar, the opposite is true. The Torah only speaks about one shofar blast on Rosh Hashanah, and we end up with one hundred. How does that happen?

In Parshat Pinchas it says,[10] וּבַחֹדֶשׁ הַשְּׁבִיעִי בְּאֶחָד לַחֹדֶשׁ מִקְרָא־קֹדֶשׁ יִהְיֶה לָכֶם כָּל־מְלֶאכֶת עֲבֹדָה לֹא תַעֲשׂוּ יוֹם תְּרוּעָה יִהְיֶה לָכֶם ("The first day of the seventh month will be established as a holy day for you. On it you should not perform any creative work. It should be for you a day of loud blasts"). This is the only reference we have in the Torah to the direct commandment of blowing the shofar on Rosh Hashanah.

In Parshat Emor it says,[11] דַּבֵּר אֶל־בְּנֵי יִשְׂרָאֵל לֵאמֹר בַּחֹדֶשׁ הַשְּׁבִיעִי בְּאֶחָד לַחֹדֶשׁ יִהְיֶה לָכֶם שַׁבָּתוֹן זִכְרוֹן תְּרוּעָה מִקְרָא־קֹדֶשׁ ("Speak to the children of Israel saying, the first day of the seventh month shall be a day of rest for you. It is a holy day of remembrance of loud blasts"). The Rabbis take this verse to refer to Rosh Hashanah that falls on Shabbat, when no actual shofar blowing takes place.

A third time the shofar is mentioned is found in Parshat Behar: וְהַעֲבַרְתָּ שׁוֹפַר תְּרוּעָה בַּחֹדֶשׁ הַשְּׁבִעִי בֶּעָשׂוֹר לַחֹדֶשׁ בְּיוֹם הַכִּפֻּרִים תַּעֲבִירוּ שׁוֹפָר בְּכָל אַרְצְכֶם ("You shall sound a shofar blast on the tenth day of the seventh month. On Yom Kippur you will sound this shofar sound throughout your land").[12] This verse teaches us that during the Jubilee year there was a commandment to blow the shofar on Yom Kippur. In each of the three verses mentioned, we have the phrase בַּחֹדֶשׁ הַשְּׁבִעִי ("in the seventh month"). The Gemara discusses[13] those verses and quotes a beraita that derives that all the blowings of the shofar in the month of Tishrei are considered one unit. Because we have three verses on the topic, whenever we are asked to blow the shofar, we must blow three sounds. The Torah obligation on Rosh Hashanah is to blow three shofar sounds, known as תְּרוּעָה.

---

10. במדבר פרק כט פסוק א
11. ויקרא פרק כג פסוק כד
12. ויקרא פרק כה פסוק ט
13. ראש השנה דף לג עמ׳ ב

However, the above mentioned beraita also teaches us that each תְּרוּעָה must be accompanied by a simpler sound, known as a תְּקִיעָה, before and after each תְּרוּעָה. In order to fulfill the mitzvah, therefore, nine sounds must be blown: תְּקִיעָה, תְּרוּעָה, תְּקִיעָה, three times. As long as we knew what the Torah meant by a תְּרוּעָה blast, that is what we did on Rosh Hashanah and on Yom Kippur that followed the Yovel.

A תְּקִיעָה is a simple unbroken sound. But how do we blow the תְּרוּעָה? The Rambam explains[14] that due to the difficulties we have experienced in early periods of our history, we forgot what was the original sound of the תְּרוּעָה. However, we have some hints. The Talmud says that the translation of the verse יוֹם תְּרוּעָה יִהְיֶה לָכֶם is יוֹם יְבָבָא יְהֵי לְכוֹן ("it should be a day of crying for you").[15]

We read in the Book of Judges:[16] בְּעַד הַחַלּוֹן נִשְׁקְפָה וַתְּיַבֵּב אֵם סִיסְרָא ("Sisera's mother bewailed [the death of her son]"). One opinion is that וַתְּיַבֵּב ("she bewailed"), means with a groaning sound (גְּנוּחֵי גָּנַח). The other opinion describes it as weeping (יִלּוּלֵי יְלֵל).[17]

We now have two possibilities of how to sound a תְּרוּעָה: like groaning or like weeping. The Gemara continues with even a third possibility: תְּרוּעָה might be a combination of moaning and weeping. Nowadays we refer to the groaning sound as a שְׁבָרִים and to the weeping sound as the תְּרוּעָה.

In order to fulfill the commandment of the Torah correctly, we need to blow at least thirty sounds: תְּקִיעָה, שְׁבָרִים־תְּרוּעָה, תְּקִיעָה three times; תְּקִיעָה, שְׁבָרִים, תְּקִיעָה three times; and תְּקִיעָה, תְּרוּעָה, תְּקִיעָה three times.[18] There is no doubt that a person who heard those thirty sounds fulfills the commandment properly. For instance, if we have to blow the shofar for someone who cannot go to shul, all we have to do is blow those thirty shofar blasts for him or her. There is no need for anything additional.

---

14. רמב"ם הלכות שופר וסוכה ולולב פרק ג הל' ב
15. תרגום אונקלוס במדבר פרק כט פסוק א
16. שופטים ה:כח
17. רש"י ראש השנה דף לג עמ' ב and רש"י שופטים פרק ה פסוק כח
18. שולחן ערוך אורח חיים סימן תקצ סעיף ב

Why, then, do we blow one hundred sounds in shul? Originally, those thirty sounds were blown in combination with the three special berachot (מַלְכֻיוֹת, זִכְרוֹנוֹת, and שׁוֹפָרוֹת) of Musaf. Over time it was noticed that many people, such as the elderly or the sick, had a hard time fulfilling the commandment of hearing the shofar because they could not stay in shul that long. Therefore, people began to blow the basic thirty sounds immediately after the public reading of the Torah. Then the elderly and sick could go home. We call those earlier shofar blasts תְּקִיעוֹת דִּמְיֻשָּׁב, "sitting-down tekiot"[19] (although customarily we do stand for these tekiot as well).[20]

The Talmud provides another reason[21] for the earlier thirty shofar blasts. Those sounds were meant to confuse the Satan (prosecuting angel) so that the Satan would not be able to prosecute the Jewish people while the main shofar blasts are blown. In short, the thirty required blasts has now grown to sixty shofar blasts: thirty after the public Torah reading and thirty additional blasts, which are integrated into the three berachot of Musaf. This gives us a higher and a more meaningful understanding of the commandment.

In some communities, the shofar is blown during the silent Amidah and also during the repetition of the Amidah. Rav Soloveitchik adopted that custom for his minyan at Maimonides School. He felt that the worshippers at Maimonides had enough understanding and knowledge to stop at the right places to hear the sound of the shofar.

The shofar blowing during the Musaf Amidah are called תְּקִיעוֹת דִּמְעֻמָּד, the standing shofar blasts. Whether in the silent Amidah or the repetition, the shofar is blown after each special blessing, at the end of מַלְכוּיוֹת, at the end of זִכְרוֹנוֹת, and at the end of שׁוֹפָרוֹת. Each time we blow ten blasts of the shofar:

תְּקִיעָה שְׁבָרִים תְּרוּעָה תְּקִיעָה
תְּקִיעָה שְׁבָרִים תְּקִיעָה
תְּקִיעָה תְּרוּעָה תְּקִיעָה

19. טור אורח חיים הלכות ראש השנה סימן תקפה; רמב"ם הלכות שופר פרק ג הלכה י
20. משנה ברורה סימן תקפה ס"ק ב
21. ראש השנה דף טז עמ' א–ב

There is a post-Talmudic custom of blowing one hundred shofar blasts corresponding to the hundred sobbings of Sisera's mother.[22] To fulfill this minhag, in most communities we listen to an additional forty blasts at the end of the service. In communities where they blow the shofar during the silent Amidah, they only need to add another ten, since the shofar was blown thirty times during the silent Amidah and thirty times in the repetition.

Why is a connection made between the sobbing of Sisera's mother and the commandment of blowing the shofar? Rav Soloveitchik explained it in the following way: Sisera's mother was an unkind woman who took great delight in her son's military exploits, success, and cruelty toward his victims. On that day she waited for her victorious son to return from battle, but he never did. As she waited anxiously, she started questioning her son's way of life, his involvement with death, destruction, and innumerable foes. She asked herself, "Couldn't my son have used his talents for constructive purposes and helped the downtrodden and the poor?" Waiting endless hours, she suddenly realized that she had brought up her son the wrong way. Her sobs were sobs of regret. She wished she could live her life over again and train her son for nobler purposes. The long wait for her son on that day awakened thoughts of repentance in her heart. Suddenly she understood how wrong she had been. Isn't this what we should feel in listening to the sound of the shofar? We should feel like Sisera's mother that we could have done better, but it's not too late for us. God has given us a second chance. We must change our way of life.

We have operated on the idea that we are not sure about the true sounds of the תְּרוּעָה and, therefore, we have to sound all possibilities. If there is one correct sound, the other sounds are invalid. However, Rav Hai Gaon states that on the contrary, all תְּרוּעָה possibilities are valid.[23] In some communities they sounded the תְּרוּעָה in one way, and in some communities they sounded the תְּרוּעָה in a different way.

---

22. תוספות ראש השנה דף לג עמוד ב

23. חידושי הר"ן ראש השנה דף לד עמוד א

Rabbi Avahu of the Gemara believed[24] that we should all blow the same uniform shofar sounds, and he introduced the custom to sound all three possibilities of the תְּרוּעָה.

Rav Soloveitchik analyzed the nature of blowing the shofar. He said the function of the first time we blow the shofar during the תְּקִיעוֹת דִּמְיֻשָּׁב together with the berachot is to fulfill our obligation to hear the shofar sounded. The second time we blow the shofar, during the musaf service, the shofar is enveloped in the berachot of the Amidah. There it fulfills a function of prayer and crying.[25] Sometimes in prayer we can organize our thoughts well and present our requests to God in a logical manner. Sometimes we are so upset that we cannot organize our thoughts at all, and we just shed tears. This is what the תְּקִיעוֹת of the Amidah of Musaf are.

Amidot of Rosh Hashanah

During Musaf on Rosh Hashanah we recite nine berachot. Rosh Hashanah is thus different from every other Musaf, which contains only seven berachot. The Gemara explains that the nine berachot of Rosh Hashanah correspond to the nine times that Hannah mentioned the name of God in her prayer, which was accepted on Rosh Hashanah. If Hannah's prayer was accepted and found mercy in God's eyes on Rosh Hashanah, we should follow the same pattern and hopefully also find mercy in His eyes.

Rav, in the time of the Gemara, composed the central berachot of the Amidah of Rosh Hashanah. They are known as תְּקִיעָתָא דְּבֵי רַב (the tekiot of Rav).[26] The three berachot of the Amidah of Musaf that distinguish it from every other Musaf are the berachot of מַלְכֻיּוֹת זִכְרוֹנוֹת וְשׁוֹפָרוֹת: of accepting God as our Sovereign; of remembrances; and about the shofar that brings to mind past, and hopefully future, salvations.

Rav's beginning of the berachah of מַלְכֻיּוֹת is what we recognize as

---

24. ראש השנה דף לד עמ׳ א

25. See רשימות שיעורים מסכת סוכה דף לח עמ׳ א.

26. ירושלמי ראש השנה פרק א הלכה ג; ירושלמי עבודה זרה פרק א הלכה ב

עָלֵינוּ. It has become so beloved that we recite it each time we finish a prayer service. The Talmud does not mention any difference between the Amidah of Musaf and the other Amidot of that day. Logically, we may assume that the Talmud intended that the nine berachot should be said in all the services of the day. From the commentary of the Rosh, we see it wasn't quite clear how many berachot were said at the different services of Rosh Hashanah. In all communities today, however, we recite seven berachot in the Amidot of Rosh Hashanah, with the exception of Musaf, in which we recite nine berachot.

How did this change come about from nine berachot to seven? The answer relates to the performance of another distinctive obligation on Rosh Hashanah. We always want to perform commandments or other obligations at the first possible opportunity. Shofar is an important mitzvah on Rosh Hashanah and is an integral part of the observance of the day. Then shouldn't we blow the shofar in Shacharit? The Talmud wonders about this.

Rashi[27] explains that the shofar used to be blown during Shacharit, but the Romans forbade it. They watched for it during Shacharit, so the Jews moved it to Musaf to fool the Romans.

Tosafot[28] offered a different explanation. Based on the Jerusalem Talmud, they explain that while for us, blowing the shofar is the fulfillment of a commandment, in the rest of the ancient world its blast was the clarion call to war. The Roman soldiers spent their evenings eating, drinking, gambling, and carousing, and went to sleep very late. At sunrise they were all fast asleep. The Jews at that time were on their way to shul. The sound of the shofar penetrated into the walls of the tents of the Roman soldiers. They did not know about the mitzvah of shofar, and they thought that the Jews were rebelling against them. They quickly ran into the streets and massacred the Jews.

The Rabbis, trying to prevent this kind of tragedy, postponed the mitzvah of shofar from Shacharit to Musaf. By that time the Roman soldiers were awake and saw the Jews in their holiday garments going

27. רש"י מסכת ראש השנה דף לב עמוד ב ד"ה בשעת השמד שנו

28. תוספות שם

to the synagogue. Even the Roman soldiers understood then that the blowing of the shofar was not a matter of rebellion but simply a matter of religious practice.

Since the shofar was originally blown in Shacharit, the Amidah of Shacharit originally contained nine berachot. As on all other holidays, the Amidah of Shacharit is the same as the Amidah of Ma'ariv and Minchah; they all contained the berachot of מַלְכֻיּוֹת, זִכְרוֹנוֹת וְשׁוֹפָרוֹת. After the Rabbis made the edict to postpone the shofar to Musaf, they removed the berachot of מַלְכֻיּוֹת, זִכְרוֹנוֹת וְשׁוֹפָרוֹת in the other עֲמִידוֹת of Rosh Hashanah. Now there were only seven berachot, and there was no longer any place in which to blow the shofar except in the שְׁמוֹנֶה עֶשְׂרֵה of Musaf. The only Amidah that was left with nine blessings was that of Musaf.

We retained vestiges from when all the Amidah services on Rosh Hashanah contained nine blessings, because the introduction to Rav's additions, the וּבְכֵן תֵּן פַּחְדְּךָ section, is still kept in the third blessing in every Amidah of Rosh Hashanah and Yom Kippur.

The opening three berachot of every Amidah are the same on Rosh Hashanah as any other שְׁמוֹנֶה עֶשְׂרֵה, but on Rosh Hashanah we expand these blessings. Rosh Hashanah starts a ten-day period, called עֲשֶׂרֶת יְמֵי תְּשׁוּבָה, of our trying to effect a change in our lives. In every Amidah during this time, we add special phrases to the first three blessings of the Amidah and to the last two blessings.

The third berachah of the שְׁמוֹנֶה עֶשְׂרֵה is the berachah of קְדֻשַּׁת ה׳, which describes God's sanctity. The fourth blessing of the שְׁמוֹנֶה עֶשְׂרֵה is the blessing of קְדֻשַּׁת הַיּוֹם describing the holiness and special character of the day. The themes of the third and fourth berachot – that God is holy (קְדֻשַּׁת ה׳) and generates holy times that we celebrate in His honor (קְדֻשַּׁת הַיּוֹם) – are intertwined. The Gemara expresses two opinions about where the additional blessing of מַלְכֻיּוֹת belongs. According to Rabbi Yochanan ben Nuri, מַלְכֻיּוֹת, the proclamation of God's kingship, should be part of the berachah of קְדֻשַּׁת ה׳ (the third berachah). Rabbi Akiva believed that מַלְכֻיּוֹת must be part of the fourth berachah. Today we follow Rabbi Akiva's view and מַלְכֻיּוֹת is included in the fourth berachah of קְדֻשַּׁת הַיּוֹם.

The berachah of זִכְרוֹנוֹת is the fifth berachah. That berachah expresses that God remembers the covenant with the Jewish people. The sixth berachah is שׁוֹפָרוֹת, which speaks about God revealing Himself to His people. This revelation took place and will take place again amid the sounding of the shofar. The seventh, eighth, and ninth berachot are the same three concluding berachot as in any other שְׁמוֹנֶה עֶשְׂרֵה.

In some places, the additions of וּבְכֵן תֵּן פַּחְדְּךָ were said through the עֲשֶׂרֶת יְמֵי תְּשׁוּבָה as well, though we do not follow this practice. These additions deal with God as the leader of the universe and all His creatures accepting His rule. In these addenda we also speak about the special role of the Jewish people, the righteous, and all those who are close to God.

מַלְכֻיּוֹת זִכְרוֹנוֹת וְשׁוֹפָרוֹת in Musaf

Each of the three extra berachot of the Musaf contains three sections. The first section interprets the idea of each berachah. The middle section contains verses from the Torah, Scriptures and Prophets expressing the core of the blessing's theme for each of מַלְכֻיּוֹת זִכְרוֹנוֹת וְשׁוֹפָרוֹת. The third section pleads with God to make those ideas come true.

מַלְכֻיּוֹת זִכְרוֹנוֹת וְשׁוֹפָרוֹת each contain ten central verses: three from the Torah, three from Psalms, and three from the Prophets, in that order, followed by a final verse from the Torah.[29]

Why are the verses not stated in biblical order: Torah, Prophets, and Scriptures? Instead they are in the sequence: Torah, Scriptures, and Prophets. The verses from Scriptures are all taken from Psalms, and King David, the author of the Psalms, lived before the other prophets. We list the verses in chronological order.

Why do we split the verses from the Torah into two sections (first

29. The Gemara gives us three reasons why there are ten verses per section. First, ten corresponds to the ten praises of God that David invokes in Psalm 150. Second, the number of verses corresponds to the Ten Commandments. Third, the number of verses corresponds to the ten utterances by which God created the universe.

three sentences, and then ending with one)? Couldn't we have said all four verses from the Torah together? To understand this, we have to realize that the first nine verses are statements of fact. God is our King. God remembers the covenant. The tenth verse is not a statement of fact. It is a request that we make, directed at God. This last verse in the berachah of מַלְכֻיּוֹת, however, is the very basis of our faith. The last verse is שְׁמַע יִשְׂרָאֵל. But the Shema also seems to be a statement and not a request. Obviously, the Rabbis interpreted the Shema differently. They translated it as follows: "Hear, O Israel! God is now only recognized by the Jewish people. We pray and hope that soon He will be the only God recognized by every human being." Rashi also adopts this interpretation of the verse.[30] Thus, the Shema is also a request and a fitting end to the berachah.

Another reason for using the Shema is that since there are only three direct verses in the Torah with the theme of God's sovereignty, we have to take a verse with an indirect theme for the fourth Torah verse.

As we further compare the berachot of מַלְכֻיּוֹת זִכְרוֹנוֹת וְשׁוֹפָרוֹת we notice that the last verse from the Torah in the berachot of זִכְרוֹנוֹת and שׁוֹפָרוֹת does not immediately follow the other nine verses, while in the berachah of מַלְכֻיּוֹת it does. Why is there this difference? The tenth verse gets a paragraph of its own when it contains a request rather than a simple statement. The different function of this tenth verse, of requesting, means that we must explain the plea to God to make those ideas come true. An explanation generates a new paragraph.

In the berachah of מַלְכֻיּוֹת (the fourth berachah) this is not so simple. The themes of the third berachah (קְדֻשַּׁת ה׳) and the fourth berachah (קְדֻשַּׁת הַיּוֹם) are closely related. We have already discussed the theme of מַלְכֻיּוֹת in the berachah of קְדֻשַּׁת ה׳ that describes God's sanctity, and we do not need to add another paragraph based around the tenth verse, because it would be redundant. That allows the fourth berachah to conclude immediately after the ten verses have been quoted because the blessing's purpose has been fulfilled.

---

30. See רש״י דברים ו:ד.

Rav Soloveitchik was strict to add a tenth verse from the Torah immediately after the first nine verses in all three of these special berachot, without waiting until the next paragraph.[31] In the berachah of זִכְרוֹנוֹת, the Rav recited the tenth verse of the Torah, וְזָכַרְתִּי לָהֶם בְּרִית רִאשֹׁנִים אֲשֶׁר הוֹצֵאתִי־אֹתָם מֵאֶרֶץ מִצְרַיִם לְעֵינֵי הַגּוֹיִם לִהְיוֹת לָהֶם לֵאלֹקִים אֲנִי ה׳, immediately after the other nine verses of the middle section of the berachah. The Ramban explains this verse as meaning that God will remember the covenant made with the Jewish people, even when they are in exile. This applies even if it takes many generations to come to fulfillment. God will remember His covenant not because the Jews have changed and have become worthy, but for His own sake. In addition, the Rav repeated the same Torah verse in the last paragraph of the berachah as a part of the request.

There is another problem in the berachah of זִכְרוֹנוֹת revolving around the verses from Psalms. The first verse is זֵכֶר עָשָׂה לְנִפְלְאֹתָיו חַנּוּן וְרַחוּם ה׳ ("He has made a memorial for His wonders. God is gracious and merciful"). Is this verse suitable for the topic of זִכְרוֹנוֹת? The point of זִכְרוֹנוֹת is that God remembers the covenant with mankind, and this is not mentioned in this verse at all. Furthermore, the very next verse in the Book of Psalms continues with the words טֶרֶף נָתַן לִירֵאָיו יִזְכֹּר לְעוֹלָם בְּרִיתוֹ ("He provides food for those who fear Him. He remembers the covenant forever"). These two consecutive verses are obviously one unit and together mention the covenant between God and man only once. If we combine them and do not use the first as one of our required three verses from the Psalms, we are short one verse. Rav Soloveitchik solved this problem by adding another verse: זָכַר לְעוֹלָם בְּרִיתוֹ דָּבָר צִוָּה לְאֶלֶף דּוֹר ("He has remembered his covenant forever, the word which He commanded to a thousand generations") as the first verse of the זִכְרוֹנוֹת Scriptures section while counting both consecutive verses mentioned above together as one quotation.

In the berachah of שׁוֹפָרוֹת, Rav Soloveitchik had the congregation recite the Torah verse לֹא־הִבִּיט אָוֶן בְּיַעֲקֹב וְלֹא־רָאָה עָמָל בְּיִשְׂרָאֵל יְיָ אֱלֹקָיו עִמּוֹ וּתְרוּעַת מֶלֶךְ בּוֹ ("God sees no wrongdoing in Jacob nor any offense in

31. See טור אורח חיים סימן תקצ״א, citing ראבי״ה.

Israel. Hashem his God is with him and the trumpeting [friendship] of the King is with them") as the tenth verse immediately following the others in the verses section of the berachah. According to the Gemara, this verse could be considered either one of the selections for the berachah of מַלְכֻיּוֹת or one of the selections for the berachah of שׁוֹפָרוֹת, because both elements (kingship and trumpeting) are mentioned in it.

In other words, Rav Soloveitchik utilized this verse twice: once as the second verse from the Torah in the berachah of מַלְכֻיּוֹת, and again as the tenth verse of the berachah of שׁוֹפָרוֹת, following immediately after the other nine verses. Then he recited, as does everyone else, וּבְיוֹם שִׂמְחַתְכֶם וּבְמוֹעֲדֵיכֶם וּבְרָאשֵׁי חָדְשֵׁיכֶם וּתְקַעְתֶּם בַּחֲצֹצְרֹת עַל עֹלֹתֵיכֶם וְעַל זִבְחֵי שַׁלְמֵיכֶם וְהָיוּ לָכֶם לְזִכָּרוֹן לִפְנֵי אֱלֹקֵיכֶם אֲנִי יְיָ אֱלֹקֵיכֶם ("and on the days of your festivals and your holidays of assembly and your New Moons, you will blow the horn over your burnt offerings and over your peace offerings, and these occasions will serve for you as a remembrance before your God. I am Hashem your God") as the verse in the last paragraph of the berachah of שׁוֹפָרוֹת as a part of the request.

If we look at the number of verses in the berachah of שׁוֹפָרוֹת, we will find that there are actually four verses instead of three from Psalms. We are permitted to add to the number of verses; that is not problematic. But why did the Rabbis choose to add an additional verse from Psalms for no special reason? The extra verse is from Psalm 150, the last psalm, in which we are instructed ten times to give praise to God. By quoting this extra verse, the Rabbis wanted to emphasize the importance of this source, which is one of the ways the Gemara derives the concept of reciting ten verses in מַלְכֻיּוֹת זִכְרוֹנוֹת וְשׁוֹפָרוֹת.[32]

Rosh Hashanah as Rosh Chodesh

On Rosh Hashanah morning when we make Kiddush we quote the verses[33] תִּקְעוּ בַחֹדֶשׁ שׁוֹפָר בַּכֶּסֶה לְיוֹם חַגֵּנוּ: כִּי חֹק לְיִשְׂרָאֵל הוּא מִשְׁפָּט לֵאלֹקֵי יַעֲקֹב ("Blow the shofar at the moon's renewal, at the time appointed for

32. ראש השנה דף לב עמוד א

33. תהלים פא:ד-ה

our festive day, because it is a decree for Israel, a judgment day for the God of Jacob"). We also recite these verses every Thursday morning as part of the psalm of the day. According to one interpretation, from the term בַּכֶּסֶה[34] (כֶּסֶה taken to mean "hidden") we derive the practice of not mentioning (hiding) the Musaf sacrifice of Rosh Chodesh in the Musaf service of Rosh Hashanah, even though Rosh Hashanah itself occurs on the new moon of Tishrei.

In the Musaf for Rosh Hashanah, the section of the שְׁמוֹנֶה עֶשְׂרֵה in which we customarily mention the sacrifices, there is no mention of the Rosh Chodesh sacrifice that we would expect to see. Since Rosh Hashanah falls on the first day of Tishrei, this is very strange. There is a hint, however, that Rosh Hashanah is also a Rosh Chodesh, because in describing the sacrifices of the day, the Musaf prayers mention מִלְּבַד עֹלַת הַחֹדֶשׁ וּמִנְחָתָהּ, "In addition to the burnt offering that is offered up each month with its meal offering."

The sacrifices of Rosh Hashanah and Rosh Chodesh are different. Those of Rosh Chodesh consist of a burnt offering of two young bulls,[35] one ram,[36] and seven lambs,[37] with their meal offerings and libations.[38] The law also required an additional male goat for a sin offering.[39] In addition to the Rosh Chodesh sacrifices there were also two daily sacrifices.[40] The Rosh Hashanah sacrifices consisted of a burnt offering of one young bull,[41] one ram,[42] and seven lambs,[43] with their meal offerings and libations.[44] The law also required one male

---

34. See תוספות ביצה דף טז עמוד א ד"ה איזהו חג.
35. עוֹלָה לה׳ פָּרִים בְּנֵי בָקָר שְׁנַיִם
36. וְאַיִל אֶחָד
37. כְּבָשִׂים בְּנֵי שָׁנָה שִׁבְעָה תְּמִימִם
38. וּמִנְחָתָם וְנִסְכֵּיהֶם: שְׁלֹשָׁה עֶשְׂרֹנִים לַפָּר. וּשְׁנֵי עֶשְׂרֹנִים לָאָיִל. וְעִשָּׂרוֹן לַכֶּבֶשׂ. וְיַיִן כְּנִסְכּוֹ
39. שָׂעִיר לְכַפֵּר
40. וּשְׁנֵי תְמִידִים
41. וַעֲשִׂיתֶם עֹלָה לְרֵיחַ נִיחֹחַ לַה׳ פַּר בֶּן־בָּקָר אֶחָד
42. אַיִל אֶחָד
43. כְּבָשִׂים בְּנֵי־שָׁנָה שִׁבְעָה תְּמִימִם
44. וּמִנְחָתָם סֹלֶת בְּלוּלָה בַשָּׁמֶן שְׁלֹשָׁה עֶשְׂרֹנִים לַפָּר שְׁנֵי עֶשְׂרֹנִים לָאָיִל: וְעִשָּׂרוֹן אֶחָד לַכֶּבֶשׂ הָאֶחָד לְשִׁבְעַת הַכְּבָשִׂים

goat for sin offerings.[45] The Torah then says that this is all "in addition to the burnt offering of the new month with its meal offering."[46] All the sacrifices of both Rosh Hashanah and Rosh Chodesh (as well as the daily sacrifices) were brought on Rosh Hashanah, but the sacrifices for Rosh Chodesh were only mentioned in a general way, without being referred to specifically. This is how Rosh Chodesh is in effect "hidden."

You might ask why the Torah keeps it a secret that Rosh Hashanah is also Rosh Chodesh Tishrei. Rav Soloveitchik once explained that Rosh Hashanah and Rosh Chodesh represent contradictory ideas and therefore cannot be mentioned together. Rosh Chodesh represents the imperfect world that we have today. According to the Rabbis, the Almighty "sinned" by making the moon a lesser light when it aspired to take the place of the sun.[47] Rosh Hashanah, however, represents the perfect world that we desire and for which we pray.

YOM KIPPUR

Yom Kippur is observed on the tenth day of Tishrei. The significance of this day goes back to Israel's history in the desert. Moshe ascended Mount Sinai to reside with God for forty days and nights and learn all of the Torah. When Moshe came down from the mountain on the 17th of Tammuz, he was shocked to see the depravity of the Jews as they danced around the golden calf. If it had not been for Moshe's fervent pleas, God would have destroyed the Jewish people. Moshe therefore ascended Mount Sinai a second time for another forty days and nights, imploring the Almighty not to reject the Jews as His nation. That second period of forty days started on the eighteenth of Tammuz and lasted until the twenty-eighth of Av. Moshe's prayers to God had an affect, and God was appeased. He told Moshe to make another set of tablets. On Rosh Chodesh Elul (the thirtieth day of

---

45. וּשְׂעִיר־עִזִּים אֶחָד חַטָּאת
46. מִלְּבַד עֹלַת הַחֹדֶשׁ וּמִנְחָתָהּ וְעֹלַת הַתָּמִיד וּמִנְחָתָהּ וְנִסְכֵּיהֶם כְּמִשְׁפָּטָם לְרֵיחַ נִיחֹחַ אִשֶּׁה לַיְיָ
47. See חולין דף ס עמ׳ ב.

Av), God's mercy triumphed, and at the end of this third period of forty days, on the tenth day of Tishrei, Moshe heard the redeeming words, סָלַחְתִּי ("I forgive them").[48] Ever since, that day has been the Day of Atonement.[49]

כָּל נִדְרֵי

In Parshat Ki Tisa[50] we are taught which ingredients we use to make the incense. All of the spices have a pleasant odor but one. Why do we use an ingredient that doesn't smell good? Is this respectful to God? The Rabbis told us that there is a good reason for it. We can learn something from it. There are many Jews have a "good aroma," meaning that they observe the commandments and do good deeds. There are Jews whose "aroma" is not so good. They are sinful crooks and cheats. But they are still Jews. Every Jew is a Jew and must be accepted. Just like the spices, of which there was one that was malodorous, so too we have some members who are "malodorous."[51] We have no right to exclude them. Every Jew is part of the community of Israel.

This principle is so important that on Yom Kippur we mention it specifically. When the actions of an individual endangered the community, the Rabbis used the weapon of חֵרֶם (excommunication). That meant that the person no longer belonged to the Jewish community and wouldn't be allowed to come to shul or even speak to anyone. It was as if the person no longer existed in the community. It was a powerful tool, and the Rabbis achieved a great deal with it. Excommunication could only be reversed if the person repented. This was so even if it took the rest of the person's life. Yom Kippur was the exception.

On Yom Kippur, if we did not allow sinners to pray with us we would have a real difficulty because there is a law, כָּל תַּעֲנִית שֶׁאֵין בָּהּ מִפּוֹשְׁעֵי יִשְׂרָאֵל אֵינָהּ תַּעֲנִית ("A fast that does not include the sinners of

48. במדבר יד:כ
49. רשב"ם בבא בתרא דף קכא עמוד א ד"ה יום שנתנו בו לוחות האחרונות
50. שמות ל:לד
51. כריתות דף ו עמוד ב

Israel is not considered a fast").[52] We cannot stand before God and ask for forgiveness, absolution, and pardon if some Jews are excluded. The ban of excommunication was lifted for one day, on Yom Kippur. This is the main reason why, in Kol Nidrei, we say, כָּל נִדְרֵי וַחֲרָמֵי ("All our vows and edicts of excommunication"), should not be valid. This is perhaps why we say, עַל דַּעַת הַמָּקוֹם וְעַל דַּעַת הַקָּהָל בִּישִׁיבָה שֶׁל מַעְלָה וּבִישִׁיבָה שֶׁל מַטָּה, אָנוּ מַתִּירִין לְהִתְפַּלֵּל עִם הָעֲבַרְיָנִים ("With God's permission and with the permission of the congregation, with the permission of the heavenly tribunal and with the permission of the earthly tribunal, we give permission to pray with the transgressors").

וִדּוּי

Another prayer central to this day is the recitation of the confessional prayer known as the וִדּוּי. The Rambam explains that it is a commandment from the Torah to recite וִדּוּי for our sins,[53] as we see in the verse וְהִתְוַדּוּ אֶת־חַטָּאתָם אֲשֶׁר עָשׂוּ ("and they should confess their sins which they committed").[54] This commandment of וִדּוּי applies all year round, not just on Yom Kippur. Whenever a Jew realizes that he has deviated from the Torah, he must take all the steps necessary for repentance, including the recitation of וִדּוּי. On Yom Kippur, we are obliged to go a step further. We have to think back on all our actions in the past year and search for all our possible iniquities. וִדּוּי therefore has become the outstanding feature of our dialogue with God on Yom Kippur.

We actually start reciting וִדּוּי on the day before Yom Kippur. The first וִדּוּי is said during Minchah, which must take place before the סְעוּדָה הַמַּפְסֶקֶת (the last meal before the fast). The Gemara quotes a beraita[55] which says that one should recite וִדּוּי before one eats and then after one eats as well, either because one might become drunk during the meal (Rashi who came from France, where they drank

52. טור אורח חיים סימן תריט

53. רמב"ם הלכות תשובה פרק א הלכה א

54. במדבר ה:ז

55. מסכת יומא דף פז עמוד ב

with every meal, was concerned about drunkenness),[56] or because one might choke during the meal. (In Spain, wine at a meal was a rarity. Thus, the Rambam thought of another danger during a meal.)[57] In the Minchah before Yom Kippur we say the weekday שְׁמוֹנֶה עֶשְׂרֵה, at the end of which we add on וִדּוּי.[58]

Even after having recited וִדּוּי during Ma'ariv of Yom Kippur, one should also recite וִדּוּי during Shacharit, Musaf, Minchah, and Ne'ilah.

Many people come to shul just before the start of Yom Kippur without having had an opportunity to pray Minchah. They quickly rise to say Minchah, including וִדּוּי, before Kol Nidrei. That does not fulfill the intent of saying the וִדּוּי before the meal. They have already eaten their meal. But it might fulfill a different obligation to recite וִדּוּי. Instead of the וִדּוּי of the שְׁמוֹנֶה עֶשְׂרֵה of Minchah, they will be saying the וִדּוּי that according to some should be recited after having begun the observance of the fast. Rav Soloveitchik required that before Kol Nidrei the congregation rise to recite וִדּוּי together. This is done to carry out the obligation of וִדּוּי after one has eaten and already begun the observance of the fast day. The beraita also tells us that the proper way to accomplish this commandment of וִדּוּי on Erev Yom Kippur is עִם חֲשֵׁכָה. Rashi interprets[59] עִם חֲשֵׁכָה as after one has eaten and has already begun the observance of the fast day. This means that there should be another וִדּוּי when Erev Yom Kippur becomes Yom Kippur.[60]

It had been the custom of many Jews, as they prepare for Kol Nidrei, to say a prayer called תְּפִלַּת זַכָּה. It contains all the ingredients of וִדּוּי. Each Jew can prepare himself for the sanctity of Yom Kippur by expressing the important sentiments brought out in this prayer .

The Gemara tells us[61] that in the silent שְׁמוֹנֶה עֶשְׂרֵה, each individual says וִדּוּי at the end of the שְׁמוֹנֶה עֶשְׂרֵה. During the repetition of the

---

56. רש"י יומא דף פז עמוד ב ד"ה שמא תטרף דעתו
57. רמב"ם הלכות תשובה פרק ב הלכה ז
58. רבינו יונה על הרי"ף מסכת ברכות דף כ עמוד א
59. רש"י יומא דף פז עמ' ב ד"ה עם חשכה
60. See בית יוסף ושולחן ערוך אורח חיים סימן תרז סעיף א.
61. יומא דף פז עמוד ב

שְׁמוֹנֶה עֶשְׂרֵה, the chazzan leads the congregation in reciting the וִדּוּי in the berachah of קְדֻשַּׁת הַיּוֹם. The Talmud does not explain the reason for this change. Rav Soloveitchik once explained it the following way: An individual who is very sincere about saying וִדּוּי and about repenting may be so embarrassed, ashamed and upset by former actions that he or she will break down and never finish the prayers. Therefore, it's best for the individual to say וִדּוּי at the end of the שְׁמוֹנֶה עֶשְׂרֵה. The chazzan, on the other hand, is our representative before God. Since he has already finished his personal prayer in the silent שְׁמוֹנֶה עֶשְׂרֵה, he understands that this recitation includes the entire congregation as צִבּוּר. As representing the Congregation of Israel, the chazzan calling to God is not as personally involved as when he talks about his own sins. He certainly can finish the שְׁמוֹנֶה עֶשְׂרֵה. Therefore, in the chazzan's repetition, he says וִדּוּי in the place where it belongs, in the berachah mentioning the special sanctity of the day, and the chazzan elicits the congregation's participation and response. This is the congregation's second opportunity to recite a וִדּוּי in each service.

There is an ancient custom on Yom Kippur that two members of the congregation stand on either side of the chazzan.[62] They may represent the assistant Kohen and the head of the Kohen's family group, who accompanied the high priest throughout the Temple service. They also may represent Aharon and Chur, who assisted Moshe in pleading with God to help His people during the battle with Amalek.[63]

Taking the comparison of Moshe, Aharon and Chur as a model, as the chazzan, representing Moshe, prepares to say וִדּוּי, he recites many reasons why God should forgive His people.

Following the וִדּוּי in the repetition of the שְׁמוֹנֶה עֶשְׂרֵה, the chazzan recites the phrase from the last paragraph of the middle berachah סְלַח וּמְחַל לַעֲוֹנוֹתֵינוּ בְּיוֹם הַכִּפּוּרִים הַזֶּה ("forgive all our sins on this Day of Atonement"). This phrase is an attempt by the chazzan to find a

---

62. See שולחן ערוך אורח חיים סימן תקסו סעיף ז; מכילתא בשלח מסכתא דעמלק א; ערוך השולחן אורח חיים סימן תריט סעיף ט.

63. טור אורח חיים הלכות תענית סימן תקסו

mitigating reason why God should forgive His people. The individual's וִדּוּי does not contain that phrase. The chazzan may make this declaration since he represents the community. The individual, however, must not minimize his or her sins or justify evil actions. The individual who wishes to repent may only turn to God, confess his sins, and ask God's forgiveness based on God's kindness and grace, not based on any rights we have. Therefore, the individual must say וִדּוּי after the שְׁמוֹנֶה עֶשְׂרֵה, where there is no request for mitigation of the impact of the confession. And in fact, that phrase does not follow the וִדּוּי of the individual.

וִדּוּי consists of two parts: the short וִדּוּי, which begins with אָשַׁמְנוּ ("We have sinned") and the long וִדּוּי, which begins with עַל חֵטְא ("For the sin that we have committed"). What is the difference between those two? Usually we assume that the short וִדּוּי speaks about sins in general without much detail, whereas the long וִדּוּי mentions individual shortcomings, such as making fun of parents and teachers. But if you look carefully, you see that the long וִדּוּי mentions many general terms for our sins, such as "sins we have committed willingly or against our will."

Rav Soloveitchik saw the distinction between the two וִדּוּיִים in the following manner: One enumerates the sins of each individual (עַל חֵטְא), whereas the other speaks about the sins of the community (אָשַׁמְנוּ). Sins of the individual include such acts as eating forbidden food. Sins of the community include such acts as not providing proper supervision for food preparation. For this reason, Rav Soloveitchik believed that two וִדּוּיִים are needed.

We have five Amidot on יוֹם כִּפּוּר: 1) Ma'ariv, 2) Shacharit, 3) Musaf, 4) Minchah, and 5) Ne'ilah. In addition to the וִדּוּי of Erev Yom Kippur, we recite וִדּוּי on Yom Kippur itself ten times. That includes twice in each service: once in the silent שְׁמוֹנֶה עֶשְׂרֵה and once in the repetition of the שְׁמוֹנֶה עֶשְׂרֵה by the chazzan. Although there is no repetition of the שְׁמוֹנֶה עֶשְׂרֵה by the chazzan in Ma'ariv, וִדּוּי is said as part of סְלִיחוֹת afterward. In all cases, both the long and short וִדּוּיִים are recited, with the exception of נְעִילָה at the end of Yom Kippur, when we only say the short וִדּוּי.

The Maggid of Dubno tells the following parable to illustrate the reason for the lack of the second וִדּוּי in Ne'ilah. A rich man built a special safe for his money in his home and hid the key. This way he was sure that no harm would come to his fortune. One day, as he took a walk, he noticed that everybody was running in the direction of his home, and smoke was rising from that direction above the whole neighborhood. He was terribly afraid that his home had caught on fire. His fear was justified: His house was on fire and about to collapse at any moment. There was no time to look for the key and unlock the safe. He quickly ran home and kicked in the door of the safe to get to his money. He grabbed the money and ran out of the burning building. Just after that, the house collapsed completely. At Ne'ilah we do not have time to examine our sins. We have to take quick and decisive action to save ourselves. A short וִדּוּי, forcefully said, could bring about Divine forgiveness.

One reason we recite וִדּוּי ten times on Yom Kippur is the special significance of the number ten. On Yom Kippur the High Priest in the Temple pronounced God's ineffable name ten times. He pronounced it three times in each וִדּוּי that he recited: The first Vidui he recited was for himself and his family; the second, for all the Kohanim; and the third, for all of Israel. And he pronounced God's name again when he determined by lot which goat was to be offered in the Temple and which would be sent off as the scapegoat.[64] The people, hearing God's name, prostrated themselves in awe and trepidation.[65]

The Sages see a connection between the ten וִדּוּיִים and the tenfold recitation of God's name. The pronunciation of God's name invoked God's aspect of mercy, assuring us of His forgiveness no matter how deeply we had fallen.

The וִדּוּי is formulated alphabetically, each letter of the Alef-Bet beginning another description of our sins. King David also made ample use of acrostics in his prayers. Psalm 145 (אַשְׁרֵי), for example, follows the order of the Alef-Bet and Psalm 119 uses each letter of the

64. רמב"ם הלכות עבודת יום הכיפורים פרק ב הלכה ו

65. יומא דף סו עמ' א

Alef-Bet sequentially, eight times, to begin each verse. King David knew that no mortal human being can adequately and comprehensively recite God's praises. Therefore, he took all the letters of the Alef-Bet to indicate that none of us can do justice to God's greatness. It is as if he said: "We ask You, God, to take all the letters of the Alef-Bet and formulate Your own praise."

Similarly, in the וִדּוּי, we admit that we cannot possibly enumerate all our shortcomings. Consequently, by saying it in the order of the Alef-Bet we tell God, "You know all our shortcomings and failures. Take the letters of the Alef-Bet and consider them as if we had mentioned them all properly ourselves."

The Gemara tells us that anyone who publicly proclaims all of his sins is a brazen person, because it is better to conceal our sins.[66] This implies that if someone announces a list of his sins, he is not truly ashamed of them but actually wants to brag about them. No one should know about your sins except you and God. The fact that in shul we say וִדּוּי out loud together seems to contradict this dictum. However, what we say in shul together is our general shortcomings, of which we are all guilty. If we want to mention our individual sins, then we must do so softly.

66. See יומא דף פו עמוד ב, based on תהלים לב:א.

Sukkot

What are the special aspects of Sukkot? There are many answers to this question. You could tell me the sukkah itself; the אַרְבַּע מִינִים consisting of the lulav, etrog, hadasim and aravot; or the mitzvah of rejoicing, which is intensified on Sukkot. You might suggest saying full Hallel each day; you could mention the נִסּוּךְ הַמַּיִם (water libation) and that it was celebrated in the time of the Temple with the שִׂמְחַת בֵּית הַשּׁוֹאֵבָה. You might think of תְּפִלַּת גֶּשֶׁם (the prayer for rain) or the הוֹשַׁעְנוֹת (when we circle the *bimah* with the אַרְבַּע מִינִים) and the special aspects of Hoshana Rabbah. That is a long list. A closer look at these items shows us that some of these are mitzvot while others are not, and some are connected to the Temple service and some are independent of the Temple service.

Sukkah is a mitzvah that is celebrated outside the Temple, and in fact, the nature of the sukkah's impermanence represents our lack of security and our total dependence on Hashem. Many of the other unique aspects of Sukkot have some connection to the way this holiday was celebrated in the Temple.

There is a מִצְוָה דְּאוֹרָיְיתָא to take the lulav on the first day of Sukkot wherever you are.[1] But in the Temple, the מִצְוָה דְּאוֹרָיְיתָא applied for seven days. Today, we take the lulav on the other days of Sukkot as well, as a מִצְוָה דְּרַבָּנָן in commemoration of the performance in the Temple. The mitzvah of lulav is not done on the Shabbat of Sukkot.

The mitzvah of שִׂמְחָה, rejoicing, has a special connection to Sukkot

1. See the section about the לוּלָב.

as celebrated in the Temple because of the verse וּשְׂמַחְתֶּם לִפְנֵי יְיָ אֱלֹקֵיכֶם שִׁבְעַת יָמִים ("Rejoice before Hashem your God for seven days").[2] As Rav Soloveitchik explained, aside from the mitzvah of שִׂמְחָה which applies equally to all three festivals (Pesach, Shavuot, and Sukkot), there is an additional aspect to the mitzvah of שִׂמְחָה which applies specifically on Sukkot in the Temple, in the presence of the Almighty.[3]

קִידּוּשׁ שֶׁל סֻכּוֹת

One aspect of Kiddush that is unique to Sukkot is the blessing recited whenever we eat in the sukkah. That berachah, בָּרוּךְ אַתָּה ה׳ אֱלֹקֵינוּ מֶלֶךְ הָעוֹלָם אֲשֶׁר קִדְּשָׁנוּ בְּמִצְוֹתָיו וְצִוָּנוּ לֵישֵׁב בַּסֻּכָּה ("Blessed are You…who commanded us to dwell in the sukkah"), is included in the Kiddush as well. There are different opinions in the Talmud about the order of the berachot within the Kiddush. Under normal circumstances, regarding Kiddush on the first night of the holiday, the Tur and Shulchan Aruch[4] say that the order of the berachot is the following: First, the berachah on the wine, next the berachah of Kiddush itself, then the berachah on the sukkah, and finally, the berachah of שֶׁהֶחֱיָנוּ. In that way, the berachah of שֶׁהֶחֱיָנוּ can cover both the holiday and the mitzvah of sukkah. This sequence is abbreviated as an acrostic: יקס״ז (יין, קידוש, סוכה, זמן).

The Rambam's practice was that when he made Kiddush in the sukkah, he stood.[5] During the rest of the year, the Rambam would sit for Kiddush, since Kiddush should be בְּמָקוֹם סְעוּדָה (in the place of the meal). For the Rambam, בְּמָקוֹם סְעוּדָה means sitting at the table. Only on Sukkot did the Rambam stand for Kiddush. He would say the berachah of לֵישֵׁב בַּסֻּכָּה, and immediately sit, and then say the berachah of שֶׁהֶחֱיָנוּ. The Rambam wanted to make the berachah of לֵישֵׁב בַּסֻּכָּה just

---

2. ויקרא כג:מ. See רמב״ם הלכות שופר סוכה ולולב פרק ח הל׳ יב.
3. See חידושי הגר״מ והגרי״ד, פ״ח מהל׳ לולב הל׳ י״ב, and see also איש ההלכה גלוי ונסתר, pp. 209–210.
4. אורח חיים סימן תרמג
5. רמב״ם הלכות סוכה פרק ו הל׳ יב

before actually sitting in the sukkah. He understood that the words לֵישֵׁב בַּסֻּכָּה should be taken literally, and the first way to demonstrate actual living in the sukkah is by sitting in it.[6]

The Rosh disagrees with the Rambam. The Rosh explains that the words לֵישֵׁב בַּסֻּכָּה mean to dwell in the sukkah, not literally to sit in it. The Rosh therefore maintains that if one wants to recite the berachah immediately before fulfilling the mitzvah (עוֹבֵר לַעֲשִׂיָּתָן), he should recite the berachah of לֵישֵׁב בַּסֻּכָּה before he walks into the sukkah. However, since the mitzvah is to eat in the sukkah and spend time in it, it is sufficient to recite the berachah after one sits down, before eating and spending time in the sukkah. Therefore, according to the Rosh, there is no reason to recite Kiddush standing rather than sitting.[7]

The Shulchan Aruch explains[8] that we recite the berachah of שֶׁהֶחֱיָנוּ at the end of Kiddush because it refers both to the holiday of Sukkot as well as to the mitzvah of sukkah, and therefore must come after the berachah on the sukkah.

There is a dispute between the Maharam of Rothenburg and the Rosh about when to recite the berachah of לֵישֵׁב בַּסֻּכָּה when eating in the sukkah and not reciting Kiddush. According to the Maharam, one should recite לֵישֵׁב בַּסֻּכָּה before the berachah on the food, because as soon as one has entered the sukkah he is obligated to recite the berachah on the mitzvah of sukkah. The Rosh, however, writes that since we customarily do not recite a berachah upon entering the sukkah unless we are eating a meal in it, the berachah of לֵישֵׁב בַּסֻּכָּה relates to the meal. Therefore, לֵישֵׁב בַּסֻּכָּה should be recited after the הַמּוֹצִיא. The Shulchan Aruch says that the custom follows the view of the Rosh.[9]

---

6. See ערוך השולחן אורח חיים סימן תרמג סעיף ג.
7. רא״ש, סוכה פרק ד סימן ג; טור אורח חיים סי׳ תרמג; רמ״א שם סעיף ב
8. שולחן ערוך אורח חיים הלכות סוכה סי׳ תרמג סעי׳ א
9. טור ושולחן ערוך סימן תרמג סעיף ג

יוֹם טוֹב שֵׁנִי שֶׁל גָּלוּיוֹת

There is a concept called יוֹם טוֹב שֵׁנִי שֶׁל גָּלוּיוֹת (the second day of a holiday that is observed outside of Israel) that was established by the Rabbis because Jews outside of Israel might not know on which day רֹאשׁ חֹדֶשׁ occurred.

It is actually a mitzvah for בֵּית דִּין, on the basis of witnesses' observations of first seeing the new moon, to declare the new month. Based on their testimony, they would inform the people, and all holidays of the month would be determined.[10] בֵּית דִּין would send out messengers to tell the people. Some places, however, were too far away for the messengers to reach in time, before the holidays had to be observed. One could not know beforehand on which day the witnesses would see the new moon and the first day of the month would be established. A month could have either twenty-nine or thirty days, so there could only be two possible days on which the new moon would occur. Therefore, בֵּית דִּין established a תַּקָּנָה (ordinance) that anyplace outside of the distance where the messengers could reach, had to observe two days (with certain exceptions) of the holidays that fell out in the month.[11] This is known as יוֹם טוֹב שֵׁנִי שֶׁל גָּלוּיוֹת (the second day of the holiday for the diaspora). Hillel the Nasi, who lived in the time of Abaye and Rava, the great Amoraim, established an astronomical computation to figure out the proper time of the new moon. His בֵּית דִּין established it, and we follow this calendar ever since.[12] Nevertheless, he was afraid that there might be a time when governments would forbid studying Torah, and it would be hard to keep track of the proper time of the holidays. Therefore, he established by תַּקָּנָה that all the places that formerly had to observe two days of the holidays (every place outside of Israel) had to continue to do so. While the first day is the true date of each holiday, the second day officially has the status of סְפֵקָא דְיוֹמָא (the nature of the day is in doubt) and it is a

---

10. רמב"ם הלכות קידוש החודש פרק א הלכה ז
11. רמב"ם הלכות קידוש החודש פרק ג הלכה יב
12. חידושי הריטב"א מסכת ראש השנה דף יח עמוד א

Rabbinic extension of the holiday on which we observe most of the practices of the first day. Even though the general rule is that we do not say berachot in a case of doubt, on יוֹם טוֹב שֵׁנִי שֶׁל גָּלוּיוֹת we say the same berachot as we do on the first day of Yom Tov, without violating laws of reciting unnecessary berachot.

Kiddush on the Second Day

Many people have a different order of reciting the berachot of Kiddush on second night of Sukkot outside of Israel. When we recite Kiddush on the second day of Sukkot, the berachah of שֶׁהֶחֱיָנוּ only refers to the holiday of Sukkot, and not also to the mitzvah of sukkah. The berachah of שֶׁהֶחֱיָנוּ doesn't have to be at the end. It can now be put closer to the Kiddush that refers to the sanctity of Sukkot. It would be, in this case, before the berachah of לֵישֵׁב בַּסֻּכָּה. The Shulchan Aruch[13] says that on the second day, the order of berachot is: יקז״ס. Having שֶׁהֶחֱיָנוּ at the end would make the berachah of לֵישֵׁב בַּסֻּכָּה an interruption between שֶׁהֶחֱיָנוּ and the Kiddush to which it refers.

The Vilna Gaon disagreed.[14] He felt that because of the doubt around the real beginning of the day of Sukkot, if the first day was not Sukkot, then the Sukkot related observances on the first day were not valid. Since שֶׁהֶחֱיָנוּ is the last berachah in Kiddush on the first day, it should be the same on the second day.

When the second day of a Yom Tov falls out just after Shabbat, we have to announce that Shabbat is over by making Havdalah and that Sukkot has started by making Kiddush. The formula is to recite the berachot in this order: יַיִן (the berachah over wine), קִדּוּשׁ (Kiddush), נֵר (light), הַבְדָּלָה. Where to put the berachah of שֶׁהֶחֱיָנוּ (זְמַן) depends on which opinion you follow in the disagreement we discussed above about שֶׁהֶחֱיָנוּ on the second night. This leaves us with the following order: Either:

---

13. שולחן ערוך ורמ״א אורח חיים סימן תרס״א סעיף א

14. מעשה רב אות ריט, and see ביאור הגר״א אורח חיים סימן תרסא ס״ק א. See also רשימות שיעורים סוכה דף נו עמוד א.

- According to the Shulchan Aruch: יקנהז״ס.[15]

Or

- According to the Vilna Gaon: יקנהס״ז.

לוּלָב

There is a mitzvah to take the lulav[16] on Sukkot[17] as the Torah says:[18] וּלְקַחְתֶּם לָכֶם בַּיּוֹם הָרִאשׁוֹן פְּרִי עֵץ הָדָר כַּפֹּת תְּמָרִים וַעֲנַף עֵץ־עָבֹת וְעַרְבֵי־נָחַל ("You must take for yourselves on the first day [of Sukkot] an etrog, branches of palm trees, a myrtle branch and the willow branches"). From this verse, we understand that the מִצְוָה דְּאוֹרַיְיתָא is to take the lulav on the first day of Sukkot, though the rabbis have extended the mitzvah for an additional six days, excepting Shabbat.

The last part of the verse, וּשְׂמַחְתֶּם לִפְנֵי יְיָ אֱלֹקֵיכֶם שִׁבְעַת יָמִים ("and rejoice before Hashem your God for seven days"), is referring to being in the Temple. From this we learn that the מִצְוָה דְּאוֹרַיְיתָא to take the lulav applies in the Temple all seven days of Sukkot.

Once the Temple was destroyed, there was no mitzvah to be performed in the Temple. After the destruction, the rabbis decreed that everyone, in Israel and out, should take the lulav for all the days of Sukkot except for Shabbat. After the destruction, the only מִצְוָה דְּאוֹרַיְיתָא left regarding lulav is on the first day. Taking the lulav on the rest of the chag is a מִצְוָה דְּרַבָּנָן established as a remembrance of the performance in the Temple.

When we perform the mitzvah of lulav we recite the berachah: בָּרוּךְ אַתָּה ה׳ אֱלֹקֵינוּ מֶלֶךְ הָעוֹלָם אֲשֶׁר קִדְּשָׁנוּ בְּמִצְוֹתָיו וְצִוָּנוּ עַל נְטִילַת לוּלָב ("Blessed

---

15. Here I want to use the Gemara's abbreviations for each of these berachot to illustrate each person's opinion: י = יין, wine; ק= קידוש, נ = נר, candle; ה = הבדלה; ז = זמן, time [שֶׁהֶחֱיָנוּ].

16. In this context, we say lulav, but we mean all four species.

17. רמב״ם הלכות שופר וסוכה ולולב פרק ז הל׳ יג-יז. The Rambam's source is a Gemara in סוכה דף מא עמ׳ א.

18. ויקרא כג:מ

are You...who commanded us to take the lulav").[19] The first time on the holiday when we take the lulav, we also recite the berachah: בָּרוּךְ אַתָּה ה׳ אֱלֹקֵינוּ מֶלֶךְ הָעוֹלָם שֶׁהֶחֱיָנוּ וְקִיְּמָנוּ וְהִגִּיעָנוּ לַזְּמַן הַזֶּה.

Rashi explains that the אַרְבַּע מִינִים are referred to as a group by the name of the largest one: the lulav. Two of the other species are bound up to it, so even though the etrog is mentioned first in the verse, the lulav has taken on a greater significance, because it includes three of the four species with it. As such, the lulav is taken up in the right hand, which is most people's stronger hand, and the etrog in the left.

In most cases, when the halachah says the right hand, it is talking about the stronger hand. In this case, the Shulchan Aruch maintains that it really means the right hand, and the lulav should be held in the right hand of even a left-handed person. But the Rama disagrees and maintains that a left-handed person should hold the lulav in his left hand.[20]

What happens outside of Israel on the second day of Sukkot? Do we say the berachah of שֶׁהֶחֱיָנוּ on the lulav then? It is a מַחֲלֹקֶת (disagreement).

There is a Gemara that relates to what we are discussing. It tells us[21] that if a person puts together a lulav for his own use before Sukkot begins, he should recite the berachah of שֶׁהֶחֱיָנוּ at that time, even though it is before the holiday begins. When he takes the lulav on the first day to fulfill the mitzvah, he should only say the berachah of אֲשֶׁר קִדְּשָׁנוּ בְּמִצְוֹתָיו וְצִוָּנוּ עַל נְטִילַת לוּלָב.

The Tur[22] quotes those who say that even though we are in doubt whether or not the first day was actually Sukkot, we could have recited the berachah of שֶׁהֶחֱיָנוּ before Sukkot began when we put the אַרְבַּע מִינִים together (as the Gemara says), so the שֶׁהֶחֱיָנוּ from the previous day over

19. The Gemara (סוכה דף לז עמוד ב) explains that we recite the berachah over the lulav, even though the mitzvah is to take all four species, because the lulav is the tallest and therefore the whole bundle is called "the lulav."

20. See שולחן ערוך ורמ"א אורח חיים סימן תרנא סעיף ג.

21. סוכה דף מו עמוד א

22. טור אורח חיים סימן תרסב

the אַרְבַּע מִינִים certainly counts. On the other hand, Rabbi Shmuel from Évreux (cited in the Beit Yosef) understands the Gemara literally. The only time you can say the berachah of שֶׁהֶחֱיָנוּ before the holiday is only when you actually prepare the item for the mitzvah. After that window of opportunity, if you did not recite the berachah then, you cannot recite the berachah until you actually perform the mitzvah. Therefore, if the first day was not Sukkot, then the berachah of שֶׁהֶחֱיָנוּ that you said when taking the lulav was not valid. Even though you said the berachah at the time you took the lulav, if the first day was not Sukkot that action had no halachic validity, nor did the שֶׁהֶחֱיָנוּ. According to this opinion, outside of Israel, we should recite a berachah of שֶׁהֶחֱיָנוּ on the second day of Sukkot over the אַרְבַּע מִינִים.

The Shulchan Aruch tells us[23] that the practice is not to recite the berachah of שֶׁהֶחֱיָנוּ over the אַרְבַּע מִינִים on the second day unless we did not have the opportunity to do so on the first day.

A berachah must be recited immediately before we perform its mitzvah. That is called עוֹבֵר לַעֲשִׂיָּתָן. However, regarding the mitzvah of lulav, this presents a problem. As soon as one picks up the אַרְבַּע מִינִים, one has already fulfilled the mitzvah. If so, how can you recite the berachah עוֹבֵר לַעֲשִׂיָּתָן?

There are a number of options to enable reciting the berachah immediately before fulfilling the mitzvah: One could pick up the lulav in one's right hand, but pick up the etrog upside down (with the pitom facing down). The halachah is that one can only fulfill a mitzvah if the object is facing "the way it grows." One can then recite the berachah and immediately turn the etrog right-side up.[24]

There are other methods of reciting the blessing עוֹבֵר לַעֲשִׂיָּתָן without performing the mitzvah first. The Shulchan Aruch also suggests, and this is the approach Rav Soloveitchik followed, placing the etrog facing up in its case, holding the other three species in the right hand, reciting the berachah and then immediately picking up the etrog and holding the four species together.

---

23. שולחן ערוך אורח חיים סימן תרסב סעיף ב
24. שולחן ערוך אורח חיים סי׳ תרנא סעי׳ ה

Even though a person fulfills the mitzvah when just holding the אַרְבַּע מִינִים, we also shake them. We do so not only when we recite Hallel, but also when we recite the berachah. If, however, there is an ill or infirm person who is not able to shake the lulav but still wants to perform the mitzvah, a person could help them recite the berachah and hold the אַרְבַּע מִינִים without shaking them.[25] Even just holding the אַרְבַּע מִינִים or shaking them a little would suffice to enable them to perform the mitzvah.

There is an important fact about lulav that also affects the berachah recited over it. It is interesting that when we say the berachah on the lulav in the morning we have fulfilled the mitzvah for the day. If we pick it up again later in the day, we are not required to recite another berachah.[26] If we go into the sukkah to eat, even several times a day, we have to recite the berachah on the sukkah each time. This is also true with many other mitzvot.[27]

The difference between lulav and other mitzvot is that those other mitzvot apply the whole day. Any time you do the mitzvah during the day, it is a mitzvah. The verse that obligates us to fulfill the mitzvah of lulav merely says you should take the lulav. Once you have taken the lulav, you have fulfilled the mitzvah for that day.

Shaking the Lulav

The Gemara tells us[28] what to do when we take the lulav: We shake it in the middle of Hallel to all four corners of the compass and above towards the heaven and down towards the earth.

The main psalm of Hallel both in size and in content is Psalm 118.[29] It starts with הוֹדוּ לַייָ כִּי־טוֹב כִּי לְעוֹלָם חַסְדּוֹ, and 29 verses later, it ends with the same verse. The Mishnah says that we shake the lulav at הודו

25. ערוך השולחן אורח חיים סי׳ תרנא סעי׳ יא
26. ערוך השולחן אורח חיים סי׳ תרנא סעי׳ יד
27. For example, if we say the blessing on putting on tefillin and wear them for an hour, and take them off for a while, when we put them back on again, they require another blessing. The same holds true for a tallit.
28. סוכה דף לז עמ׳ ב
29. תהלים פרק קיח

לַייָ at the beginning and at the end. Beit Hillel added that we also shake the lulav at אָנָּא יְיָ הוֹשִׁיעָה נָּא, which is verse 25. Beit Shammai says we should also shake the lulav at אָנָּא יְיָ הַצְלִיחָה נָּא. That is the second half of the same verse, but we follow Beit Hillel's view, and only shake the lulav for the first half of the verse.

The Gemara also provides the reason for shaking the lulav in every direction. Rabbi Yochanan says that it is to indicate we are praying to the One who owns all the four corners of the world and to the One who owns the heavens and the earth. Rabbi Chama bar Ukva said in the name of Rabbi Yossi son of Rabbi Chanina that the shaking itself was a prayer, asking for God's intervention.

In Hallel we celebrate with the אַרְבַּע מִינִים. We have just gone through a very tense time during the יָמִים נוֹרָאִים. We experienced God's judgement of all living beings. We didn't know if we would come out guilty or exonerated. Now at Sukkot, we can experience the joy of being vindicated.[30] This is the first reason for shaking the lulav during Hallel: to express our joy with our אַרְבַּע מִינִים.

Why were these specific four plants chosen to express our joy? On Sukkot, God judges the world and decides how much rain and water we will merit during the year.[31] These plants grow near the water, and when we do a mitzvah with them, the water is blessed. That is why we rejoice while davening with these plants.

Tosafot[32] explain why we shake the lulav in Hallel, as well as Hillel's position about when to shake the lulav, by referring to three verses in Chronicles I:16 (33–35). The three verses are:

לג אָז יְרַנְּנוּ עֲצֵי הַיָּעַר מִלִּפְנֵי ה׳ כִּי־בָא לִשְׁפּוֹט אֶת־הָאָרֶץ. לד הוֹדוּ לַה׳ כִּי טוֹב כִּי
לְעוֹלָם חַסְדּוֹ. לה וְאִמְרוּ־הוֹשִׁיעֵנוּ אֱלֹקֵי יִשְׁעֵנוּ, וְקַבְּצֵנוּ וְהַצִּילֵנוּ מִן הַגּוֹיִם: לְהֹדוֹת
לְשֵׁם קָדְשֶׁךָ, לְהִשְׁתַּבֵּחַ בִּתְהִלָּתֶךָ.

The first verse (33) says that after "God comes to judge the world," we celebrate with "the trees of the forest," עֲצֵי הַיָּעַר. This refers to the

30. מדרש תנחומא פרשת אמור, cited by רא"ש סוכה פרק ג סימן כו.

31. ראש השנה דף טז עמ׳ א

32. תוספות סוכה דף לז עמוד ב ד"ה בהודו

lulavim that fill our shuls. The next two verses tell us where we shake the lulav: when we recite הודו לַייָ כִּי טוֹב (34) and when we recite וְאִמְרוּ הוֹשִׁיעֵנוּ אֱלֹקֵי יִשְׁעֵנוּ (35) – in other words, אָנָּא יְיָ הוֹשִׁיעָה נָּא.

The first four verses of Psalm 118 (that starts הודו לַייָ כִּי טוֹב) are recited by the chazzan. In response to each verse, the congregation says הודו לַייָ כִּי טוב כִּי לְעוֹלָם חַסְדּוֹ. Each time either the chazzan or the congregation says this phrase, that party shakes the lulav. We also shake the lulav when we recite this phrase twice at the end of Hallel. In addition, the chazzan also shakes the lulav when reciting the verse יֹאמַר־נָא יִשְׂרָאֵל כִּי לְעוֹלָם חַסְדּוֹ.[33] Moreover, we follow Beit Hillel's opinion and shake the lulav the two times we say אָנָּא יְיָ הוֹשִׁיעָה נָּא. To recap: during Hallel the chazzan shakes the lulav six times and the congregation eight.[34]

There are different views about how to fulfill the Gemara's directive of shaking the lulav to the four directions and up and down:

- The Rambam[35] says to shake it outward three times, then bring it in and shake three times, in each of the six directions (for a total of 36 shakes).
- The Tur cites the Ba'al HaItur who says that you need to wave the lulav in and out a total of three times in each direction (and no other shaking is necessary).
- Another custom cited by the Ba'al HaItur is that you don't have to wave it in all four directions at all; it is enough to wave it out and wave it in, wave it up and wave it down.

The Shulchan Aruch cites the first opinion, and the Rama cites the second.[36] There are many customs regarding the order of shaking as well:[37]

---

33. רמ"א אורח חיים סימן תרנא סעיף ח
34. ערוך השולחן אורח חיים סימן תרנא סעיף כב
35. רמב"ם הלכות לולב פרק ז הלכה י
36. שולחן ערוך ורמ"א אורח חיים סימן תרנא סעיף ט
37. ערוך השולחן אורח חיים סימן תרנא סעיף כז

- The Shulchan Aruch says to start from the east and move clockwise: east, south, west, north, up and down.
- The Magen Avraham says start with east, south, and north, then up, down, and west.
- A Sephardic custom is to shake starting with south, then north, west, east, up and down.
- The Ari suggests south, north, east, up, down and west.
- The Tur mentions[38] a custom: east, north, south, west, up and down.

The Aruch Hashulchan mentions[39] that as long as you hold the lulav and the etrog together and shake in all six directions, the order is not so important.

הוֹשַׁעְנוֹת

Another aspect of Sukkot that has a strong connection to the Temple is related to the aravot (willow branches), which is independent of the aravot that are part of the lulav. The Mishnah[40] explains that in the time of the Temple, they used to gather willow branches to bring to the Temple and stand them up on the sides of the altar so the tops leaned over the top of the altar. Every day during Sukkot they blew the shofar and marched around the altar one time, saying אָנָּא ה׳ הוֹשִׁיעָה נָּא, אָנָּא ה׳ הַצְלִיחָה נָּא ("Please, God, save us; Please, God, grant us success"). On Hoshana Rabbah (The seventh day of Sukkot) they would go around the altar seven times. The Gemara[41] says that this observance with the aravot is an oral law transmitted to Moshe (הֲלָכָה לְמֹשֶׁה מִסִּינַי).

Outside of the Temple, there is also a practice involving aravot which is independent of the aravot in the lulav. This practice dates back to the time of the prophets; it is a dispute in the Gemara whether it was a formal institution of the prophets (יְסוֹד נְבִיאִים), or a custom

---

38. טור אורח חיים הלכות לולב סימן תרנא
39. ערוך השולחן אורח חיים סימן תרנא סעיף כז
40. סוכה דף מה עמוד א
41. סוכה דף מד עמוד א

established by the prophets (מִנְהַג נְבִיאִים). Rashi explains the ramification of this dispute. If it was a מִנְהַג נְבִיאִים, we do not recite a berachah when we perform it. If it was a יְסוֹד נְבִיאִים, then we would say a berachah when we performed this act. We fulfill this practice of the prophets on Hoshana Rabbah, when we beat the aravot.[42]

We have another practice today which is of later origins. We take the lulav each day of Sukkot and circle the bimah one time while reciting special piyutim. On Shabbat, since we do not take the lulav, we just recite piyutim. On the seventh day, Hoshana Rabbah, we take the lulav with a bunch of aravot (called הוֹשַׁעֲנוֹת) and go around the bimah seven times. We observe the practice of הוֹשַׁעְנוֹת without reciting a berachah before it. This practice, going around the bimah with the lulav or aravot and reciting piyutim, is known as הוֹשַׁעְנוֹת. The Mishnah tells us that when they went around the altar in the Temple they would recite אָנָּא ה׳ הוֹשִׁיעָה נָּא, אָנָּא ה׳ הַצְלִיחָה נָּא and Rabbi Yehudah used to say אֲנִי וָהוֹ הוֹשִׁיעָה נָּא. Our piyutim are based around these words.

Rashi explains[43] the reason we observe the custom of הוֹשַׁעְנוֹת is to remind us of the ceremony of נִסּוּךְ הַמַּיִם that was performed during the time of the Temple. Every day during Sukkot, the people came to witness the ceremony of נִסּוּךְ הַמַּיִם. On Shemini Atzeret, they began to pray for rain. (They specifically didn't mention rain until then, because having rain during Sukkot itself would spoil the mitzvah of sukkah and would be considered a bad sign.) The text of הוֹשַׁעְנוֹת that we recite begins:

הוֹשַׁע נָא לְמַעַנְךָ אֱלֹקֵינוּ הוֹשַׁע נָא: לְמַעַנְךָ בּוֹרְאֵנוּ הוֹשַׁע נָא לְמַעַנְךָ גּוֹאֲלֵנוּ הוֹשַׁע נָא: לְמַעַנְךָ דּוֹרְשֵׁנוּ הוֹשַׁע נָא ("Save us for Your sake, our God, save us. Save us for Your sake, our Creator, save us. Save us for Your sake, our Redeemer, save us. Save us for Your sake, our Seeker, save us").

This prayer seems strange. We ask God to help us for His sake. Why don't we ask God to save us for our sake, because we are in exile? This formulation is based on a Midrash. When we Jews are in exile, God takes Himself into exile too, and when we return, He too returns.

---

42. תוספות סוכה דף מד עמוד ב ד״ה כאן במקדש כאן בגבולין

43. סידור רש״י סימן רכד

That is why we pray to save us for His sake – He is suffering, as it says in Isaiah,[44] בְּכָל־צָרָתָם לא לוֹ צָר ("In all their distress He is distressed") and in Psalms, עִמּוֹ אָנֹכִי בְצָרָה ("I am with him in his distress").[45] The *Otzar Hatefillot*[46] explains that Rabbi Elazar HaKalir composed the הוֹשַׁעְנוֹת.

There is one more practice that some people observe on Sukkot that reminds us of the experience before the Temple was destroyed. That is שִׂמְחַת בֵּית הַשּׁוֹאֵבָה. The Gemara explains[47] that there was a ceremony in the Temple that occurred beginning on the second night of Sukkot, and every subsequent night of Chol Hamoed. Everyone gathered in the Temple, and they set up lights all over. There were a large candelabras of gold set up in the Temple. They made a grand ceremony about lighting it. All of Jerusalem was filled with lights – all the streets, all the courtyards – and there was much dancing. It was said that whomever has not witnessed this event has not seen true happiness. Many people today recreate a שִׂמְחַת בֵּית הַשּׁוֹאֵבָה in memory of this event with singing, dancing and feasting.

שְׁמִינִי עֲצֶרֶת

The holiday of Shemini Atzeret is full of contradictions. Is it part of Sukkot? Or is it its own holiday, a רֶגֶל בִּפְנֵי עַצְמוֹ?

In Vayikra chapter 23, we find the definition of the holiday of Sukkot, lasting seven days. The first day is defined as a מִקְרָא־קֹדֶשׁ, on which creative work is prohibited: בַּיּוֹם הָרִאשׁוֹן מִקְרָא קֹדֶשׁ כָּל־מְלֶאכֶת עֲבֹדָה לֹא תַעֲשׂוּ.[48] We are commanded to bring sacrifices for the seven days of the holiday, and then another day is added at the end of the verse: שִׁבְעַת יָמִים תַּקְרִיבוּ אִשֶּׁה לַיי בַּיּוֹם הַשְּׁמִינִי מִקְרָא־קֹדֶשׁ יִהְיֶה לָכֶם וְהִקְרַבְתֶּם אִשֶּׁה לַיי עֲצֶרֶת הִוא כָּל־מְלֶאכֶת עֲבֹדָה לֹא תַעֲשׂוּ.[49] On the eighth day of this seven-day

44. ישיעה סג:ט
45. תהלים צא:טו; Also see תענית טז ע׳ א ובמגילה יט ע׳ א
46. אוצר התפילות עמ׳ א׳ מסדר הושענות
47. סוכה דף נא עמוד א
48. ויקרא כג:ז
49. ויקרא כג:לו

holiday, we again have a מִקְרָא־קֹדֶשׁ, and we again bring a sacrifice and are prohibited from doing creative work. What does it mean to have an eighth day of a seven-day holiday?

The Midrash explains[50] that Hashem added an additional day to the holiday in order to have the Jewish people remain with Him, as their departure was difficult for him: קָשֶׁה עָלַי פְּרֵדַתְכֶם.

In this description, it appears that Shemini Atzeret is simply an additional day of the holiday of Sukkot. However, the Torah records one way in which Shemini Atzeret is entirely different and separate from Sukkot – in the sacrifices that are offered. Over the seven days of Sukkot, there is a descending series of sacrifices, as described in the book of Bamidbar,[51] and as mentioned in the Musaf davening. On the first day, thirteen bulls are brought, along with two rams and fourteen lambs. While the number of rams and lambs remains constant all seven days, the number of bulls decreases by one every day until the seventh day, when seven bulls are brought. If Shemini Atzeret were simply a continuation of Sukkot, we would expect to bring six bulls, two rams, and fourteen lambs. However, on Shemini Atzeret, one bull, one ram, and seven lambs are offered – in other words, it is not part of the series at all.[52] In fact, this set of sacrifices is much more similar to the sacrifices brought on Rosh Hashanah[53] than to the Sukkot offerings. From this we see that Shemini Atzeret is a separate holiday, a רֶגֶל בִּפְנֵי עַצְמוֹ.

The Talmud in Tractate Sukkah 48a lists six aspects of our observance that indicate that Shemini Atzeret is a separate holiday.[54]

1. פַּיִס: In the Beit Hamikdash, the assignment of the Kohanim to the Temple service was done by a lottery, and the Shemini Atzeret lottery was separate from that of Sukkot.

---

50. רש״י ויקרא פרשת אמור כג:לו
51. במדבר כט:יג-לד
52. במדבר כט:לה-לח
53. See the section on Blowing the Shofar in the יָמִים נוֹרָאִים chapter.
54. These are abbreviated as פז״ר קש״ב. Rashi explains each term.

2. זְמַן: We recite the שֶׁהֶחֱיָנוּ blessing on Shemini Atzeret, which we don't do, for example, on the last days of Pesach.
3. רֶגֶל: Rashi explains this to mean that Shemini Atzeret does not share the mitzvah of sukkah with the previous seven days.[55]
4. קָרְבָּן: As mentioned before, the Shemini Atzeret sacrifices are separate from those of Sukkot. Avudraham explains[56] that the total of seventy bulls offered over the seven days of Sukkot represent the seventy nations of the world, while the single bull offered on Shemini Atzeret represents the singular nation of Israel.
5. שִׁיר: The psalm sung by the Levi'im in the Beit Hamikdash was different for Shemini Atzeret.
6. בְּרָכָה: This may refer to the fact that we refer to Shemini Atzeret separately in the davening, or it may refer to the fact that the nation of Israel gathered together and were blessed by the king on Shemini Atzeret.

There is a difference of opinion about how to refer to Shemini Atzeret in the davening. The majority opinion, which includes Rashi,[57] R. Yosef Karo,[58] and the Vilna Gaon,[59] is that it is called שְׁמִינִי חַג הָעֲצֶרֶת הַזֶּה. The Rama[60] differs slightly from this, saying that we should just say שְׁמִינִי הָעֲצֶרֶת הַזֶּה because it is not referred to as a חַג in the Torah. And the Magen Avraham has a different order of words,[61] calling it שְׁמִינִי עֲצֶרֶת הַחַג הַזֶּה.

The Torah readings for the different holidays are listed in the

55. Tosafot (ראש השנה דף ד עמוד ב; סוכה דף מח עמוד א) give another explanation: If a person is in mourning for a relative before Sukkot, Shemini Atzeret reduces the 30-day mourning period (*sheloshim*) by an entire week. Sukkot reduces the *sheloshim* by a week, and Shemini Atzeret reduces it by an additional week.
56. ספר אבודרהם יום שמיני ושמחת תורה
57. רש"י סוכה דף מו עמ' ב ושמיני לברכה
58. שולחן ערוך אורח חיים סי' תרסח סעי' א
59. Quoted in the משנה ברורה סימן תרסח ס"ק ג.
60. שולחן ערוך אורח חיים סי' תרסח סעי' א
61. מגן אברהם סימן תרסח ס"ק א

Talmud.[62] It says that on Shemini Atzeret we read from Devarim chapter 14, starting with כָּל הַבְּכוֹר, as we do on the last day of Pesach. Rashi changes that slightly,[63] saying that we start earlier, at עַשֵּׂר תְּעַשֵּׂר, because this section talks about the fall season, which is relevant to this holiday. This is what we do. The Haftarah is from מְלָכִים א פרק ח, which discusses the blessing of the king for the nation.[64] However, in Israel, the reading of Shemini Atzeret is replaced with Parshat Vezot Haberachah, because Simchat Torah and Shemini Atzeret are all one holiday in Israel.

In the Musaf of Shemini Atzeret we recite the prayer for rain.[65] This is another indication that this holiday is separate from Sukkot, because we specifically don't pray for rain on Sukkot so that rain will not prevent us from eating in the sukkah.

Outside of Israel, many people eat in the sukkah on Shemini Atzeret, another reminder of how ambiguous this holiday is. The reason for eating in the sukkah is the question of whether the day is Shemini Atzeret or actually the seventh day of Sukkot. The Gemara tells us that on Shemini Atzeret we should eat in the sukkah but not recite the blessing. The Avudraham poses the question:[66] if you are going to eat in the sukkah because of the doubt, why do you not also take the lulav and etrog without a blessing? He explains that the mitzvah of sitting in the sukkah is דְּאוֹרָיְיתָא all seven days of the holiday, making it important to perform in cases of doubt. However, the mitzvah of lulav is only mandated in the Torah for the first day of the holiday. All other days, we do it because in commemoration of what was done in the Beit Hamikdash. As it is not a דְּאוֹרָיְיתָא, it does not need to be performed out of doubt.

Outside of Israel, the holidays of Simchat Torah and Shemini

---

62. מגילה דף לא עמ׳ א

63. רש״י מגילה דף לא עמ׳ א קורין כל הבכור

64. The Haftarah of Simchat Torah in the diaspora is read on Shemini Atzeret in Israel, where Simchat Torah and Shemini Atzeret are the same day.

65. שולחן ערוך אורח חיים סי׳ תרסח סעי׳ ב

66. ספר אבודרהם יום שמיני ושמחת תורה

Atzeret are celebrated on consecutive days. In Israel, the holiday of Simchat Torah is combined with the holiday of Shemini Atzeret and celebrated on the same day. Simchat Torah is not mentioned in the Torah or the Talmud, although its Torah reading is mentioned as the reading for the second day of Shemini Atzeret. The practices of Simchat Torah as we know them started in the time of the Geonim.[67] Simchat Torah is the only time that we read the Torah at night, and there is never an explanation given as to why we do this.

The הַקָּפוֹת, the processions around the bimah, are not mentioned in the Talmud. They are first mentioned by Rabbi Isaac Tyrnau in the 14th–15th century. We do these on Simchat Torah evening and day. Chasidim also do them on the evening of Shemini Atzeret. The הַקָּפוֹת are similar to the הוֹשַׁעֲנוֹת done on Hoshana Rabbah, where we circle the bimah with all the Torahs from the ark seven times.

The person who is called to the aliyah for the last eight sentences in the Torah is called Chatan Torah; this is considered a great honor. Immediately after finishing the end of the Torah, we start over with the reading of the beginning of Bereishit. The person called to that aliyah is called Chatan Bereishit, also a great honor. We begin the Torah immediately to show that we are not only happy to finish the Torah but also to start it again.[68]

The Haftarah is from the first chapter of the book of יְהוֹשֻׁעַ, the first book of the prophets. It is almost a continuation of the end of the Torah.

---

67. ספר החילוקים בין בני מזרח ומערב סימן מח

68. רמ"א אורח חיים סי' תרסט סעי' א

הַגָּדָה שֶׁל פֶּסַח

יְצִיאַת מִצְרַיִם (the Exodus from Egypt) is one of the most important events in Jewish history. This event was so significant that God made it a commandment to remember it daily.[1] This affects other mitzvot as well. For example, the Rambam says:[2] "Even though the mitzvah of tzitzit is not observed at night, we recite the paragraph about tzitzit at night because it mentions the Exodus from Egypt, and there is a commandment to mention the Exodus from Egypt both during the day and during the night." The Gemara says that we must mention the Exodus from Egypt when we recite Kiddush.[3] And the most obvious mitzvah related to the Exodus from Egypt is the seder on Pesach.[4]

IN EVERY GENERATION

The seder that we observe is quite old, and has changed remarkably little through the generations. The Gemara[5] tells us that: בְּכָל דּוֹר וָדוֹר חַיָּב אָדָם לִרְאוֹת אֶת עַצְמוֹ כְּאִלּוּ הוּא יָצָא מִמִּצְרַיִם ("In every generation one is obliged to imagine that he himself actually left Egypt"). The Rambam takes it one step further and says a person must demonstrate that it

1. רמב"ם הלכות קריאת שמע פרק א הלכה ג. It is also a fulfillment of the Divine covenant made with Avraham in בראשית טו:יג,יד,טז
2. רמב"ם שם
3. פסחים קיז
4. Rashi on דברים טז:ג
5. פסחים קטז עמ' ב

is as if he personally was released from the slavery of Egypt. The goal of the seder is to enable us to achieve this feeling.[6]

MITZVOT OF THE SEDER

Matzah

Eating matzah on the night of the 15th of Nissan is a mitzvah from the Torah.[7] By eating a כְּזַיִת (the volume of an olive)[8] of matzah one fulfills the requirement.

Telling the Story of יְצִיאַת מִצְרַיִם

There is another mitzvah from the Torah to tell the story of יְצִיאַת מִצְרַיִם on the night of the fifteenth of Nissan.[9] In addition, as part of the mitzvah of telling the story of the Exodus, one must express thanks and praise to God for His taking us out of Egypt. The recitation of Hallel at the seder fulfills this element of the mitzvah.[10] Rav Soloveitchik explained that this is an integral part of the mitzvah of telling the story.

Since סִיפּוּר יְצִיאַת מִצְרַיִם is a mitzvah, we could ask why we don't recite a berachah over it. Rav Soloveitchik said that whenever the mitzvah itself consists of or contains a berachah, such as בִּרְכַּת הַמָּזוֹן, there is no בִּרְכַּת הַמִּצְוָה beforehand. In this case, the mitzvah of סִיפּוּר יְצִיאַת מִצְרַיִם is framed by the berachot of Kiddush beforehand and אֲשֶׁר גְּאָלָנוּ ("who redeemed us") afterward, so there is no בִּרְכַּת הַמִּצְוָה needed.[11]

---

6. רמב"ם הלכות חמץ ומצה פרק ז הל' ו'
7. רמב"ם הלכות חמץ ומצה פרק ו, הלכה א
8. It is a small amount and the minimum amount that is considered eating. משנה כלים פרק יז משנה ח and ברכות דף לט עמ' א.
9. הלכות חמץ ומצה פרק ז, הלכה א
10. See רשימות שיעורים ברכות דף יב עמוד ב: - בגדר מצות זכירת יצ"מ וסיפור יציאת מצרים.
11. From an email response of his grandson, Rabbi Mayer Twersky.

קָרְבַּן פֶּסַח

There are two more performances that will apply to the seder when the Temple service in Jerusalem is reinstituted. These observances are: eating the קָרְבַּן פֶּסַח and eating the קָרְבַּן חֲגִיגָה שֶׁל אַרְבָּעָה עָשָׂר (korban chagigah of the fourteenth of Nissan). The Gemara describes them, though today we only have vestiges of them that appear on the seder plate.

The קָרְבַּן פֶּסַח is a mitzvah that is performed for a prearranged group of people who share the meat of the sacrifice at the seder together.[12] The קָרְבַּן פֶּסַח must be sacrificed on the Temple mount on the fourteenth of Nissan and must be eaten that night before midnight. It can only be eaten in Jerusalem.[13] It must be roasted whole and eaten together with the maror and the matzah.[14] Its bones should not be broken. If we can't fulfill the mitzvah of קָרְבַּן פֶּסַח this year, we should have a broiled food on the seder plate to remind us of this korban.

There were two sacrifices called קָרְבַּן חֲגִיגָה related to Pesach. The korban chagigah of the fourteenth of Nissan and the regular קָרְבַּן חֲגִיגָה. The regular חֲגִיגָה had nothing to do with the seder ceremony. This sacrifice was offered to fulfill a separate mitzvah from the Torah. A קָרְבַּן חֲגִיגָה was offered on each of the major holidays, including Pesach. The קָרְבַּן חֲגִיגָה for Pesach was usually sacrificed on the first day possible which was the fifteenth of Nissan, though it could be brought until the end of Pesach. This קָרְבַּן חֲגִיגָה was eaten on the holiday as part of a regular holiday celebration.

On Pesach, though, there was another sacrifice, known as the חֲגִיגָה of the fourteenth, which was sacrificed with the קָרְבַּן פֶּסַח on the fourteenth day of Nissan. This was eaten at the seder before the קָרְבַּן פֶּסַח. The korban chagigah of the fourteenth of Nissan was established because there is a requirement to eat the קָרְבַּן פֶּסַח on a full stomach, and not break any of the korban's bones.[15] This חֲגִיגָה was eaten before

---

12. רמב"ם הלכות קרבן פסח פרק ט הלכה א
13. רמב"ם הלכות קרבן פסח פרק ד הל' ג
14. הלכות קרבן פסח פרק ח הלכה א
15. פסחים דף סט עמוד ב - ע עמוד א

the קָרְבַּן פֶּסַח, and enabled the קָרְבַּן פֶּסַח to be eaten when a person was satiated. This also reduced the likelihood of breaking the bones of the קָרְבַּן פֶּסַח. If we can't fulfill the mitzvah of קָרְבַּן פֶּסַח this year, we will have another broiled food on the seder plate to remind us of the korban chagigah of the fourteenth of Nissan.[16]

The Mishnah says that at the seder we should have the vegetable for dipping, the charoset, the matzah, the maror and two cooked foods to remind us of the קָרְבַּן פֶּסַח and the קָרְבַּן חֲגִיגָה.[17] The kinds of cooked foods that we use to symbolize these korbanot differ according to custom. As far as the actual practice, you should follow the minhag of your family.

Maror

When there is a Temple in Jerusalem, then there is a mitzvah to bring a קָרְבַּן פֶּסַח on the 14th day of Nissan, and eat the korban on the eve of the 15th of Nissan (at night) together with matzah and maror.[18] When there is no Temple, and therefore no קָרְבַּן פֶּסַח, maror is not a mitzvah from the Torah yet remains a Rabbinic mitzvah, and we must eat it.

OTHER ASPECTS OF THE SEDER

The seder must begin as soon as possible after nightfall, when the קָרְבַּן פֶּסַח may be eaten.[19] After all, we hope to be able to offer the קָרְבַּן פֶּסַח again, and a person must feel as if reliving the original Pesach. In light of this, the Shulchan Aruch instructs us to set the table beforehand, but not start the seder until dark.[20]

Hallel after Maariv in Shul

There is one custom that could delay the start of the seder a bit.

---

16. פסחים דף קיד עמ׳ ב
17. פסחים דף קיד עמוד א
18. פסחים דף קכ עמוד א
19. See תוספות פסחים דף צט עמוד ב ד״ה עד שתחשך.
20. שולחן ערוך אורח חיים סימן תעב סעיף א

Masechet Sofrim[21] quotes Rabbi Shimon ben Yehotzadak listing the days on which we recite the complete Hallel, and this list includes the night of Pesach. Some authorities, including the Shulchan Aruch,[22] maintain that Hallel should be recited before the seder in the synagogue. During the seder, we do not recite a berachah for Hallel since Hallel is split into two parts. But if one recites Hallel with a berachah in shul, it is not necessary to recite the berachah in his home because he already recited it in shul beforehand. The Rama says that we don't say Hallel in shul at all on the eve of the seder.

Rav Soloveitchik[23] gave a different explanation for why some recite Hallel twice on the night of the seder, in shul and at home. On the night of the seder, there is a double requirement to recite Hallel: because of the קָרְבַּן פֶּסַח and the mitzvah of סִפּוּר יְצִיאַת מִצְרַיִם on the one hand, and because of the obligation to recite Hallel on Yom Tov on the other hand. This obligation includes the night as well as the the following day. The Rav further explained that reciting Hallel in shul on the night of the seder has the following advantages:

- It is a distinct Hallel for the holiday of Pesach, which is separate from the Hallel of סִפּוּר יְצִיאַת מִצְרַיִם.
- It allows us to publicize the miracle in a way that we cannot do at home (פִּרְסוּם הַנֵּס).
- Reciting Hallel in shul allows us to recite the berachah that we cannot recite at the seder because of the interruption in that Hallel.

הֲסִיבָה – Leaning to the Left Side

The Gemara tells us that one of the ways of demonstrating our feelings of freedom at the seder is through הֲסִיבָה (leaning to the left side). Rashi explains[24] that this is the manner of free people. The Rambam

21. מסכת סופרים פרק כ הלכה ז
22. שולחן ערוך אורח חיים סימן תפז סעיף ד
23. See *Shiurim Lezecher Abba Mari*, vol. 1, p. 15; Rav Yitzchak Abba Lichtenstein, *Haggadah Siach HaGrid*, sections 71–72 (עמ׳ פט-צב).
24. רש״י ד״ה אפילו עני שבישראל לא יאכל, פסחים דף צט עמוד ב

summarizes the mitzvah of הֲסִיבָּה:[25] "When do we need to lean? When we eat the כְּזַיִת (volume of an olive) of matzah and when we drink these four cups [of wine]. As far as the rest of the eating and drinking, if you lean, it is praiseworthy, but if you don't, it is not necessary." The Shulchan Aruch adds that when eating the Korech matzah together with the bitter vegetable one also needs to lean.[26]

Women at the Seder

Even though they are time-bound mitzvot, women are obligated to fulfill all the mitzvot of the seder.[27] The seder is a means of thanking and praising God for saving us and for appreciating His acts of grace. Even though women are generally exempt from Hallel, the Hallel at the seder is an exception. Here it seems that a woman has the same level of obligation to recite Hallel, both before and after the meal, as does a man.

Rabbi Avira stated[28] that the Israelites were taken out of Egypt as a reward for the righteous women of that generation who brought food and encouragement to their husbands in the fields. They stood up to Pharaoh and did not kill the male Jewish babies. And when God saved the Jews on the shores of the sea, the women were the first to recognize Him.

Keeping the Children's Interest

There are a number of practices whose purpose is specifically to stimulate the interest of the children in what is occurring during the seder. We have activities for the children; we encourage the children to ask questions; and while we can't begin the seder until nightfall, we nevertheless try to not overly delay the beginning. One example of a practice intended to keep the children's interest is letting the children

---

25. רמב״ם הלכות חמץ ומצה פרק ז הל׳ ח
26. שולחן ערוך אורח חיים סימן תעה סעיף א
27. שולחן ערוך אורח חיים סימן תעב סעיף יד
28. סוטה דף יא עמוד ב

steal the afikomen.[29] Another activity which is intended to pique the children's curiosity is how, at certain points in the seder, we remove the seder plate from its normal position.[30] The Karpas, the vegetables which we dip before the meal, was introduced for this reason also.

In fact, pouring the second cup at this point in the seder serves this purpose as well. The Shulchan Aruch says that we pour the second cup of wine before the מַה נִּשְׁתַּנָּה so that the children will ask why are we drinking a second cup of wine before the meal when we normally do not do so.[31] The Mishnah Berurah explains that by pouring a second cup of wine now, it will stimulate the children to ask other questions about all the strange things they notice about this night.[32]

The Beit Yosef[33] quotes the Kol Bo, saying that some sections appear in the vernacular so people not versed in the Hebrew can understand.

FOUR CUPS OF WINE

The Talmud requires drinking four cups of wine during the seder; each cup is drunk over a separate mitzvah.[34] Everyone is required to drink the cups of wine, including women and children who are old enough to understand.[35] The Yerushalmi,[36] quoted by Rashi, explains the source of our drinking four cups at the seder:

- Rabbi Yochanan in the name of Rabbi Benayya says that the four cups correspond to the four terms expressing redemption in the two verses (Exodus 6:6–7)[37]: "Therefore say to the children of

29. פסחים קט עמוד א
30. פסחים דף קטו עמוד ב
31. שולחן ערוך אורח חיים הלכות פסח סימן תעג סעיף ז
32. משנה ברורה שם ס"ק סט
33. בית יוסף אורח חיים סימן תעג
34. פסחים דף קיז עמוד ב
35. פסחים דף קח עמוד ב
36. ירושלמי פסחים פרק י הלכה א
37. ו) לָכֵן אֱמֹר לִבְנֵי־יִשְׂרָאֵל אֲנִי ה׳ וְהוֹצֵאתִי אֶתְכֶם מִתַּחַת סִבְלֹת מִצְרַיִם וְהִצַּלְתִּי אֶתְכֶם

Israel, "I am God, and I will **bring you out** (וְהוֹצֵאתִי) from the suffering of Egypt, and I will **save you** (וְהִצַּלְתִּי) from their work demands, and I will **redeem you** (וְגָאַלְתִּי) with an outstretched arm and with great judgements. And I will **take you** (וְלָקַחְתִּי) for Me as a nation and I will be for you a sovereign, and you will know that I am your Sovereign who took you out of the suffering in Egypt."

- Rabbi Yehoshua ben Levi says that the four cups correspond to the four times that "cup" is mentioned in connection with Pharaoh in Genesis 40.
- Rabbi Levi says that they correspond to the four times that foreign governments (Persia, Media, Greece and Edom) ruled us.
- The Rabbis say that they correspond to the four calamities that God will bring upon the nations of the world in the future. Rabbi Avin adds that in consequence of those, God will provide Israel with four cups of comfort (which is a specific reference to God's bringing redemption to the Jews).

Fifth Cup of Wine

Our version of the Talmud only mentions four cups of wine.[38] The Gemara states: "The Rabbis taught: On the fourth cup, finish reciting the Hallel, and recite the הַלֵּל הַגָּדוֹל on it. These are the words of Rabbi Tarfon." The Rif has a different version of this text. In his text, הַלֵּל הַגָּדוֹל is recited over a fifth cup according to Rabbi Tarfon. The textual basis for this fifth cup comes in the verse that follows the source for the other four cups, Exodus 6:8:[39] "And I will **bring you** (וְהֵבֵאתִי) to the land that I promised to give to Abraham, Isaac and Jacob." וְהֵבֵאתִי is a fifth term expressing redemption.

The Rambam mentions the fifth cup as well: "And one can pour

מֵעֲבֹדָתָם וְגָאַלְתִּי אֶתְכֶם בִּזְרוֹעַ נְטוּיָה וּבִשְׁפָטִים גְּדֹלִים

ז) וְלָקַחְתִּי אֶתְכֶם לִי לְעָם וְהָיִיתִי לָכֶם לֵאלֹקִים וִידַעְתֶּם כִּי אֲנִי ה׳ אֱלֹקֵיכֶם הַמּוֹצִיא אֶתְכֶם מִתַּחַת סִבְלוֹת מִצְרָיִם

38. פסחים דף קיז עמ׳ ב - קי״ח עמ׳ א

39. וְהֵבֵאתִי אֶתְכֶם אֶל־הָאָרֶץ אֲשֶׁר נָשָׂאתִי אֶת־יָדִי לָתֵת אֹתָהּ לְאַבְרָהָם לְיִצְחָק וּלְיַעֲקֹב

a fifth cup and recite over it הַלֵּל הַגָּדוֹל...and this cup is not obligatory like the other cups."[40] This seems to be the opinion of many Rishonim.

The Netziv in his commentary Ha'amek Davar[41] explains that the four cups represent the process of the Jews transitioning from being slaves to free people who can devote themselves by their free will to God. The first cup represents the beginning of the process where the Jews physically stopped being slaves and the fourth cup represents the stage of being ready to become God's people. The fifth cup, according to the Netziv, corresponds to a higher level of spiritual achievement that not everyone can attain. Therefore, the fifth cup is optional but not mandatory. However, there are also reasons for not drinking a fifth cup.

Drinking Extra Wine during the סֵדֶר

The Tur[42] mentions two concerns about drinking extra cups of wine: First, one may not eat after the afikoman. Perhaps this also includes drinking wine unnecessarily. In addition, the Tosefta[43] states that one should stay up as long as one can studying the laws of Pesach. Drinking an extra cup of wine will impede one's ability to do so. The Shulchan Aruch states only that one may not drink wine after the four cups, although the Rama adds that one who has a strong desire to drink a fifth cup of wine may recite הַלֵּל הַגָּדוֹל over it and drink it.[44]

The four cups are drunk throughout the seder when completing four mitzvot:

- Kiddush is recited over the first cup.
- We tell the story of the Exodus over the second cup.
- Birkat Hamazon is recited over the third cup.

---

40. רמב"ם הלכות חמץ ומצה פרק ח הל' י'
41. שמות פרק ו פסוק ו-ז
42. אורח חיים סימן תפא
43. סוף מסכת פסחים
44. שולחן ערוך ורמ"א אורח חיים סימן תפא

- Hallel (except the first two paragraphs, recited earlier) is recited over the fourth cup.

THE FIRST CUP: KIDDUSH

On an ordinary Shabbat, one can recite Kiddush earlier than its official time, thereby adding on to Shabbat.[45] However, on Pesach we have to wait for dark before we begin Kiddush.[46]

Kiddush at the seder is usually a straightforward event. There can, however, be additions to it if Pesach falls out on Shabbat or just after Shabbat.

If Pesach falls out on Shabbat, then we add the paragraph of וַיְכֻלּוּ[47] to the beginning of the Kiddush. We also add the phrases that mention Shabbat to the regular text of the Kiddush for Yom Tov. The mention of Shabbat is necessary because Kiddush must reflect the special character of the day.

When Pesach falls out just after Shabbat, we have to announce that Shabbat is over by making הַבְדָּלָה in the Kiddush.[48] We use an existing flame for a הַבְדָּלָה candle and recite the berachah of בּוֹרֵא מְאוֹרֵי הָאֵשׁ. On a holiday we also have an extra allotment of holiness that accompanies us on this day, just like on Shabbat, so the berachah over spices is unnecessary.[49] We still have to express our gratitude for being able to reach this special occasion and being able to enjoy the closeness to God on a holiday like this. The berachah of שֶׁהֶחֱיָנוּ, referred to as זְמַן (time), accomplishes that.

Our practice of reciting Kiddush today follows the opinion of Rav in the Gemara about the order of reciting the Kiddush elements. The formula is to recite the berachot in this order: יַיִן (the berachah over wine), קִדּוּשׁ, נֵר (light), הַבְדָּלָה and שֶׁהֶחֱיָנוּ (זְמַן). This is abbreviated in Hebrew as: יקנה״ז.

---

45. רמב״ם הלכות שבת פרק כט הלכה יא
46. בית יוסף אורח חיים סימן תעב ס״ק ב
47. בראשית ב:א-ג
48. פסחים דף קב עמוד ב
49. רשב״ם פסחים דף קב עמוד ב ד״ה ושמואל

KARPAS

Karpas[50] is often translated as celery, but is actually any vegetable[51] over which one says a berachah of בּוֹרֵא פְּרִי הָאֲדָמָה.[52] Before we eat the karpas, we pour water over our hands and dry them but do not recite the berachah of עַל נְטִילַת יָדַיִם that we usually recite when we pour water over our hands for food. Then we dip the karpas vegetable in salt water[53] or vinegar.[54] The Rambam[55] requires dipping the karpas in חֲרֹסֶת to remind us of the mortar our ancestors used as slaves, as he does any dipping requirement of the seder. The Rashbam[56] and Tosafot[57] disagree with the Rambam because the karpas does not commemorate slavery as the maror does.

We know from the Gemara that the reason for the karpas is to awaken the children's curiosity about what is happening at the seder and encourage them to ask questions. Today, karpas as a question stimulator is just as relevant, but the children will probably ask questions for entirely different reasons. That enables us to fulfill the mitzvah of telling them how God took us out of Egypt.

What our children will notice is probably that we usually wash over bread and here we wash over a vegetable. When we wash, we usually say a berachah of עַל נְטִילַת יָדַיִם. Here we wash and don't say עַל נְטִילַת יָדַיִם. Maybe some children will question why here we eat so

---

50. Some sources say that the word כַּרְפַּס symbolizes the hard work (פֶּרֶךְ) that 600,000 Jews suffered (ס in gematria is sixty. Sixty times 10,000 is 600,000).

51. The Mishnah Berurah (סימן תעג ס״ק כ) says that we should use a food that has the same berachah as the maror that is eaten later in the seder, but it is preferable not to use a type of bitter herb for the karpas.

52. שלחן ערוך, אורח חיים סי׳ תעג סעי׳ ד

53. If the seder falls out on Friday night, the salt water should be prepared before Shabbat. If you didn't, you could still mix it once the seder starts because it is needed for the seder. מגן אברהם סימן תעג ס״ק ה, ט״ז אורח חיים סימן תעג ס״ק ג

54. שולחן ערוך אורח חיים סימן תעג סעיף ו

55. רמב״ם הלכות חמץ ומצה פרק ח הלכה ב

56. רשב״ם פסחים דף קיד עמוד א ד״ה מטבל בחזרת

57. תוספות שם ד״ה מטבל

little. And finally, our children might be used to saying a final berachah after eating something that is not a part of a meal. Here we do not. There are potentially a lot of questions. The challenge is how to relate them to the seder narrative.

Why do we wash our hands before we dip and eat the karpas? Originally, in the time when we offered sacrifices, people were very careful about טוּמְאָה that was on a person's hands and that could affect the status of food. The Gemara[58] says that you need to perform נְטִילַת יָדַיִם before you dip things in liquid so your hands won't convey טוּמְאָה to the food. But today, we are no longer concerned about טוּמְאָה. The Taz explains that as a result, we generally don't wash our hands before we dip food. If we did, the washing would be obligatory, and would require a berachah. Today, we wash our hands as a reminder of what we once did. Therefore, we wash our hands and don't make a berachah before we dip the karpas in the salt water. And this could cause the children to ask why we are doing things differently tonight.[59]

Now we must wonder why we eat less than a כְּזַיִת (the volume of an olive) of the karpas. We only have to eat enough to stimulate the questions of the children. If we eat a כְּזַיִת we would have to say a berachah after it. We don't want to say a berachah after it, because there is a question about whether the maror needs its own berachah. When we eat the karpas, we have in mind to exempt the maror as well, which would not work if we make a berachah after the karpas. However, if we eat less than a כְּזַיִת of karpas, while we would have to say a berachah beforehand, we will not be required to say a berachah afterwards. Since we do not recite a berachah afterward,[60] the berachah that we recite before eating the karpas also serves as the berachah for the maror, since there is a doubt about whether it requires its own berachah.

58. פסחים דף קטו עמוד א

59. ט"ז אורח חיים סימן תעג ס"ק ז

60. שולחן ערוך אורח חיים, סימן תעג, סעיף ו

NUMBER OF MATZOS - יַחַץ

After we eat the karpas, we take the middle matzah of the three that are on the seder plate and break it in two. This is called יַחַץ. We put aside one piece for the afikoman and place the other piece between the other two whole matzot. The order in which we perform the breaking of the matzah, long before saying Hamotzi, is described by the Tur.[61]

לֶחֶם עֹנִי and לֶחֶם מִשְׁנֶה

The reason for having two loaves on Shabbat is because, referring to the manna, the Torah says that God gave to the Jews in the desert: לֶחֶם מִשְׁנֶה – a double portion of bread.[62] This is also true on Yom Tov.[63]

Does this requirement apply at the seder? At this point, we need to understand what the matzah symbolizes. The Torah calls it לֶחֶם עֹנִי.[64] What exactly does that mean? There are three possibilities:[65]

- עֹנִי means poverty. In that case we still don't know from the Hebrew construction whether we are saying that (1) the bread (לֶחֶם) is poor, or that (2) it is a poor man's bread.
- Another possibility is that the word עֹנִי could have a different source. It could come from the word ענה, meaning to recite. Then (3) לֶחֶם עֹנִי means the bread over which we recite many things.

All three interpretations of these words have halachic ramifications. The matzah that we eat at the seder must be made with water, and not oil or honey or milk, because the bread itself must be "poor."[66] Additionally, we break the matzah, because it is the way of a poor person to eat broken pieces of bread. According to the Rambam, this

61. טור אורח חיים סימן תעג
62. שמות טז:כב
63. שולחן ערוך אורח חיים סימן תקכט סעיף א
64. דברים טז:ג
65. פסחים דף קטו עמ׳ ב – קטז עמ׳ א
66. רמב״ם הלכות חמץ ומצה פרק ה הלכה כ

requirement overrides the usual requirement of לֶחֶם מִשְׁנֶה on Yom Tov.[67] According to others, however, we fulfill both requirements by starting with three matzot. Even after we break one to fulfill the requirement of לֶחֶם עֹנִי, we are left with two whole matzot for the requirement of לֶחֶם מִשְׁנֶה.[68] Regarding the third meaning of לֶחֶם עֹנִי, "bread over which we recite many things," that is why we keep the matzah on the table when we recite the Haggadah.[69]

מַגִּיד - THE SECOND CUP OF WINE

The Mishnah describes the part of the seder that revolves around the second cup of wine: Pour the second cup of wine and ask the four questions. The Rambam understands that the four questions are actually an introduction to the telling of the Exodus and the beginning of the mitzvah of סִפּוּר יְצִיאַת מִצְרַיִם. The questions involve the children in this mitzvah.[70]

The Four Questions: מַה נִּשְׁתַּנָּה

The first three questions are: מַה נִּשְׁתַּנָּה הַלַּיְלָה הַזֶּה מִכָּל הַלֵּילוֹת? "What is different about this night from all other nights?" שֶׁבְּכָל הַלֵּילוֹת אָנוּ אוֹכְלִין חָמֵץ וּמַצָּה, הַלַּיְלָה הַזֶּה - כֻּלּוֹ מַצָּה. "On all other nights we eat chametz and matzah, and on this night only matzah." שֶׁבְּכָל הַלֵּילוֹת אָנוּ אוֹכְלִין שְׁאָר יְרָקוֹת - הַלַּיְלָה הַזֶּה (כֻּלּוֹ) מָרוֹר. "On all other nights we eat other kinds of vegetables, this night (only) bitter vegetables." שֶׁבְּכָל הַלֵּילוֹת אֵין אָנוּ מַטְבִּילִין אֲפִלּוּ פַּעַם אַחַת - הַלַּיְלָה הַזֶּה שְׁתֵּי פְעָמִים. "On all other nights we don't dip the vegetables even once before we eat them, this night we dip twice."

The fourth question was different in the time of the Beit Hamikdash from what it is today. The Mishnah records the fourth question as: שֶׁבְּכָל הַלֵּילוֹת אָנוּ אוֹכְלִין בָּשָׂר צָלִי שָׁלוּק וּמְבֻשָּׁל הַלַּיְלָה הַזֶּה כֻּלּוֹ צָלִי, "On all

67. ביאור הגר"א אורח חיים סימן תעג ס"ק יא; see also הלכות חמץ ומצה פרק ח הלכה ו.
68. משנה ברורה סימן תעג ס"ק יח; שולחן ערוך אורח חיים סימן תעג סעיף ד
69. See שולחן ערוך ורמ"א סימן תעג סעיף ז; משנה ברורה שם ס"ק עו.
70. רמב"ם הלכות חמץ ומצה פרק ז הלכה ג

other nights we eat roast, cooked or stew meat, but on this night only roasted." Today we replace that question with: שֶׁבְּכָל הַלֵּילוֹת אָנוּ אוֹכְלִין בֵּין יוֹשְׁבִין וּבֵין מְסֻבִּין - הַלַּיְלָה הַזֶּה כֻּלָּנוּ מְסֻבִּין, "On all other nights, we eat either sitting or reclining, this night we all recline."

The Mishnah continues that we have to answer according to the capabilities of the child to understand.

The Gemara says that if the child is wise, then the son asks, but if not, then his wife asks the questions, and if that is not possible, he asks himself. Furthermore, even if there are just two people at the seder, and they both know the answers, they still have to ask the מַה נִּשְׁתַּנָּה of each other.

Rav Menachem M. Kasher addresses[71] the differing number of questions. He says that while it seems that four is a special number in the haggadah, maybe this is not the case regarding מַה נִּשְׁתַּנָּה. Possibly, in the time when there was a Temple and a קָרְבַּן פֶּסַח, there was still a question about הֲסִיבָה as well as a question about the קָרְבַּן פֶּסַח. Rav Kasher suggests that there is another meaning for the word הֲסִיבָה. It could come from the word סָב (surround), as when everyone sat around together in a defined group (מְסֻבִּין) to eat the Pesach sacrifice. Later, when we could no longer eat the sacrifice together, the term took on the meaning of reclining, but even before reclining became a formal obligation, they asked this question: Why on this night are we all מְסֻבִּין, meaning, why are we eating the Pesach sacrifice together in one group?

Start with Disgrace and End with Glory

We begin the answer with a description of how the history of the Jewish people מַתְחִיל בִּגְנוּת (began in a humiliating circumstance), וּמְסַיֵּם בְּשֶׁבַח (and we end the account with the glory of the Jewish people now). Explaining the above mentioned Mishnah, the Gemara[72] describes the dialogue between parent and child. Rav says that מַתְחִיל

71. הגדה שלמה מאת הרב מנחם מ. כשר מהדורה שלישית הוצאת מכון תורה שלמה ירושלים תשכ"ז עמ' 115–116 הלילה הזה כולנו מסובין

72. פסחים דף קטז עמוד א

בְּגְנוּת refers to the fact that our ancestors originally worshipped idols. Abraham's father was an idol worshipper, and Abraham came to recognize the folly of this and discovered the existence of Hashem. This opinion is the reason we recite the section of מִתְּחִלָּה עוֹבְדֵי עֲבוֹדָה זָרָה הָיוּ אֲבוֹתֵינוּ ("In the beginning our ancestors were idol worshippers") in the Haggadah. Shmuel disagrees with Rav and says that מַתְחִיל בִּגְנוּת refers to our being slaves in Egypt. This opinion is the reason we recite the section of עֲבָדִים הָיִינוּ לְפַרְעֹה בְּמִצְרָיִם ("We were slaves of Pharaoh in Egypt") right after the four questions.[73] We observe both opinions.

Rav Yitzchak Zev Halevi Soloveitchik[74] points out that both Rav and Shmuel, who disagree about the meaning of "beginning with humiliating circumstances and concluding with the glory of the Jewish people," are trying to show that the purpose of starting the haggadah with the Jewish people in a disgraced position is to set off the counterpoint of the redemption leading up to our accepting God as our King and our receiving the Torah.

אֲרַמִּי אוֹבֵד אָבִי

The last point of the Mishnah is that we elaborate on the Exodus (סִפּוּר יְצִיאַת מִצְרַיִם) with an interpretation of the story of as it is found in the recounting of the bringing the בִּכּוּרִים (the first crops to the Temple).[75] When bringing the בִּכּוּרִים we also tell the story of the Exodus. There we explain the events beginning from the circumstances leading to Yaakov and his family going down to Egypt and continuing until the new Jewish nation was led to the Promised Land. Since the Torah, in the course of describing בִּכּוּרִים, told us what we should say, we analyze that text of בִּכּוּרִים and explain it as part of our telling the story.

The purpose of this section is to tell of the very beginning of the exile that was foretold to Avraham at the בְּרִית בֵּין הַבְּתָרִים (Covenant

73. פסחים דף קטז עמוד א

74. Also known as the Brisker Rav, in חידושי הגרי"ז על התורה סימן רטו.

75. דברים כו:ה-ט

of the Parts).[76] The exile is considered as starting with Yitzchak, but the servitude began in Yaakov's time (our ancestor) when he went to Lavan's house (the Aramite) after escaping from Esau.[77]

This explanation is reinforced by the selection where we recite, צֵא וּלְמַד מַה בִּקֵּשׁ לָבָן הָאֲרַמִּי לַעֲשׂוֹת לְיַעֲקֹב אָבִינוּ. שֶׁפַּרְעֹה לֹא גָזַר אֶלָּא עַל הַזְּכָרִים וְלָבָן בִּקֵּשׁ לַעֲקוֹר אֶת הַכֹּל (Let's look at what Lavan the Aramite wanted to do to Yaakov, our ancestor. Pharaoh only instituted a decree to kill the male children, but Lavan tried to uproot everyone).

Telling and Remembering the Exodus

There are two mitzvot dealing with the Exodus from Egypt: the mitzvah of remembering the Exodus from Egypt which is observed every day, and the mitzvah of telling the story of the Exodus which is only observed on the night of the fifteenth of Nissan. Rav Chaim Soloveitchik explained that there are three differences between the two mitzvot: 1) The mitzvah of "remembering" entails just mentioning briefly that we left Egypt, while the mitzvah of סִפּוּר יְצִיאַת מִצְרַיִם involves telling all that happened to our ancestors in Egypt at great length. 2) The mitzvah of remembering is only incumbent on oneself, while סִפּוּר יְצִיאַת מִצְרַיִם requires telling the story to one's children and to others. 3) Remembering the Exodus is not an independent mitzvah; it is part of the mitzvah of Shema, in which we accept God's yoke by mentioning God taking us out of Egypt. סִפּוּר יְצִיאַת מִצְרַיִם is an independent mitzvah. R. Chaim's grandson, R. Joseph B. Soloveitchik, added that the obligation to remember the Exodus doesn't require one to praise God, but the mitzvah of סִפּוּר יְצִיאַת מִצְרַיִם also includes the requirement to express thanks and praise to God for His taking us out of Egypt. Hallel on the night of the seder fulfills that requirement.[78]

---

76. בראשית פרק טו: ט-כא
77. מלבי"ם דברים פרק כו: ארמי אובד אבי
78. See *Shiurim Lezecher Abba Mari*, vol. 1, p. 14, note 4.

Rabban Gamliel

The Mishnah[79] adds another requirement to what we must say at the seder. רַבָּן גַּמְלִיאֵל הָיָה אוֹמֵר: כָּל שֶׁלֹּא אָמַר שְׁלֹשָׁה דְבָרִים אֵלּוּ בְּפֶסַח, לֹא יָצָא יְדֵי חוֹבָתוֹ, וְאֵלּוּ הֵן: פֶּסַח, מַצָּה, וּמָרוֹר. (Rabban Gamliel used to say, Anyone who does not mention these three things [at the seder] does not fulfill his obligation: the קָרְבַּן פֶּסַח, the matzah and the maror.) In other words, one must give the reason for these three mitzvot, as the Mishnah goes on to explain, and as we recite them in the Haggadah. What is the meaning of Rabban Gamliel's statement – what obligation does he mean?

The Rambam includes this requirement among the other requirements of סִפּוּר יְצִיאַת מִצְרַיִם.[80] According to the Rambam, one who does not explain the reason for these mitzvot has not properly fulfilled the mitzvah of סִפּוּר יְצִיאַת מִצְרַיִם. On the other hand, Tosafot explain that the obligation to give the reasons for the mitzvot of קָרְבַּן פֶּסַח, matzah and maror relates to these three mitzvot themselves.[81] In other words, according to this perspective, these mitzvot are not fulfilled merely by eating the foods, but one must also explain their symbolism.

Hallel in the Seder

The Hallel at the seder is different from any other Hallel that we say, because it is divided into two parts and separated by the seder meal. That leads us to ask some questions. It might be that the two parts of Hallel have different purposes or even different levels of obligation. Is reciting Hallel on the eve of the seder a Torah or Rabbinic obligation?

---

79. פסחים דף קטז עמוד א-ב

80. רמב"ם הלכות חמץ ומצה פרק ז הלכה ה. See also חידושי הגר"ח פסחים דף קטז עמוד א.

81. תוספות פסחים דף קטז עמוד א ד"ה ואמרתם. Tosafot write that although the halachah that one must recount the reason for the mitzvah is stated with regard to the mitzvah of קָרְבַּן פֶּסַח, we derive the obligation to recount the reasons for matzah and maror from קָרְבַּן פֶּסַח, since they are compared to each other in the Torah.

That revolves around a statement in the Mishnah[82] that was carried over to the Haggadah:

בְּכָל דּוֹר וְדוֹר חַיָּב אָדָם לִרְאוֹת אֶת עַצְמוֹ כְּאִלּוּ הוּא יָצָא מִמִּצְרַיִם, שֶׁנֶּאֱמַר: וְהִגַּדְתָּ לְבִנְךָ בַּיּוֹם הַהוּא לֵאמֹר, בַּעֲבוּר זֶה עָשָׂה ה׳ לִי בְּצֵאתִי מִמִּצְרָיִם ("In every generation one is obligated to see oneself as if he personally left Egypt, as it says, 'Tell your children that day saying because of this God took me out of Egypt…'") .לְפִיכָךְ אֲנַחְנוּ חַיָּבִים לְהוֹדוֹת, לְהַלֵּל, לְשַׁבֵּחַ, לְפָאֵר,...וְנֹאמַר לְפָנָיו שִׁירָה חֲדָשָׁה: הַלְלוּיָהּ ("Therefore, we must thank Him (לְהוֹדוֹת) and praise Him (לְהַלֵּל) and exalt (לְשַׁבֵּחַ) and glorify Him (לְפָאֵר) etc. and we will recite a new song to Him. Praised be the Lord!")

The next passages in the Haggadah are the first two paragraphs of the Hallel. The recitation of the Hallel fulfills the requirement of וְנֹאמַר לְפָנָיו שִׁירָה חֲדָשָׁה, reciting a new song.[83]

Tosafot in Megillah[84] state that Hallel at the seder is a Rabbinic obligation, while the Rambam[85] indicates that it is a Torah obligation. One can reconcile these two views if we explain that the first two chapters of Hallel that we say together with the telling of the story of leaving Egypt are a Torah-level requirement, and a fulfillment of the מִצְוַת סִפּוּר יְצִיאַת מִצְרַיִם. But the rest of the Hallel which we recite after the meal is a Rabbinic-level obligation, and this is what Tosafot are discussing.[86]

The Gemara talks about the part of Hallel we recite before the meal. How much of it should we say? Beit Shammai says to say the first chapter. Beit Hillel says to say the first two chapters.[87] The Netziv explains this disagreement. Beit Shammai felt that the thanks to God was recited while the Jews were eating the קָרְבַּן פֶּסַח at the first seder in Egypt. They had not yet left Egypt. They were still under Pharaoh's

---

82. פסחים דף קטז עמ׳ ב

83. See the section on סִפּוּר יְצִיאַת מִצְרַיִם and Telling and Remembering the Exodus.

84. תוספות מגילה דף כא עמ׳ א ד״ה לאתויי

85. ספר המצות מצות עשה קנז

86. הגדה של פסח שי״ח הגרי״ד חלק ע׳

87. פסחים דף קטז עמוד א

shadow. But things had dramatically changed. They were eating the קָרְבַּן פֶּסַח which was an expression of throwing off Pharaoh's power over them. They certainly had to praise God, but they needed to continue to pray for the rest of the redemption. After midnight, they would be witnesses to additional freedom, and then they would be ready to recite the rest of the Hallel. Beit Hillel felt that once the process had begun, it would not stop. God had intervened in the natural forces of history and was revealing Himself in the process of redeeming the Jewish people. Once we start reciting praise, we can continue to sing about בְּצֵאת יִשְׂרָאֵל מִמִּצְרַיִם ("As Israel left Egypt").[88]

The Berachah on Redemption: אֲשֶׁר גְּאָלָנוּ

This berachah, which we recite before we drink the second cup of wine, offers thanks to God and prays that He bring us back to our land, so we can again offer the sacrifices as He decreed.

The Gemara tells us[89] that we end this portion of the seder with the berachah for redemption. Rabbi Tarfon says it consists of what we know as the first part of the blessing: בָּרוּךְ אַתָּה ה׳ אֱלֹקֵינוּ מֶלֶךְ הָעוֹלָם, אֲשֶׁר גְּאָלָנוּ וְגָאַל אֶת אֲבוֹתֵינוּ מִמִּצְרַיִם, וְהִגִּיעָנוּ לַלַּיְלָה הַזֶּה לֶאֱכֹל בּוֹ מַצָּה וּמָרוֹר ("Blessed are You Hashem our God, King of the universe who has redeemed us and redeemed our ancestors from Egypt and brought us to this night to eat on it the matzah and maror"). Rabbi Akiva adds on what we recognize as the rest of the blessing: כֵּן ה׳ אֱלֹקֵינוּ וֵאלֹקֵי אֲבוֹתֵינוּ יַגִּיעֵנוּ לְמוֹעֲדִים וְלִרְגָלִים אֲחֵרִים הַבָּאִים לִקְרָאתֵנוּ לְשָׁלוֹם, שְׂמֵחִים בְּבִנְיַן עִירֶךָ וְשָׂשִׂים בַּעֲבוֹדָתֶךָ. וְנֹאכַל שָׁם מִן הַזְּבָחִים וּמִן הַפְּסָחִים אֲשֶׁר יַגִּיעַ דָּמָם עַל קִיר מִזְבַּחֲךָ לְרָצוֹן, וְנוֹדֶה לְךָ שִׁיר חָדָשׁ עַל גְּאֻלָּתֵנוּ וְעַל פְּדוּת נַפְשֵׁנוּ בָּרוּךְ אַתָּה ה׳, גָּאַל יִשְׂרָאֵל ("So too, Hashem our God and God of our ancestors, bring us in peace to other holidays and festivals as they come: happy in the rebuilding of Your city, and rejoicing in Your worship. And then we will eat there from the sacrifices and the korban Pesach whose blood will be sprinkled on the altar in accordance with Your will. And we will thank You with a new song of redemption and for the freedom of our souls. Blessed

---

88. הגדה של פסח עם פירוש אמרי שפר

89. פסחים דף קטז עמ׳ ב

are You, the Redeemer of Israel"). Rashbam explains[90] that Rabbi Tarfon is ending the section of the haggadah with an expression of thanks. As such, it is a single idea and only needs to be a short berachah. A short berachah, like a berachah that we recite before we eat a fruit or before we perform a mitzvah, does not need a conclusion. Rabbi Akiva believed that the discussion of the most significant example of God's saving us from trouble and giving us the Torah could not be complete unless we took the opportunity to ask God for the fulfillment of the promise of the future redemption. Rabbi Akiva asked that we be able to witness the rebuilding of the Temple and the restoration of the Temple service. He continued to ask that we should be able to thank Him and recite Hallel over His salvation.

This kind of berachah, where we thank God for the past and pray to Him for the future is considered a complex berachah. That kind of berachah requires a concluding blessing.

There is a question about the order of the text in this berachah: Do we say וְנֹאכַל שָׁם מִן הַזְּבָחִים וּמִן הַפְּסָחִים (and we will eat from the zevach sacrifices and from the Pesach sacrifices), or is the order reversed? Seemingly, we should say הַזְּבָחִים first because that refers to the חֲגִיגָה שֶׁל אַרְבָּעָה עָשָׂר (korban chagigah of the fourteenth of Nissan),[91] which was eaten before the קָרְבַּן פֶּסַח. However, the Maharil[92] argues that because we always have a קָרְבַּן פֶּסַח on this day, but we don't always eat the חֲגִיגָה שֶׁל אַרְבָּעָה עָשָׂר, we should say הַפְּסָחִים first. A compromise view is that of the Bach, citing R. Yaakov (Mahari) Weil. He says[93] that if Erev Pesach falls out on Shabbat, we don't offer the חֲגִיגָה שֶׁל אַרְבָּעָה עָשָׂר. Therefore, when Pesach falls out on Motza'ei Shabbat (Erev Pesach falling out on Shabbat),[94] you should say הַפְּסָחִים first. As a result, you will see in many Haggadot that the order is reversed for Motza'ei Shabbat, מִן הַפְּסָחִים וּמִן הַזְּבָחִים.

---

90. רשב"ם ותוספות פסחים דף קטז עמ' ב
91. פסחים דף ע עמ' א
92. ספר מהרי"ל (מנהגים) סדר ההגדה אות ל
93. ב"ח אורח חיים סימן תעג ס"ק לו
94. מגן אברהם סימן תעג

BERACHOT OVER THE MATZAH

As mentioned earlier, at the seder there is a requirement of לֶחֶם עֹנִי which impacts the usual requirement of לֶחֶם מִשְׁנֶה. We must have a broken matzah for the mitzvah of eating matzah. Is this also the matzah over which we recite the berachah of הַמּוֹצִיא? The Gemara[95] says that we put the broken matzah together with the whole matzah, and recite the berachah, because of the requirement of לֶחֶם עֹנִי. To which berachah is the Gemara referring? Tosafot[96] cite two opinions on the matter. According to R. Menachem of Joigny and R. Yom Tov, both the berachah of עַל אֲכִילַת מַצָּה and the berachah of הַמּוֹצִיא are recited on the broken matzah. The second opinion in Tosafot, that of Ri (R. Isaac of Dampierre), is that the berachah of הַמּוֹצִיא is recited on the whole matzah while the berachah of עַל אֲכִילַת מַצָּה is recited on the broken matzah.

According to Tosafot, we recite the berachot over three matzot, so that even after one is broken we are left with two whole matzot for לֶחֶם מִשְׁנֶה. The Rambam has a different view.[97] According to the Rambam, one takes two pieces of matzah like on any Yom Tov, but because of לֶחֶם עֹנִי he breaks the one and places the whole and broken matzah together to recite the הַמּוֹצִיא. The לֶחֶם עֹנִי rule overrides the לֶחֶם מִשְׁנֶה rule, so we do not need two whole matzot, but we still recite the הַמּוֹצִיא on the whole piece out of respect, and the עַל אֲכִילַת מַצָּה on the broken piece because of the specific לֶחֶם עֹנִי requirement.[98]

The Mishnah Berurah[99] cites the view that is commonly described in most Haggadot. We take three matzot, of which the top and bottom are whole. The middle one is the one we broke during יַחַץ. When we recite the הַמּוֹצִיא, we intend that the berachah relate to both the top and bottom whole matzot for לֶחֶם מִשְׁנֶה. Then we are done with that

95. ברכות לט עמ׳ ב

96. תוספות פסחים קטז עמ׳ א ד״ה מה

97. רמב״ם הלכות חמץ ומצה פרק ח הל׳ ו

98. See R. Yitzchak Abba Lichtenstein, *Haggadah Siach HaGrid*, section 58 (עמ׳ סח-סט).

99. משנה ברורה סימן תעה ס״ק ב

requirement, so we drop the bottom matzah. Next, we recite the עַל אֲכִילַת מַצָּה over the top and the broken middle matzah to fulfill the לֶחֶם עֹנִי requirement, after which we break the top and (formerly) middle matzot, distribute them and eat them.

Most people follow the custom of the Mishnah Berurah. Rav Soloveitchik followed the position of the Rambam and the Vilna Gaon. There are many positions, and all of them have a basis. As both the Ramban and Rav Hai Gaon expressed, widespread customs have a validity of their own, and you do not have to change from the custom your family has been observing to a different custom.

Maror

Maror is a bitter vegetable, and the Gemara gives a number of examples of what can be used, but the primary vegetable used was חַסָּא, which means lettuce, and which is the maror of choice.[100] All parts of the leaf could be used, but not the root.[101] The Gemara said that eating חַסָּא may be dangerous, because it contained קפא, which is either a poison found in the leaf,[102] or a certain bug that infested it.[103] While in common practice, most people were not concerned about the likelihood of harm from eating this plant, the Gemara didn't want any harm to come from performing a mitzvah.[104] As a result, they required dipping the lettuce used for maror in חֲרֹסֶת that could negate the effects of this poison or bug.

When the קָרְבַּן פֶּסַח was eaten, it was a mitzvah from the Torah to eat it together with matzah and maror.[105] When there is no קָרְבַּן פֶּסַח, then matzah remains an independent mitzvah from the Torah while maror becomes a מִצְוָה מִדְּרַבָּנָן. We first eat the maror by itself, and then together with the matzah, in commemoration of the way Hillel ate it

100. פסחים דף לט עמ׳ א
101. שולחן ערוך אורח חיים תעג סעיפים ה-ו
102. רש״י פסחים דף קטו עמוד ב ד״ה צריך לשקועיה
103. תוספות שם ד״ה קפא
104. רא״ש פסחים י:כה בשם ה״ר יונה
105. פסחים קכ עמ׳ א; רמב״ם, הלכות חמץ ומצה פרק ז הלכה יב

when there was a קָרְבַּן פֶּסַח. The amount that we have to eat of maror is a כְּזַיִת, the minimum amount that is considered eating.[106]

Maror is connected integrally to other parts of the seder. We have seen that it is connected to the mitzvah of קָרְבַּן פֶּסַח and of matzah. The mitzvah of סִפּוּר יְצִיאַת מִצְרַיִם, around which the whole seder revolves, must be performed when there is matzah and maror in front of us. The matzah reminds us of the freedom, but the maror reminds us of the bitter experience we had before God took us out of Egypt. Because leaning is a sign of freedom, we don't lean when we eat the maror.

Maror is also connected to something else in the seder: חֲרֹסֶת. The חֲרֹסֶת is a mixture of nuts, fruit and spices mixed with a liquid and it is used as a dip for the maror. There are different recipes, but the Gemara tells us that it should be thick like the mud our ancestors worked with in Egypt and acidic to remind us of the verse תַּחַת הַתַּפּוּחַ עוֹרַרְתִּיךָ, "Under the apple tree I roused you," which refers to the redemption of the Jewish people in Egypt.[107] Some people put in fruit of the kind to which Israel is compared, like figs, nuts, dates and pomegranates or nuts, almonds, apples,[108] and spices like cinnamon and ginger that aren't easily ground up. When these spices are finely chopped up, they remind us of the mortar. The Tur also writes that one should add wine or vinegar, in memory of the blood.[109]

We find in the Mishnah[110] a disagreement about the nature of חֲרֹסֶת. The anonymous author of the Mishnah says that חֲרֹסֶת is brought to the table with the matzah and maror, even though it is not a mitzvah. Rabbi Elazar bar Tzadok, however, says that חֲרֹסֶת is a mitzvah, because it commemorates the mortar that the Jews used in Egypt.[111] This thematically connects חֲרֹסֶת to maror, because the mortar reminds us of the bitter life we lived in Egypt.

---

106. שולחן ערוך אורח חיים סימן תעה, סעיף א

107. שיר השירים ח:ה; רש"י פסחים דף קטז עמוד א

108. תוספות פסחים דף קטז עמוד א ד"ה צריך לסמוכיה

109. טור ורמ"א אורח חיים סימן תעג סעיף ה

110. פסחים דף קיד עמ' א

111. פסחים דף קטז עמוד א: חרוסת זכר לטיט

We dip the maror in the חֲרֹסֶת before we eat it. We don't leave it in the חֲרֹסֶת for too long. Then shake off the excess חֲרֹסֶת so it can still taste bitter. We eat a כְּזַיִת of maror without doing הֲסִיבָה (leaning) and then eat another כְּזַיִת of maror together with the matzah for Korech. This combines the elements of remembering the bitter oppression with the symbol of freedom of God taking us out from Egypt.[112]

THE FOURTH CUP OF WINE

The Mishnah tells us that we pour the fourth cup of wine, finish reciting the Hallel and recite the בִּרְכַּת הַשִּׁיר (the berachah of the song).[113] The Gemara asks what בִּרְכַּת הַשִּׁיר is. Rav Yehudah says that it is the berachah of יְהַלְלוּךָ ה׳ אֱלֹקֵינוּ ("All Your works will praise You, our God"), which we customarily recite at the end of Hallel. Rabbi Yochanan says בִּרְכַּת הַשִּׁיר is נִשְׁמַת כָּל חַי ("The soul of every living thing"), which is the conclusion of the expanded version of פְּסוּקֵי דְזִמְרָא that we say on Shabbat and Yom Tov.[114] Then, Rabbi Tarfon says after finishing Hallel we say הַלֵּל הַגָּדוֹל. The Gemara has to define what הַלֵּל הַגָּדוֹל is. After some discussion, it concludes that it is Psalm 136. We recognize it as starting with הוֹדוּ לַייָ כִּי־טוֹב כִּי לְעוֹלָם חַסְדּוֹ. It is called הַלֵּל הַגָּדוֹל because it describes how Hashem provides food for those in need.[115]

There are different opinions about how the Hallel at the seder should end: The Rambam follows Rav Yehudah's opinion and recites Hallel with the conclusion of יְהַלְלוּךָ ה׳ אֱלֹקֵינוּ.[116] The Rambam requires only one version of בִּרְכַּת הַשִּׁיר.

The Rashbam explains that בִּרְכַּת הַשִּׁיר includes two elements: both יְהַלְלוּךָ and נִשְׁמַת. יְהַלְלוּךָ should be recited after we complete the

112. רמב"ם הלכות חמץ ומצה פרק ז, הלכה יב

113. פסחים דף קיז עמוד ב

114. Rav Soloveitchik used to say that from נִשְׁמַת כָּל חַי through יִשְׁתַּבַּח is all part of the same berachah.

115. פסחים דף קיח עמוד א

116. רמב"ם הלכות חמץ ומצה פרק ח הלכה י

festival Hallel (הַלֵּל הַמִּצְרִי), and נִשְׁמַת should be recited after we recite הַלֵּל הַגָּדוֹל.[117]

Tosafot[118] accepted the position of reciting both נִשְׁמַת and יְהַלְלוּךָ ה׳ אֱלֹקֵינוּ, like the Rashbam. Tosafot explain that נִשְׁמַת is called בִּרְכַּת הַשִּׁיר because it follows פְּסוּקֵי דְזִמְרָה on an ordinary Shabbat, and פְּסוּקֵי דְזִמְרָה is a song (שִׁיר). Then Tosafot bring in a new element: the position of R. Chaim Kohen who requires reciting only one concluding berachah. R. Chaim Kohen maintains that יְהַלְלוּךָ is recited without its concluding berachah, and then נִשְׁמַת is recited with its conclusion. His view is based on the fact that the text of the Gemara refers to בִּרְכַּת הַשִּׁיר, which implies a single berachah rather than two.

The Shulchan Aruch follows the view of R. Chaim Kohen that only one concluding berachah is recited, but differs with R. Chaim Kohen about which berachah it is. According to the Shulchan Aruch, after Hallel, we do not recite יְהַלְלוּךָ. Instead, we proceed to recite הַלֵּל הַגָּדוֹל, followed by נִשְׁמַת and יִשְׁתַּבַּח, until the words מֵעַתָּה וְעַד עוֹלָם. However, instead of saying the concluding berachah, we now say יְהַלְלוּךָ.[119] This is one version that is followed in many Haggadot today. The Magen Avraham[120] cites those who follow the opinion of R. Chaim Kohen, and conclude with the regular ending of יִשְׁתַּבַּח. This is the other version that you will find in Haggadot today.

What is strange here is that we recite two versions of Hallel. Normally when we recite Hallel, we recite only one version. What is it that makes us say both הַלֵּל הַמִּצְרִי and הַלֵּל הַגָּדוֹל on the night of the seder? Rav Soloveitchik explained as follows.[121] We are compelled to say פְּסוּקֵי דְזִמְרָא every day to thank Hashem for renewing the act of creation every day. But הַלֵּל הַמִּצְרִי is only for special occasions. The Gemara[122] that says when a person sees the place where a miracle happened to him,

---

117. רשב״ם פסחים דף קיח עמ׳ א: ד״ה יהללוך ועוד ד״ה ור׳ יוחנן אמר
118. פסחים דף קיח עמ׳ א ד״ה רבי יוחנן אמר נשמת כל חי
119. שולחן ערוך אורח חיים סימן תפ סעיף א
120. See מגן אברהם סימן תפ ס״ק ב ומשנה ברורה ס״ק ה.
121. See *Haggadah Siach HaGrid*, בענין ברכת השיר.
122. ברכות דף נד עמוד א

he should recite a berachah. The Rosh[123] proves from this Gemara that if a number of miracles occurred to a person, when he comes to a place of one of them, he should recite a berachah to give thanks for all of the miracles that happened to him, even for the ones that did not occur at that place.

On the night of the seder we are obligated to see ourselves as if we ourselves were redeemed from Egypt and give thanks for being redeemed. That is why we recite הַלֵּל הַמִּצְרִי. Additionally, we must give thanks for the creation of the world and of man as well. That's the reason we say הַלֵּל הַגָּדוֹל during the seder.

Rav Chaim Soloveitchik suggested a different solution to the question of what berachah to recite at the conclusion of Hallel.[124] Rav Chaim's solution to fulfill both opinions about which berachah is recited is to end הַלֵּל הַמִּצְרִי with יְהַלְלוּךָ without its final berachah. He immediately says הַלֵּל הַגָּדוֹל and ends it with נִשְׁמַת. Then he combines both berachot to end with: בא״י מֶלֶךְ מְהֻלָּל בַּתִּשְׁבָּחוֹת קֵל הַהוֹדָאוֹת אֲדוֹן הַנִּפְלָאוֹת הַבּוֹחֵר בְּשִׁירֵי זִמְרָה מֶלֶךְ קֵל חֵי הָעוֹלָמִים ("Blessed are You Hashem, King who is praised with exaltations, Lord to whom thanks is directed, Master of wonders, who chooses songs of praise, King, Lord who gives life to the world"). And with this he fulfilled the two opinions.

---

123. רא״ש מסכת ברכות פרק ט סוף סימן א

124. *Haggadah Siach HaGrid*, p. 96.

Epilogue

In this volume on the siddur, we dealt with various issues. In this conclusion, I would would like to reiterate a few of the points that have been discussed regarding the development of the siddur.

One of the early berachot that we mentioned starts with the words אֱלֹקַי נְשָׁמָה שֶׁנָּתַתָּ בִּי טְהוֹרָה הִיא ("My God, the soul that you placed in me is pure"). This means that our souls have not been stained by sins. Can we really say that? Are not our souls always contaminated by iniquities?

Christians believe that souls are contaminated by sin. Every human being is born with sin, and only baptism can rid us of it. Jews don't believe that. Anything created by the Almighty is perfect and radiates sanctity. We are all created pure and perfect, because nothing coming from God is deficient. The only stains on our souls are of our own doing, and only we ourselves can remove them. Therefore, we declare proudly, "The soul that you gave me is pure."

The Greeks and the Romans, we have noted, did believe in the existence of gods, but in their understanding the immortal God had nothing in common with mortal humans. The gap between God and humanity is so great, they thought, that nothing could bridge it. They believed that God had no interest in the fate of humanity, so He put the powers of nature in charge of it. This is called deism. The pagans believed that the planets were the seat of the powers. Each planet represented a different power; Mars, for example, governed military success. While pagan philosophers understood that statues were merely images and not gods, the masses failed to make this fine distinction. For them there was no difference between the statue and the force it represented.

Jews also understand this problem. However, we solved it in a different way, which is called monotheism: אָמַר רַבִּי יוֹחָנָן: כָּל מָקוֹם שֶׁאַתָּה מוֹצֵא גְבוּרָתוֹ שֶׁל הַקָּדוֹשׁ בָּרוּךְ הוּא שָׁם אַתָּה מוֹצֵא עַנְוְתָנוּתוֹ ("Rabbi Yochanan said: Wherever you find the greatness of the Holy One, Blessed be He, there you will also find His humility").[1] We cannot bridge the gap between God and His creatures, but in His miraculous way He is in close contact with the human race.

The Rabbis wanted every Jew to understand this basic philosophy of Judaism. Therefore, in our prayers we are often confronted by this problem and its solution.

In the first berachah of the Shema in the morning, we praise God's creative powers. Suddenly, without transition, we turn to God and beg, "Master of the universe, in Your great mercy, have pity on us." Then, as if we did not even notice this interruption, we continue our praise of God. This example shows that our ancestors were well aware of the problem we have described. That God is great is the theme of this berachah, but we neither understand how great God is nor how He will help us. In the middle of God's praises, we switch over to a petition to throw light on our problem. We have faith that our prayer will penetrate the very heavens and we will merit God's attention.

Another example of our belief that God maintains an active involvement in the affairs of the individual is found in the first paragraph of Hallel, which is chapter 113 of Tehillim. We say מִי כַּיְיָ אֱלֹקֵינוּ הַמַּגְבִּיהִי לָשָׁבֶת. הַמַּשְׁפִּילִי לִרְאוֹת בַּשָּׁמַיִם וּבָאָרֶץ ("Who is like Hashem, our God, who sits enthroned so high, yet turns so low to see the heavens and the earth?"). In short, on one hand, God is above the heavenly heights, and on the other hand, God lowers Himself to our level.

This problem is the basis of a major difference between Judaism and Christianity. Since there is such a wide gap between humanity and God, we can easily understand how the idea of a semi-divine mediator between God and humanity developed. Judaism rejects this notion as

---

1. מגילה דף לא עמ׳ א

idolatry. This idea is expressed in the Musaf of Rosh Hashanah. The benediction of מַלְכֻיּוֹת proclaims God to be the King of the universe. This berachah includes the phrase שֶׁהֵם מִשְׁתַּחֲוִים לְהֶבֶל וָרִיק וּמִתְפַּלְלִים אֶל אֵל לֹא יוֹשִׁיעַ ("they bow to vanity and nothingness and pray to a god who cannot help them"). As we noted, Christians took offense and banned this phrase, though we have reinstituted it.

Another basic issue in Jewish philosophy is theodicy, the justice of God. In Hebrew we call this problem צַדִּיק וְרַע לוֹ רָשָׁע וְטוֹב לוֹ (the righteous suffer and the evil seem to prosper). This theme occupies much of the Bible. In the period of the Babylonian exile there arose a group of people who thought that they had found a solution to this problem. Zoroastrianism declared the existence of two gods, the god of light and the god of darkness. It stated that there is an eternal struggle between these two opposing forces. If the god of light triumphs, there is peace, prosperity, and good health. If the god of darkness triumphs, misfortune fills the world.

This was a very popular religion since it had a simple solution for all problems. At the very beginning of the first berachah of the morning Shema, we quote a verse in which the prophet Isaiah proclaims[2] that there is only one God, יוֹצֵר אוֹר וּבוֹרֵא חֹשֶׁךְ עֹשֶׂה שָׁלוֹם וּבוֹרֵא אֶת הַכֹּל ("Who forms light and creates darkness, who makes peace and creates everything"). Actually, this verse ends, עֹשֶׂה שָׁלוֹם וּבוֹרֵא רָע ("who makes peace and creates evil"). We believe there is only one Power in the world. What seems to us as bad is not necessarily so. Sometimes it is the result of not fulfilling our mandate to care for the environment. Sometimes it is the result of humanity exerting its gift of free will, albeit inappropriately. Sometimes an act that seems bad is not, in another context. Nevertheless, we do not believe that evil comes from an independent power who struggles with God for dominance. Thus the Rabbis used the daily prayers to teach the Jews the errors of this religion.

The interference of the gentiles with our Divine services changed our prayer book to a great extent. Kaddish is one of the most basic

---

2. ישעיהו מה:ז

prayers, yet if not for the gentiles, we would not have this prayer, in addition to some other beautiful and devotional expressions of our faith. During the Second Temple period, life was difficult for the Jews. On the one hand there were the holy writings with the Divine promise of a glorious future, the Messianic Era. On the other hand, there was the reality of defeat and death. This contradiction between bitter reality and beautiful dreams weakened the faith of many Jews. The Rabbis felt they had to do something to strengthen the faith of the Jewish people.

At the end of the regular davening, they called their congregants together and taught them verses from Bible, highlighting the joys of the next world. One of the worshippers would get up and intone the prayer that we today call Kaddish, asking the Almighty to turn what they had learned into reality. The common people who participated in this daily lecture did not know Hebrew, so therefore Kaddish was said in Aramaic.

They actually said more than what we say in Kaddish today. In this early Kaddish, all parts of the redemption are spelled out as follows: בְּעָלְמָא דִּי הוּא עָתִיד לְאִתְחַדְתָּא וּלְאַחְיָא מֵתַיָּא, וּלְאַסָּקָא לְחַיֵּי עָלְמָא, וּלְמִבְנֵי קַרְתָּא דִּירוּשְׁלֵם, וּלְשַׁכְלֵל הֵיכָלֵיהּ בְּגַוַּהּ, וּלְמֶעְקַר פּוּלְחָנָא נוּכְרָאָה מֵאַרְעָא, וּלְאֲתָבָא פּוּלְחָנָא דִּשְׁמַיָּא לְאַתְרֵהּ, וְיַמְלִיךְ קוּדְשָׁא בְּרִיךְ הוּא בְּמַלְכוּתֵיהּ וִיקָרֵהּ, וְיַצְמַח פֻּרְקָנֵהּ וִיקָרֵב מְשִׁיחֵהּ, "in the world which He will renew; and revive the dead and raise them to eternal life; rebuild the city of Jerusalem and dedicate His Temple in its midst; uproot idol worship from the land and bring back the service of God to its place. The Holy One, Blessed be He, will rule with His kingship and glory, and bring the flourishing of the Redemption and hasten the coming of the Messiah."

The Romans and early Christians did not like this version of Kaddish. They knew very well to whom we referred when we spoke about idol worship. The rulers of the Eastern Roman Empire therefore strictly prohibited the recitation of the various aspects of the Redemption. They did not object to the mention of God's Kingdom; they also prayed for the coming of the Kingdom of God. But the mention of everything else was strictly forbidden. Our Kaddish today is a censored prayer. The Jews had no choice but to abide by the Roman command.

However, the original version of Kaddish was preserved on two occasions: at a סִיּוּם (meal celebrating the completion of a tractate of the Talmud) and at a funeral. The Romans strictly prohibited learning Torah. Those who did not live up to the Roman edict were cruelly put to death. To this day on Yom Kippur during the repetition of the Musaf and on Tishah B'Av in the Kinot, we recite the martyrdom of the ten great scholars who were murdered by the Romans. A סִיּוּם therefore had to be celebrated in great secrecy. This gave our ancestors the opportunity to recite the entire Kaddish. At a funeral, an unabridged version of Kaddish could be recited since the Romans did not honor the Jews by attending their funerals.

Another prayer that was very unpopular with the Christians, was Kedushah, the song of the angels as taught to us by the prophets. Isaiah tells us[3] that the Seraphim praised God with the threefold recitation of the Divine attribute קָדוֹשׁ. This attribute is repeated three times to serve as a substitute for the grammatical form of the superlative. Jonathan ben Uzziel interprets this as indicating God's superiority in three realms: in the heavens, in this world, and in the next world. But there is only one God.

The Christians, however, claimed that this threefold mention of the adjective "holy" is a reference to their doctrine of the trinity. According to them, the Jews falsified the meaning of the verse in Isaiah. Therefore, the Christians prohibited the recitation of Kedushah. What were the Jews to do? To say Kedushah might mean execution; not to say it would mean giving in to their enemies. This is the way the Jews solved the problem: they omitted Kedushah as long as they knew that the king's spies were alert and listening carefully. The spies knew that Kedushah had to be recited standing, so once the Jews sat down, the spies relaxed.

The Jews outsmarted their enemies by sitting down and quoting the verses of Kedushah. How could they do this? They made it a study session and added the translation and interpretation of the Targum. Thus, by adding on the element of Torah study, the Jews fulfilled their

---

3. ישעיהו ו:ג

obligation to say Kedushah without violating the law requiring that we stand for it. All this is contained in the prayer וּבָא לְצִיּוֹן גּוֹאֵל. This, then, is another section that became a part of our prayers through the evil intentions of our foes.

Another example is found after the berachot recited at the beginning of the day, where we add the section לְעוֹלָם יְהֵא אָדָם יְרֵא שָׁמַיִם בַּסֵּתֶר ("A person should always fear God in private"). This part of our prayer we also owe to our enemies. An early Babylonian king was a fanatical adherent of Zoroastrianism. Under no circumstances would he permit the proclamation of the oneness of God as expressed in the Shema. Spies were posted in all synagogues, so the Rabbis advised their followers to proclaim the unity of God secretly in the privacy of their house. The evil king died at a young age and the Jews were sure that his premature death was God's punishment for interfering with their daily prayers. The Rabbis retained this daily prayer even after his death in order to remember the miracle.

During the years of persecution the Jews also included the beginning and end of the Shema in the Kedushah. The spies never realized that they were being fooled. They were aware that the Shema was recited sitting, so when it came to the Kedushah and everyone stood up, the spies paid little attention and the Jews got away with it.

A central part of our Shabbat and holiday services is the Haftarah, when we chant a section from Prophets. This is yet another example of outside interference that resulted in a permanent addition to our liturgy. The reading of the Torah on Shabbat and Yom Tov goes back to the early history of the Jewish people; Moses and Ezra instituted it as part of our service. When was the reading of the Haftarah instituted? Why was there a need to do so? On which days do we add the reading of the Haftarah to the reading of the Torah? It is an enigma.

The reading of the Haftarah may simply be a continuation of the Torah reading. By reading the Torah so often in shul, the average person became acquainted with the laws of the Torah, and that made him or her a better Jew. Centuries later, when Prophets, the second part of the Bible, had been canonized, the Rabbis wanted the people to know this and be proficient in it as well. There was no better way to accomplish this than by making the reading of the Prophets a regular part of the synagogue service.

One theory, which has become very popular, connects the reading of the Haftarah with the uprising of the Jews against their Hellenistic Syrian oppressors.[4] The Syrians did not want to annihilate the Jews, but they wanted them to forget their spiritual heritage and become part of the Hellenistic culture that was embraced by the whole Near East. They forbade the study of the Torah, and as a result many Jews abandoned their faith completely. The Rabbis had to act quickly to prevent this lack of knowledge. They therefore substituted the reading of the Prophets for the reading of the Torah. There was always a similarity between the selection from Prophets and the weekly Torah reading. This way, the Jews retained the knowledge of the Torah portions. For some reason the Syrians did not object to the reading of Prophets. In their eyes these were historical documents and had no relation to their religious beliefs. The Hellenists long ago passed from the stage of history, but their oppression of the Jewish religion has, ironically, enriched and beautified our religious services.

Rav Soloveitchik considered the introduction of the Haftarah as a parallel to the introduction of Kaddish. The Haftarah, just like Kaddish, was introduced to strengthen the faith of the ordinary Jew during the Second Commonwealth. This explains the great number of berachot after the reading of the Haftarah. These berachot, just like the Kaddish, deal with the Messianic Era.

As the various textual versions of the liturgy developed and the various customs took shape, Rav Soloveitchik has pointed out, we often deviated from the law. One of the laws is that we are not permitted to quote incomplete verses. Each verse forms an entity that is not to be altered, unless a teacher is instructing students. The Rav pointed out that too often we ignore this halachic ruling.

Most of us commence the sanctification of the Sabbath evening Kiddush by saying יוֹם הַשִּׁשִּׁי. וַיְכֻלּוּ הַשָּׁמַיִם וְהָאָרֶץ וְכָל צְבָאָם ("...the sixth day. The heavens... were completed"), even though everybody

---

4. אבודרהם שחרית של שבת

realizes that יוֹם הַשִּׁשִּׁי is only a fragment of a verse. Rav Soloveitchik used to say the whole verse.

In the Shabbat morning Kiddush, many people start with the words עַל־כֵּן בֵּרַךְ יְיָ אֶת יוֹם הַשַּׁבָּת וַיְקַדְּשֵׁהוּ ("therefore God blessed the day of the Shabbat and made it holy"), even though a glance at the Torah would convince them that this is the last half of a verse.[5]

When we return the Torah scroll to the ark, most people recite the words וְזֹאת הַתּוֹרָה (And this is the Torah), and end with the words עַל פִּי ה׳ בְּיַד מֹשֶׁה (in accordance with Hashem's command through Moses). However, the second part is only half of a verse. Rav Soloveitchik used to omit this ending.

Each berachah has a special text coined by the Rabbis of the Talmud, and this text should never be changed. Rav Soloveitchik strictly adhered to this rule. In most congregations outside Israel, when the Priestly Blessing is recited on Yom Tov, the conclusion of the previous berachah, הַמַּחֲזִיר שְׁכִינָתוֹ לְצִיּוֹן ("who returns His presence to Zion"), is changed to שֶׁאוֹתְךָ לְבַדְּךָ בְּיִרְאָה נַעֲבֹד ("because it is You alone whom we worship"). Rav Soloveitchik objected to this change. The conclusion of the blessing was established to be הַמַּחֲזִיר שְׁכִינָתוֹ לְצִיּוֹן. This conclusion cannot be changed arbitrarily a few times a year, but must remain the same all year round.

Though Rav Soloveitchik corrected these "errors" in his synagogue, they will not be corrected by most worshippers who continue the practice of their ancestors. But the discussion of these problems will contribute to a better understanding of our liturgy.

In this book we have dealt with one of the basic practices in Judaism: prayer. We started out with a few basic ideas of the prayers, and then investigated the prayers in chronological order. Hopefully, the discussions in this book will raise questions in the minds of the reader, give a deeper understanding of the prayers, and make the time set aside for prayers a highlight of one's daily activities. The fact that in recent years many books have been written and published on the

5. שמות פרק כ פסוק יא: כִּי שֵׁשֶׁת־יָמִים עָשָׂה יְיָ אֶת־הַשָּׁמַיִם וְאֶת־הָאָרֶץ אֶת־הַיָּם וְאֶת־כָּל־אֲשֶׁר־בָּם וַיָּנַח בַּיּוֹם הַשְּׁבִיעִי עַל־כֵּן בֵּרַךְ יְיָ אֶת יוֹם הַשַּׁבָּת וַיְקַדְּשֵׁהוּ

prayers shows that many contemporary Jews look to these prayers for guidance in these difficult times. The ideas expressed in this volume are meant to strengthen the dedication and faith of the reader. In place of a formal conclusion, we will discuss a Midrash concerning King David.

According to the Talmud,[6] King David asked the Almighty to let him know the date of his death and the age that he would reach. The Almighty refused his request. However, God did let him know that his life would come to an end on a Shabbat. What good did it do David to know that he would die on a Shabbat? This information made it possible for him to study Torah all Shabbat long, making it impossible for the angel of death to claim his soul. The rest of the week David could engage in his usual activities without worrying. Does that mean that David could acquire eternal life by warding off the angel of death on Shabbat?

We don't know any human who could evade death. God did not promise any human being eternal life and King David was no exception. In the story we are not speaking about the human David. The human David had to die like anybody else. Here David is actually a symbol for the Jewish people. The issue here is whether it is possible to cheat death and continue one's existence after God determines that our time has come to leave this world.

It is indeed possible to extend a life indefinitely. If we study Torah and don't sin, we can even stave off the angel of death. David the human was tricked. Finally distracted from his Torah study, he did die. But the congregation of Israel has another fate. David, representing the Jewish people, will live forever. As long as the Jewish people remain true to God and the Torah, we have our covenant with God. This assures us as a people an eternal existence that David the person could not enjoy.

This fact has been proven in every era of Jewish history. The Romans, for example, destroyed the Temple. They knew that as long as David, personifying the Jewish people, studied Torah, he would be

---

6. שבת דף ל עמוד א

immortal, so they strictly prohibited the study of the Torah. The Jews never accepted this Roman edict. Their spiritual leaders courageously faced death, but they kept the torch of Torah study burning. The Jewish people knew that as long as they continued with the study of the Torah, they were invincible and would live forever. Emperor Hadrian outlawed Torah study, but the ten martyrs ignored this and bestowed immortality upon Israel.

Any Jew who opens a siddur, enters a synagogue, attends a Talmud lecture, or listens to the reading of the Torah, bars the path of the angel of death and prevents him from destroying the Jewish people. When David learns Torah, there is no Final Solution. The dialogue between David and God is our prescription for Israel's immortality. Millions have died, but we will never cease to exist.

When the First Temple was dedicated by King Solomon, he was ready to bring the Ark into the Holy of Holies to signify the fact that the Shechinah dwelled in the midst of Israel. However, the gates of the sanctuary would not open, and no power on earth could open them. What a disappointment! After all the sacrifices made by the Jewish people to have such a magnificent building as an expression of their relationship to God, the Almighty rejected the Temple as the abode for His Divine Majesty. In desperation, Solomon turned to God and begged Him not to reject the face of His anointed and to remember the kindness of David. Immediately the gates were thrown open and the Ark could be placed in its proper location. From the Talmud we see that the happenings of that day demonstrated clearly that David had been forgiven.

I would like to suggest a reason for the events on that fateful day. Solomon may have thought that it was his doing that brought the Jewish people close to God. The Almighty therefore taught him a lesson: It was not because of his piety and learning that Jerusalem was chosen for the Temple, but rather because of David's lifelong dedication to God.

The Frankonian Jews had a saying that expresses our philosophy of life in a simple way: "Wer sich geniert zu essen und zu oren ist auf dieser und auf jener welt verloren" – "Whoever is too shy to eat or to pray is lost in this world and the next world." Jews had been living in Frankonia (the northern part of Bavaria) for at least a thousand years. There were 125 Jewish communities there until the Holocaust. They led simple lives and were not great scholars. Kitzingen, my home town, was in Frankonia. Most Jews eked out a simple living as cattle dealers and small traders because they were not permitted to engage in any other profession. The authorities went so far as to prohibit the establishment of any new Jewish family in town, so if a Jewish couple wanted to get married, they had to wait for another family to die first.

The Jews of Frankonia were constantly driven from town to town since the Middle Ages, and they had to find living quarters in the small villages surrounding the larger cities. Simple folk, they were determined to remain faithful to the Jewish religion and to hand down their traditions to future generations. Usually the rabbi was in charge of a larger community and its surrounding towns, and it was his obligation to make sure that there was no child without a Jewish education.

It was a difficult life, but it had its rewards. Those rewards were, primarily, the hours spent in shul and words of wisdom the rabbis taught them. In 1861, Emancipation came even to the Frankonian Jews, who had had such a restricted life. Of course, the Frankonian Jews were "free" only for about seventy years.

The Nazis did not find it difficult to reawaken the anti-Semitic feelings and hatred of the general population. The majority of Frankonian Jews were what we today call "Orthodox." But in those days, "Orthodox," "Conservative," and "Reform" didn't mean much. They just loved Hashem and were ready to accept any sacrifice for Him.

American Jews are not restricted in any way, and we must be grateful for this. Many of the students in the Hebrew day schools are the descendants of Frankonian Jews who emigrated to America in the latter part of the nineteenth century and the first part of the twentieth. They must have heard from their parents and grandparents how important Judaism was in their parents' lives. I think that the rapid growth of Hebrew day schools, and their success in influencing today's youth, is certainly a result of the determination of the Frankonian Jews to remain loyal to Hashem no matter what.

Until the Holocaust, it was more or less accepted that the main enemy of the Jewish people was assimilation. The Jewish people lost more people by assimilation than by pogroms. After the decimation of the Jewish people, those proportions changed. As an example of the loss of a Jewish family, let us look at Heinreich Heine. He was the scion of a well-known Jewish banking family and was born around the beginning of the nineteenth century in Dusseldorf. At that time, Dusseldorf was under French administration, and Jews were comparatively free.

As a youth, Heine was not interested in Jewish tradition but tried to become part of German culture. He loved everything German, although he never denied that he was Jewish. He was one of Germany's greatest poets. Even today, we cannot but admire his beautiful rhymes.

All this changed when Germany occupied Dusseldorf and sent "Jews back to the ghetto." The return of Dusseldorf to Germany was the greatest misfortune in Heine's life. He felt so German and he was so enamored by Germany's thinkers and poets. His greatest aspiration was to become a professor at a German university, but he knew he had to pay a price for that. He bought a ticket of admission into German society: baptism. This betrayal of his people did not help him, for his ambition was never fulfilled. At the same time, Germans enjoyed his prose and his poetry, but all this did not do him any good.

Since admission into the intellectual life of Germany was denied to him, he started feeling like a Jew, and he began to appreciate the ethical code of Judaism. He began to write poems on Jewish themes. One of these was "Lorelei." It was put to music, and every German sang it. Even the Nazis could not force the people to abandon the joy of this poem, so the Nazis simply called it a folk song.

In German legend, Lorelei was a woman who sat upon the hills surrounding the Rhine River and sang. The sailors of the Rhine who heard her would lose sight of where they were, and many of them shipwrecked and died. In my opinion, this fable was an allegory for the fate of the Jewish people. Lorelei symbolizes German culture. In enjoying German culture, Jews lost sight of their Judaism and became "shipwrecked." Thousands of Jews lost their continuity with Jewish culture and spiritual values of Judaism.

In the United States, many Jews mistakenly think that there is no price for admission to American culture. Indeed, baptism isn't demanded of us, but ignorance, intermarriage, lack of education, and imitation of Christian ways can lead to the same results. Today, many Jewish leaders are worried that in a generation or two we might share Heine's fate. But we don't have to pay a price of admission to Judaism. This is our birthright. We needn't follow other peoples' cultures, and we have no reason to be ashamed of our past. On the contrary, the roots of Western civilization are found in our sacred literature. If we understand our own traditions, it can bring us closer to God and a sense of fulfillment. That is more than enough to satisfy our yearning for spirituality and closeness to a people who have lived beyond time.

Rabbi Isaiah Wohlgemuth

Appendix 1

A Brief Biography of Rabbi Isaiah Wohlgemuth

Rabbi Isaiah Wohlgemuth (1915–2008) was part of a "greatest generation" of post–World War Two Jewish leadership who helped to rejuvenate an American Jewish community badly in need of educational direction. During his tenure at the Maimonides School, Wohlgemuth attracted three generations of young people to the warmth of the Torah. He was a gentle man and a beautiful teacher with a brilliant mind and a clear philosophy. He represented, with Rav Joseph B. Soloveitchik, a vision of Torah deeply rooted in traditional sources and also directed at the betterment of all humankind.

Rabbi Wohlgemuth was ordained at the Hildesheimer Rabbinical Seminary in Berlin. In 1935, he returned home to Kitzingen, in the district of Bavaria, where he became the youngest pulpit rabbi in Germany at the time, taking over for his father who had just passed away. In 1938, his synagogue was among the thousands devastated on Kristallnacht. Rabbi Wohlgemuth was confined to Dachau. After his release in 1939, he was able to escape to a relative in New York City. Shortly thereafter, he came to Boston where he embraced the ideals of Rav Joseph B. Soloveitchik in the teaching of Torah and Yiddishkeit. It was also here that he met his wife Bertha Oberndoerfer, *z"l*. They were married in 1943. Rabbi Wohlgemuth developed a close relationship with Rav Soloveitchik, founder of the Maimonides School, who took a particular interest in Rabbi Wohlgemuth's *tefillah* course and insisted that no student graduate without it.

Rabbi Isaiah Wohlgemuth was, above all, a master teacher whom few could match and who was able to instill a love of learning into all his students. He cared and empathized with each of his students and they reciprocated with their admiration and respect.

It was this loving relationship with his students that contributed determinately to the popularity of Rabbi Wohlgemuth's famed *Beurei HaTefillah* course, compiled into his Guide to Jewish Prayer.

Rabbi Wohlgemuth's classroom and this book are his legacy to us.

Appendix II

Reminiscences of Rabbi Wohlgemuth's Students

These extracts, some constructed from interviews with Maimonides School graduates who took Rabbi Wohlgemuth's *Beurei HaTefillah* course, are an indication of the special feeling of admiration that Rabbi Wohlgemuth's memory evokes. Rabbi Wohlgemuth's students cherish the influence he exerted – and continues to exert – on their lives. His philosophy of teaching was simple – you have to love the child, then the child learns to love you and wants to learn everything from you.

- "Rabbi Wohlgemuth had a very soft demeanor, and even when he was being harsh, you could tell that underneath, he was cracking up. There was an impishness about him. He peppered our classes with games and exercises."
- Rabbi Wohlgemuth davened regularly with the Maimonides School high-school student minyan. "When I pray today, I often feel as if Rabbi Wohlgemuth is with me."
- "Everything he taught us was practical. He had an infectious way of teaching. We took away a love of Torah and Jewish tradition as well as an appreciation of general culture."
- "Rabbi Wohlgemuth's *Beurei HaTefillah* class was the one in which we paid the most attention, the one whose notes we have saved over the years."

- "The world of Jewish text is a difficult one to open up. Some people take to it naturally, some struggle with it, but he made the text accessible to everyone."
- "I not only remember the halachic, philosophical and aggadic teachings he left us with, but I have used them over the past decades nearly every day. I can't think of the first bracha of the Amidah without thinking – do I really have the merits of our forefathers or not, or the million other parts of the Tefillah where understanding and kavanah were built on Rabbi Wohlgemuth's teachings."
- "It was about taking prayers seriously, intellectually as well as emotionally. Prayers are very emotional and private, but Rabbi Wohlgemuth put a kind of intellectual structure and rigor to it."
- "This is the man who imbued us with a depth of understanding of prayer. Without those teachings our relationship to the text, history and poetry of the siddur would be weak facsimile of what we know prayer to be. This was the man, who, as the consummate teacher, knew how to be not only a scholar of knowledge, but a mentor and, above all, a kind and caring friend. He truly loved each of us, and we knew it – by his gentle smile, his listening eyes and by his special (and uncannily timed) chuckle."

Appendix III

Index of References to Rabbi Joseph B. Soloveitchik